The Definitive Guide to Point and Figure

A Comprehensive Guide to the Theory and Practical Use of the Point and Figure Charting Method

Jeremy du Plessis

HARRIMAN HOUSE LTD

3A Penns Road
Petersfield
Hampshire
GU32 2EW
GREAT BRITAIN

Tel: +44 (0)1730 233870
Fax: +44 (0)1730 233880
Email: enquiries@harriman-house.com
Website: www.harriman-house.com

First published in Great Britain in 2005 by Harriman House.
Reprinted 2006

The right of Jeremy du Plessis to be identified as the author has been asserted
in accordance with the Copyright, Design and Patents Act 1988.

ISBN 1-897-59763-0
978-1-897597-63-7

British Library Cataloguing in Publication Data
A CIP catalogue record for this book can be obtained from the British Library.

Printed and bound by Cambridge Printing, University Printing House, Cambridge.

Designated trademarks and brands are the property of their respective owners.

About the Author

Jeremy du Plessis CMT, FSTA

Jeremy trained as an automotive engineer, then an economist, but gave them both up to become a Technical Analyst. In 1983 he founded Indexia Research and pioneered the development of PC-based technical analysis software with the Indexia range of technical analysis systems. During the 1980s he developed a number of technical tools and indicators under the banner of Indexia, which are still used in software to this day.

He is an expert on Point and Figure charts, and the Indexia software was the first PC-based system to draw them correctly and clearly in the early 1980s. He lectures the Point and Figure module for the Society of Technical Analysts and sets the Point and Figure syllabus for the International Federation of Technical Analysts. He has taught Technical Analysis, and in particular Point and Figure, to thousands of professional traders and investors over the last 20 years. In 2001, after running Indexia Research for nearly 20 years, he agreed to merge the company with Updata plc, where he is now head of Technical Analysis and the designer of the Updata Technical Analyst software.

He is a Fellow of the Society of Technical Analysts (FSTA) in the UK, and a member of the American Market Technicians Association (MTA). He is a holder of the Chartered Market Technician (CMT) designation awarded by the MTA.

To Lynne

Contents

3. Understanding Point and Figure Charts 113

4. Projecting Price Targets

6. Point and Figure Charts of Indicators   335

7. Optimisation of Point and Figure Charts   353

11. Conclusion   457

12. References and Further Reading   463

Appendix A – Construction of 2-Box Reversal Charts   467

Appendix B – Construction of 1-Box Reversal High/Low Charts   475

Appendix C – Construction of Log Scaled Charts   489

Appendix D – Codes and Instrument Names   493

Appendix E – Dividing your Stocks into Bullish and Bearish   497

Index   505

Instruments

The following instruments have been covered:

Charts

Charts are actual Point and Figure charts of Indices, Shares, Stocks, Exchange Rates and Commodities from a number of International Markets.

Figures

Figures are diagrams which have been drawn to illustrate a particular aspect of Point and Figure charts.

Tables

Preface

What this book is about

This book is about Point and Figure charts; anyone wishing to practise Technical Analysis of the markets should be fully conversant with them. They may be the oldest method of charting the market in the Western world, but that does not mean they should be ignored in our modern world. On the contrary, once you understand more about them, you will wonder how you survived without them.

Who this book is for

I have written this book so that it can be used and enjoyed by all levels of reader. Newcomers may find that they do not need another text, as this book starts with the basics and covers everything that they need to get a grip of Point and Figure Charts. Expert Technical Analysts, who are familiar with Point and Figure charts, are likely to find that the book covers things they may not be aware of, at the same time reminding them of things they may have forgotten. I have tried to show as many examples as possible.

Structure of the book

The first thing you will notice about Point and Figure charts is that they look completely different from any other type of chart you may be familiar with; the main reason being that there is no time-scale along the horizontal axis. To understand why this is the case, it is essential that you read chapter 1 – *Introduction to Point and Figure charts*. Thereafter it is suggested that you read the book sequentially because each new chapter builds on the chapters before and assumes that you have accumulated that knowledge.

If you are new to Technical Analysis

If you are new to Technical Analysis, you should read the section, Introduction to Technical Analysis, which explains what Technical Analysis is all about, and why and how charts are used. If you are an experienced Technical Analyst, you may skip the chapter and go straight to chapter 1 – Introduction to Point and Figure charts.

A summary of each chapter is given below.

Chapter 1 – Introduction to Point and Figure Charts

Chapter 1 explains the history and development of Point and Figure charts and how they came to get their name. It is essential that you read this chapter as it sets the scene and explains why Point and Figure charts look the way they do, and helps you understand more about them. You will find with this knowledge that all other aspects of Point and Figure charts become clearer.

Chapter 2 – Characteristics and Construction

Chapter 2 follows on directly from chapter 1 and starts by explaining the characteristics that describe a Point and Figure chart. It then explains in detail how to construct one. You may be surprised to learn that there are quite a few different ways – all valid – to construct a Point and Figure chart. Even if you have software drawing the charts for you, it is important to understand the various methods and the implications of using them. Some software, unfortunately, does not draw them correctly and unless you know what is right, you may be using charts that are incorrect without knowing it. Full details of arithmetic as well as log scale construction methods are provided, as well as the difference between using tick-by-tick data and end-of-day data.

Chapter 3 – Understanding Point and Figure Charts

Chapter 3 is about understanding Point and Figure charts and the patterns associated with them. Instead of listing dozens of theoretical patterns, you are encouraged to understand how the patterns develop and what happens when they do. There are differences in the pattern make-up depending on the construction method. Chapter 3 explains those differences and compares and contrasts them. The chapter explains how Point and Figure charts generate buy and sell signals, and when signals should be ignored. Trend lines are essential to Point and Figure analysis and a full explanation of their use is given.

Chapter 4 – Projecting Price Targets

Chapter 4 covers one of the unique features of Point and Figure charts; the ability to project price targets using both the vertical and horizontal count methods. A full explanation of the calculation, as well as where and how to apply the counts, is given. Once again, different construction methods result in different ways of calculating the targets. The implications of targets being exceeded or not achieved is explained and also how this adds to the analysis of the chart as a whole. There is a full explanation of risk-reward ratios and how they can be established on a Point and Figure chart.

Chapter 5 – Analysing Point and Figure Charts

Chapter 5 explains how to analyse a Point and Figure chart. It explains how to approach the chart and how to decide what Point and Figure parameters to use when drawing the chart. It explains the implications of altering the parameters. You are then taken through an exhaustive step-by-step analysis of the FTSE 100 Index and the NASDAQ Composite using two construction methods. Finally, there is an explanation of how to use stops with a Point and Figure chart.

Chapter 6 – Point and Figure Charts of Indicators

Chapter 6 describes the benefits of drawing Point and Figure charts of indicators – calculated lines – such as relative strength, on-balance volume and oscillators. It explains that Point and Figure is simply a method of charting data and it should be used for drawing charts other than just price charts.

Chapter 7 – Optimisation of Point and Figure Charts

Chapter 7 discusses the case for and against optimisation; how Point and Figure parameters may be optimised and what the benefits or disadvantages are of doing so. A number of examples of optimised parameters are given and it is shown how these can be used to assist analysis.

Chapter 8 – Point and Figure's Contribution to Market Breadth

Chapter 8 covers Point and Figure's contribution to market breadth, namely, bullish percent. It explains how the chart is calculated and how to read it.

Chapter 9 – Advanced Point and Figure Techniques

Chapter 9 covers advanced Point and Figure techniques such as the use of moving averages, Parabolic SAR and Bollinger Bands on Point and Figure charts. It explains how using these techniques can enhance the readability of the charts.

Chapter 10 – Chart Examples

Chapter 10 is there to answer the complaint so often levelled at authors; that there are not enough real-life examples. Chapter 10 contains a number of chart examples from a number of markets with a brief explanation of each to help you understand how to approach a Point and Figure chart.

Chapter 11 – Conclusion

Chapter 11 concludes the book with a summary of the major points made in the text.

Chapter 12 – References and Further Reading

There are many fine texts that preceded this one. Many have been used as references and you are encouraged to read as many as possible.

Figures and charts in the book

Throughout the book you will see references to figures as well as charts.

- *Figures* are diagrams I have drawn to illustrate a particular aspect of Point and Figure charts.

- *Charts* are actual Point and Figure charts of indices, equities (stocks), exchange rates and commodities from a number of international markets.

The colour used throughout the book makes reading the charts so much easier.

The name and origin of the instrument used in any chart is not important. A chart is a chart, no matter which market and which country it has come from. When looking at the charts, try to ignore the instrument name. Do not assume that if you do not trade the particular instrument, the chart is of no use to you. Point and Figure techniques apply across all instrument types in the same way.

Introduction

The question I ask myself before reading a book such as this, is what qualifies the author to write on the subject?

I am not going to pretend that I started trading stocks when I was at junior school. I can't even pretend that it was at high school; there were many more exciting things to do at that age. I confess that I did not pay my way through university from the proceeds of trading either. In fact, I graduated in 1975 and settled down to the life of an automotive engineer, blissfully unaware that the stock market even existed. I was 27 before I became aware of financial markets, when I returned to university in Britain to take an economics degree.

Some may therefore regard me as a relative novice. I only have 25 years of Technical Analysis behind me. It was in 1979 that I was first introduced to the subject and in 1980 I bought a copy of How Charts can Help you in the Stock Market by William Jiler, which I read many times over. I tinkered with charts without really understanding too much about them, but I knew enough to tell me that this was what I wanted to do for the rest of my life.

After graduating in economics, I returned to South Africa and joined my brother who was coincidentally in partnership with a South African Technical Analyst, Tony Henfrey, publishing a Technical Analysis newsletter on gold and gold shares. It was there that I was introduced to Point and Figure charts and have been intrigued by them ever since. We had a team drawing and updating both Point and Figure charts as well as bar charts, by hand in large chart books every day. We also used basic arithmetic and exponential moving averages as well as momentum indicators, all of which were calculated by hand and logged in large journals from which the charts were drawn. It took more than half of the day to produce the charts, leaving the balance of the day for analysis. Eventually we bought a very basic computer (pre-IBM) that we used to generate some of the calculations for our hand drawn charts.

I learnt a lot about Technical Analysis and how markets worked during that time. We had a stockbroker two floors above us with a Reuters Ticker or Telex machine, as well as a number of Reuters Stockmasters. I would run up the stairs a number of times a day to record the latest prices so we could update our charts – in pencil, because the market had not yet closed – to see what the latest position was. The stockbroker was typical of the time; tea was served to anyone in reception. It was a gathering place; a place to chat about the markets. The same faces were there day after day. We called them the 'old boys'. They sat there watching the ticker; some of them updating a few hand drawn charts. Very often, those charts were Point and Figure charts. They had been around a long time and I learned so much from them.

At the time, we also had a very good relationship with a broker on the floor of the exchange and seeing and experiencing the live open-outcry trading taught me a lot about how markets worked. We were able to speak directly to the floor and get a feel for what was happening. They liked the chartists because our information combined with the floor intuition could give them a head start.

Commodities were big then as well, especially metals. Trading LME silver was an exhausting and very emotional experience. To be called up at 8pm, when you had a long position, only to be told that silver was nearly limit down in New York, was chilling to say the least. The decision was to either ignore the outside LME trading or try to open a contrary position in the US market. It was bracing stuff.

Our intra-day charts were mostly Point and Figure charts because they were easy to update and it didn't matter if you missed the occasional price. Although manually updating charts tells you more about the emotions of the market than electronically drawn charts, I realised that the only way forward for the company was to computerise. The IBM PC had just been released and it seemed a good use for the computer, although not everyone thought so, and I was told that charting could never be computerised. I didn't believe it and decided to spin off a separate company, Indexia Research, with the specific aim of computerising Technical Analysis for our internal use. Together with a brilliant computer programmer, John Johnson, we worked on the first program and, in early 1983, we saw the first chart drawn. It was a revelation. The chart took 12 seconds to draw! We were so excited that we took the rest of the day off because we couldn't believe how quick it was. Although 12 seconds is laughable now, remember that to produce the same chart by hand would have taken an hour. Being able to change the periods of moving averages in seconds convinced us that we were on the right track and soon all Technical Analysis would be done by computer.

We used the software we had written for our own analysis and produced charts and advisory reports from the PC. Word soon spread that we had produced a Technical Analysis system and we started to see a demand from other market analysts for a similar program. So, we decided to give it a name, Indexia Research Market Analyser, IRMA for short, and start selling it. But how? We had no experience of producing and selling software. What about a manual? How did we stop the program from being copied? All these things crossed our minds but, being young and naïve, we forged ahead.

Our first system was written for a German designed MS-DOS-based PC, the NCR DecisionMate V, mainly because it had a 640x400 full colour resolution compared to only 320 x 200 for the IBM. The problem was that we had to sell a PC as well as the software and that was not easy. There was a big demand from brokers and banks who were fitted with IBM PCs and were not prepared to go down the NCR route. So, we produced a monochrome IBM version (I refused to allow anyone to see our charts in low resolution IBM colour). Soon every broker and bank in South Africa had an Indexia program, together with a growing band of private users that quickly grew into thousands.

In 1986, we released a new version of the program called INDEXIA II at an investment show in Johannesburg. Nothing like it had been seen before. It had many innovative features as well as a number of Indexia indicators I had developed, the Indexia Market Tracker being one of them. It was very successful and proved to be just what the market wanted. In order to expand the business, we opened up agencies in the UK and Australia, but neither of these markets matched the sales of South Africa. The UK, in the 1980s, was behind South Africa in terms of Technical Analysis and we struggled to make it acceptable to the British investor.

I eventually decided that the only way to make Indexia and Technical Analysis acceptable in the UK was to move; so John and I moved the company and our families to the UK. The strategy worked and soon we had released a more powerful version INDEXIA II Plus.

Throughout the 1990s Indexia software was regarded as the best Technical Analysis software available and, in 2001, Indexia won the first Shares Magazine annual award for the best Investment software.

Then in 2001 I agreed that Indexia join forces with a public company, Updata plc. It was a difficult decision to make, but having weighed up all the options, I realised that together we would be more progressive; Updata's programming resources combined with Indexia's reputation and Technical Analysis knowledge would make a formidable team and indeed it has. As head of Technical Analysis at Updata plc I was able to design an all-new Technical Analysis program, Updata Technical Analyst, which many regard as the leading Technical Analysis software. Its compatibility with major services such as Bloomberg has brought me into contact with some of the world's leading Technical Analysts from whom I have continued to learn.

Another book on Point and Figure?

You could be excused for asking why there is a need for yet another book on Point and Figure charts. I have read many excellent texts and there are some yet unread. This book has been over 20 years in the making for no other reason than that it was easier to put off today what could easily be accomplished tomorrow. If I had finished it 20 years ago, it would have been one of a handful. Now there are dozens. The interesting thing is that, no matter how many times I read about the same technique in different books, I pick up something new each time due to the way the author is able to articulate it. I hope that the same will apply to this book. I have consciously and sub-consciously used information I have gained from reading other books. I have listed these in the References section at the end and thank the authors for their assistance.

I am, however, disappointed that of the many fine Point and Figure books available today, none cover the original 1-box reversal charts in any detail. These are where Point and Figure charts began and they still have a place today. This book goes into more depth on traditional Point and Figure charts than any other book I have read. The aim is to ensure that you understand the history, development, calculations and the analysis of Point and Figure charts. You really need these basics to fully appreciate and apply this technique. Given all the facts, you, as the reader, may go out and apply every technique and assess for yourself whether it is of any benefit to you. Many believe that no knowledge of the construction and make-up is required because we all have computers to draw the charts. This is wrong. If you do not understand what is behind a Point and Figure chart you should not use them.

Do not presume that this book can replace all the other fine books on Point and Figure charts. It cannot. It can only supplement them. Although I believe this to be a complete work, you will gain further knowledge by reading some or all of those listed in the References section at the back of this book.

Desert Island charts

I have often described Point and Figure charts as my 'desert island' charts. This has nothing to do with a special pattern I have discovered – as a student on a course once thought – but more to do with their usefulness. In the UK there is a radio program called 'Desert Island Discs' where celebrities nominate the songs they would most like to hear if stranded on a desert island. So just like we all have our favourite book, or our favourite song, I have my favourite chart. If I were ever shipwrecked on a desert island with only one chart to guide me through the markets, it would have to be a Point and Figure chart. No other single chart has the ability to cut through the chaff and show what is really going on.

Technical Analysis software

Although, at the start of my Technical Analysis career, I drew Point and Figure charts by hand, I no longer think it is necessary – unless of course you draw one just to 'keep your hand in'. I believe that computers can draw them more clearly, more accurately, with more flexibility and certainly a lot more quickly. As the designer and project manager of the Updata Technical Analyst software, I can recommend no other. Updata Technical Analyst does what every Point and Figure analyst requires in a clear and, most importantly, accurate way. Speed and flexibility is key to good Point and Figure analysis, as you will see, and good PC software can do this so much better than an internet-based system can.

The Point and Figure charts used throughout this book are taken from Updata Technical Analyst. More information may be obtained from www.UpdataTA.com in the USA or www.Updata.co.uk in the rest of the world, from where you can download a trial. You will find that being able to draw and analyse charts while you are reading this book will help your understanding. With the introduction in 2004 of a version of Updata Technical Analyst that works with Bloomberg Terminal, it is used increasingly by some of the world's leading market professionals. Indeed, some of the charts in this book were provided by professionals using Bloomberg data.

Acknowledgements and thanks

I would not be at this point in my career today without the help of many people: my wife Lynne, who has given me so much support over the years; my daughter Angelique and son Daryl, who encouraged me to finish this book; my brother Dennis, who introduced me to a career in Technical Analysis and has encouraged me through it during good times and bad; John Johnson, who was my business partner for over 20 years, and whose creative genius created the range of Indexia Technical Analysis software systems and most especially Point and Figure charts, long before Technical Analysis software was generally available for the PC; Tony Henfrey, who taught me the basics of Technical Analysis and how to understand charts; David Linton, Chief Executive of Updata plc, who gave me a free hand to create the Technical Analysis program of my dreams without any restrictions and gave me time to complete this book; Sami Khan of Updata whose brilliant mathematical mind turned much of my theoretical ramblings into the best computerised Point and Figure charts available today, and Nigel Shaw and Andrew McKendrick who helped him to create the world's best Technical Analysis software system; John Cameron whose advice and encouragement helped me to keep going; the many authors over the last 100 years or more, whose writings I have digested and which have helped me to write a book on Point and Figure charts; finally the thousands of nameless individuals who supported me, the Indexia Technical Analysis software and then the Updata Technical Analyst software for over 20 years, and whose suggestions I have noted, and in many cases have unashamedly used in the software and this book. Without all these people, I would not be in this very exciting business today and would certainly not have written this book.

Most especially, I would also like to thank Sami Khan, David Linton and Tony Smith for patiently and studiously reading through the text to see if it made sense and giving valuable comment and advice.

Finally any errors, omissions and plain incompetence are entirely my own.

Jeremy du Plessis CMT, FSTA

Berkhamsted, United Kingdom 2005

Any comments on the book will be gratefully received at PointandFigure@updata.co.uk

Introduction to Technical Analysis

In order to fully understand Point and Figure charts, it is essential that the reader understands the basics of Technical Analysis. This brief introduction simply lays the foundations of Technical Analysis and explains the philosophy behind it. If you are new to Technical Analysis, it is essential that you also read one or more of the excellent texts on the subject, such as Murphy or Pring listed in the References section.

Experienced readers may skip this section and go straight to chapter 1 – Introduction to Point and Figure Charts.

Technical Analysis of markets has been around for well over a hundred years, but what really popularised it was the advent of the IBM PC and the Technical Analysis software that followed in the early 1980s. This allowed private investors to start doing their own analysis and compete on equal or better terms with the professionals. Societies and associations of Technical Analysts[1] gained popularity and met regularly to discuss the subject and publish journals. Most countries now have their own organisations and there is an International Federation of Technical Analysts, which holds a worldwide conference once a year. Even universities are starting to embrace Technical Analysis and offering courses, but anyone thinking that Technical Analysis is a short-cut to riches should think again; it is not. Technical Analysis is a method that requires time and effort to be spent on it to be profitable.

Technical Analysis and the 'F' word

Technical Analysts are not normally appreciative of the 'F' word being used in their presence, however there are some who tolerate it and indeed some who embrace it. This author believes, however, that there is no place for 'fundamental' analysis if Technical Analysis is used, but there are those who use both methods. Either way, they are very different and although this is a book on Technical Analysis, it is important to understand the difference.

Fundamental Analysts look at macroeconomic, microeconomic and business factors in order to determine the direction of the market and the prospects for a particular share. The objects of their research include company reports and economic statistics.

Technical Analysts, on the other hand, look at price and volume changes to deduce from these the direction of the market and the prospects for the price of any instrument; the only measure that truly counts if you are an investor.

Technical Analysts argue that all these known and less known factors are reflected in the price and if good, the price will rise, and if they are bad, the price will fall. Technical Analysts argue that fundamental analysis lags the market to be of any use.

---

[1] Web sites: Society of Technical Analysts (STA) www.sta-uk.org , Market Technicians Association (MTA) www.mta.org, International Federation of Technical Analysts (IFTA) www.ifta.org

There are, of course, stories that Technical Analysts love to tell. There is the one about the Technical Analyst and the Fundamental Analyst having lunch one day. Accidentally, the Fundamental Analyst knocks his steak knife off the table and it goes straight into his foot. The Technical Analyst looks at him and says, "That must have hurt, why didn't you move your foot?" The Fundamental Analyst replies, "I thought it would go back up again". No matter how good the fundamentals are, a price in a strong downtrend is unlikely to reverse back up again without demand behind it.

Another is told about a broker who phones his client and says, "Hi, Bob, I have some good news and some bad news". Bob replies, "Oh dear, give me the bad news first". The broker says, "You know that share I told you to buy yesterday? Well, it has halved in price this morning". "Oh no," says Bob, "What's the good news?" "The fundamentals are still good", replies the broker.

Well, he's probably right. The fundamentals probably are still good because they have not had time to change. As John Maynard Keynes once remarked, when criticised for altering his position, "When the facts change, I change my mind. What do you do, Sir?" For a Technical Analyst, the facts are the price. If the price breaks up through a price level, a Technical Analyst may recommend buying. However, if, for some reason, the price pulls back again and goes in the other direction, Technical Analysts will change their view and recommend selling – unlike the broker, who, despite the change in direction, tells his client that the fundamentals are still good. Technical Analysts are often criticised for changing their view, but in fact a speedy adaptation to the movement in the price is the strength of Technical Analysis.

What is Technical Analysis?

Technical Analysts have never been very good at explaining what Technical Analysis is, so it is not surprising that it is often misunderstood. Technical Analysis in the Western world goes back to the 19th century, when Charles Dow, of Dow Jones fame, laid some of the foundations for the subject. Since then, its history has been well-documented, and books from the first half of the 20th century are excellent reading for anyone wishing to understand more about the subject and its rich history. So what is Technical Analysis and why is it is the best way to analyse markets?

When asked, most people will tell you that Technical Analysis is about charts, but it is likely that they don't know why. A book by Robert Edwards and John Magee, one of the definitive Technical Analysis texts, described (Technical Analysis) as follows:

"Technical Analysis is the Science of recording, usually in graphic form, the actual history of trading (meaning price changes, volumes etc.) in a certain share, or commodity etc. and then deducing from that pictured history, the probable future trend."

The definition is correct, but it doesn't explain what Technical Analysis actually is. It's a bit like explaining that a car is a pile of steel, glass and rubber that gets you from A to B. A car may be made of these things, but the definition does not communicate what a car really is; a mode of transport.

Technical Analysis is the art of recognising repetitive shapes and patterns within a data series represented by charts. It is the understanding that these patterns are created by price changes which are in turn created by the market participants like you and me. The patterns created by the market participants repeat themselves because human nature is constant; just like fashions repeat, so market action repeats itself.

The important point to remember is that it's people that create the price – their fear and greed, their hopes and prayers, and the opinions of the market participants. The price, and therefore the chart, is the weighted average sum of everyone's feeling or opinion about a particular share, future or commodity. It's better than an opinion poll, because everyone with the slightest interest in the share makes their mark by participating in the buying or selling thus making the price go up or down. A chart, therefore, is a study of human behaviour, and that is the key to Technical Analysis.

Technical Analysis is a bit like trying to cross the Champs Elysées in Paris. The safe way to do it is to wait on the pavement for a few people to gather. Someone will take a step off the pavement and step back as a car rushes past. And so it will continue. Individuals test the road until the small group on the pavement becomes more powerful than the cars and start holding up the traffic. Then, and only then, will the Technical Analyst step out and walk across the road. Technical Analysts need some indicator that things are now in their favour, before they act.

But why do Technical Analysts draw charts? The reason is that they can't interview all the market participants every day. All they can do is take the price and accept that at the end of the day – when all the 'fighting' has stopped – the price represents the best estimate as to the value of the company in question. It is then far easier and more informative to draw a chart of this price on a day-to-day basis than simply to write down the price. A chart can show things that the numbers cannot. For example, charts can show trends (and in 90% of cases markets do trend).

So, charts represent price movement, but what causes the price to move? It's simple. If there are more buyers than sellers, the price will go up. If there are more sellers than buyers, the price will go down. These are the simple laws of demand and supply that we all understand. The markets are driven by the constant fight between the buyers and the sellers. It has little to do with PE ratios, what a government minister has just said, or who a company's directors are. It is the interaction of the market participants and how they feel about all the available information that drives the price.

Trend

Trend is vital to good Technical Analysis. There is nothing unusual about that. You will hear economists, company analysts and accountants using the word 'trend' – trend in earnings, trend in the sales, trend in the exchange rate. Trends in fashion too. Anyone who has read *Memoirs of Extraordinary Popular Delusions and the Madness of Crowds* by Charles Mackay will have read about trends that have occurred in human behaviour, whether it is the price trend of tulip bulbs or the trend – one could say fashion – of going on the crusades. Trends do exist and are an integral part of human nature.

James Dines, in his 1972 book, *How the Average Investor can use Technical Analysis for Stock Profits*, placed trends into four psychological phases.

1. Cognitive or awareness stage

This is where the public are aware that a trend exists, but they are hesitant to get involved for one reason or another. It's like the start of a new fashion trend. You see it in the street, but wouldn't wear it yourself. You need to see confirmation that it exists and is not a one-off. You are aware that the market has been rising but, having been caught out before you are hesitant to get involved again.

2. Mobilisation stage

This is when the public start moving with the trend or the fashion and even the most hesitant get involved. Having seen the trend, they want to be part of it. They see others wearing the latest fashion and start to do so themselves. Having continually heard about profits that others are making in the market, you overcome your hesitation and get involved yourself.

3. Confirmation stage

This occurs when, having become involved, the public see confirmation that the trend exists and are now convinced by it. It's the "things are different this time, the old rules no longer apply" stage and complacency sets in. This stage was evident in the internet boom of the late 1990s. It's when you have taken up the fashion yourself and see others wearing it as well. Having become involved with the market you start to make the gains that others have been making. You feel secure.

4. Equilibrium stage

This occurs when the expectations are no longer met and the trend has to retreat dramatically to bring back equilibrium again. These expectations could be profit-related. Investors used to making 20% a month become disappointed with only 10%! It's when the fashion you have been wearing doesn't look that good anymore and when you step out you feel like a fool.

During this phase, the stock market can retreat significantly, as it did in the years following the technology boom top in March 2000.

Think how these phases apply to the analogy of crossing the road. The pioneers start, the crowd follows and everyone is happy, except the motorists, who, after waiting for a while, get impatient and start moving forward to prevent the pedestrian trend from continuing.

Technical Analysts are therefore most concerned with trends and trend lines. You just have to look at any chart and you will see that prices do move in trends. Human beings are trend followers. Technical Analysts observe these trends and act when important trends are broken.

Support and resistance

In addition to prices moving in trends, Technical Analysts also look for support and resistance levels. Support occurs at a level at which the market participants believe the price will rise and, consequently, where the demand is. Resistance occurs at a level at which the market participants believe that price cannot rise further and, consequently, where the supply is. Technical Analysts don't look for fundamental reasons why certain areas are support and resistance areas, they simply observe that they are. In fact, they occur mostly for psychological reasons. Let's have a look at how it might work: Figure 1 shows a hypothetical price on the decline.

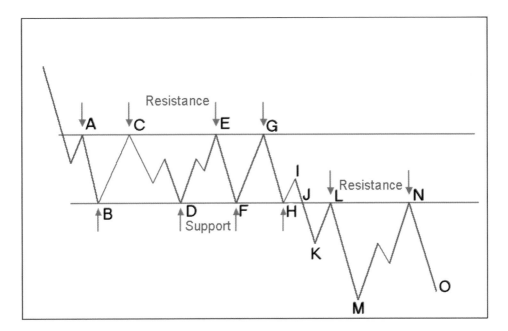

Figure 1: Support and resistance

The price is in a downtrend. It pauses, reacts back up to point A, and then falls to point B. Technical Analysts do not reason why it did this; it is simply understood that supply and demand caused the price to move in this way. At point A, buyers were not prepared to pay any more and so the price declined to B, where the buyers were prepared to start buying again.

You have to remember that the market is made up of lots of participants with differing views and objectives. Buyers who bought at point B may take profits at point C. However, there is another group who bought at point A, are pleased that the price has risen back to the same level at point C, and are pleased to get out of their position. This collective view causes a resistance level at point C and causes the price to move down from point C.

Remember, buyers at point B made a good gain when they sold at point C, and so when it gets down to point D they start buying again. This creates a support level, where buyers are prepared to take an interest again. This demand pushes the price back up again. Once again, at point E, they start selling, reinforcing the resistance level at that level. This causes the price to decline again until it reaches support at point F, where the same short-term traders, who have bought at B and D before, start buying again.

Point G is as far as the price gets again because the short-term traders have become confident that it will not go higher, and so the resistance at that level gets stronger. It declines again to point H and, once again, the buyers come back again, creating support for the price. The price bounces to point I and then falls back to point J. The same buyers who bought at point H are pleased that they now have a second chance to buy at the same price at point J, but this time, the sellers are in charge and force the price below point J. It is important to consider how the participants feel about this. Buyers had become confident buying at the same level and making a profit, so much so, that they probably were buying increasingly more each time. For the first time, they are in a losing position.

Some will sell their positions immediately, creating a selling frenzy that pushes the price down. Others will, however, hope and pray that the price will rise back to the price they paid. Point K is the point where the price has become oversold. That is, it has fallen too far too quickly, and short-term traders looking for a quick profit start buying. This forces the price back up to point L briefly, where the new buyers take a quick profit and some of the B, D, F, H and J buyers sell to break even. The move to point L is short-lived as so many sellers appear. So, the level at point L, which was a support level, now becomes a resistance level. The price falls to point M.

There is no reason why the price stops at point M. It could be at any level. It is simply a point where demand exceeds supply and the price is driven back up again. It is important to pause and consider the psychological make-up of the participants. There will be a large group who bought at the B, D, F, H and J levels and are still holding their positions. What is going through their minds is 'if only the price can reach the price I paid, I will sell out and never buy another thing again'! This creates even more resistance at the L level, which is the same level as the previous support. So, when the price does eventually rise back to that level, those who have been praying start selling at point N, reinforcing the resistance level and forcing the price down again to point O or lower. The level at points L and N will remain a strong resistance until there are no sellers left at that level.

The important point about this scenario is to understand that levels of support and resistance do occur on charts and that they occur for psychological, not fundamental reasons. When support is broken, it is important to recognise and understand that support becomes resistance to any up movement and that this is also caused by psychological reasons. Although not shown in the diagram, resistance, once broken becomes support to any down movement. So support and resistance alternate. This is not just a theory, it actually happens in real life, as the chart of Whitbread plc (a FTSE 100 company) below will testify.

Notice how resistance areas become support areas once the price breaks above the resistance, and support areas become resistance areas once support is broken. As explained, these are created by the emotions of fear and greed that influence market players. There are thousands of private scenarios being played out. There is no point in trying to analyse each and every one. Simply observe and predict where the price will be supported and where it will be resisted. You can see that there is support for the price around the 780 mark and resistance around the 850 mark. Should the resistance break, then the next resistance is at around 1130, a price tested twice several years ago.

Chart 1: Whitbread plc showing support and resistance levels

Price patterns

In addition to looking at trends, support and resistance, Technical Analysts also look for price patterns. These patterns help us to predict whether a trend has reversed or whether it will continue. They are not rigid patterns, and perhaps Technical Analysts made a mistake when they decided to give them names, like double-tops and head and shoulders, because then the uninformed take hold of them and recite them without understanding how and why they are created. These patterns are created by crowd psychology as well.

Let's see how it happens, referring to Figure 2.

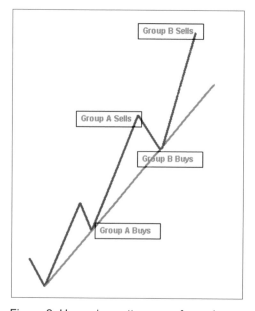

Figure 2: How price patterns are formed

The price finds a level where it starts to move up. Very few people get on the first leg up. After the first move up, profit-taking forces the price back and Group A buys. The point where Group A buys allows a trend line to be drawn from the bottom to this point. The price runs up and Group A, who are then showing a good profit, sell, causing the price to fall back again. When they think the price is at bargain levels, Group B, who missed out before, buys. The price runs back up again and Group B eventually sells for a profit and are pleased with themselves.

The price falls back to the psychological trend – the red trend line – in Figure 3. Group C, the largest group, usually small players, who have missed the whole move from the bottom, buy in the circled area. Instead of rising, however, the price continues down, breaking the uptrend line. Remember, however, that none of these participants are consciously aware that the trend line exists. Consider the psychological state that members of Group C are in. Their first foray into the market has left them holding a paper loss. Many will be praying that the price gets back to the level they paid so they can get out at break-even. The 'cheapness' of the price however attracts the attention of Group B, who notice that the price is in the same area that they had made a profit from before. Group B therefore buys as well and the price moves up again allowing a new trend line to be drawn. It is the line where there is currently demand. As the price reaches the level paid by Group C, it is held back by selling from Group C, who have just suffered the trauma of the price falling below the level they bought at. So, Group C sells to break even, placing resistance on any further up move, and the price falls back again. This allows a downtrend line to be drawn from the top. It is the line where there is currently supply. Look at Figure 3. The price is trapped in a triangular pattern bounded by the neckline and the downtrend line. It is a point of resolve, where either the demand from buyers or supply by sellers must take the upper hand. Also notice that a head and shoulders pattern has been traced out by the antics of the various groups. There is a head and two clear shoulders supported by a neckline.

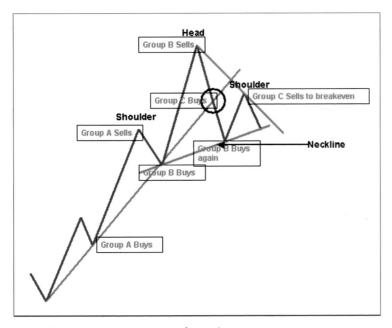

Figure 3: How price patterns are formed

Figure 4 shows what happens next. Instead of rising, the price falls, breaking the neckline in the circled area, indicating that the supply is greater than the demand. The price falls back and a new Group D, who have not yet participated, buy. Again the price moves up slightly, hitting the downtrend line where Group B, thankful that they can break even, sell. This selling pressure forces the price to fall again and another new group E buys. Once again, the demand, this time by Group E, drives the price back up and Group D, who have seen paper losses, use the opportunity to sell at a small loss, thankful to get out. This halts any further up movement and the price falls further until another new group F finds it cheap enough to buy. It is likely that Group F will consist of many members of Group A, who have seen the price come back to the level where they bought and made profits previously.

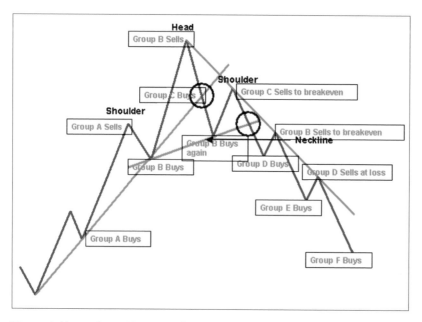

Figure 4: How price patterns are formed

The process continues in Figure 5. The price moves up and Group E, thankful to get out at break-even, sell, forcing it down again. As this happens, Group F, who can't believe their luck, come in and support it by buying more at the same level they bought before. The price moves up again. Group F who are now aware of previous levels where the price had turned down, sell for a profit, and the cycle starts all over again.

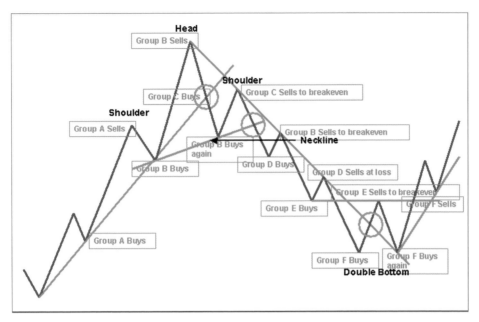

Figure 5: How price patterns are formed

Notice that in constructing this scenario, two very important patterns are created, namely, a head and shoulders top and a double-bottom.

Don't expect every scenario to play out in this form. There are thousands of permutations, but remember that patterns chartists observed 100 years ago still present themselves to this day. Why? Because people with the same habits and the same emotions are still behind the price moves. As you become more involved with charts and the technical analysis of them, so you will sub-consciously read them as if they are a picture of the emotions of the players in the market.

Finally

The brilliant thing about Technical Analysis that makes it so much more powerful than any other analysis method is that you can change your analysis time horizon by changing the time-frame of data you use, switching to weekly, monthly or even 1 minute price changes. Try asking a Fundamental Analyst for a short-term and medium term view.

Technical Analysis is the best method of analysis because:

- It is based on fact (the price), not estimates.

- Real people with real emotions drive the price.

- It keeps you on the right side of the trend – long in an uptrend and short in a downtrend.

- It lets you know when you are wrong and allows you to change your mind.

- It allows you to change your analysis time horizon by changing the time-frame of the chart.

Technical Analysis is a vast subject. It is not the intention of this book to cover every aspect, but rather just the Point and Figure method.

Emotion – the Analyst's greatest enemy

Without doubt, the greatest cause of bad decisions is emotion and, unfortunately like everyone else, Technical Analysts are subject to emotion when making their decisions. How many times have you spent an hour deciding which share to buy, only to be told that the fundamentals are poor? You change your mind about buying, only to see the price rise in the weeks following. How many times have you decided to sell your shares and then seen a glowing report in the newspapers predicting on ongoing bull run? You decide not to sell and, within days, the price falls dramatically.

These are the sorts of emotions that any investor is subjected to constantly. If you are a Technical Analyst in the corporate world, you may have additional pressure from your superiors who are not believers in Technical Analysis. Your advice may therefore be unpopular. Stick to your guns, however much pressure you get. In the end, it will pay off – you will be right and they will be wrong. Above all, do not listen to market gossip and rumour. So often, rumours are started by those who have bought into a share and then encourage the price to rise by spreading stories on how good the share is.

Finally, trading, and investing, isn't easy. If it were, it wouldn't be profitable.

Chapter 1

Introduction to Point and Figure Charts

Point and Figure charts are unique to Technical Analysis. Their roots are in the markets and have fascinated Technical Analysts for over a hundred years. Chart 1-1 below shows a Point and Figure chart of Whitbread plc, the same company shown in Chart 1 in the previous chapter.

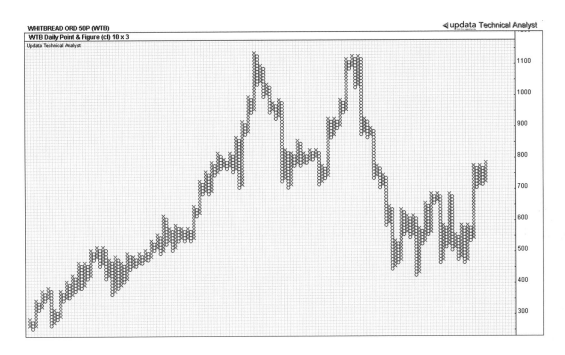

Chart 1-1: Point and Figure chart of Whitbread plc

It is not often that a discipline – in this case Technical Analysis – can claim complete ownership of a technique, with the knowledge that other disciplines could not use it even if they wanted to.

So unusual are Point and Figure charts that most students of Technical Analysis avoid them completely. This author has dedicated the last 20 years to educating and encouraging the wider use of Point and Figure chart analysis. One thing that makes them clearer to students is an understanding of where they came from and how they developed.

History and development

No one really knows precisely where the Point and Figure charts came from, or who invented them. They weren't always called Point and Figure charts, as you will see. Writing in 1933, Victor De Villiers and Owen Taylor state that the Point and Figure Method is over 60 years old. Some have therefore attributed them to Charles Dow, which seems to be the easy option, as Dow is regarded by many as the father of Technical Analysis. It is unlikely that any one person invented Point and Figure charts. In fact they probably weren't invented at all. It is more likely that they were born out of necessity – a need to be able to record price movement quickly and efficiently whilst on the move. 'On the move' being not at your desk, but standing on the trading floor or in front of the ticker tape machine in the broker's office, as most private traders would have been. What the trader wanted was a general idea of what the share price was doing. The most obvious way therefore, was to simply write down the prices on the back of a cigarette packet or notebook as the share traded as follows:

$9\frac{3}{4}$ $10\frac{1}{4}$ $11\frac{1}{2}$ $11\frac{1}{4}$ $12\frac{1}{2}$ $12\frac{1}{4}$ $13\frac{1}{4}$ 15 $16\frac{1}{2}$ 15 $14\frac{1}{4}$ $13\frac{1}{2}$ 12
$10\frac{1}{4}$ 10 $11\frac{3}{4}$ $11\frac{1}{2}$ 14 15 16 17 $19\frac{1}{2}$ 20 $21\frac{3}{4}$ 19 $18\frac{3}{4}$ $19\frac{1}{2}$ 20

It was not long before he[2] realised that there was no point in writing down all the fractions[3], because firstly it took more time, and secondly the fractional changes were irrelevant to the general trend, which is what he was trying to see. He therefore left out the ¼'s, the ½'s and the ¾'s, so his record of the day's trading started to look like this:

9 10 11 11 12 12 13 15 16 15 14 13 12 10 10 11 11 14 15 16 17 19 20 21 19 18 19 20

He now had a record of what the share was doing, but this is what it would look like at the end of a busy trading session.

9 10 11 11 12 12 13 15 16 15 14 13 12 10 10 11 11 14 15 16 17 19 20 21
19 18 19 20 21 19 18 19 20 20 21 23 20 19 16 15 13 12 10 10 8 9
11 11 14 15 16 17 15 11 12 12 13 12 12 13 15 16 15 13 12 10 10 11 11
14 15 16 17 19 20 21 19 20 20 23 24 21 22 22 20 19 19 20 22
20 21 20 21 20 19 19 20 19 20 20 21 22 21 20 20 21 21 22 21
20 19 19 18 19 19 20 19 20 19 19 18 18 17 18 17 16

---

2 'he' has been used for convenience, because firstly it is unlikely that any 'she's' were trading on the floor 120 years ago and secondly writing 'he or she' interrupts the flow of the text. Many of the world's best Technical Analysts are women and the author hopes that they do not take offence.

3 U.S. markets have always traded using fractions rather than decimals.

It would have been a mass of numbers. The only thing he could glean from it was the first price of the day, 9, and the last price of the day, 16. He could not see, at a glance, how it had traded during the day; what the high or low was; or where most of the trading had taken place. So, he had to come up with a better way of recording the prices. How about writing down the numbers in columns so that the highest and lowest price could easily be seen? Logically, he decided on a rising column for rising prices and a falling column for falling prices. Taking the first few prices from our series, his tabulation would have looked something like this.

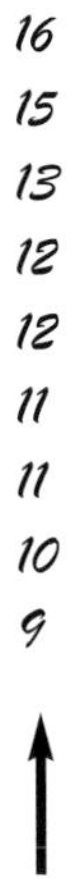

16

15

13

12

12

11

11

10

9

↑

Figure 1-1: Table of rising prices

It didn't take him long to work out that it was unnecessary to write down a price twice if it traded at the same price in succession. So, the double 11s and 12s disappeared. He also realised very quickly that when the price changed direction he would have to move across to the next column and write the number in the next free space. So, having written '10 11 12 13 15 16' in the first column as the price was rising, when the price fell back to 15, he realised he would have to move to the next column to write '15' and then '13 12 10' as the price fell further. See Figure 1-2:

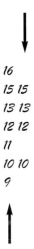

16
15 15
13 13
12 12
11
10 10
9

Figure 1-2: Table of rising and falling prices

This immediately showed a flaw in the method. In the first column, he initially missed out 14 because the price had not traded at 14, but that meant there was nowhere to put 14 in the second down-column as the price traded at 14 on the way down. So, he had to ensure that all price levels were recorded even though the price never traded at that level and hence one of the basic tenets of the method was established the charts take no account of gaps. See Figure 1-3, which shows the construction of the first 3 columns.

```
        17
16      16
15  15  15
14  14  14
13  13  13
12  12  12
11  11  11
10  10
9
```

Figure 1-3: Table of rising and falling prices

As the columns grew longer, and more columns appeared as the price changed direction, he realised that squared paper would assist in keeping the tables neat and regular and so his record (remember it was not intended to be a chart) started to look like Figure 1-4. The figures written into squares brought the word 'box' into the language, although he had no idea at this stage that, firstly, he was drawing a chart and, secondly, that it would one day be called Point and Figure, he would refer to the 14 box, or that the price had increased by 2 boxes.

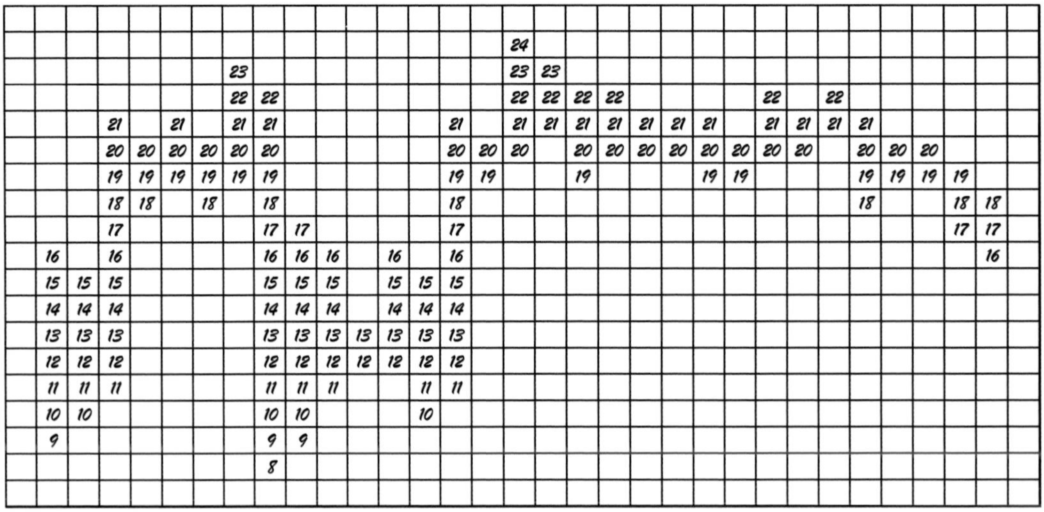

1	2	3	4	5	6	7	8	9	10	11	12	13	14	15	16	17	18	19	20	21	22	23	24	25	26	27
												24														
					23							23	23													
					22	22						22	22	22	22				22		22					
21		21			21	21					21	21	21	21	21	21			21	21	21	21				
20	20	20	20	20	20						20	20	20	20	20	20	20	20	20	20	20	20	20			
19	19	19	19	19	19						19	19			19			19	19	19	19	19	19			
18	18		18		18						18									18					18	18
17					17	17					17														17	17
16	16				16	16	16		16		16															16
15	15	15			15	15	15		15	15	15															
14	14	14			14	14	14		14	14	14															
13	13	13			13	13	13	13	13	13	13															
12	12	12			12	12	12	12	12	12																
11	11	11			11	11	11			11	11															
10	10				10	10				10																
9					9	9																				
					8																					

Figure 1-4: Early record of prices

Figure 1-4 shows how a Figure chart was born. It is important to note that it was not started as a method of charting, but more as a sequential price recording method.

Traders now had a way of recording price movements that had a number of benefits:

1. They could trace what the price had done during the day by following the columns.

2. They could easily see what the high of the day was (24).

3. They could easily see the low (8).

4. They could see where it closed on the day (16).

5. They could see where most of the trading had taken place by looking at the most filled in row (20).

6. It was a portable system that could be written on the back of an envelope and did not require the plotting rigours and precise time and price scaling of a line or bar chart. Thus, time is not an ingredient of the method.

In an editorial in the Wall Street Journal in 1901, Charles Dow described what we have seen above as the Book method because it was plotted from the ticker, often referred to as the market book.

Once traders realised that they were, in fact, drawing charts, the name 'Figure Chart' began to be used. Perhaps the best printed example of exactly how a trader would have drawn a Figure Chart[4] is shown by George Cole in his 1936 book. See Figure 1-5 below.

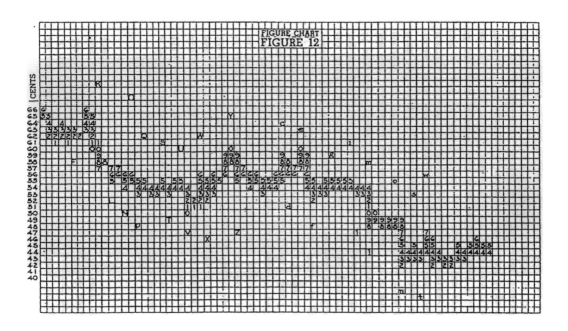

Source: Cole, Geo W., Graphs and the Application to Speculation, Peoria 1936

Figure 1-5: Early Figure chart

Note that he had a vertical scale, choosing to write down the price units only. Note also, that he entitled it 'Figure Chart'[5].

---

[4] In fact George Cole made some plotting errors in this chart. Once you become familiar with Point and Figure construction, see if you can spot where he went wrong.

[5] The inserted letters above and below the chart are reference points in Cole's text and have no relevance here.

Some traders would have found it tedious to write down the price all the time, preferring instead to 'tick off' or 'mark off' the price with a dot, a tick or cross as it hit a particular price level (Figure 1-6). These charts constructed with ticks or crosses started to appear towards the end of the 19th century and into the 20th. It is almost as if there were several groups developing the charts to their own specification, often not realising that others were doing the same.

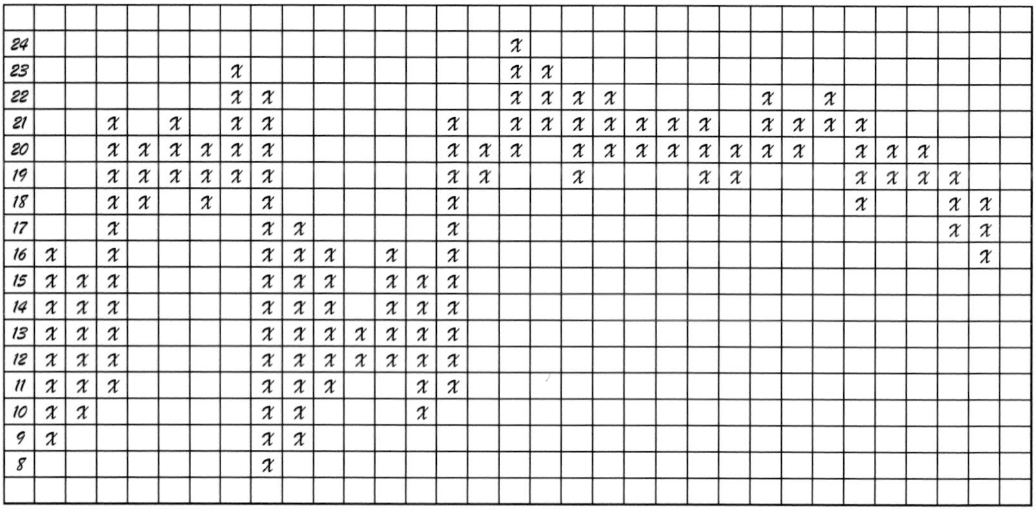

	1	2	3	4	5	6	7	8	9	10	11	12	13	14	15	16	17	18	19	20	21	22	23	24	25	26	27	28
24																X												
23						X										X	X											
22						X	X									X	X	X	X				X		X			
21			X		X	X	X				X					X	X	X	X	X	X	X	X		X	X	X	X
20			X	X	X	X	X	X			X	X	X			X	X	X	X	X	X	X	X		X	X	X	
19			X	X	X	X	X	X			X	X				X			X	X					X	X	X	X
18			X	X		X		X			X					X									X		X	X
17			X					X	X		X																X	X
16	X		X					X	X	X		X		X		X												X
15	X	X	X					X	X	X		X	X	X		X	X	X		X	X	X						
14	X	X	X					X	X	X		X	X	X		X	X	X		X	X	X						
13	X	X	X					X	X	X	X	X	X	X		X	X	X	X	X	X	X						
12	X	X	X					X	X	X	X	X	X	X		X	X	X	X	X	X	X						
11	X	X	X					X	X	X			X	X		X	X	X			X	X						
10	X	X						X	X				X			X	X				X							
9	X							X	X							X	X											
8								X								X												

Figure 1-6: Chart constructed with crosses

In 1898, an anonymous writer, calling himself 'Hoyle', published what he called a 'pamphlet' entitled *The Game in Wall Street and How to Play it Successfully*. In it, he described and demonstrated *'the method of keeping records of the fluctuation in the price of stocks'*. His method shown in Figure 1-7 is exactly the Figure method described above.

The method of keeping the records of the fluctuations in the price of stocks as shown on the charts in this book is as follows :

Suppose St. Paul sells at 85 then goes to 86 and to 87. Then the price turns and reacts to 85 again. Then it turns again and goes to 86, 87, 88, 89. Then reacts to 87. Then goes up to 90 and down to 89. The record should be made each day in the order in which the changes occur,

```
                              90
                89            89      89
                88     88     88
87              87     87
86       86     86
85       85
```

the corresponding quotations should always be on the same horizontal line.

Source: Hoyle, The Game in Wall Street, J.S., reprinted by Fraser Publishing

Figure 1-7: Fluctuation chart

Although he described the Figure method in detail, Hoyle's charts were actually drawn with price scales, and instead of numbers, he had 'ticks' as if he was ticking off the prices as they occurred. Figure 1-8 is an example of a Fluctuation chart from Hoyle's booklet. The fact that this appeared in a book suggests that it must have been in common usage at that time.

Hoyle states that the "*study of fluctuations or records of daily ups and downs in prices of stocks furnishes a key to an understanding of this whole business*". They are "*the smoke and dust of battle that hides the plans of the general from the men in the thick of the fight*".

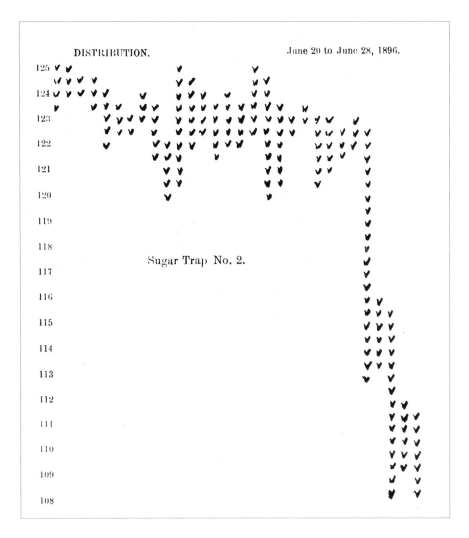

Source: Hoyle, The Game in Wall Street, J.S., reprinted by Fraser Publishing

Figure 1-8: Fluctuation chart

Although there is no evidence to support the theory, one can imagine that these charts could have been referred to as tick charts, a name that lives on to this day in describing any chart that records prices as they occur, rather than in equal time intervals.

The method of ticking off the price with ticks did not, however, seem to be that widespread. There is more evidence of the use of the letter X, but this did not mean the demise of Figure charts. Richard Wyckoff, writing under the name 'Rollo', in 1910 clearly shows a chart constructed with figures, showing the Amalgamated Copper panic of 1903 (Figure 1-9). There is no mention of using Xs or ticks.

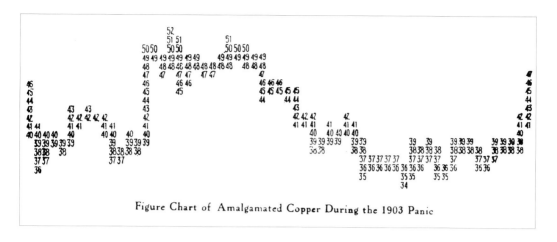

Source: Rollo Tape, Studies in Tape Reading and the Application to Speculation, 1910, reprinted Fraser Publishing

Figure 1-9: Early Figure chart

The next mention of Point and Figure charts was in 1932, when Richard Schabacker published his Technical Analysis epic, entitled, *Technical Analysis and Stock Market Profits*. Although the book is mainly about Bar and Line charts, he included a short section headed '*Point and Figure charts*', which he referred to as a "*corruption of the ticker chart*". A ticker chart was one where the prices were not grouped by time. This type of chart is referred to as a Tick chart nowadays. Schabacker also states that Point and Figure charts are similar to minor move charts, where a vertical line continued to be drawn until the price reversed by a prescribed amount. At that point, a short horizontal line was drawn and another vertical line was drawn in the other direction. Although he does not show one, these appear to be similar to Manhattan swing charts and are related to Point and Figure charts because they take no account of time.

Interestingly, Schabacker states that "*this type of chart has many names, but it is usually known as the Figure or the Point chart*". He concluded the section by saying that Point or Figure charts "*offer the practical trader no advantages over the ordinary vertical line chart*" [bar chart].

In 1933, Richard Wyckoff mentioned and showed a Figure chart (Figure 1-10) in his book *Stock Market Technique No.1* and challenged the reader to interpret it. When you compare the charts you can see that the construction method is exactly the same as that in his 1910 book. He made no mention of any chart constructed with ticks or crosses.

Can you read this chart?

To 64
↑

It shows all the one point movements of Atchison around 18 — its low point in July 1932, where it turned upward for a rise to 64.

```
31                                                                          31
30  30                                                                      30
29  29  29  29                                                              29
    28  28  28                                              28  28  28
            27                                              27  27  27
        26  26                                              26
        25  25                                    25        25
            24                                    24  24  24
            23      22                23  23  23  23
            22  22                    22  22  22
            21  21  21          21    21
                20  20  20  20  20    20
                    19  19  19  19
                    18
```

The action of Atchison at that time gave *ten distinct buy signals* from 18 to 24. It kept *urging* you to buy.

If you *know* these signals you have an understanding of Stock Market Technique. If not you can learn them.

Such a chart gives you *better* and *more re-*

liable information than any insider or other adviser can give you. Its forecasts and predictions work out to a high percentage of accuracy.

If you had bought 100 shares of Atchison when this chart told you to buy, around 20, you could have sold it at 60 within six weeks — a profit of $4,000.

Source: Wyckoff, R.D, Stock Market Technique Number One, reprinted by Fraser Publishing

Figure 1-10: Figure chart construction example

Also, in 1933, the first book dedicated to Point and Figure charts appeared. De Villiers' booklet, entitled *The Point and Figure Method of Anticipating Stock Price Movements – Complete Theory and Practice*, appears to be the first text dedicated to the Method, indicating that it was by then widespread enough to sell a book describing it. In the book, De Villiers shows an example of a chart constructed with figures, which he calls the Figure Method, as well as one constructed with Xs and numbers at key levels, which he calls the Point Method (Figure 1-11).

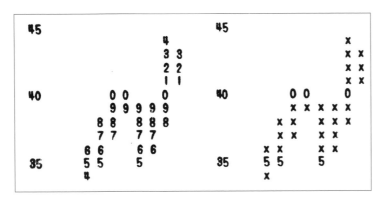

Source: De Villiers, V, The Point and Figure Method of Anticipating Stock Price Movements, 1933, Reprinted by Windsor Books

Figure 1-11: Early Figure chart and early Point chart

He states that he prefers the Point Method, but does say that Figure charts do have the advantage that the analyst can see the repetition of the figures at a particular level more easily than in Point charts. He goes on to say that Figure charts are *"old fashioned"*, so, by 1933, Point charts – as De Villiers calls them – were starting to replace Figure charts, but it does show that even into the 1930s Figure charts were still being used. There is no doubt, however, that Point charts were becoming more widespread, reinforced by that fact that throughout De Villiers' book the charts he shows are those constructed with Xs instead of Figures.

In doing away with figures written in each square, Point and Figure chartists had to have another way of seeing what the price level was. They introduced a vertical price scale so that the price could be marked off quickly as it moved, but they also considered the 5 and 10 levels so important that they wrote the numbers five (5) and zero (0) in the squares at these levels. See Figure 1-11.

The original price series, used here as an example, started off as rows of numbers, then the trader started to use columns of numbers, then the columns became Figure charts, then Tick charts and finally Xs replaced the numbers and the ticks, which resulted in Point charts where Xs, 5s and 0s were used instead of figures.

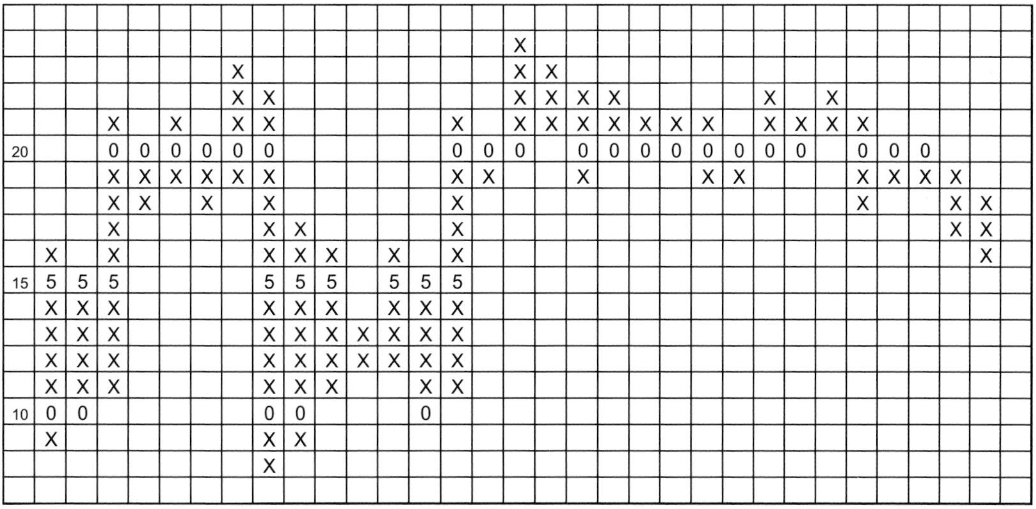

```
                           X
        X                  X X
        X X                X X X X        X     X
      X   X                X           X X X X X X X       X X X X
 20   0 0 0 0 0 0          0 0 0       0 0 0 0 0 0 0 0     0 0 0
      X X X X X X          X X         X             X X     X X X X
      X X     X            X           X                     X
      X                    X X         X                     X X
      X                    X X X       X                     X
 15   5 5 5                5 5 5       5 5 5
      X X X                X X X       X X X
      X X X                X X X X X X X
      X X X                X X X X X X X
      X X X                X X X       X X
 10   0 0                  0 0         0
      X                    X X
                           X
```

Figure 1-12: Point chart example

Writing again in 1933, this time with Owen Taylor in a much more comprehensive work, De Villiers does not refer to, or show, Figure charts at all. All the charts shown in the book are constructed with Xs, 5s and 0s as shown in Figure 1-12.

In Wyckoff's 1934 work, *Stock Market Technique No.2*, he showed the charts constructed with Xs, 5s and 0s (Figure 1-13), just as De Villiers and Taylor had done in 1933, which was a complete change from Wyckoff's book, written a year earlier. So, with Wyckoff persuaded to move to crosses, we can conclude that Figure charts had virtually ceased to exist.

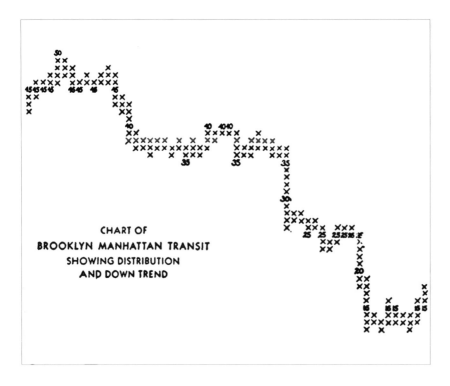

Source: Wyckoff, R.D, Stock Market Technique Number Two, reprinted by Fraser Publishing

Figure 1-13: Early Point chart

In 1936, George Cole's pioneering work, *Graphs and the Application to Speculation*, refers to, and shows, a hand-written Figure chart, shown in Figure 1-5 on page 33. He states, however, that some practitioners prefer a chart constructed with Xs instead of Figures and shows an example of a chart constructed with Xs, where each X is half a point. See Figure 1-14[6]. What is interesting however is that he did *not* include 5s and 0s at the 5 and 10 levels on the chart. Cole does not refer to De Villiers or Taylor, but does say the method of Figure charts was originated by Charles Dow.

---

[6] Once again, the letters above and below the chart are irrelevant.

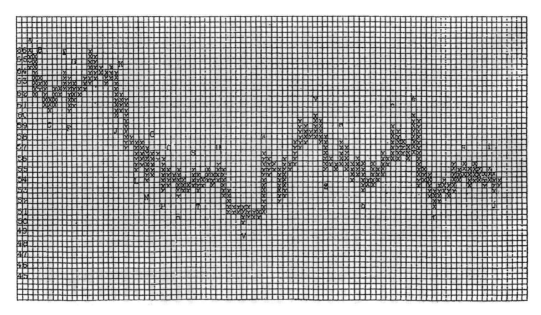

Source: Cole, Geo W., Graphs and the Application to Speculation, Peoria 1936

Figure 1-14: Early Point chart

It is safe to assume that Figure charts gave way to Point charts constructed with Xs for two reasons:

1. Writing down numbers had become tedious.

2. If a fractional chart was required like a half point chart in Figure 1-14, they would have to have written down all the ½'s as well, which would have made the chart unreadable.

There appears to have been another lull in writing until two very important works appeared: A.W. Cohen's 1947 work, entitled *Stock Market Timing*, later re-titled as *The Chartcraft Method of Point & Figure Trading* and re-titled again as *How to use the Three Point Reversal Method of Point and Figure Stock Market Trading*; as well as Alexander Wheelan's 1954 booklet, *Study Helps in Point and Figure Technique*.

The two books could not have been more different if they had tried. Cohen's was the very first occurrence of a completely new plotting method which will be discussed in a later chapter. Significantly, the traditional chart constructed with Xs – and sometimes 5s and 0s at key levels – was dispensed with, in favour of a chart constructed with the letters X and O[7], where Xs designated up-moves and Os designated down moves. It gave a completely new

---

[7] For readability, Xs and Os should be read as Ex's and Oh's rather than crosses and noughts. So an X is an 'Ex' rather than a cross, and an O is an 'Oh' rather than a nought.

meaning to Point and Figure charts and their interpretation. Figure 1-15 shows our original price series constructed with Xs and Os.

```
                                              X
                                 X            X  O
                                 X  O         X  O  X  X                    X        X
                    X       X    X  O      X  X  O  O  X  O  X  X           X  O  X  O
 20                 X  O  X  O  X  O        X  O  X        O  X  O  O  O  X  X  O        O  X  X
                    X  O  X  O  X  O        X  O           O              O  O           O  X  O  O
                    X  O     O     O        X                             O                 O  X
                    X                    O  X              X              O                    O  O
           X        X                 O  X  O           X                                         O
 15        X  O     X                 O  X  O      X  O  X
           X  O     X                 O  X  O      X  O  X
           X  O     X                 O  X  O  X  X  O  X
           X  O     X                 O  X  O  X  O  O  X
           X  O     X                 O  X  O        O  X
 10        X  O                       O  X              O
           X                          O  X
                                      O
```

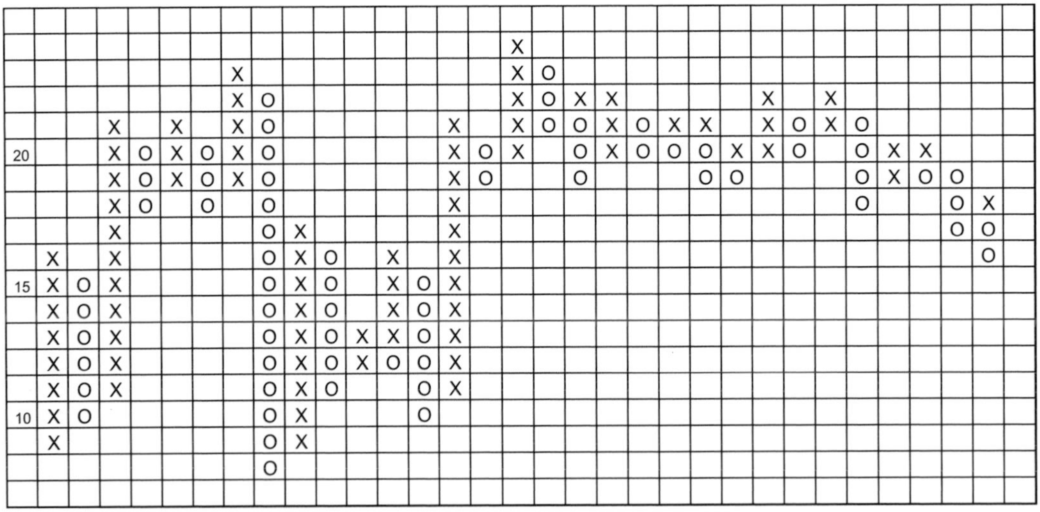

Figure 1-15: Point and Figure chart example

It is easy to see why Cohen preferred charts constructed with Xs and Os. Charts constructed with Xs, 5s (fives) and 0s (zeros) suffer from two problems:

- It is confusing, having Xs going up as well as down. Anyone looking at the chart has to work out whether the first column is a rising or falling one, before analysis can take place. This is a waste of time and prone to mistakes.

- It is also somewhat off-putting to see rows of 0s and 5s amongst the Xs as they can be mistaken for support and resistance levels – which they are not – leading to incorrect interpretation.

Although the X and O method was clearer, some authors, namely Alexander Wheelan in 1954, still used charts with Xs, 5s and 0s. Nowhere did he use the X and O method. In fact, to this day, the X-only method is still the best method when a certain type of Point and Figure chart – called a 1-box chart – is drawn. The X-only method (without the 5s and 0s) makes the 1-box chart clearer than the X and O method does. The X and O method is, however, the clearest for all other types of Point and Figure chart.

Books on Point and Figure charts have continued to appear over the last 20 years, from authors such as Aby (1996), Blumenthal (1975), Burke (1990), Dorsey (2001), Markstein (1972), Zieg (1997) and others. Their excellent texts are listed in the References section on page 465. Most have, however, ignored the history and therefore the original methods of construction, leading newcomers to Point and Figure to believe that there is only one type of Point and Figure chart, constructed in only one way. This book will address that issue.

So, that is the history and development of Point and Figure charts. You may find it useful to read it again, because no other method has such a clear development path. It is the understanding of the psychology that caused this development path that is important when it comes to interpreting Point and Figure charts. It is almost as if it is the mouthpiece or the voice of the market. The chart moves only when the market moves and only when there is significant movement in the price. It is like watching a ticker tape or the trading of a particular stock on the floor, which sadly does not exist in most major markets anymore. It is a graphic representation of the supply and demand, the fear and greed that is part of the market.

Where did Point and Figure charts get their name?

There has been much discussion and speculation about the origin of the name Point and Figure, and, although it is not that important, it is worth looking at the written evidence.

Charles Dow described the early charts constructed with figures as the 'Book Method'. They were so called because the charts were plotted from the ticker, also known as the market book, in a sequential process.

As stated earlier, Hoyle did not give the method a name, other than to describe them as 'fluctuation records'. Although he described the recording of figures, Hoyle's charts were drawn with price scales, and instead of numbers he used 'ticks', as if he was ticking off the prices as they occurred.

Richard Wyckoff describes and shows a Figure chart of Amalgamated Copper during the 1903 panic, but says nothing about Points. So, by 1903 the Book Method had become known as Figure charts.

It is clear, therefore, where the word 'Figure' came from. Figures were used to plot the prices as they occurred. There is, however, some confusion and speculation as to where the word 'Point' originated.

Wyckoff referred to one-point Figure charts in 1933, where the lower case 'p' and upper case 'F' were deliberate. The charts were Figure charts, plotting one point.

In his 1933 book, entitled *Point and Figure Charts*, De Villiers states that although he uses Point charts exclusively, Figure charts do have the advantage that the analyst can see the repetition of the figures at a particular level more easily than in Point charts. This implies that there were two types of chart: Figure charts constructed with figures; and Point charts where the figures are replaced by Xs. Throughout the book, De Villiers refers to the Point and Figure method, but when referring to charts he refers to them as Points and Figures (note the plural).

This implies that the words 'Point' and 'Figure' relate to the two methods – the Point method and the Figure method. It is likely therefore, that when referring to his charts the analyst referred to his Points and Figures charts and possibly the combination of the two, using Xs with 5s and 0s, was referred to as Point and Figure.

In an apparent complete contradiction, however, writing with Owen Taylor in 1933, De Villiers clearly states that the name, Point and Figure, came from plotting one point in figures. This is confusing, since in the same year he had earlier referred to Figure charts or Point charts in a book with the same title. In De Villiers and Taylor, they refer to Point and Figure (singular) charts and do not refer to them as separate Point charts or Figure charts. This could have been Taylor's influence, but it does seem that this was the earliest joining of the two methods into one name and then searching for a reason for doing so. De Villiers and Taylor chose to explain the name as plotting one point in figures. On the evidence this does not seem a good explanation.

In the first of his *Stock Market Technique* books also published in 1933, Wyckoff discusses Figure charts constructed with Figures and states that the *"one point figure chart"* is the standard for stocks.

Although it was clear from a number of sources that Figure charts were losing favour to Point charts, it still does not explain the name Point and Figure.

George Cole refers to, and shows, a Figure chart similar to De Villiers'. He also states that some practitioners prefer a chart constructed with Xs instead of Figures and shows an example of a Figure chart constructed with Xs where each X is half a point. He calls this chart a *"One half point Figure Chart"*. One presumes that if each X had been worth one point he would have referred to it as a *"One point Figure chart"*. This is a similar naming convention to that used by Wyckoff in 1933. It is possible, therefore, that Point and Figure got its name in one or all of three ways:

1.   As De Villiers and Taylor explained in 1933, the charts got their name by plotting one point in figures. This is, however, a flawed reason because it does not explain what the chart would have been called if each X were half a point, as many were.

2.   The name came from a distortion of the full name *'One point Figure chart'* where each X represents one point, or the *'Half point Figure chart',* where each X represents half a point, as Cole and Wyckoff seem to suggest, although neither of them ever referred to their charts as Point and Figure charts.

3.   Writers and practitioners referring to their *'Point or Figure charts'* or their *Point and Figure charts* meaning their Point charts and/or their Figure charts, which represented the same thing, and this became distorted to Point and Figure charts. This theory is supported by the fact that De Villiers entitled his 1933 book *Point and Figure charts* but never actually referred to them as Point and Figure in the book, but rather as Point charts

and Figure charts as separate types of chart. However, the final piece of conclusive evidence comes from Point and Figure sceptic, Richard Schabacker, who heads a section in his 1932 book as 'Limitations of Point or Figure charts'. Note the use of the word 'or'. All the way through the section, he refers to Point or Figure charts as if the analyst had the choice of one or the other but probably kept both. As you have read earlier, he headed another section 'Point and Figure charts', but said that this type of chart is usually known as the Figure chart or the Point chart.

The evidence, therefore, seems to favour the third way. Of course, it does not really matter where and how it got its name, because the method we know today is called the Point and Figure method and the charts we draw and analyse are called Point and Figure charts. It is interesting however to show that it was an evolving technique that may well keep evolving. Towards the end of this book, some new Point and Figure techniques, such as moving averages on Point and Figure charts as well as Point and Figure charts of indicators, are covered.

Before moving to the next chapter on Point and Figure construction, here are a few examples of what Point and Figure charts look like. Remember they work just as well for stocks, indices, futures, commodities, bonds and currencies – in fact any financial instrument. Don't worry about trying to understand the charts at this stage; they will be explained in later sections. The purpose is to get a 'feel' for the charts.

Chart 1-2 is a traditional Point chart of Intel Corp, where Xs are used for up- and down-columns. It is drawn in the early De Villiers style of showing 5s and 0s at the 5 and 10 levels. You can see now having these rows of numbers can make the chart confusing.

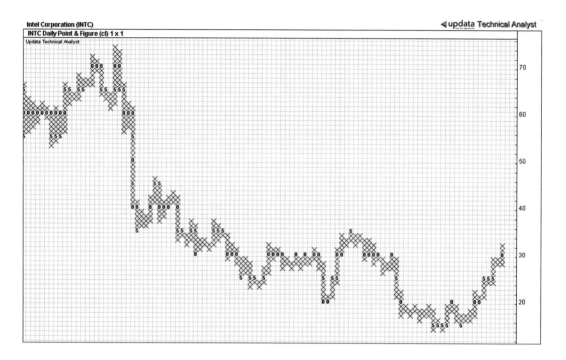

Chart 1-2: Computer drawn Point chart with 5s and 0s of Intel Corp.

Chart 1-3 is a traditional Point chart of Euro Dollar, where Xs are used for up- as well as down-columns. This version is favoured for 1-box charts, which you will learn about later.

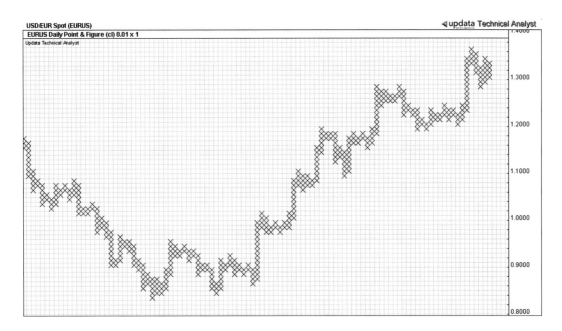

Chart 1-3: Computer drawn Point chart of Euro Dollar

Chart 1-4 is a Point and Figure chart of the Gold price, constructed using the Cohen method of Xs and Os. Notice, however, that some of the Xs and Os are replaced by numbers. Because Point and Figure charts don't have a time-scale, some analysts use a number to show the start of each month instead of an X or O. A, B and C are used for October, November and December.

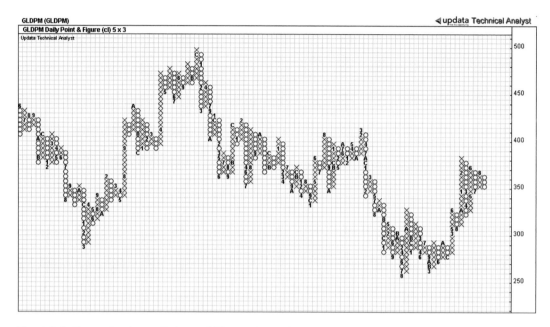

Chart 1-4: Computer drawn Point and Figure chart of gold pm fix showing month numbers

Finally, Chart 1-5 shows a Point and Figure chart of Reckitt Benckiser plc constructed with Xs and Os which are coloured blue and red to identify the columns and make the chart easier to read.

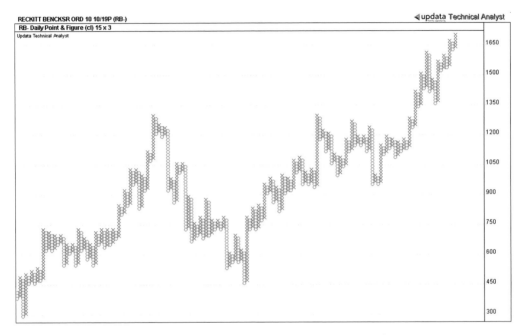

Chart 1-5: Computer drawn Point and Figure chart of Reckitt Benckiser plc

The *voice* of the market

Point and Figure charts are the *voice of the market*. They are the only charts that come directly from the trading floor and are plotted as and when the price changes. Of course, all charts come from the market, but remember that Point and Figure charts only change when the price changes. All other charts having time-scales must move forward as time passes, whether the price is changing or not. When the market is quiet, Point and Figure charts do not move. When the market is busy and the price is moving up and down, Point and Figure charts show that movement.

Point and Figure charts plot every price box size tick by tick, telling you exactly what is going on. It's like the market talking to you. When analysing Point and Figure charts, that's exactly what you get from the charts – your own squawk box. Each minor and major battle between bulls and bears is played out on the chart and is there for you to see and analyse. If nothing is happening, the chart falls silent as well.

Chapter 2

Characteristics and Construction

Already you will have seen that Point and Figure charts are different from any other type of chart. In order to define them however, certain characteristics must be enumerated and discussed. These characteristics are also important for the understanding and interpretation of the charts.

Characteristics of Point and Figure charts

Point and Figure charts have the following unique features, all of which are explained in greater detail below:

- They are usually[8] constructed with Xs and Os[9] instead of lines or bars.

- Xs represent sequential up movements in price.

- Os represent sequential down movements in price.

- The Xs and Os are called 'boxes'.

- Each X and O represents a discrete price interval, which is called the 'box size'.

- Price changes below this interval are ignored when plotting the chart.

- A column of Xs changes to a column of Os (and vice versa) when the price changes direction by a given number of boxes. This is called the 'reversal size'.

- The columns of Xs and Os represent demand and supply.

- The chart sensitivity can be varied to show the short, medium and long-term position using the same data.

- No record is made of price gaps.

- Price is scaled on the vertical Y axis.

- There is no time-scale along the horizontal X axis.

- Time plays no part in the construction or analysis of Point and Figure charts.

- Although there is no time axis, Point and Figure charts are two-dimensional charts.

- Volume plays no part in the construction or analysis of Point and Figure charts.

- Point and Figure charts are named according to their box and reversal size.

---

[8] Sometimes it is better to use Xs only. This is clarified later.

[9] Meaning the letter X and the letter O.

Constructed with Xs and Os

You will recall that early Point and Figure charts were constructed with numbers or figures and that these numbers were replaced by Xs, which were eventually replaced with Os and Xs. Every time you look at a Point and Figure chart, you must visualise this. You will learn that it is often better to construct some Point and Figure charts using Xs only.

Up moves and down moves

Xs are used to indicate up moves in price and Os are used to indicate down moves. Using two different letters makes Point and Figure charts very readable. You can instantly see the general trend, and within that general trend you can see the intermediate pullbacks against the trend represented by alternate columns of Xs and Os. Computer-drawn Point and Figure charts allow Xs and Os to be drawn in different colours, normally blue for up and red for down.

Xs and Os called boxes

You have seen why they are called boxes, because on squared paper the Xs and Os are drawn in 'boxes'. You will find, when you look at construction, that the word 'box' is used to describe the Point and Figure chart.

Box size

You will recall that early Figure charts ignored any fractional movement. This meant that a figure could only be written down when the price reached that level. The same applies to Point and Figure charts constructed with Xs and Os. Each X and O is given a sensitivity value before the chart is constructed. This is called the *box size*. It may be 1 point, ½ a point, or it may even be 50 points. No matter what value is assigned, you may not plot an X or O until the price has reached the next interval. For example, if each X and O is 50 points, then the values of ascending Xs would be 50, 100, 150, 200 and so on. A price move from 50 to 99 would be ignored because it had not reached 100. It is important to note that the 'box' represents the price and not the line. Point and Figure charts are plotted differently from line or bar charts. With line or bar charts the price scale is represented by lines, so a price of 100 is on the horizontal line at 100. With Point and Figure charts however, 100 is a square with an X or an O above the 100 line. This often confuses students of Point and Figure and will be seen when the construction procedure is explained.

Reversal size

The reversal size is an important part of Point and Figure chart construction. It is the number of boxes required to change from a column of Xs to a column of Os or from a column of Os to a column of Xs. Depending on the type of Point and Figure chart you are drawing, the reversal size can be 1-box, which is the original method, 3-box, 5-box, or any other value. It is, however, important to note that this terminology has changed for the better over the years. Cohen and others before him referred to 3-point reversal charts, meaning that the box size was 1 point and so a reversal of 3 boxes was 3 points. This was fine when Point and Figure charts were constructed with a box size of 1-point, but started to get confusing when the box size was, say, 5 points. The reversal was then referred to as a 15-point (5 x 3) reversal chart. You will however still hear Point and Figure analysts talk of their 3-point reversal charts, meaning their 3-box reversal charts.

Variable sensitivity

One of the unique characteristics of Point and Figure charts is that the sensitivity to price changes can be varied by varying the box size – that's the number of points that each X and O represent – as well as the reversal size – the number of Xs or Os required to convert from a column of Xs to Os or Os to Xs. This will be explained in much greater detail later.

Gaps

Point and Figure charts do not record gaps. If the price jumps from 10 to 15, each price on the way to 15 (that is 11, 12, 13 and 14) is recorded by an X. As you saw in the development of Figure charts, you cannot leave out a price row just because the price did not print there. The reason is that it may be required in the future if the price trades at that level later in the chart.

Price on Y-axis but no time on X-axis

Point and Figure charts have a vertical y-axis scale for price, but no horizontal x-axis scale where time would usually be shown. Point and Figure charts are constructed as and when new prices are received, with no regard to time. Time is therefore not a factor in the construction or interpretation. Only when the instrument trades at a new price is the Point and Figure chart updated, provided the condition for plotting an X or O is fulfilled. This means that whereas line and bar charts assign equal importance to every time interval, whether that be days or minutes, Point and Figure charts do not. Instead, their second dimension is related to the changes in direction of the price. So, you will not find a time or date scale on a Point and Figure chart, but you may find references to dates. Some Point and Figure analysts place the number of the month into a box instead of an X or O to signify the start of a new month. The only reason for doing this is to have a reference point. It has no influence on the analysis of the chart at all. Most modern software allows you to read off approximate dates making the use of these month numbers redundant.

Two-dimensional charts

It is important to be clear that Point and Figure charts are not one-dimensional, as many believe. It is true that they do not have a time-scale, but that does not cause them to be one-dimensional. They are, in fact, two-dimensional. This usually comes as a shock to those who have a basic knowledge of Point and Figure charts. A chart has two dimensions when it has two axes: a y-axis and an x-axis. In bar and line charts, price is scaled on the vertical y-axis and time is scaled along the x-axis. With Point and Figure, price is scaled on the vertical y-axis and the number of columns of Xs and Os is scaled along the horizontal x-axis. The x-axis therefore measures the number of changes in direction because each time the price changes direction, a column of Xs becomes a column of Os and vice versa. This has important implications for the analysis and understanding of Point and Figure charts and trend lines, as you will see.

No volume

There is no room for volume in Point and Figure charts. Volume, although a valuable ingredient in market analysis, is not required in Point and Figure construction or analysis. Point and Figure charts, however, do cater for volume in a different way. Rather than recording number of shares or contracts traded, Point and Figure charts record number of price reversals, which could be thought of as activity volume.

Demand and supply

Because Point and Figure charts divide intermediate uptrends into columns of Xs and downtrends into columns of Os it is easier to see the buying pressure, or the demand, by the length of the column of Xs, and the selling pressure, or supply, by the length of the columns of Os. The equilibrium of these two forces is an important part of Point and Figure analysis, which is discussed in chapter 3.

Naming Point and Figure charts

It is customary now to name Point and Figure charts with the box and reversal size. The person looking at the chart needs these two parameters to understand the chart. A Point and Figure chart, where the box size is 10 and the number of boxes required to change columns is 3, is referred to as a 10 x 3 (10 by 3) Point and Figure chart. This convention leaves no room for doubt, when looking at a Point and Figure chart, as to what the box and reversal are.

Point and Figure construction

Many students of Point and Figure ignore the construction chapters because modern software does it for them. Whether or not you intend to draw Point and Figure charts by hand, it is vital that you understand the construction, as this explains the behaviour and psychology behind them. That aside, you may not know that there are a number of ways to construct Point and Figure charts and that these methods are not mutually exclusive. So, do not ignore the rest of this chapter. You will come out knowing a lot more about the whole meaning of Point and Figure charts. This book is designed as a complete reference work, which brings together all the known Point and Figure construction methods for the first time. It would therefore be remiss to leave out any method and the accompanying examples.

Now that there is an accepted way of drawing Point and Figure charts, using Xs and Os, construction may be tackled. Unfortunately, under the umbrella of Point and Figure, there are a number of different Point and Figure charts, each of which is constructed, and consequently interpreted, in a different way.

It was established earlier that true Point and Figure charts require intra-day tick data because they were originally constructed from the tape or from the floor, so this construction method will be looked at first, where all the price changes during the day are available and every price is considered in the order it is received.

Remember, up movements in price are designated by plotting a column of Xs and down movements by plotting a column of Os. Point and Figure charts plot discrete movements only, so in order to construct a Point and Figure chart, you must decide what value each X and O will have. This is the box size. Traditionally it was 1 point or 1c or 1p, but this is hardly practical when plotting a Point and Figure chart of the Dow Jones Industrial Average, or an exchange rate. So, the value you assign to each X and O must be decided by considering the instrument in question and deciding what price moves you wish to isolate. This will depend on the range and level of the prices in question. For example, you might use 50 points for the FTSE 100 Index, 100 for the Dow, or .001 for an exchange rate, and so on, but this will be covered in detail later. It is important to use 'rounded' values like 1, 2, 5, 10, 15, 20, 25, 50, 100 etc. or multiples of these. Don't be tempted to use values like 7 or 13 or 38 just because the chart will fit on the sheet of paper you are using.

In addition to deciding on the box size, there is another factor in the construction of Point and Figure charts. You must decide by how much the price must reverse in order to change from an X to an O or O to an X. In practice, this amounts to the number of boxes required to change direction. This is called the *reversal*. Traditionally the reversal has been 1-box, 3-box or 5-box, where to record a change in direction the price must reverse by either the value of 1-box, 3 boxes or 5 boxes. These will be dealt with in turn as the construction for each is different.

1-box charts provide the detail of the price action and are vital for understanding the demand and supply forces involved. 3-box charts provide more of a summary of the price action, without showing the detail that the 1-box charts show, and are vital for assessing the short, medium and long-term trend. Finally, 5-box charts show the main long-term trend with none of the detail shown in 3-box charts.

1-box reversal charts

If you followed the history and development of Point and Figure charts in the previous chapter, you will know that the 1-box reversal is the original type of Point and Figure chart. Unfortunately, it is a method that seems to have been forgotten and, when it is remembered, the charts are usually presented incorrectly, immediately destroying their character and usefulness. This is caused by a basic misunderstanding of how Point and Figure charts developed. With the previous chapter read and digested, you are well on your way to a full understanding of Point and Figure charts.

A 1-box reversal means that if the price reverses by the value of one box, an up-column changes to a down-column or a down-column changes to an up-column. Remember, up-columns are usually represented by Xs and down-columns by Os. So, each time the price reverses by the value of at least one full box you move across by one column and start plotting in the opposite direction, changing from an X to an O or an O to an X.

Why change columns when price reverses?

Cast your mind back to the development of Point and Figure charts discussed in the previous chapter. Consider why you move to the next column when the price changes direction. The only reason you move across to the next column is to avoid plotting an X on top of an O and vice versa. There is no other reason. Remember when discussing the development of Point and Figure charts, early Figure charts were shown. When the price rose to 16 in the first column and then fell back to 15, they had to move the next column to write the number 15. See Figure 2-1. This was done to avoid writing 15 in the space already occupied by 15 on the way up. It is as simple as that. This is one reason why understanding the development of these charts is so important.

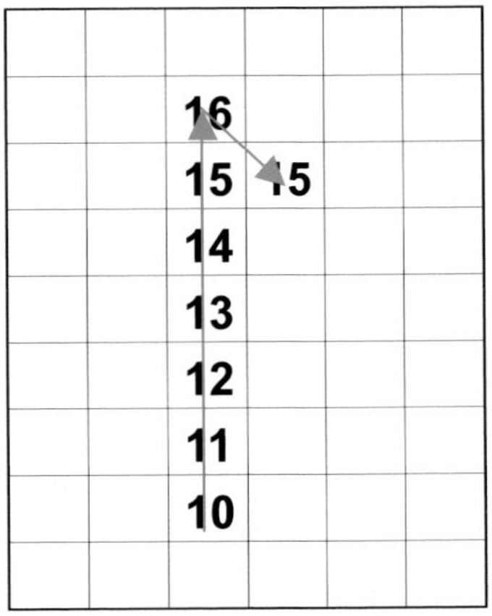

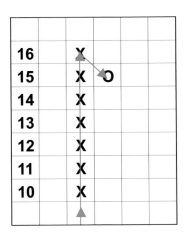

Figure 2-1: Development of a 1-box reversal chart

The red arrow shows the direction of the price and hence the plotting sequence.

Now look at the same chart now using Xs and Os. See Figure 2-2.

16		X			
15		X	O		
14		X			
13		X			
12		X			
11		X			
10		X			

Figure 2-2: Development of a 1-box reversal chart

You can see why the O has to be placed in the second column, in order not to overwrite the X in the same row in the first column.

If the price now continues down from 15 to 14, another O is plotted in the same column, so there are two Os in the second column. See Figure 2-3 overleaf.

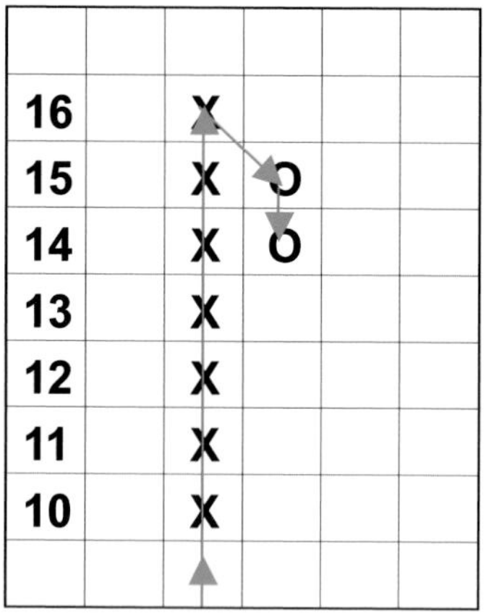

16 X
15 X O
14 X O
13 X
12 X
11 X
10 X

Figure 2-3: Development of a 1-box reversal chart

Consider what happens if the price then goes back up to 15. You would have to place an X in the 15 row, but you can't place it in the second column, because there is an O there already, so you would have to start a third column and place the X in the 15 row in the third column. See Figure 2-4.

16 X
15 X O X
14 X O
13 X
12 X
11 X
10 X

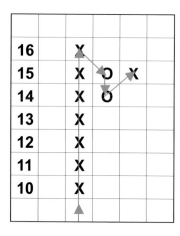

Figure 2-4: Development of a 1-box reversal chart

Again, the red arrow shows the direction of the price and hence the plotting sequence.

If the price continued to rise to 16 you would place another X in the first available space, which is row 16, column 3. See Figure 2-5 opposite.

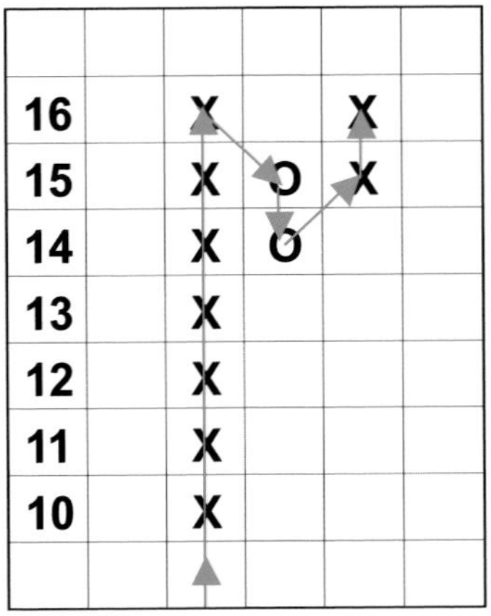

16	X		X	
15	X	O	X	
14	X	O		
13	X			
12	X			
11	X			
10	X			

Figure 2-5: Development of a 1-box reversal chart

You could now be forgiven for thinking, therefore, that it is impossible to have an X and O in the same column. Most students of Point and Figure have had this drummed into them and believe it to be the case, but it is wrong. With 1-box reversal charts, it is possible to have an advancing X and declining O in the same column. In order to get this across to new students of Point and Figure, it is necessary that the condition is given a name and that name is *one-step-back*.

One-step-back

One-step-back can only occur in 1-box reversal charts. There is a case where it is not necessary to move one column across when the price changes direction. It occurs when the price reverses direction by the value of one box only and then reverses back in the opposite direction.

For example, if you are plotting a column of Xs and the price reverses by one box, you move across to the next column to plot the O. You have to move across to the next column because there is no room to plot the O in the current column of Xs. Now you have a new second column with one O in it. See Figure 2-6.

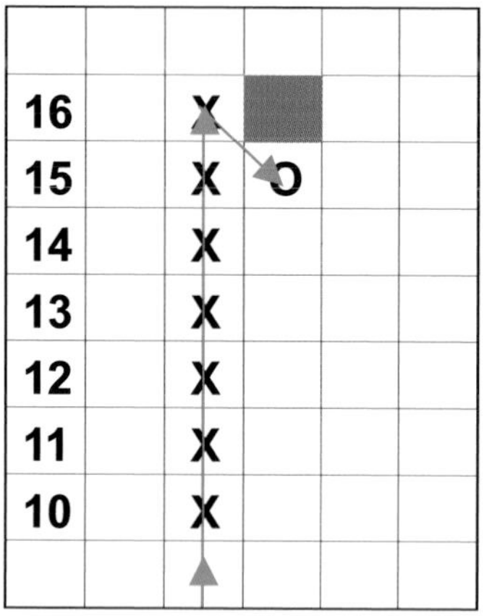

16	X			
15	X	O		
14	X			
13	X			
12	X			
11	X			
10	X			

Figure 2-6: Development of a 1-box reversal chart showing one-step-back

Consider now what happens if the price rises from 15 to 16 without first falling to 14. You need to plot an X representing 16, but you do not need to move to the third column to do this, because there is room above the O in the second column, shown by the shaded area in Figure 2-6. The chart therefore becomes Figure 2-7.

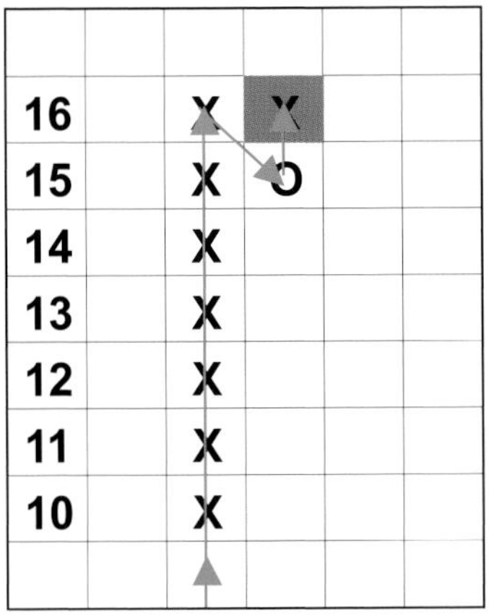

Figure 2-7: Development of a 1-box reversal chart showing one-step-back

Therefore, contrary to many beliefs, it is possible to plot an X and an O in the same column.

The one-step-back is a powerful sign. When the price reverses by just one box, it may be the start of a correction or just be a temporary aberration in the trend, so you need to wait for the next plot in the column to tell you whether the trend is going to continue from the previous column or whether it is a true reversal. If it is a temporary change, the price will reverse back and when it does, the next X or O must be plotted in the same column.

It means that any supply during the uptrend is quickly absorbed and the demand takes control again. Consider the analogy of walking up a steep hill. At some stage you may wish to pause, take a breath, even steady yourself to strengthen your resolve by taking a step back, before determinedly stepping forward again to continue the ascent. The process of steadying yourself and then, instead of turning back down the hill, continuing up strengthens your resolve.

Plotting an X and O in the same column may seem strange (even incorrect) and difficult to do, but it is important for the Point and Figure chart as a whole, especially with regard to the width of the patterns and the counts that will be discussed later.

Figure 2-8 and Figure 2-9 overleaf show the wrong way and the right way to construct a 1-box reversal Point and Figure chart. Unfortunately, the wrong way, where a new column is started every reversal, is sadly seen all too often.

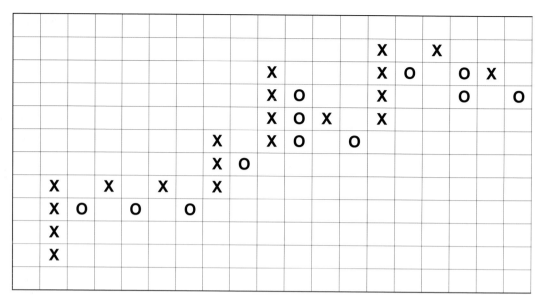

Figure 2-8: Incorrect construction of a 1-box reversal chart

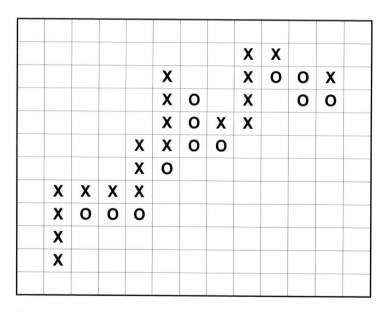

Figure 2-9: Correct construction of a 1-box reversal chart

Notice the difference between the two charts. Figure 2-9, the correct chart, shows the congestion areas more clearly than Figure 2-8, the incorrect one. Notice also that the width of the charts is different. This has important implications for analysis of congestion and establishing price targets, which will be dealt with later.

One-step-back also applies to downtrends, where an X corrects the downtrend and an O follows in the same column as the downtrend continues.

Using other box sizes

All the Point and Figure examples considered so far have assumed a box size of 1 point. That is how the original Point and Figure charts were constructed, although occasionally ½ point charts were used. The problem is 1 point or ½ point charts are far too restrictive and far too sensitive for many of today's instruments. With the Dow Jones Industrial Average at 10,000, you would not be that interested in 1 point movements because the Dow doesn't move 1 point at a time. It is more likely that you would be interested in 50 point or 100 point moves. Consequently, when constructing any Point and Figure chart, consideration has to be given to the value placed on each X and O. You therefore need to understand how to construct a 1-box reversal chart when the box size is greater than 1.

Construction example of 1-box reversal chart

Table 2-1 shows 50 prices from which the procedure to construct a 1-box Point and Figure chart will be outlined. Because the prices are in the thousands rather than tens, you should use a box size of 10, but note this is not always the case. It will be discussed in greater depth in a later chapter. It means that any movement less than 10 is ignored. The 1-box reversal chart is therefore called a 10 x 1 Point and Figure chart. This means that each X and O is worth 10 points and the reversal required to change from an X to an O is 1 box. Don't concern yourself at this stage why the chosen box size is 10, as the choice of the box size will be discussed in more detail on page 278.

Day no.	Price		Day no.	Price
1	1100		26	1122
2	1105		27	1133
3	1110		28	1125
4	1112		29	1139
5	1118		30	1105
6	1120		31	1132
7	1136		32	1122
8	1121		33	1131
9	1129		34	1127
10	1120		35	1138
11	1139		36	1111
12	1121		37	1122
13	1129		38	1111
14	1138		39	1128
15	1113		40	1115
16	1139		41	1117
17	1123		42	1120
18	1128		43	1119
19	1136		44	1132
20	1111		45	1133
21	1095		46	1147
22	1102		47	1131
23	1108		48	1159
24	1092		49	1136
25	1129		50	1127

Table 2-1: Table of prices for construction examples

The first thing you have to do is to decide whether the first box will be an X or an O. It will be an X if the initial price trend is up and an O if the initial price trend is down.

- Take note of the first price, 1100, and look at the second price. If the 2nd price is 1110 (remember you are interested in 10 point movements) or higher then the 1st plot is an X. If it is 1090 or lower, the first plot will be an O.

- If the 2nd price is not one full box (10 points in our example) away from the 1st price, which is the case in this example, then ignore that price, look at the 3rd price and apply the rule. Continue doing this until you find a price that has either risen or fallen by at least 10 points from the first price. In this example, the second price of 1105 does not satisfy the condition because it is only 5 points away from the first price, but the 3rd price of 1110 is 10 points higher than the first price. This allows you to start the Point and Figure chart by plotting two Xs in the 1100 and 1110 boxes, ignoring the 2nd price. See Figure 2-10.

1140							
1130							
1120							
1110	X						
1100	X						
1090							

Figure 2-10: Construction example of a 1-box reversal chart

Immediately you can see that the Point and Figure chart does not plot every price, only those that satisfy the construction conditions.

Now you have the start of your Point and Figure chart, you can continue through the rest of the price series, but stop to think what it is you are doing. Because this is a 10 x 1 Point and Figure chart, it means you are not interested in any prices less than 10 points away from the *last plotted box*.

IMPORTANT NOTE:

It is always the *last plotted box* that is considered when deciding whether to fill the next box or change columns. Do not make the mistake of considering the last price. Once a price is used to plot an X or O, the price itself is discarded and no record is kept. It is not possible to look at a Point and Figure chart and know what price generated any X or O.

- The 4th price is 1112, which is ignored because it is not 10 points higher than the last plotted box of 1110.

- The 5th price is 1118, which is also not 10 points higher than the last plotted box of 1110.

- The 6th price is 1120. This is 10 points higher than the last plotted price of 1110 and so an X can be placed into the 1120 box. See Figure 2-11.

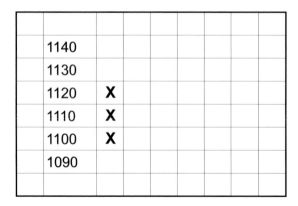

Figure 2-11: Construction example of a 1-box reversal chart

The 7th price is 1136. That one is also easy; simply place an X in the 1130 box. See Figure 2-12. Only one X can be plotted, despite the 16 point price rise, because to plot two Xs, the price would have to have risen to 1140.

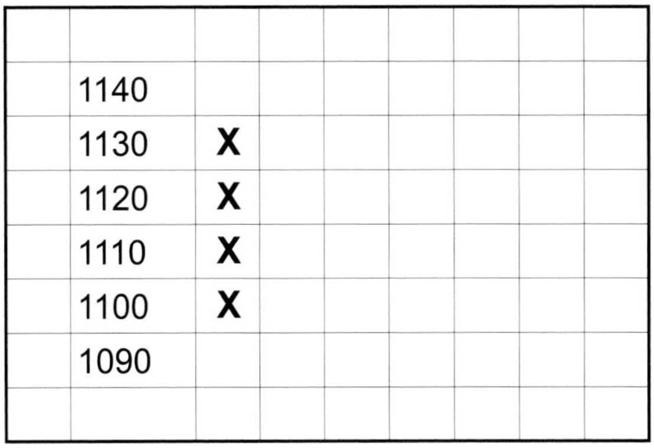

1140								
1130	X							
1120	X							
1110	X							
1100	X							
1090								

Figure 2-12: Construction example of a 1-box reversal chart

• The 8th price is 1121. Remember, the last plotted box was 1130. This means that to plot another X, the price must be 1140 or higher, or to plot an O it must be 1120 or lower. So even though the price has fallen by 15 points, the price has not reversed by 10 points from the last plotted box of 1130, so the 8th price is ignored.

• The 9th price is 1129. Again, this is ignored.

• The 10th price is 1120. This is 10 points away from the last plotted box of 1130, so you must place an O in the 1120 box, which means you must move to the next column to find a vacant box.

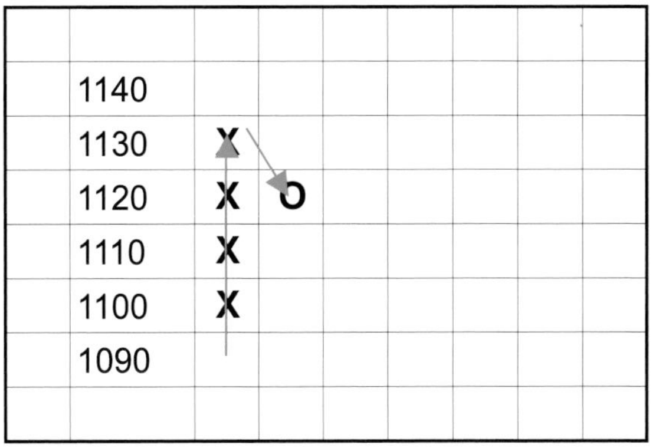

1140								
1130	X							
1120	X	O						
1110	X							
1100	X							
1090								

Figure 2-13: Construction example of a 1-box reversal chart

- The 11th price is 1139, which is 19 points higher than our last plotted box of 1120, so you must plot an X in the 1130 box. You can't extend it as far up as the 1140 box, because the price has not reached 1140. The important thing is that this time you do not have to change columns, because the 1130 box in column 2 is vacant. You can, therefore, remain in the same column and plot the X above the O. See Figure 2-14. Remember the one-step-back discussed on page 62.

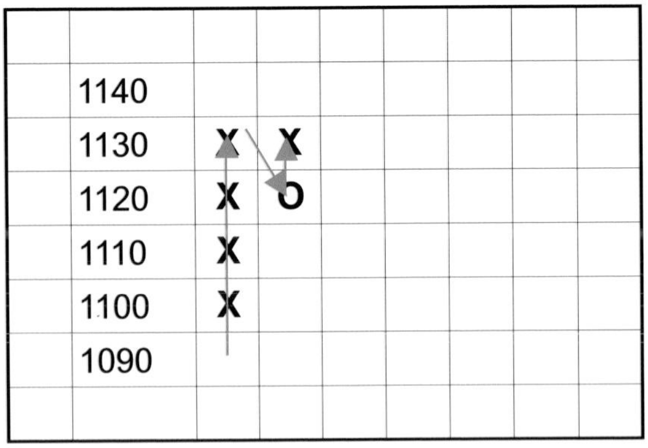

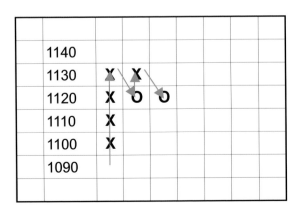

Figure 2-14: Construction example of a 1-box reversal chart showing one-step-back

- The 12th, 13th and 14th prices are neither 1140 or higher, nor 1120 or lower and so they are all ignored.

- The 15th price is 1113, which is 17 points lower than the last plotted box of 1130. This means you must place an O in the 1120 position only. You can't extend as far down as 1110, because the price has not reached 1110. You also can't remain in the same column because the 1120 box is already occupied. You must therefore move to the third column to plot the O in the 1120 box. See Figure 2-15.

Figure 2-15: Construction example of a 1-box reversal chart

- The 16th price is 1139, which is 19 points higher than the last plotted box of 1120. This means you must place an X in the 1130 position only. You can't extend as far up as 1140, because the price has not reached 1140. Again, the one-step-back rule applies and you can place the X in the same column without moving across. See Figure 2-16.

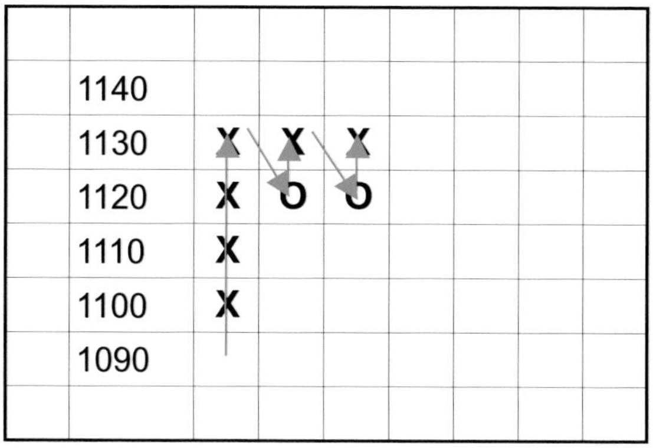

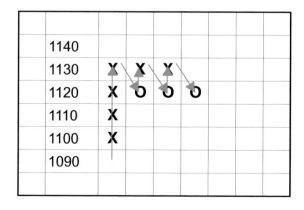

Figure 2-16: Construction example of a 1-box reversal chart

- The 17th, 18th and 19th prices are neither 1140 or higher, nor 1120 or lower and so are ignored.

- The 20th price is 1111, which 19 points lower than the last plotted box of 1130, so you must place an O in the 1120 box, but not the 1110 box. If you look at Figure 2-16, you can see that to do this, you have to move across to column 4. See Figure 2-17.

Figure 2-17: Construction example of a 1-box reversal chart

It is worth pausing here to look at the chart. Notice how many times the price has reached the 1130 level, only to be forced back again. This is an example of the fight going on between the bulls and the bears.

- The 21st price is 1095, which is 25 points lower than the last plotted box of 1120. This means you must fill the 1110 and 1100 boxes. As there is space in the same column, you can simply place the two Os below the previous O. See Figure 2-18.

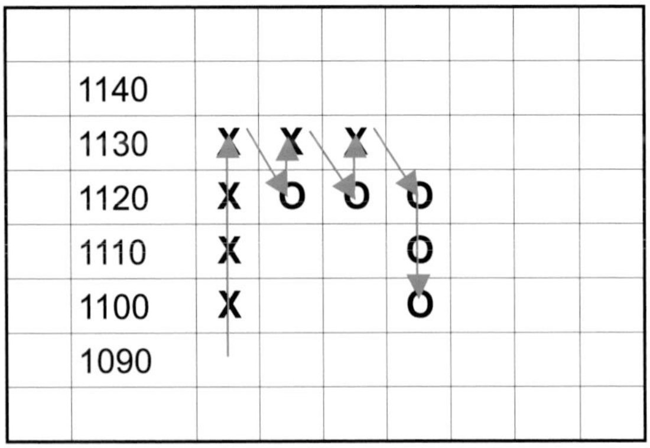

1140							
1130	X	X	X				
1120	X	O	O	O			
1110	X			O			
1100	X			O			
1090							

Figure 2-18: Construction example of a 1-box reversal chart

- The 22nd, 23rd and 24th prices are neither 1110 or higher, nor 1090 or lower, so they are ignored.

- The 25th price is 1129, which is 29 points higher than the last plotted box of 1100, so you must place an X in the 1110 box and the 1120 box. You are plotting two Xs. To do this you must move across to the next column. See Figure 2-19.

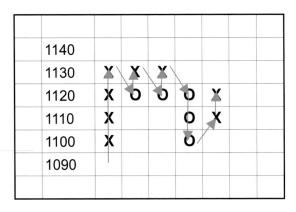

1140							
1130	X	X	X				
1120	X	O	O	O	X		
1110	X			O	X		
1100	X			O			
1090							

Figure 2-19: Construction example of a 1-box reversal chart

Figure 2-19 shows the chart after the first 25 prices, but notice that there are only 13 Xs and Os. It is important to remember that there does not have to be an X or O for every price. Sometimes, the price change does not fulfil the condition for a new X or O.

The above may have been tedious to follow, but, as stated before, much of the power of Point and Figure charts comes from a full understanding of what is behind their construction. If you have had difficulty in understanding the plotting, try to think of it in terms of filling and emptying glasses.

Filling and emptying glasses

Plotting Point and Figure charts is like filling and emptying glasses of water. Imagine the boxes are straight-sided glass tumblers. When plotting a column of Xs, you are *filling* a glass and only once it is full do you plot the X, stack the full glass on top of the previous one and pick up an empty glass to start filling again. When plotting a column of Os you are *emptying* a glass and only when the glass is empty do you plot the O, stack the empty glass and pick up a full one ready to start emptying it.

Let's look at an example. Let's assume you are plotting a column of Xs (a rising column) and have plotted the 1120 box. This means that the 1120 glass is full but the 1130 glass is empty. If the price rises to 1125, this means that the 1130 glass is half full and so the 1130 box cannot yet be plotted. If the price rises to 1129, the 1130 glass is almost full but still not completely. If the price rises to 1130, the 1130 glass is now full. The X can be placed in the 1130 box and the glass 'put down'. An empty 1140 glass is then 'picked up'. Most students find this concept easy to grasp, but have difficulty with down-columns of Os and emptying glasses.

If you are plotting a column of Os (a falling column) and have plotted the 1120 box, it means that the 1120 glass is empty, you have 'put it down' and 'picked up' the *full* 1110 glass. If the price falls to 1115, this means that you have 'poured out' half the water from the 1110 glass that is now half full. If the price falls to 1111, the 1110 glass is almost empty. If the price falls to 1110, the 1110 glass is empty and can be 'put down' and an O placed in the 1110 box. If you are having difficulty completing the following example, think about filling and emptying glasses.

Using the half-completed template in Figure 2-20, and the last 25 prices in Table 2-1, complete the Point and Figure chart and see whether yours looks like the one in Figure 2-21.

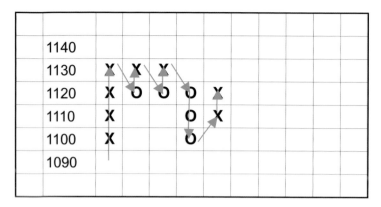

Figure 2-20: Construction example of a 1-box reversal chart

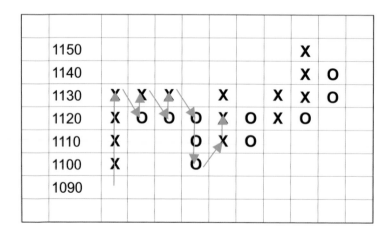

Figure 2-21: Construction example of a 1-box reversal chart

Table 2-2 below shows the prices and boxes that were plotted.

Day no.	Price	Plot Box	X/O		Day no.	Price	Plot Box	X/O
1	1100	1100	X		26	1122		
2	1105				27	1133	1130	X
3	1110	1110	X		28	1125		
4	1112				29	1139		
5	1118				30	1105	1110	O
6	1120	1120	X		31	1132	1130	X
7	1136	1130	X		32	1122		
8	1121				33	1131		
9	1129				34	1127		
10	1120	1120	O		35	1138		
11	1139	1130	X		36	1111	1120	O
12	1121				37	1122		
13	1129				38	1111		
14	1138				39	1128		
15	1113	1120	O		40	1115		
16	1139	1130	X		41	1117		
17	1123				42	1120		
18	1128				43	1119		
19	1136				44	1132	1130	X
20	1111	1120	O		45	1133		
21	1095	1100	O		46	1147	1140	X
22	1102				47	1131		
23	1108				48	1159	1150	X
24	1092				49	1136	1140	O
25	1129	1120	X		50	1127	1130	O

Table 2-2: Table of prices showing where Xs and Os have been recorded to construct a 1-box chart

If you have managed to do this, you have mastered the construction of 1-box reversal Point and Figure charts and you can now move on to 3-box reversal charts.

3-box reversal charts

Soon after Point and Figure charts became more widely used, there came a need for a less sensitive chart. The 3-box reversal chart, sometimes called 3-box minimum reversal chart, was the answer. The first reference to these charts was made by De Villiers in 1933, which suggests that they must have been well established by this time. They are not a substitute for 1-box charts, but rather a complement to them.

A 3-box reversal chart means exactly what its name implies. A change from an X to an O or an O to an X is only undertaken if the price reverses (changes direction) by the value of at least 3 boxes. It has the effect of condensing the price movement by getting rid of minor reversals during a prevailing trend. 3-box charts, therefore, give more weighting to the prevailing trend. The chart can never have less than 3 Xs or 3 Os in any column and, consequently there can never be an X and O in the same column, so no one-step-back exists in 3-box charts.

Constructed from 1-box charts

Traditionally, 3-box charts were constructed at the end of the trading day directly from the 1-box chart. The original prices were no longer available, simply the trader's 1-box representation of what the price did during the day. The day's movement from the 1-box chart was transferred to the 3-box chart which showed months, perhaps years of trading history.

Unique asymmetric filter

3-box charts consider the value of 3 boxes when a reversal is being determined, but the value of 1 box when a continuation of trend is being determined. This gives greater weighting to the prevailing column and hence the trend. If the current column is an X column, the price needs only to increase by the value of 1 box to generate a new X, but in order to generate a change of column to an O column, the price must fall by the value of 3 boxes. This is a unique feature of Point and Figure charts where the reversal size is greater than 1. The price is 'filtered' differently, depending on whether the price change is in the direction of the current column, and therefore the trend, or against it.

It is here that many an unwary Point and Figure student gets confused and caught. Say that you are plotting a 1 x 3 Point and Figure chart and the price is at 12. See Figure 2-22. Remember 1 x 3 means each box is worth 1 point and the price must reverse by the value of 3 boxes, which is 3 points, in order to change direction.

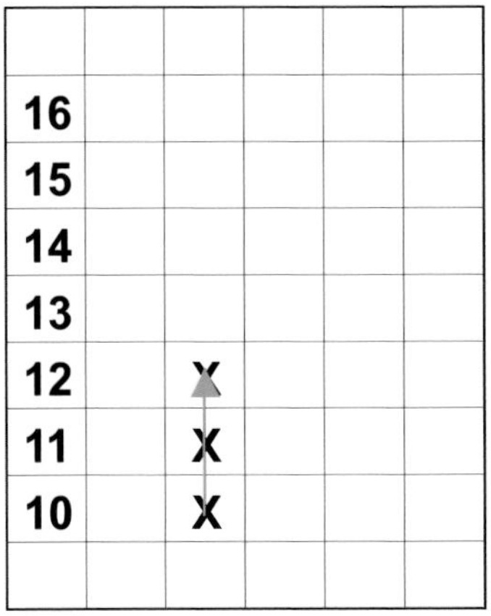

16
15
14
13
12 X
11 X
10 X

Figure 2-22: Development of a 3-box reversal chart

If the price rises to 13, you must plot the 13 box, even though this is a 3-box reversal chart, because in the direction of the current column you take the single box moves. See Figure 2-23.

16
15
14
13 X
12 X
11 X
10 X

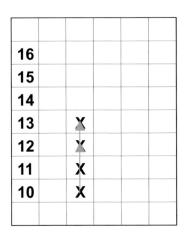

Figure 2-23: Development of a 3-box reversal chart

If the price falls to 11, you have nothing to plot (see Figure 2-24), because in order to change from a column of Xs to a column of Os, the price must reverse by 3 boxes, or 3 points from the last plotted box, which in this case is 13. So the price has to fall to 10 or less in order to plot a column of Os.

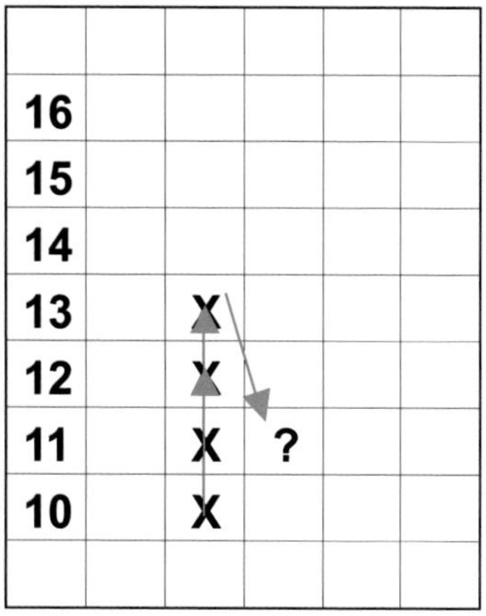

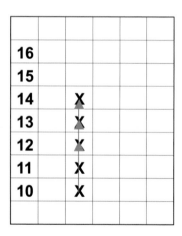

Figure 2-24: Development of a 3-box reversal chart

If the price rises to 14, you must plot another X because 14 is one X above 13. See Figure 2-25.

16					
15					
14	X				
13	X				
12	X				
11	X				
10	X				

Figure 2-25: Development of a 3-box reversal chart

If the price then falls to 11, that is now 3 points away from the last plotted box of 14. This is a reversal of 3 boxes or, in this case, 3 points. You must now change columns and plot 3 Os in the second column, taking you down to 11. See Figure 2-26.

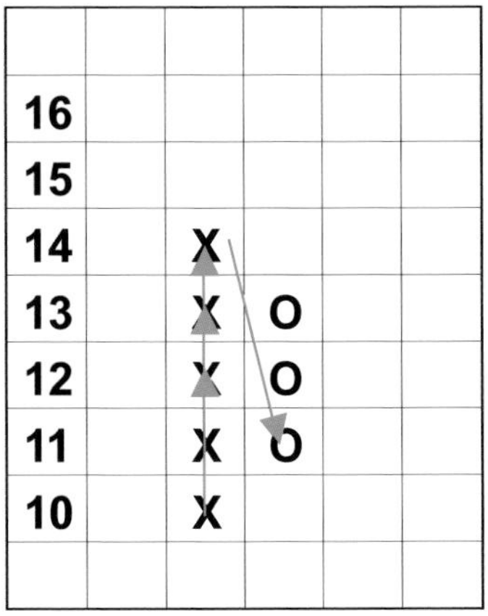

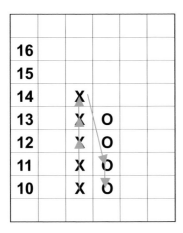

16					
15					
14	X				
13	X	O			
12	X	O			
11	X	O			
10	X				

Figure 2-26: Development of a 3-box reversal chart

You can see that in 3-box reversal charts, the minimum number of boxes in any column is 3, so there can never be an X and O in the same column. This is because a new column must be started on every reversal to avoid plotting an X on top of an O, and vice versa, when there is a reversal.

The position now is that the last plotted box is 11. What if the price rose to 13? 13 is only two boxes above 11 so there would be no plot at all. The price would have to rise to 14 before you could make a plot. In doing so, you would have to change to a new column and plot 3 Xs.

But what if the price fell to 10? Remember if you are plotting in the direction of the column, in this case a down-column of Os, you must take every 1 box move. So, if the price continued falling to 10, you would plot an O in box 10. See Figure 2-27.

16					
15					
14	X				
13	X	O			
12	X	O			
11	X	O			
10	X	O			

Figure 2-27: Development of a 3-box reversal chart

So remember, when you are plotting a 3-box reversal chart, you have to look at either plotting another box in the direction of the current column, or a new column of at least 3 boxes, if the price has reversed.

Consider the value of the box

It is important to note that when attempting to establish a reversal (change in columns), the value of 3 boxes is calculated from the last plotted box and not from the last recorded price. For example, if you are plotting a 10 x 3 chart and the last price in a rising market (a column of Xs) is 547, you would place an X in the 540 box. Once this is plotted, the figure of 547 is discarded and the value of the last box (540 in this case) is retained. So, in order to change columns and plot a column of Os, the price must reverse by at least 30 (10 x 3) points from the last plotted box, which means the price must reach 540-30 = 510, not 547-30 = 517. This will become more evident in the example below.

Example of a 10 x 3 Point and Figure chart

The best way to illustrate the plotting of a 3-box reversal chart, and the difference between the 1-box and 3-box method, is to plot a chart using the same set of data in Table 2-1 on page 66, used for the 1-box reversal chart example.

As before, the box size is 10. This means that any movement less than 10 is ignored. The chart you are going to construct is called a 10 x 3 Point and Figure chart. This means that each X and O is worth 10 points and the reversal required to change columns is 3 boxes or 30 points from the last plotted box.

As with 1-box charts, the first thing you have to do is to decide whether the first box will be an X or an O. It will be an X if the initial price trend is up and an O if the initial price trend is down. The procedure is the same as that outlined when the 1-box chart was plotted and results in 2 Xs being plotted using the first 3 prices. See Figure 2-28 opposite.

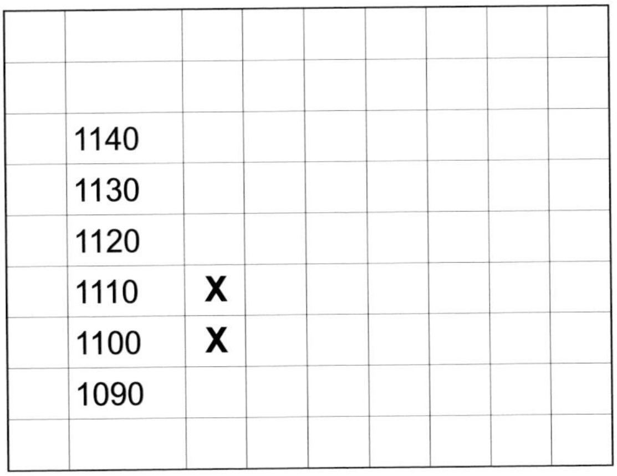

1140							
1130							
1120							
1110	**X**						
1100	**X**						
1090							

Figure 2-28: Construction example of a 3-box reversal chart

Like the 1-box charts, 3-box charts do not plot every price, only those that satisfy the construction conditions.

You now have the start of the Point and Figure chart and can continue through the rest of the price series ignoring any price moves that are less than 10 points away from the last plotted box. Do not make the mistake of considering the last price.

- The 4th price is 1112, but it is ignored because it is not 10 points higher than the last plotted box of 1110.

- The 5th price is 1118, which also is not 10 points higher than the last plotted box.

- The 6th price is 1120. This is 10 points higher than the last plotted box of 1110 and so an X can be placed into the 1120 box. See Figure 2-29.

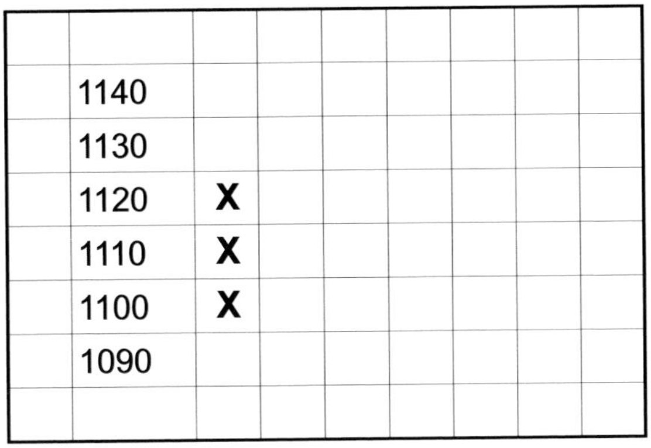

1140							
1130							
1120	**X**						
1110	**X**						
1100	**X**						
1090							

Figure 2-29: Construction example of a 3-box reversal chart

- The 7th price is 1136, so another X can be placed in the 1130 box. See Figure 2-30.

1140							
1130	X						
1120	X						
1110	X						
1100	X						
1090							

Figure 2-30: Construction example of a 3-box reversal chart

- The 8th price is 1121. Remember, the last plotted box was 1130. This means that to plot another X the price must be 1140 or higher, or to plot an O it must be 1100 or lower – that is 3 boxes, or 30 points, lower. It is neither, so the 8th price is ignored.

- The 9th price is 1129. Again, this is ignored.

- The 10th price is 1120. This is 10 points away, and against the price direction of the last plotted box of 1130, but, because you are plotting a 10 x 3 chart, the price must reverse by 3 boxes or 30 points to change columns. It has not done this, so it is ignored.

- The 11th price is 1139, which is neither 10 points above nor 30 points below the last plotted box of 1130, so it is ignored. Remember, what you are doing now is looking for 1140 or higher to plot another X or 1100 or lower to plot 3 Os.

- The 12th, 13th, 14th, 15th, 16th, 17th, 18th, 19th and 20th prices are neither 1140 or higher, nor 1100 or lower and so they are all ignored.

- The 21st price is 1095, which is 35 points lower than the last plotted box of 1130. This means there has been a reversal in the price of at least 30 points, which is enough to plot a column of Os. You plot this by moving to the next column and plotting three Os down to the 1100 box. See Figure 2-31. Remember, you can't plot down to the 1090 box because the price has not reached 1090. Think about emptying a glass of water. In this case, the glass is half full because it is at 1095.

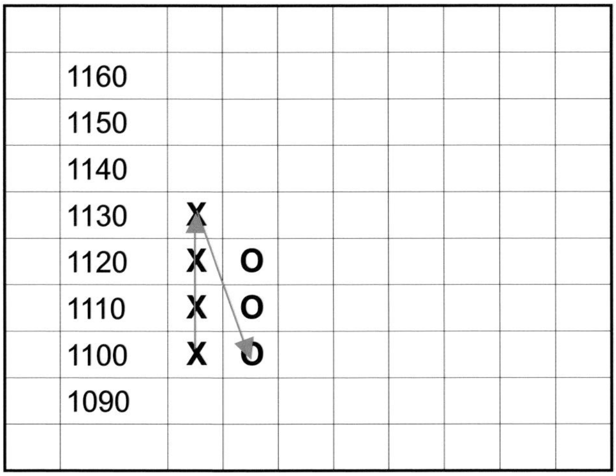

1160								
1150								
1140								
1130	X							
1120	X	O						
1110	X	O						
1100	X	O						
1090								

Figure 2-31: Construction example of a 3-box reversal chart

- The 22nd price is 1102. This is neither 10 points below the last plotted box of 1100 nor the 30 points needed to plot a new column of Xs in the other direction, so it is ignored.

- The 23rd price is 1108 and is ignored as well, as is the 24th price of 1092. Remember, with the last plotted box having been 1100, you either have to see a new price of 1090 or lower to plot an O, or a reversal price of 1130 or higher to plot 3 Xs.

- On the same basis, the 24th and 25th prices are ignored as well.

Figure 2-31 above shows the chart after the first 25 prices. Notice that there are now only 7 Xs and Os, so much of the price movement has been condensed and filtered out.

As before, there are 25 prices left to plot. It is suggested that you use the template in Figure 2-31 to complete the chart and see if yours looks like the completed chart in Figure 2-32.

1160								
1150			X					
1140			X					
1130	X		X					
1120	X	O	X					
1110	X	O	X					
1100	X	O						
1090								

Figure 2-32: Construction example of a 3-box reversal chart

Table 2-3 shows the prices and boxes that were plotted.

Day no.	Price	Plot Box	X/O		Day no.	Price	Plot Box	X/O
1	1100	1100	X		26	1122		
2	1105				27	1133	1130	X
3	1110	1110	X		28	1125		
4	1112				29	1139		
5	1118				30	1105		
6	1120	1120	X		31	1132		
7	1136	1130	X		32	1122		
8	1121				33	1131		
9	1129				34	1127		
10	1120				35	1138		
11	1139				36	1111		
12	1121				37	1122		
13	1129				38	1111		
14	1138				39	1128		
15	1113				40	1115		
16	1139				41	1117		
17	1123				42	1120		
18	1128				43	1119		
19	1136				44	1132		
20	1111				45	1133		
21	1095	1100	O		46	1147	1140	X
22	1102				47	1131		
23	1108				48	1159	1150	X
24	1092				49	1136		
25	1129				50	1127		

Table 2-3: Table of prices showing where Xs and Os have been recorded to construct a 3-box chart

It is important now, to compare your 10 x 3 chart in Figure 2-32 with the 10 x 1 chart in Figure 2-21 on page 74. Notice how the 3-box reversal chart condenses the price movement by filtering out minor movements.

Constructed from the 1-box chart

As stated earlier, 3-box charts were originally compiled from the 1-box charts. Referring to Figure 2-21, the procedure is to work your way across the 1-box chart from left to right noting first the direction of the current column and whether there has been a reversal of three boxes against it. The first column rise of 4 Xs must be plotted on the 3-box chart ending at 1130. Column 2 with one X and O is ignored, as is column 3. Column 4 has three Os down to 1100 and so this reversal must be plotted on the 3-box chart. Column 5 has three Xs up to 1130 and this must also be moved to the 3-box chart. Column 6, with two Os is ignored, as is column 7, with two Xs. Column 8 extends the last X in the 3-box chart by two further Xs to 1150 and must therefore be plotted. Column 9 is ignored because it only has two Os.

This method is only useful if you are plotting a 1-box chart by hand first and wanting a 3-box chart as well. If you have no intention of using 1-box charts, you may simply plot the 3-box chart from the original price data.

Characteristics of 3-box reversal charts

You can now see that 3-box reversal charts are very different from 1-box charts. The main difference is in the unique asymmetric filter. You have learnt that all Point and Figure charts filter the price by ignoring any movement below the box size. This is very effective in eliminating noise from the data.

1-box charts apply the same filter to the price in both directions. In other words, you add a box to an existing column if it has moved in the same direction as the column, but you also add a box to a reversal column if it has reversed by the box size.

You should now understand this is not the case with 3-box reversal charts. 3-box charts apply a 1-box filter in the direction of the current column, but a 3-box filter against the direction of the current column. For example, if you are plotting a 50 x 3 Point and Figure chart and the current column is an X column, every 50 point increase in price from the last box plotted is added to the X column, but in order to change columns and plot a column of Os, the price must fall by the value of 3 boxes or 150 points!

The converse is true if the current column is an O column. Any fall in price of 50 points or 1 box results in a new O box, but the price must rise by the value of at least 3 boxes to change columns and plot a new column of Xs.

So, 3-box charts are giving more emphasis to the current trend, defined by the latest column – either uptrend Xs or downtrend Os – and ignoring any 'minor' reactions against that trend which are less than 3 boxes.

This is entirely unique. All other price-filtering mechanisms are symmetrical, taking no account of the prevailing trend when assessing the filter. For this reason, the reversal against the trend – the appearance of a new column in the opposite direction – can be used as a trailing stop, which will be covered later.

5-box reversal charts

5-box reversal charts appeared at the same time as 3-box charts, but they are rarely used today. The principle is exactly the same as that for 3-box charts, but the price must reverse by the value of 5 boxes in order to change columns. This has the effect of condensing the Point and Figure chart even more. The minimum number of boxes in any column is therefore 5. Originally they were also constructed from the 1-box chart.

They tend to be used when analysing very volatile instruments, or by traders who wish to remain within the trend and are prepared to accept larger drawdowns before they are alerted to a change in direction. They are also used to obtaining the long-term picture.

Using the same prices as before, the 5-box reversal chart is shown in Figure 2-33 below.

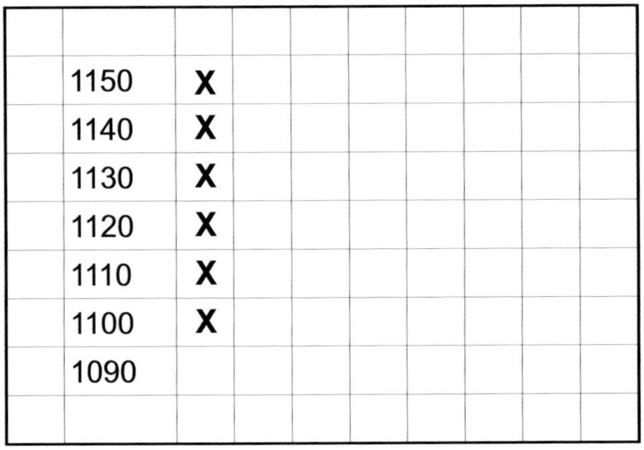

1150	X							
1140	X							
1130	X							
1120	X							
1110	X							
1100	X							
1090								

Figure 2-33: Construction example of a 5-box reversal chart

Notice the chart is even more compressed, so much so that there are no columns of Os at all. This is because at no time did the price reverse by 5 boxes or more. It is easy to see when comparing the 1-box reversal chart in Figure 2-21, the 3-box reversal chart in Figure 2-32 and the 5-box reversal chart in Figure 2-33, that not only are they compressing and filtering the price movement, but they are also changing the sensitivity, and in effect, changing the time horizon of the chart. This point about changing the time horizon is a unique feature of Point and Figure charts, because using the same set of data, you can alter the sensitivity and hence the time horizon even though there is no time axis. There is more about this later.

The same unique asymmetric filter is present in 5-box reversal charts, but of course the filter is now 5 boxes against the current trend.

2-box and other reversal charts

Although original Point and Figure charts were either 1, 3 or 5-box charts, there is absolutely no reason why other reversals cannot be used. The arrival of the Personal Computer made changing from one to the other so easy that other reversals can be produced instantly.

2-box reversal charts

Of all the 'other' reversals, the 2-box is the most popular for a number of reasons:

1. Some traders find 1-box reversal charts too sensitive and difficult to use.

2. 1-box charts are often plotted incorrectly, negating their usefulness.

3. For short-term traders, 3-box reversal charts allow too much drawdown before a change in direction is signalled and are, in effect, too insensitive and slow for short-term trading.

4. Traders want the asymmetric filter to keep them in the trend, without making that filter too severe.

2-box charts answer all the above. They are less sensitive than 1-box charts, but not as coarse as 3-box charts. They also have an asymmetric filter, which 1-box charts do not have.

The construction of 2-box charts is exactly the same as for 3-box charts, except that the price only has to reverse by the value of 2 boxes to change columns. The construction of 2-box charts using the same set of data is covered in Appendix A. You should familiarise yourself with it because 2-box charts have not been written about before and it is important that you have a reference point. The resultant 2-box chart from the sample data is shown in Figure 2-34. Compare this with 1 and 3-box reversal charts shown earlier.

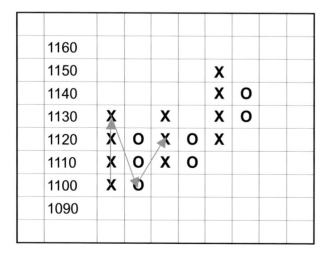

Figure 2-34: Construction example of a 2-box reversal chart

Characteristics of 2-box reversal charts

2-box charts have the same characteristics as 3-box charts, but they are more sensitive. They have the asymmetric filter but the difference between the with-trend filter is only slightly different from the against-trend filter. They can be thought of as one step forward, two steps back, whereas a 3-box chart is one step forward, three steps back.

2-box charts apply a 1-box filter in the direction of the current column, but a 2-box filter against the trend. For example, if you are plotting a 50 x 2 Point and Figure chart and the current column is an X column, every 50 point increase in price from the last box plotted is added to the X column. In order to change columns and reverse against the X column however, the price must fall by the value of at least 2 boxes or 100 points. The converse is true if the current column is an O column. Any fall in price of 50 points results in a new O box, but the price must rise by the value of 2 boxes to change columns and plot a column of Xs.

In a similar way to 3-box charts, 2-box charts are giving more emphasis to the current trend, but only slightly more. This is what makes them favoured by short-term traders as you have seen. As with 3-box charts, the appearance of a new column in the opposite direction can be used as a trailing stop, where the stop is only 2 boxes away.

Other box reversals

As stated previously, there is no fixed rule about reversals. There is no reason why you can't use a 7-box reversal chart provided you understand what this means. It means that the prevailing trend is of more importance to you than any reversal of less than 7 boxes. This means that you will not be alerted to a change in direction until there is considerable reversal against the trend.

The computer gives you the opportunity of experimenting with different box sizes and reversals, which was not available to those early traders.

Summary so far

Figure 2-35 below shows all four reversal methods constructed so far, using the same set of data. It is a good idea to look at them together and notice the differences.

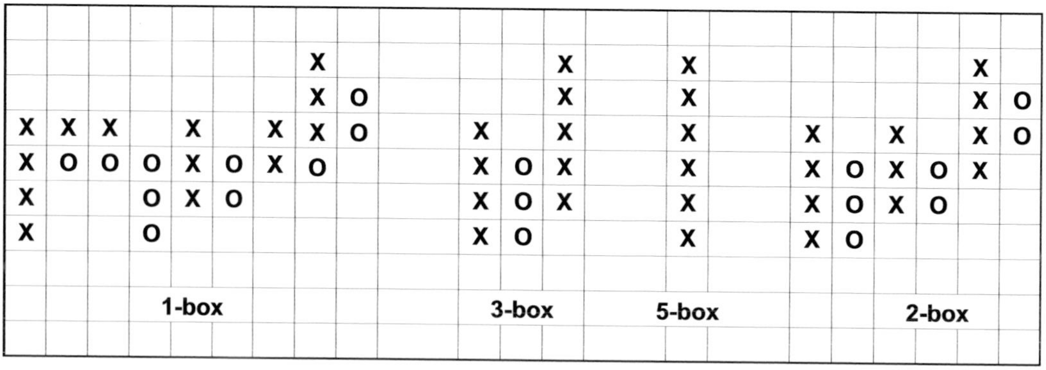

1-box

				X			
				X	O		
X	X	X		X	X	X	O
X	O	O	O	X	O	X	O
X			O	X	O		
X			O				

3-box

		X
		X
X		X
X	O	X
X	O	X
X	O	

5-box

X
X
X
X
X
X

2-box

				X	
				X	O
X		X		X	O
X	O	X	O	X	
X	O	X	O		
X	O				

Figure 2-35: Example charts constructed using 1-box, 3-box, 5-box and 2-box reversals

All these construction methods have assumed that tick data is available, although it is not a requirement as you will see later. The construction methods are summarised below:

1-box reversal charts

- 1-box reversal charts plot every full box movement in the price in both directions.

- Normally, a new column is started each time there is a reversal, except when there is a temporary reversal of 1 box only – called one-step-back.

- 1-box charts are the only charts that can have an X and O in the same column.

- The value of the box – not the price – is taken into account when determining the next plot.

- Price changes smaller than the box size are ignored.

- There are no gaps on the chart. If the price gaps away, all boxes must be filled in.

3-box reversal charts

- 3-box reversal charts plot every full box movement in the price only if it is in the direction of the current column.

- A new column is started each time there is a reversal of the value of 3 boxes or more.

- Price reversals less than the value of 3 boxes are ignored.

- 3-box charts can never have an X and O in the same column, because the minimum number of boxes in any column is 3.

- The value of the box is taken into account when determining the next plot – either the same column or the reversal.

- Price changes less than the box size are ignored.

- There are no gaps on the chart. If the price gaps away, all boxes must be filled in.

5-box reversal charts

- 5-box reversal charts plot every full box price movement only if it is in the direction of the current column.

- A new column must be started every time there is a reversal of 5 boxes or more.

- Reversals less than the value of 5 boxes are ignored.

- 5-box charts can never have an X and O in the same column, because the minimum number of boxes in any column is 5.

- The value of the box is taken into account when determining the next plot – either the same column or the reversal.

- Price changes less than the box size are ignored.

- There are no gaps on the chart. If the price gaps away, all boxes must be filled in.

2-box reversal charts

- 2-box reversal charts plot every full box movement in the price only if it is in the direction of the current column.

- A new column is started every time there is a reversal of the value of 2 boxes or more.

- Price reversals less than the value of 2 boxes are ignored.

- 2-box charts can never have an X and O in the same column, because the minimum number of boxes in any column is 2.

- The value of the box is taken into account when determining the next plot – either the same column or the reversal.

- Price changes less than the box size are ignored.

- There are no gaps on the chart. If the price gaps away, all boxes must be filled in.

You may already be asking yourself, with four possible construction methods, which one do you use and when. This will be made clear in the coming chapters. At this stage, a few more aspects of construction need to be covered to ensure you have a full grounding in the subject.

The move from intra-day to end-of-day – the great debate

Point and Figure charts are, and always will be, an intra-day charting mechanism. This surprises many students who often ask whether Point and Figure charts can be used with real-time data. Only a lack of understanding of the Point and Figure method can prompt such a question. The answer is a resounding yes. It is where Point and Figure charts came from – the floor and the ticker – in the first place. For most traders and investors however, it is neither practical nor possible to plot all intra-day price changes, so the end-of-day Point and Figure chart was created.

It is unclear when end-of-day Point and Figure charts emerged, but in 1933, De Villiers and Taylor state that *"Point and Figure charts compiled from the newspaper will rarely show complete patterns"*. They advise, therefore, that it is *"absolutely essential that you record all of the full figure fluctuations"*. Alexander Wheelan is even more scathing about end-of-day data, condemning *"the practice as being thoroughly unsound and unsatisfactory"*, and advising readers that they would be *"better off by using some other charting method instead of Point and Figure"*.

Both are too strong. Of course, taking every price change during the day will produce much more information on which to base decisions, but Point and Figure is not only a short-term tool. It is not just for traders, but investors too. It can and should be used for both medium-term and long-term analysis as well. This being the case, it is just not practical to store tick data for every instrument for 10 or 20 years and then use that data to construct your chart. Besides the inconvenience of manipulating such a large amount of data, the management of so many prices across a wide range of instruments would be inconceivable. For example, many US stocks trade many times per second and each of these trades would have to be stored for the period you wish to draw the Point and Figure chart.

This means that there is a place for Point and Figure charts using end-of-day data, alongside the traditional intra-day tick data we have discussed so far. Most Point and Figure chartists use end-of-day data because of the expense and inconvenience of using intra-day tick data. Whilst on this subject, it should be noted that 1 minute, 15 minute, 30 minute, 60 minute or, in fact, any fixed time-frame data may be used as well.

This section however, will concentrate on Point and Figure charts using end-of-day data and how this affects the construction of the charts.

One of the problems of using end-of-day data is that there are four pieces of information with which to assess the day's trading. How these are used greatly affects the resultant Point and Figure charts.

There are two customary ways to construct Point and Figure charts using end-of-day data:

- Close only method using end-of-day close price.

- High/low method using daily high/low prices.

Close only method

Using the end-of-day close is now the most common method of drawing Point and Figure charts for medium term traders and investors. The method is simple and the data is easily obtainable from a variety of sources.

The end-of-day close price is used instead of taking all the intra-day price changes during the day. The construction is the same as the intra-day charts we have constructed so far. In other words, you use just one price per day instead of a number of prices.

It is vital to understand that with end-of-day or daily Point and Figure charts you either plot Xs or Os each day. You cannot, under any circumstances, make any plot that results in an X *and* an O on the same day. The chart is drawn at the end of the day, taking the day's close as the figure from which the plot will be considered.

Whilst the close only method provides some very satisfactory Point and Figure charts, some believe that they suffer from ignoring all the intra-day movement that may be important to the analysis. It's a bit like using a line chart instead of a bar or candle chart.

Plotting close only end-of-day Point and Figure when data is being received in real-time

An end-of-day Point and Figure chart means just that. It is constructed at the end of the day with the price at the close of the day; that is why they are called end-of-day or daily Point and Figure charts.

That is fine and easily understood, but there is confusion amongst those fortunate enough to have a real-time feed and hence real-time daily Point and Figure charts. In this case, when a daily or end-of-day Point and Figure chart is drawn, it uses the last price it receives during the day either to continue with the current column or to create a new column if the price reverses by the prescribed amount.

No matter how many prices are received each day, the Point and Figure chart is constructed by clearing any Xs or Os plotted so far during the current day, taking the chart back to where it was at the close of the previous day. Each new price is then considered as if it were the only price received, and Xs or Os are plotted – but not both. It is *impossible* to plot both an X and an O during the same day on a daily Point and Figure chart. Some believe that the columns of Xs and Os should follow the price up and down during the day until the close. This is *incorrect* for a daily chart. A chart plotted like this is a tick-by-tick Point and Figure chart described in the previous section, and if this is what you require, then your whole chart must be constructed with tick data.

At the risk of repetition, a daily/end-of-day Point and Figure chart is constructed during the day by taking the latest price as it is received and comparing it to the last X or O plotted on the previous day. Xs or Os are then plotted according to whether the column is continued or reversed. This means that an X or O could be removed from the chart later in the day. A breakout that occurred in the morning may not remain in the afternoon. When a Point and Figure chart is drawn by hand, the Xs or Os plotted during the day are plotted in pencil so that they can be rubbed out every time a new price is received. Ink is only used when the closing price is confirmed.

High/low method

The deficiency of end-of-day Point and Figure charts was recognised by A.W. Cohen in 1948. He turned the world of Point and Figure upside down when he came up with an all new method of dealing with end-of-day prices. He advocated the high/low Point and Figure chart, where the daily high and low are used in the construction and the close is ignored completely. This went a long way to satisfying the criticism being levelled at end-of-day Point and Figure charts.

High/low Point and Figure charts are more difficult to construct than close only charts, but the rules are relatively straight forward. Step through each point below:

1. Take note of the direction of the current column. Is it an X or O column?

2. If the column is an up-column (you are in a column of Xs) then look at the high for the day you are about to plot.

3. If the high is high enough to plot a new X, then plot the X using the high price and ignore completely the low for the day.

4. If, however, the high does not yield a new X, look at the low to see if there has been a reversal. If there is a reversal, then change columns and plot the required number of Os.

5. If the high does not yield a new X and the low does not result in a reversal, ignore the day completely.

6. If instead the column is a down-column (you are in a column of Os), then look at the low for the day you are about to plot.

7. If the low is low enough to plot a new O, plot the O using the low price and ignore completely the high for the day.

8. If the low does not yield a new O, look at the high to see if there has been a reversal. If there is a reversal, then change columns (if required) and plot the required number of Xs.

9. If the low does not yield a new O and the high does not result in a reversal, ignore the day completely.

What this effectively means is that trend always takes precedence over reversal when deciding whether to plot the high or the low.

The high/low method can be used with any reversal size, although it is most popular with 3-box reversals. Because 1-box high/low charts are not used that often, their construction has been placed in Appendix B for those who are interested to follow it through. You are probably saying to yourself 'no more construction', but don't worry – this is the last one.

Example of a 10 x 3 Point and Figure chart using high/low prices

Table 2-4 shows 50 high/low prices from which a high/low Point and Figure chart may be constructed. Because the prices are in the thousands you should use a box size of 10. This means that any movement less than 10 is ignored. The chart will be called a 10 x 3 Point and Figure chart (h/l), which means that each X and O is worth 10 points and the reversal required to change columns is 3 boxes. The (h/l) tells the person looking at the chart that it is constructed with high/low prices instead of close only.

Day no.	Day's high	Day's low		Day no.	Day's high	Day's low
1	1100	1099		26	1125	1120
2	1105	1102		27	1136	1129
3	1115	1109		28	1127	1124
4	1115	1110		29	1141	1133
5	1124	1115		30	1107	1100
6	1131	1110		31	1133	1128
7	1136	1130		32	1125	1118
8	1129	1115		33	1132	1126
9	1129	1121		34	1128	1123
10	1125	1113		35	1140	1135
11	1141	1134		36	1119	1100
12	1122	1118		37	1125	1120
13	1132	1123		38	1114	1108
14	1143	1135		39	1130	1124
15	1113	1108		40	1115	1110
16	1140	1136		41	1119	1111
17	1128	1121		42	1124	1116
18	1141	1126		43	1120	1117
19	1139	1133		44	1134	1129
20	1112	1096		45	1137	1130
21	1096	1087		46	1149	1143
22	1105	1100		47	1135	1130
23	1110	1105		48	1162	1153
24	1095	1089		49	1139	1132
25	1132	1127		50	1130	1125

Table 2-4: Table of daily high/low prices for construction examples

The procedure to construct a 10 x 3 Point and Figure chart using the high/low data in the Table 2-4 is as follows:

As before, the first thing you have to do is to decide whether the first box will be an X or an O. It will be an X if the initial price trend is up and an O if the initial price trend is down.

- Take note of the 1st high/low, 1100/1099, and look at the 2nd high/low, 1105/1102. If the 2nd high is 1110 or higher then the first plot is an X. If it is not 1110 or higher, then compare lows. If the 2nd low is 1090 or lower, then the first plot is an O. Neither applies in this case, so the 2nd high/low is ignored.

- Look at the 3rd high/low, 1115/1109, and apply the rule. The 3rd high is 1115, which is more than 10 points higher than the first high, so the Point and Figure chart can be started by plotting two Xs in the 1100 and 1110 boxes, ignoring the 2nd price. You could also have started at 1090, but this is not important.

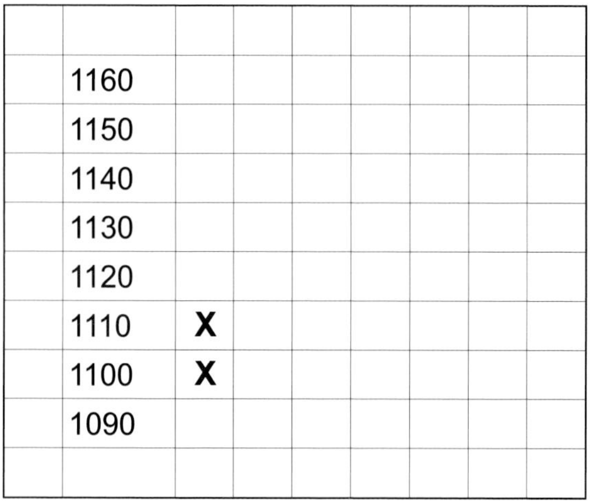

1160						
1150						
1140						
1130						
1120						
1110	**X**					
1100	**X**					
1090						

Figure 2-36: Construction example of a 3-box reversal chart using daily high/low

- The 4th high/low is 1115/1110. It is important when plotting high/low Point and Figure charts to have in your mind the figures you are looking for. You need the price required to continue the column and the price required to reverse it. In this case, you are looking for a high of 1120 or higher to plot a new X, but if that cannot be done you are looking for a low, which generates a 3-box reversal. In this case, it is 1080, which is 1110 less 30. Neither occurs and the 4th high/low is ignored.

- The 5th high/low is 1124/1115 so an X may be placed in the 1120 box (not shown).

- The 6th high/low is 1131/1110 so another X is placed in the 1130 box and the low is ignored. See Figure 2-37 overleaf.

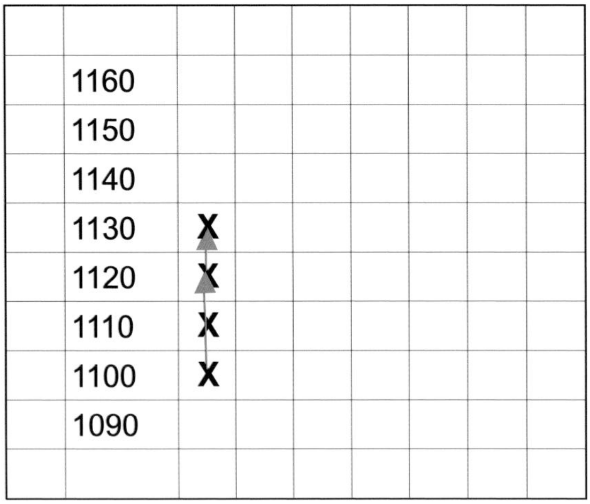

1160								
1150								
1140								
1130	X							
1120	X							
1110	X							
1100	X							
1090								

Figure 2-37: Construction example of a 3-box reversal chart using daily high/low

- The 7th high/low is 1136/1130. This does not produce a new X in the 1140 box, nor does it produce a reversal, so the 7th price is ignored.

- The 8th high/low is 1129/1115. This does not produce a new X in the 1140 box, nor does it produce a reversal, so the 8th price is ignored.

- The 9th high/low is 1129/1121. No new X and no reversal, so the 9th high/low is ignored.

- The 10th high/low is 1125/1113. There is no new X and no reversal, so the 10th high/low is ignored.

- The 11th high/low is 1141/1134. This does produce a new X in the 1140 box. See Figure 2-38.

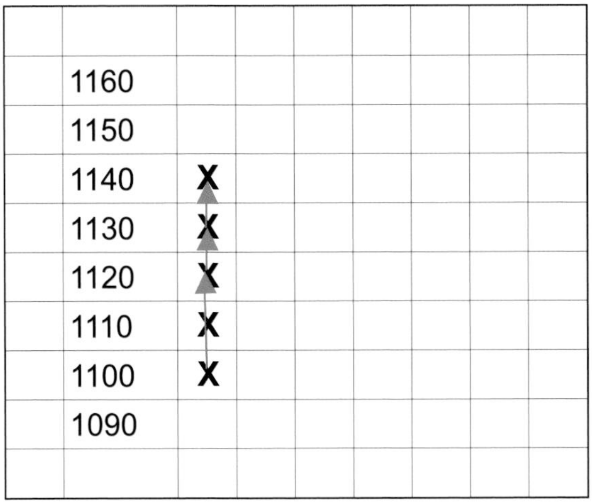

1160							
1150							
1140	**X**						
1130	**X**						
1120	**X**						
1110	**X**						
1100	**X**						
1090							

Figure 2-38: Construction example of a 3-box reversal chart using daily high/low

- The 12th high/low is 1122/1118. Your last plot was an X in the 1140 box. The high is not 1150 or higher, so you must look at the low for a reversal down to 1110. The low is 1118, so no reversal takes place and the 12th high/low is ignored.

- The 13th and 14th high/low are also ignored.

- The 15th high/low of 1113/1108 does not produce a new X, so the low is checked and this does produce a reversal of three boxes and a new column of Os down to 1110. See Figure 2-39.

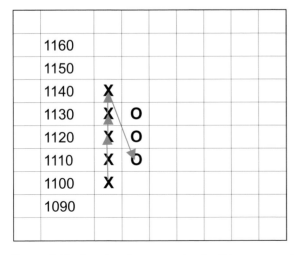

1160							
1150							
1140	**X**						
1130	**X**	**O**					
1120	**X**	**O**					
1110	**X**	**O**					
1100	**X**						
1090							

Figure 2-39: Construction example of a 3-box reversal chart using daily high/low

- The 16th high/low of 1140/1136 does not produce a lower O, but the high does produce a 3-box reversal and a new column of Xs is plotted up to 1140. See Figure 2-40.

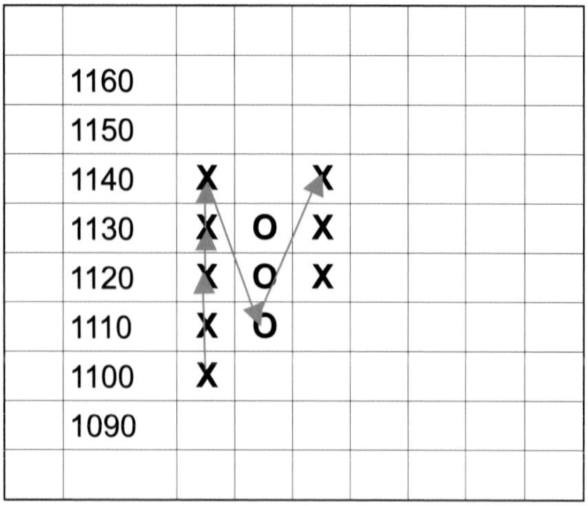

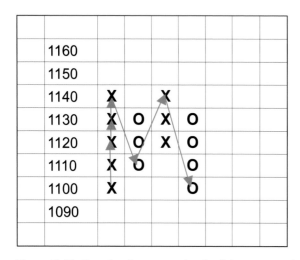

Figure 2-40: Construction example of a 3-box reversal chart using daily high/low

- The 17th, 18th and 19th do not produce a new X, nor do their lows produce a new O and so they are ignored.

- The 20th high/low is 1112/1096. The high does not produce a new X but the low does produce a 3-box reversal down to 1100. See Figure 2-41.

Figure 2-41: Construction example of a 3-box reversal chart using daily high/low

- The 21st high/low of 1096/1087 produces another O at 1090. See Figure 2-42 below.

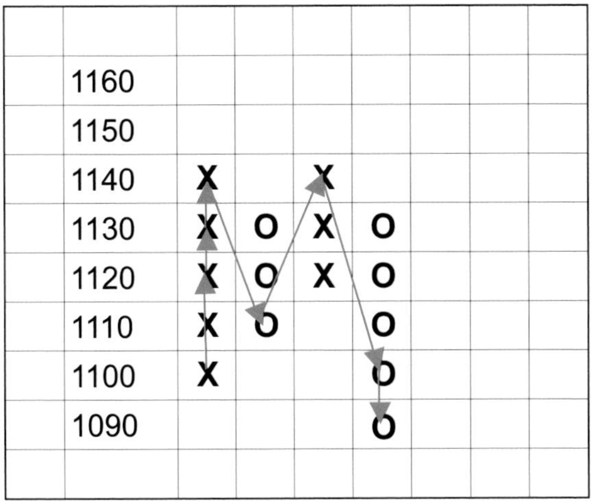

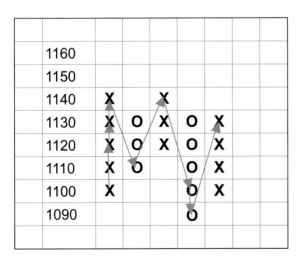

Figure 2-42: Construction example of a 3-box reversal chart using daily high/low

- The 22nd high/low of 1105/1100 does not produce a new O, nor does it produce a 3-box reversal. Remember, you are looking for a low that is 1080 or lower, or a high that is 1120 or higher. This means the 23rd and 24th high/lows can also be ignored.

- The 25th high/low is 1132/1127. The low does not reach 1080 or lower, but the high does produce a new column of Xs up to 1130.

Figure 2-43: Construction example of a 3-box reversal chart using daily high/low

Figure 2-43 shows the chart after the first 25 prices. Because it is a 3-box reversal chart, it is more compressed than the 1-box chart shown in Appendix B. Once again, you should complete the exercise. The finished chart should look like the chart in Figure 2-44.

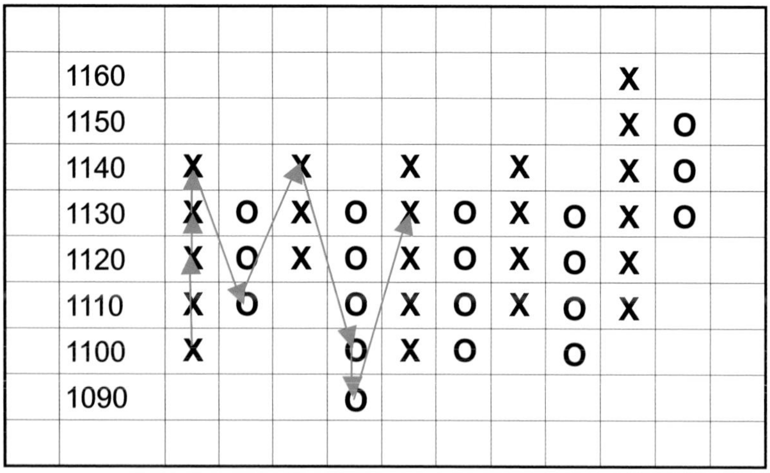

1160									X		
1150									X	O	
1140	X		X		X		X		X	O	
1130	X	O	X	O	X	O	X	O	X	O	
1120	X	O	X	O	X	O	X	O	X		
1110	X	O		O	X	O	X	O	X		
1100	X			O	X	O		O			
1090				O							

Figure 2-44: Construction example of a 3-box reversal chart using daily high/low

You have now seen how to construct a 3-box, end-of-day Point and Figure chart using high/low data.

Plotting high/low end-of-day Point and Figure when data is being received in real-time

The points made about real-time daily charts using close only on page 93 apply to high/low Point and Figure charts as well. Only one price, either the high or (not and) the low may be used to update the chart at the end of the day, so the issue of daily high/low Point and Figure charts using real-time data must be understood too.

When a daily or end-of-day Point and Figure chart is drawn in real-time, it uses the latest high or the low to either continue with the current column or create a new column, if the price reverses by the prescribed amount. No matter how many times the High and Low change during the day, the Point and Figure chart is constructed by clearing any Xs or Os plotted so far during the current day, taking the chart back to where it was before the open of the current day. Each new high or low is then considered as if it was the *only* price received, and Xs or Os are plotted – but not both. As with close only charts, it is impossible to plot both an X and an O on the same day. Some believe that the columns of Xs and Os should follow the high and low up and down during the day until the close. This is totally incorrect for a daily chart.

A daily (end-of-day) high/low Point and Figure chart is constructed during the day by taking the current high or low, according to the high/low plotting rules and comparing it to the last X or O plotted prior to the open of the current day. This does, therefore, mean that an X or O could be removed from the chart later in the day. At the end of the day, when the market has closed, either the high or the low is used to plot X or an O on the chart, according to the high/low construction rules.

The only difference between this and a close only end-of-day Point and Figure chart is in the case of the high/low version, either the high or the low is plotted, because the close is ignored.

Problems with the high/low method

At first glance, the high/low method of plotting Point and Figure charts using end-of-day data seems to solve the problems of close only charts not taking into account the intra-day movements. The fact, as you have seen when constructing, is that the high/low method also has a problem, which occurs when the high and low both generate a plot. If you are plotting a column of Xs, the high takes precedence, so you must look at the high to see if it generates a new X. If it does, you plot that X and ignore the low.

But what if the high generates a new X and the low also generates a reversal column of Os? The rule says you must ignore the low even though it does produce a reversal. It is a problem, but it is insurmountable if you are using end-of-day data, for the simple reason that you do not know whether the high or low occurred first.

The converse is true if you are plotting a column of Os. In this case, the low takes precedence, so you must look at the low to see if it generates a new O. If it does, you plot that O and ignore the high. However, if the high and low are such that the low generates a new O and the high generates a 3-box reversal of Xs, you still have to ignore the high.

It is just as well to note that it does not occur that often, and if it does, there is usually a follow-through the next day confirming whether the high or low has taken control and a column of Xs or Os takes precedence.

End-of-interval time-frame Point and Figure charts

There is a half-way house between tick Point and Figure charts constructed using every tick as it is received, and end-of-day Point and Figure charts which use a summary of the day's trading, either end-of-day close or end-of-day high/low. A third type of data, called intra-day or interval data, is available, composed by summarising the data for a chosen interval – 1 minute, 5 minute, hourly, or any time-frame – into high, low and close for that interval. So, 1 minute interval data in an 8 hour day, would result in 480, high, low, close (HLC) packets, which represent the HLC for each minute. A 1 minute Point and Figure chart is then constructed using either the close at the end of each minute or the high/low each minute, giving a far more detailed chart than one constructed with end-of-day close or end-of-day high/low. This opens up a huge range of Point and Figure charts to use, because you could draw a 5 minute chart, a 10 minute, an hourly, or any intra-day time-frame you wish to nominate.

The advantage of these intra-day interval Point and Figure charts over end-of-day charts is that the direction of the price during the day is known. Depending on the interval time-frame chosen, the sequence in which the high and low are hit can be seen and charted. During a day, column changes can, and will, occur as new end-of-interval prices are received. Remember that it is not possible to have intra-day column changes with end-of-day Point and Figure charts as only one price per day is used to construct the chart.

Fixed time interval data like this is easier to store, because there is a fixed number of data points per day, so back data is far easier to obtain. Remember, there is a distinct difference between tick data and fixed interval time-frame data. Tick data has no fixed time interval. The busier the market, the more trades will go through and the more ticks will be received and plotted. Tick data is suited to Point and Figure charts because there is no fixed time interval. The data is plotted as it is received, with no regard to time. Interval data, even if it is 1 minute interval data, is received every minute, so your Point and Figure chart uses a summary of the ticks for that minute.

There are many Point and Figure purists who insist on using tick data only. Their commitment is to be applauded. If the data is available for the period you require, then tick data is the best. However, interval data is far easier to manage and the difference between 1 minute data and tick data is insignificant, especially if you use the high/low construction method.

Interval Point and Figure charts are not as detailed as tick Point and Figure charts, but they are far more detailed than end-of-day Point and Figure charts as they show the path of the price during the day.

Log scale Point and Figure charts

All the Point and Figure charts described so far have been constructed using a uniform box size. In other words, throughout the chart, the box value has remained constant. The chart is therefore an arithmetic scaled chart. In many cases, however, this is not suitable, especially where the price of the instrument has risen or fallen by large percentages.

Prior to the use of computers, Point and Figure analysts arbitrarily changed the size of the box at certain key levels to cater for large rises and falls. For example, they may use a box size of 0.5 when the price is below 50, then 1 when the price is between 50 and 100 and so on. There were no strict rules, but the attempt was to change the sensitivity of the chart as the price increased or decreased. This method does, however, create a number of problems:

• It is too arbitrary.

• The changes in box size are not smooth, but happen suddenly at specific levels.

• Construction becomes much more difficult because box sizes are changing. This is especially so when plotting at the change-over level.

• It is doubtful that trend lines across the change-over point are valid because of the step change in the box size.

• Counts (discussed in a later chapter) are difficult to work out because the box values change halfway through the count.

It was in fact a sensible attempt at a log scaled chart without getting too deeply into complex mathematics. The advent of personal computers for Technical Analysis has, however, allowed the construction of genuine log scaled Point and Figure charts.

In order to understand how to construct a log scale Point and Figure chart, you first need to understand the difference between log and arithmetic scaling.

• On an arithmetic scale chart, the same vertical distance (10 boxes) throughout the chart equates to the same arithmetic difference in price – the same number of points – but a different percentage change in price.

• On a log scale chart the same vertical distance (10 boxes) equates to the same percentage change in price but a different points change in price. In other words, 10 boxes at the top of the chart represents a different number of points from 10 boxes at the bottom of the chart.

• On an arithmetic scale chart, actual price changes are plotted, so the size of each box is the same throughout the chart.

• On a log scale chart, each box has a different points size because they represent percentage changes.

Each box being a different size does not mean each X and O is a different physical size, it means that each X and O represents a different points value.

To draw a log scaled Point and Figure chart, you must take the log of the starting price, then increment that logged value[10] by an equal amount for each box. The amount you choose is decided by the percentage increase you wish to use. The price level for each box is determined by reversing the process – taking the anti-log or exponential of the logged figure. The price, therefore, increases by a fixed percentage at each box level. The percentage difference between one box and the next is dependent on the size of the increment in the logged value. What this means is that each X and O represents the same percentage change in price, although the percentage increase in price is marginally different from the percentage decrease in price.

To construct a log scale Point and Figure chart, therefore, you must choose a percentage box size rather than a points box size. For example, if you choose a box size of 1%, this means that each box is 1.01 times bigger than the previous. The log of 1.01 gives you the logged box size of .00995. For more details on the construction of box values, please see Appendix C.

The result is a logarithmic chart and the effect is that each box size is always 1% greater than the previous and each is 1% of the current price; so at the 500 level the box size is 5 points, at the 1000 level, it is 10 points and so on. In this way, you have a Point and Figure chart where the value of the Xs and Os increases as the price rises and decreases as it falls.

Unless you have a computer to draw them for you, it is very difficult to construct these charts by hand and this is the reason why they were never attempted before personal computers made it easy. You will be relieved, therefore, that there is no construction exercise.

---

[10] There are a number of ways to take the log of a value. The two most common being log base 10 and log base e, or ln, as it is called. Appendix C explains how to construct a log scaled Point and Figure chart using ln.

Naming log scaled Point and Figure charts

Instead of the physical box size, log scaled Point and Figure charts are named by the percentage box size. A 1% x 3 is a log scaled 1% by 3-box reversal chart.

Chart 2-1 shows a 2 x 3 chart of Vodafone plc, a FTSE 100 Telecoms stock, on an arithmetic scale. Throughout the chart, the value of each X and O is 2 points.

Chart 2-2 shows 2% x 3 chart of Vodafone plc on a log scale. The chart has a 2% box size so every box throughout the chart has the same percentage value but has a different points value. At point A on the chart the box size is approximately 0.3, at point B it is approximately 0.98, at point C it is 7.2 and at point D it is 2.2.

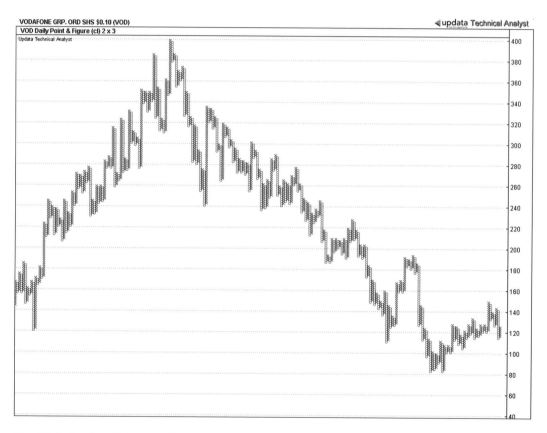

Chart 2-1: 2 x 3 of Vodafone plc – arithmetic scale chart

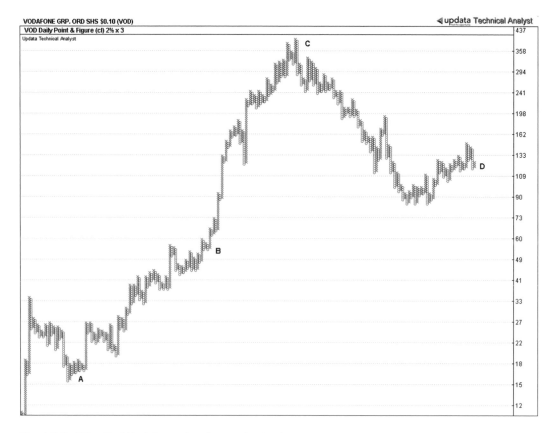

Chart 2-2: 2% x 3 of Vodafone plc – log scale chart

Choosing between log and arithmetic

There is no strict rule as to whether arithmetic is better than log or vice versa. There are those who swear by log scaled charts and those who never use them. It very much depends on what it is you are trying to analyse. If you are analysing a share that has risen from 100 to 1200 and has gone back to 10, it is impossible to find an arithmetic box size that will allow sensible analysis of the *whole* move because a box size of 1, although ideal when the price is 100, is far too sensitive when the price is at 1200. However, it does depend on what it is you are trying to do. If you want to see the whole performance of the instrument, then the only chart that will make any sense is a log scale chart. If you are not interested in the fact that it peaked at 1200, then there is no need to draw a log scale chart. An arithmetic chart with a box size relevant to the current price will be more applicable.

Marconi plc, formerly GEC, is one of those companies whose share price rose to dizzy heights during the dotcom boom, only to plummet in the years following. In fact, after various corporate actions, the high was £6,250 or 625,000p and fell to 270p – that's a fall of

99.9%. Chart 2-3 shows a line chart of Marconi on an arithmetic scale. No analyst would be able to analyse the share's current position from the chart, so a log scale chart (Chart 2-4) would be used.

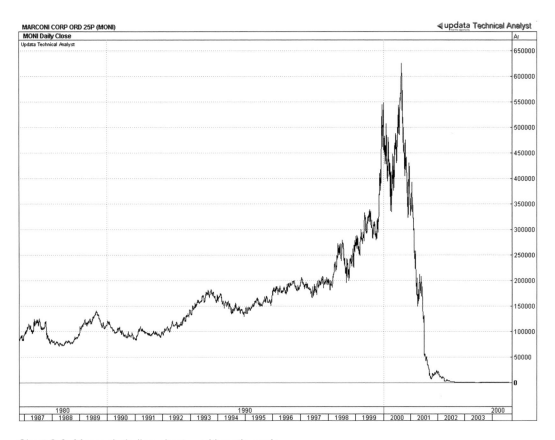

Chart 2-3: Marconi plc line chart – arithmetic scale

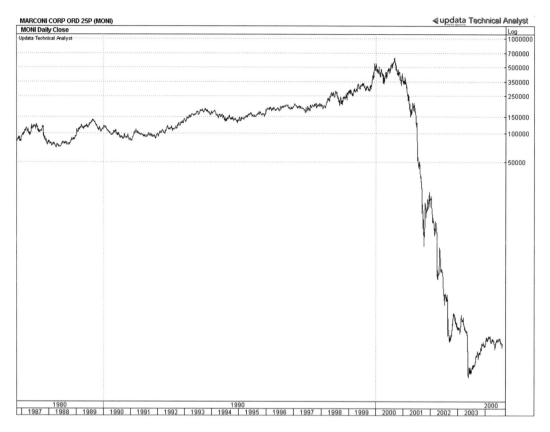

Chart 2-4: Marconi plc line chart – log scale

This is the same reasoning behind using log or arithmetic scale Point and Figure charts. Log scale Point and Figure charts are useful in the same way as they are when using line or bar charts. They tend to be used for long-term analysis or where there has been a large rise or fall in the price. It should be noted that the shape of log scale and arithmetic charts is different as would be expected with bar or line charts. Log scale charts show percentage changes whereas arithmetic charts show absolute changes. The easy way to think about it is that short-term traders are more interested in the points they make rather than the percentages, whereas longer-term investors are more interested in percentage returns.

Stops and log scale Point and Figure charts

One advantage of log scaled Point and Figure charts is that a reversal from a column of Xs into a column of Os is like triggering a percentage trailing stop. For example, in a 1% x 3 Point and Figure chart, a reversal of 3 boxes is equivalent to a 3% (actually 2.97%) stop loss being triggered from the last plotted X; a reversal in a 2% x 3 Point and Figure charts is equivalent to 6% (actually 5.77%) stop loss. Many traders close positions at certain percentage retracements. In a log scale Point and Figure chart set to the right percentage, these stops are triggered whenever a reversal occurs.

Point and Figure construction summary

You may have found this chapter tedious and may have given up halfway through and will not be reading these words, but one thing is certain: anyone who has persevered will have gained an invaluable knowledge and insight into Point and Figure charts. Those who skipped this chapter, or failed to follow it through, will never really get to grips with Point and Figure charts, the idiosyncrasies of the data required and the various construction methods. For those who have reached this summary, there are a number of things to note:

- True Point and Figure charts require intra-day tick data which show the path the price has taken during the day.

- End-of-day Point and Figure charts are possible using either the close or the high/low at the end of the day.

- End-of-day Point and Figure charts cannot show the path the price has taken during the day. Either an X or an O can be plotted each day, but not both.

- In between tick and end-of-day Point and Figure charts, are the interval Point and Figure charts which are constructed by taking the close or high/low at the end of each interval, which could be every minute, every 10 minutes or every hour – in fact, any fixed time-frame.

- Traditionally the box reversal was 1, 3 or 5 boxes, but there is a growing use of 2-box reversal charts because of the advantages they have over 1-box and 3-box charts, namely the asymmetric filter and the greater sensitivity.

- 1-box reversal charts can have an X and O in the same column. This is called the one-step-back. Other reversals cannot.

- Charts may be constructed on arithmetic or log scales.

Chapter 3

Understanding Point and Figure Charts

Before you can use Point and Figure charts, you need to understand what the charts are telling you. Because no time is involved in their construction, the chart can show one thing only: uncontaminated supply and demand. Uncontaminated, because the chart is not showing anything else – no time, no volume, nothing else which may distort the true interaction of the demand from buyers or supply by sellers. Remember, a Point and Figure chart does not change unless the price changes by the pre-determined amount. The passage of time, which causes all other chart types to 'move', makes no difference to a Point and Figure chart. Remember also that, in order to move the price, volume is required, so that although Point and Figure charts don't use volume they do indirectly show volume by way of the changing price.

Point and Figure charts show the market interaction extremely clearly. Demand pushes up a column of Xs and supply pushes down a column of Os. It's as simple as that. A Point and Figure chart is, therefore, a picture of the market's fear and greed, accumulation and distribution, and this gives rise to support and resistance levels created by these emotions. The support and resistance levels are created when the price reaches a level of equilibrium, where supply and demand are balanced. This is the change-over point. It is the point at which demand gives way to supply and an O is plotted, or supply gives way to demand and an X is plotted.

Point and Figure signals

One of the great advantages of Point and Figure charts is the unambiguity of the buy and sell signals they generate. Of course, not every signal will result in a profit, but the fact that the signals are unambiguous makes the charts easier to interpret. These buy and sell signals are created by demand overcoming a resistance level or supply overcoming a support level. This can be seen in many ways, from simple patterns to quite complex ones. Furthermore, the terminology used to identify many of the patterns has changed over the years. Although this terminology does not affect the way the patterns work, it is important to understand the differences and the changes. There are also differences in the way patterns are treated in 3-box and 1-box charts; so instead of dealing with them separately, they are dealt with together so that you can compare and contrast them.

Double-top and bottom patterns

If, on a second attempt, demand, represented by a new column of Xs, overcomes supply and the column of Xs breaks above the previous column of Xs (above the blue line in Figure 3-1), this is the most basic Point and Figure buy signal. This pattern is essentially a 3-box reversal pattern that has little or no significance in 1-box reversal charts. Originally, the pattern was called a semi-catapult, and that name was applied to the pattern whether it appeared in 3-box or 1-box charts, although the two charts tend to have a completely different look. Since

Cohen's work on 3-box charts, however, it has become widely known as a double-top[11] buy signal. It is an unfortunate name because many will associate double-tops and double-bottoms with M and W patterns, which occur as reversal patterns at the ends of trends in bar and line charts. The Point and Figure double-top (note the hyphen) and double-bottom patterns give buy and sell signals, respectively, when the double-top or double-bottom is breached, as you will see.

Because Cohen ignored 1-box charts completely, it is best to refer to the pattern in Figure 3-1 as a double-top when looking at 3-box charts and to the pattern in Figure 3-2 as a semi-catapult when referring to 1-box charts. They are, in fact, the same pattern created from exactly the same data and in both cases the signal occurs when, after a small correction, an X is plotted above the highest X in the pattern. But recall that 1-box charts offer more detail than 3-box charts and so the chart will look different. For this reason it is just as well to differentiate by using separate names.

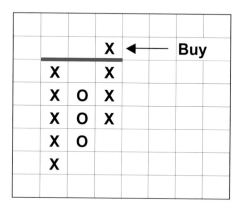

Figure 3-1: Continuation double-top buy signal in 3-box reversal charts

---

[11] In a double-top pattern, the breakout column of Xs must break above the previous column of Xs. Prior to the breakout there will have been two level Xs in a row, with an empty box between, hence the name double-top. In a double-bottom pattern there will have been two Os in a row.

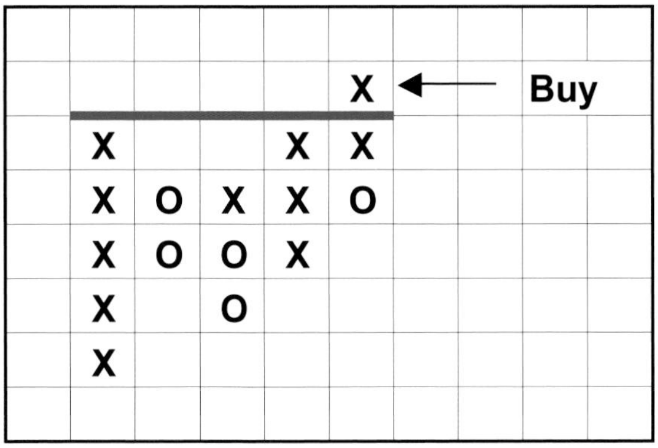

				X	←	Buy
X			X	X		
X	O	X	X	O		
X	O	O	X			
X		O				
X						

Figure 3-2: Equivalent semi-catapult in 1-box reversal charts

Whereas there is only one version of the 3-box double-top pattern (Figure 3-1), there can be many different variations of the 1-box semi-catapult pattern (Figure 3-2). This is because there are a number of ways in which the price can oscillate before breaking out. The essential ingredient, however, is that there must be an advance, which is pushed back, then at some stage – the catapult point marked with the arrow – the price breaks above the highest column in the pattern.

Figure 3-3 shows a small sample of semi-catapult patterns in 1-box charts.

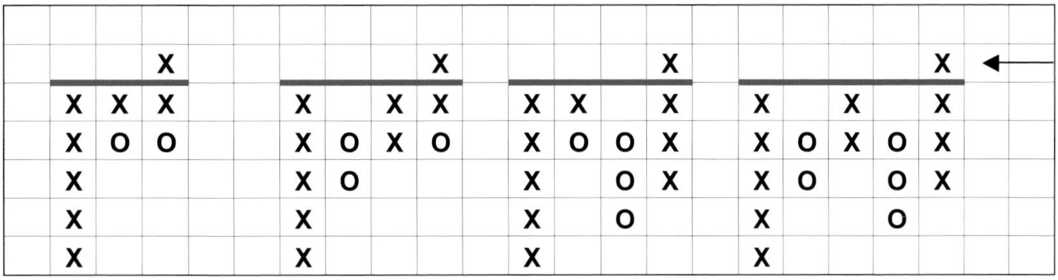

		X				X				X				X	←
X	X	X		X		X	X	X	X		X	X		X	X
X	O	O		X	O	X	O	X	O	O	X	X	O	X	O	X
X				X	O		X		O	X	X	O		O	X
X				X			X		O		X			O	
X				X			X				X				

Figure 3-3: Variations of bullish semi-catapults in 1-box reversal charts

Conversely, if supply, represented by a new column of Os, overcomes demand and the column of Os breaks below the previous column of Os (below the red line in Figure 3-4), this is the most basic Point and Figure sell signal. It is called a double-bottom sell signal in 3-box charts and a semi-catapult in 1-box charts. The signal occurs when an O is plotted below the lowest O in the pattern.

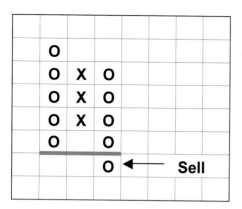

Figure 3-4: Continuation double-bottom sell signal in 3-box reversal charts

1-box variations of the semi-catapult sell are shown in Figure 3-5 below. These are the inverse of those shown in Figure 3-3.

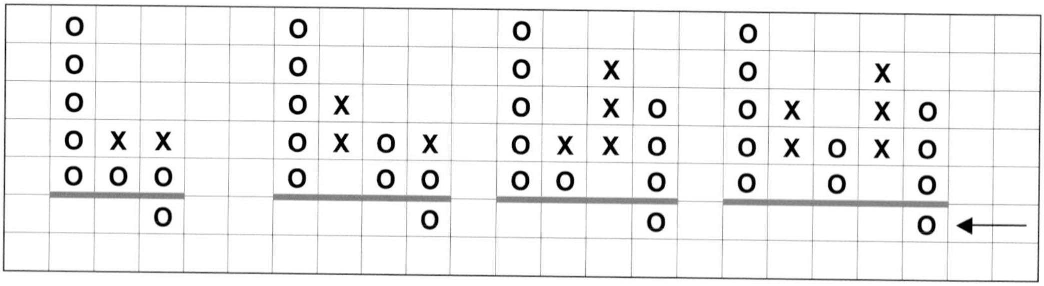

Figure 3-5: Variations of bearish semi-catapults in 1-box reversal charts

Continuation as well as reversal

In 3-box charts, it is important to note that double-top and double-bottom patterns can be either continuation or reversal patterns. That is to say, they can either occur after a pause during an up or downtrend, or at the end of a trend as a trend reversal. There is no distinction between them other than that continuation patterns shown in the previous Figure 3-1 and Figure 3-4 comprise at least 3 columns, and reversal patterns shown in Figure 3-6 and Figure 3-7 opposite comprise at least 4 columns. This is simply because a continuation pattern requires that the same column type (X or O) leaves the pattern as entered it. Therefore, a column of Xs entering the pattern leads to a reversal of a single column of Os, which in turn leads to a second column of Xs leaving the pattern in the direction the pattern was entered. The same applies to a double-bottom pattern where a column of Os enters and a column of Os leaves after a single reaction column of Xs.

Double-top and double-bottom reversal patterns in Figure 3-6 and Figure 3-7 below have at least 4 columns because, by definition, the column type leaving the pattern is the opposite to that entering the pattern. The buy and sell signals are the same, except that the buy and sell signals generated from a continuation pattern are more reliable because they are in the direction of the prevailing trend. Reversal signals, on the other hand, are a complete change of mood and may initially be unreliable, or at least should be treated with caution.

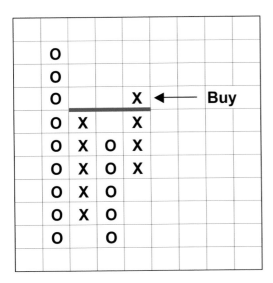

Figure 3-6: Reversal double-top buy signal in 3-box charts

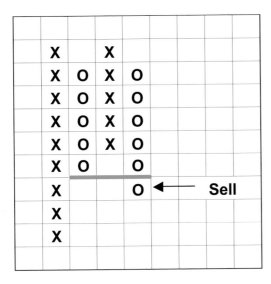

Figure 3-7: Reversal double-bottom sell signal in 3-box charts

Reversal patterns in 1-box charts

In 1-box charts, continuation and reversal patterns have different names. As you have seen, continuation patterns are called semi-catapults but reversal patterns are called fulcrums and take on many forms that are discussed in more detail on page 137. However, they need to be introduced here to explain 1-box reversal patterns.

For a reversal to occur, there must be a move into a pattern and a move out in the opposite direction. As you have seen, in Figure 3-6 and Figure 3-7, this is quite straightforward in 3-box charts, but in 1-box charts there are many variations, as shown in Figure 3-8.

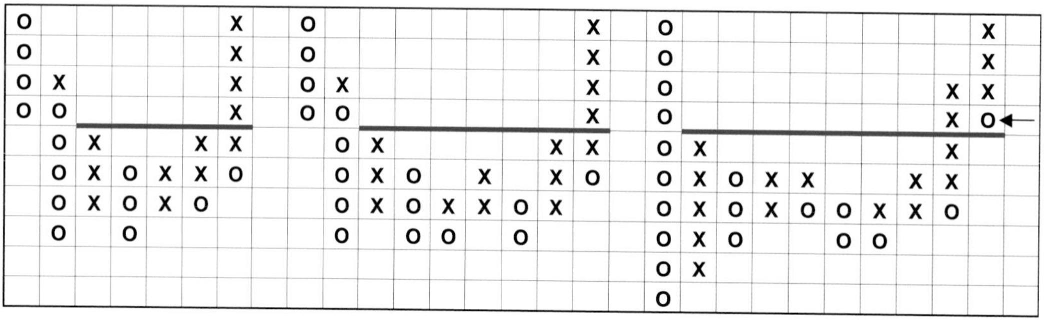

```
O        X    O                    X    O                          X
O        X    O                    X    O                          X
O  X     X    O  X                 X    O                    X  X
O  O     X    O  O                 X    O                    X  O←
   O  X     X  X    O  X        X  X    O  X                    X
   O  X  O  X  X  O    O  X  O     X  O    O  X  O  X  X     X  X
   O  X  O  X  O       O  X  O  X  X  O  X    O  X  O  X  O  O  X  X  O
   O     O          O     O  O     O          O  X  O        O  O
                                              O  X
                                              O
```

Figure 3-8: Variations in bullish fulcrum patterns in 1-box charts

The patterns shown in Figure 3-8 all translate into reversal double-top patterns in 3-box charts and this illustrates how many more variations there are in 1-box charts. 1-box charts issue buy signals when the price breaks above the high X in the pattern. They give sell signals when the price breaks below the low O in the pattern.

You will have noticed so far that in 3-box charts there is always a column in the opposite direction between the breakout column and the previous column in the same direction. This means that the minimum number of columns in a double-top or bottom pattern is three. This is not the case with 1-box charts, the reason being that these can have an X and O in the same column during the one-step-back process as discussed on page 62. Every time there is a one-step-back in an uptrend, there will be two Xs adjacent to one another. If the trend continues, and a second column of Xs breaks above the previous X, this is a reinforcement of the uptrend and is regarded as a continuation, or weak buy signal, shown by the thin blue lines in Figure 3-9 opposite. It is more a case of 'all is well' signal rather than 'act now' signal.

As the trend matures, it will eventually encounter resistance and some sideways congestion will occur. The breakout of this sideways congestion is called a semi-catapult and is regarded as a strong buy, shown by the thick blue line. The semi-catapult, as you have seen already, is in most cases equivalent to a double-top buy signal in a 3-box reversal chart.

What defines a pattern as a semi-catapult, and therefore adds to its strength, is white space: unfilled boxes across the top of the pattern. In chapter 5 you will see that, when analysing 1-box charts, the Os have been dispensed with and the chart is constructed using the original Point method of Xs only. This makes pattern identification much easier and is recommended. However, for the understanding it is better to distinguish between Os and Xs at this stage.

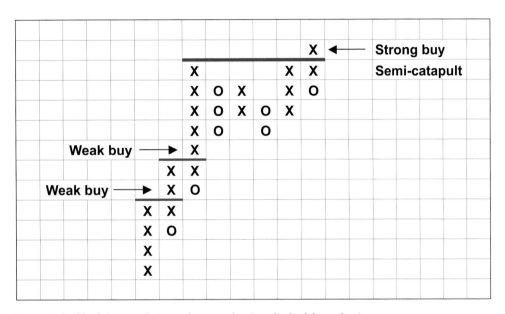

Figure 3-9: Weak buy and strong buy semi-catapults in 1-box charts

Figure 3-10 shows a downtrend in a 1-box chart. Weak sell signals occur on the continuation after a one-step-back, shown by thin red lines. A strong sell occurs on the breakdown from the semi-catapult.

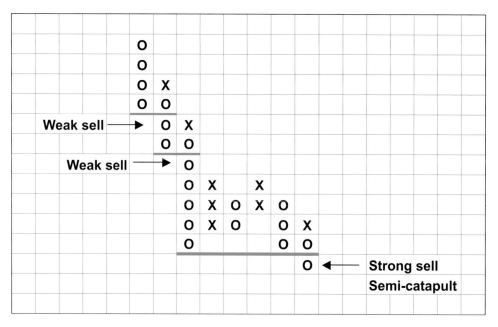

Figure 3-10: Weak sell and strong sell semi-catapults in 1-box charts

Signals may be graded according to the width of the semi-catapult. A simple 3 column semi-catapult is not going to be as strong as a 6 column one.

Chart 3-1 is a 50 x 1 Point and Figure chart of the FTSE 100 Index showing all the uptrend semi-catapult buy signals designated by a horizontal blue line, as well as the weak one-step-back buy signals designated by a red horizontal line.

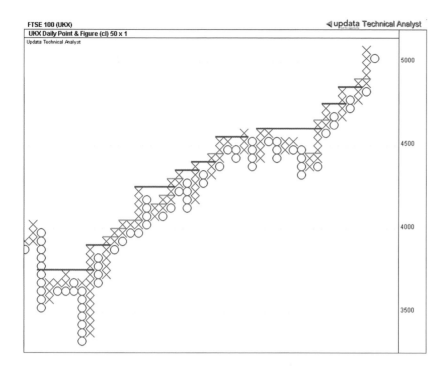

Chart 3-1: 50 x 1 of the FTSE 100 Index showing weak and strong buy signals

All Point and Figure patterns which generate buy and sell signals are built around the basic patterns discussed above. In the case of 3-box charts it is the double-top and double-bottom, and in the case of 1-box charts it is the semi-catapult and fulcrum. Some authors go on to list tables of patterns, but the need to learn patterns indicates a lack of true understanding of how a pattern is created. Although a number of patterns are shown and discussed below, it is to illustrate how and why the patterns are created. There is no point trying to learn dozens of patterns; it is better to understand what causes them.

Triple-top and bottom patterns

As stated earlier, all Point and Figure patterns which generate buy and sell signals are built around the two basic double-top and double-bottom patterns; however, the stronger the resistance or support, the more important the subsequent buy or sell signal. Consequently, a triple-top[12] buy (Figure 3-11) or triple-bottom sell (Figure 3-12), where the level breached has been attained twice already, will lead to a stronger move.

[12] You will have seen that in a double-top pattern, the breakout column of Xs must break above the previous column of Xs. In a triple-top, it must break above two columns of Xs. Prior to the breakout there will have been three Xs in a row, hence the name triple-top.

The reason that the wider pattern generally leads to a stronger and more reliable signal is that the battle for control has taken three upthrust columns instead of two. Having been forced back twice, demand from the bulls eventually manages to overcome supply on the third attempt by breaking up above the resistance level. This catches the bears off-guard because they will have built-up confidence every time they managed to push the bulls back when the price reached the same level as the previous column of Xs. Bears taking out shorts on the blue line resistance level will find that they are on the wrong side and have to cover (buyback their shorts). It is this process that leads to potentially good moves.

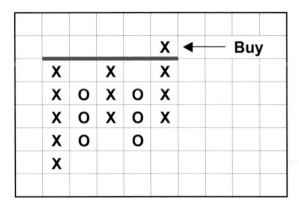

Figure 3-11: Continuation triple-top buy signal in 3-box reversal charts

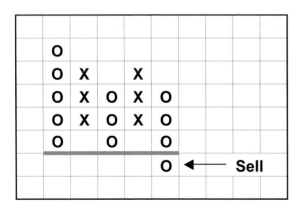

Figure 3-12: Continuation triple-bottom sell signal in 3-box reversal charts

Once again, the opposite applies when considering a sell signal as in Figure 3-12. The battle for control has taken three downthrust columns instead of two. The bears, having been forced back twice, eventually manage to overcome bullish demand by breaking down below the support level on the third attempt. This time it is the bulls who are caught off-guard. They will have gained confidence because every time the bears pushed down a column of Os the bulls gained control again at the same level as the previous column of Os. Bulls taking out longs on the red line support level will find that they are now on the wrong side and will have to close their longs quickly.

1-box charts

In 1-box charts there is no distinction between the patterns as there is with 3-box double-top/bottom and triple-top/bottom patterns. The only difference is that the 1-box continuation semi-catapults and 1-box reversal fulcrums are wider, as shown in Figure 3-13.

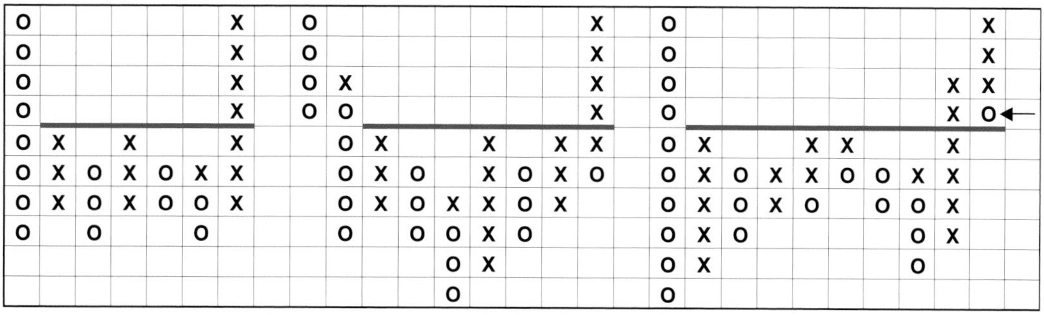

```
O        X  O              X  O                    X
O        X  O              X  O                    X
O        X  O  X           X  O                 X  X
O        X  O  O           X  O                 X  O ←
O  X  X  X     O  X     X  X  X  O  X        X  X     X
O  X O X O X X  O  X O  X O X O  O  X O X X O O X X
O  X O X O O X  O  X O X X O X   O  X O X O    O O X
O     O    O    O     O O X O    O  X O       O  X
                      O  X       O  X          O
                      O          O
```

Figure 3-13: Variations in bullish fulcrum patterns in 1-box charts

In each case the patterns shown in Figure 3-13 translate into 3-box triple-top patterns. Obviously if the patterns were inverted, they would translate into triple-bottom patterns.

There are dozens of variations of these basic patterns. There is no need to list them all, provided you understand how the basic patterns are formed and what they represent. Remember, they represent the fear and greed leading to distribution and accumulation within a range where one side of the pattern – support or resistance – gives way. The wider the pattern and the more times the levels are tested, the stronger the resultant signal and subsequent move in that direction. Just like double-top and bottom patterns, triple-top and bottom patterns can be continuation, as well as reversal patterns.

Compound patterns

There is no point looking for the perfect pattern, you won't find it. Instead, you will see combinations and variations of the standard patterns like the ones below. The important thing in Point and Figure analysis is 'looking left' and understanding what creates the patterns. Look left on the chart and make a subjective decision as to the support or resistance being offered by previous columns of Xs or Os, remembering that the more times a level has held, the stronger it will be. Figure 3-14 has probably been given a special name by someone, but the name is not important. What is important is that this is just a variation of the triple-top. In fact, the diagram in Figure 3-14 would be a semi-catapult if it was a 1-box reversal chart.

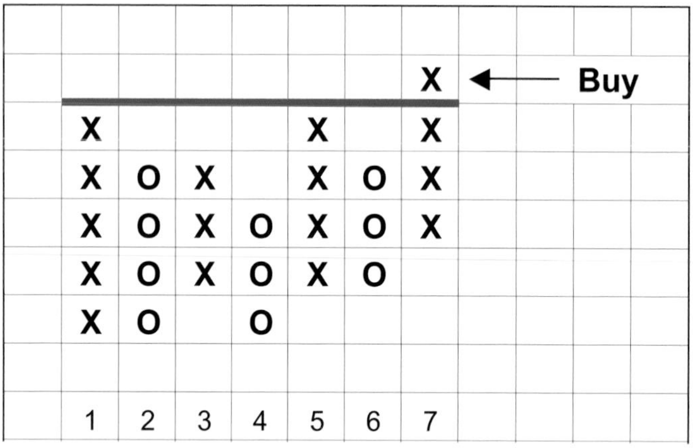

					X	←	Buy		
X			X		X				
X	O	X		X	O	X			
X	O	X	O	X	O	X			
X	O	X	O	X	O				
X	O		O						
1	2	3	4	5	6	7			

Figure 3-14: Variation of triple-top buy signal in a 3-box reversal chart

In Figure 3-14, column 3 fails to reach the level of column 1, which has bearish implications, but column 5 breaks above column 3, generating a double-top buy signal. However, looking left shows that column 5 has only reached the level of column 1. If column 1 is the highest level reached in the near-term, then it is advisable to wait until that level is broken first. This does occur in column 7 and so the pattern becomes an extended triple-top pattern. There are literally thousands of variations of the pattern, once more columns are considered. Figure 3-15 opposite shows what could be loosely termed a multiple top pattern. Notice that it is composed of double-top and triple-top patterns.

Knowing when to ignore signals

It is sometimes advisable to ignore the minor double-top buy and bottom sell signals, especially as the pattern becomes larger and more complex, as shown in Figure 3-15.

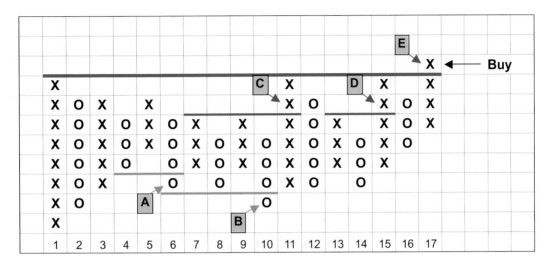

Figure 3-15: Knowing when to ignore signals

A number of minor signals in the context of a bigger pattern can be selectively ignored.

- The first signal, marked A, is a double-bottom sell in column 6, where the O goes below the previous column of Os. The analyst may, however, look left and see that there is an O in column 2, which is one price box lower, and decide to ignore the minor double-bottom signal. This decision would be made by considering how the pattern was entered. If the pattern was entered from below with a column of Xs, as is the case with this pattern, it is unlikely that a simple double-bottom sell signal will reverse the trend. If, however, it was entered from above, with a column of Os before column 1, then the double-bottom sell at A is a continuation signal and should be taken.

- The next signal is a triple-bottom sell, marked B, where the O in column 10 goes below the previous two columns. Once again, looking left shows the O in column 2 as support and, although this is a triple-bottom sell, it may also be ignored.

- Progressing along the pattern, the third signal is a triple-top buy, marked C, in column 11. Looking left again shows Xs at this level in columns 3 and 5 as well as another in column 1. Although it is a triple-top buy, it is weakened by the presence of Xs to the left, in columns 1, 3 and 5, and may therefore be ignored.

- A minor double-top, marked D, is shown in column 15 and ignored by looking left again. As more of these signals occur within the pattern, so more support and resistance is built up, making it easier to spot which signals should be ignored.

- Finally, the signal marked E is a multiple top buy signal in column 17, breaking the Xs in columns 1, 11 and 15. The buy is taken because looking left shows the demand has exceeded the supply for the first time in the overall pattern.

This example shows that although Point and Figure signals are unambiguous, a certain amount of subjectivity must be applied. That subjectivity is only possible if you are able to go inside the chart, so to speak, and understand the psychological make-up of the bulls and bears within the pattern.

Remember, in all cases, the patterns work in the reverse as well.

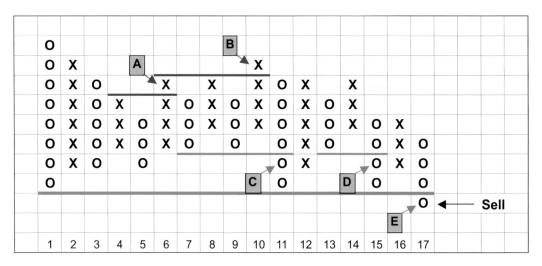

Figure 3-16: Knowing when to ignore signals

Exactly the same scenario takes place in Figure 3-16, but in reverse. The signals are marked as before.

Importance of reassertion of control

What all these patterns are showing us is the reassertion of control by one group over another. In fact, the more times the bears can overcome the bulls, preventing an X column breakout, the more important the eventual X column breakout becomes. Similarly the more the bulls can overcome the bears, preventing an O column breakout, the stronger the sell signal becomes. It is the act of reaching a support or resistance level only to be forced back that makes the subsequent breakout more significant, and hence the trend, stronger. As in life, being able to reassert yourself after a setback makes you that much stronger.

The strength of the pattern

Knowing whether the pattern is likely to be a continuation or reversal pattern has important implications for Point and Figure analysis. Whilst the pattern is being formed, there are clues to the strength of the pattern and the subsequent breakout. Strength is influenced by two things:

- Sloping sides

- Breakout and pullback

Upside and downside triangles – sloping bottom or sloping top

An up-sloping bottom (Figure 3-17) makes any compound pattern bullish to the upside because the slope means that the demand is coming in at higher levels on each reaction. A down-sloping top (Figure 3-18) makes the pattern bearish because supply is coming in at lower and lower levels. These triangles are known as upside and downside triangles. They are much harder to spot in bar and line charts.

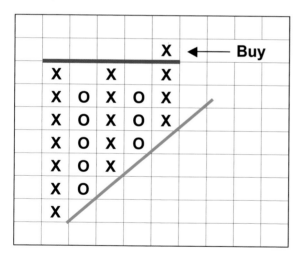

Figure 3-17: Continuation upside triangle in 3-box charts

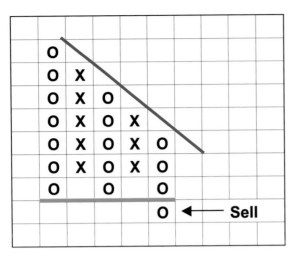

Figure 3-18: Continuation downside triangle in 3-box charts

It is important to note that the signal is not generated until the breakout from the pattern occurs, but the sloping bottom or top gives you a clue to the direction of the breakout. These are very similar to triple-top and bottom patterns seen earlier and like those patterns, they can be continuation, as they are in Figure 3-17 and Figure 3-18 above, or reversal, as they are in Figure 3-19 below and Figure 3-20 opposite. The only difference, as explained earlier, is that a reversal pattern has a different column type entering the pattern from that leaving the pattern.

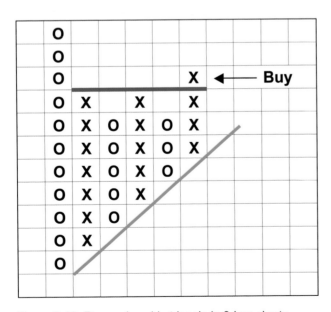

Figure 3-19: Reversal upside triangle in 3-box charts

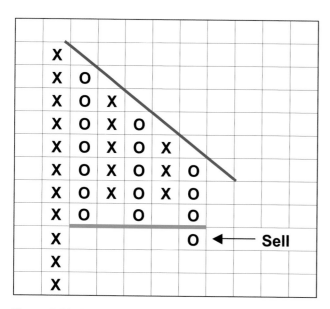

Figure 3-20: Reversal downside triangle in 3-box charts

Remember these are much more likely to be seen in their neat form in 3-box charts. The same pattern in a 1-box chart will have more price action and may not be quite as easy to spot. The upside triangle in Figure 3-17 on page 129 may translate into Figure 3-21 in a 1-box reversal chart. This pattern falls into the category of a semi-catapult discussed earlier.

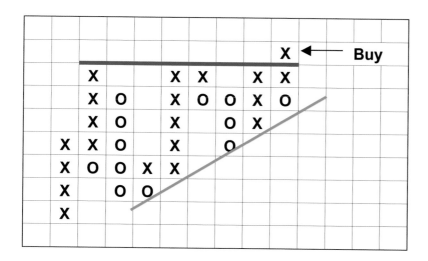

Figure 3-21: Semi-catapult or continuation upside triangle in 1-box charts

Like all patterns, upside and downside triangles can fail as the chart of the S&P 500 Index in Chart 3-2 shows. The perfect upside triangle within a strong trend failed to break up and instead broke below the sloping bottom triggering a sell signal. This reinforces the view that while the pattern provides you with the likelihood of the break, the signal only comes when a double-top or double-bottom signal is issued. The pattern in the chart is identical to that in Figure 3-17 until the part where it does not break up.

Chart 3-2: 5 x 3 of S&P 500 Index showing failed upside triangle

Symmetrical triangles – sloping top and sloping bottom

When you see a sloping top and bottom in a pattern, this indicates uncertainty on the part of the participants and therefore the direction of the breakout cannot be predicted with any degree of certainty. There is some evidence that the breakout is more likely to be in the direction of the underlying trend, and this tends to be the case with smaller patterns. The bigger the pattern the more likely it is to be a reversal pattern.

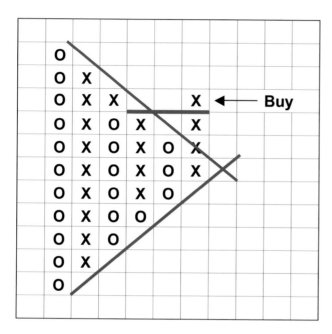

Figure 3-22: Buy signal following a symmetrical triangle

The important thing to note with these symmetrical patterns is that the signal is not given by the break of the trend line. As in all Point and Figure Analysis, the signal is generated when a breach of a previous column occurs. The buy shown in Figure 3-22, and sell shown in Figure 3-23, occur after a double-top and double-bottom breakout, respectively. You may wonder why looking left and seeing resistance does not cause you to ignore the signal. It really depends what the greater pattern looks like. If it is simply a triangle, then the signal should not be ignored, especially if the signal is with the main trend.

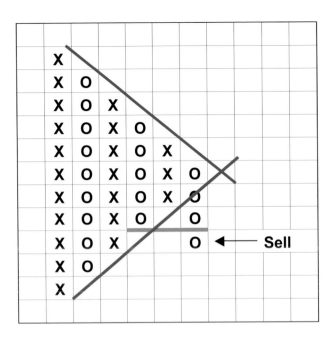

Figure 3-23: Sell signal following a symmetrical triangle

The patterns shown so far are idealised, so when you look at a real chart they may not be quite as clear. Chart 3-3 of Whitbread plc shows two patterns with sloping sides. Pattern A is a typical upside triangle with up-sloping bottom and flat top, similar to the ones in Figure 3-17 and Figure 3-19.

Pattern B shows a typical symmetrical triangle with sloping top and bottom, similar to Figure 3-22. It is not a perfect pattern but it is still a symmetrical triangle with a break to the upside. Note that the signal only comes with the break of the triple-top.

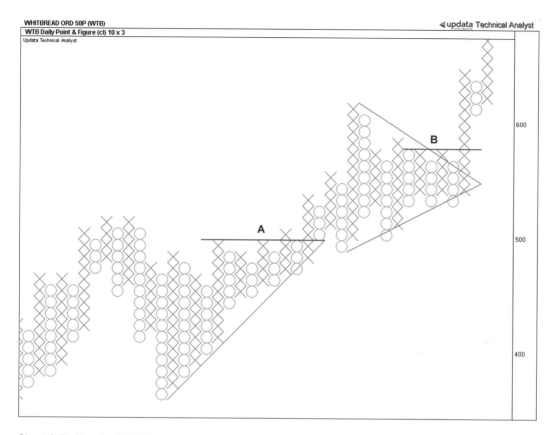

Chart 3-3: 10 x 3 of Whitbread plc showing upside and symmetrical triangles

The breakout and pullback

The second factor which influences the strength of a pattern is the ability to breakout, then pullback into the pattern and finally breakout again. It is one of the strongest signals you can get in Point and Figure charts and enhances the first breakout signal. It occurs when the price breaks out of a multiple top or bottom pattern by one or two boxes but then, instead of continuing, it pulls back into the pattern, before breaking out again.

It is important when considering any pattern to think about the psychological make-up of the participants. The bulls are euphoric that they have managed to overcome the bears at the breakout. The bears take the opportunity of the higher prices to sell and push the price back down below the breakout point. The bulls are so keen to buy the stock that they once again overcome the bears to push the stock to a new high. It is the determined demand that makes the pattern so much stronger.

3-box catapult patterns

The breakout and pullback pattern was first described as a 3-box pattern by Cohen and given the name, catapult. Unfortunately, this is a slightly confusing name as you will see when 1-box charts are discussed below.

Strict rules as to what constitutes a 3-box catapult are not necessary; to qualify, all it needs is the following, referring to Figure 3-24 and Figure 3-25:

- A triple or multiple-top/bottom breakout. A double-top/bottom is not enough. The pattern prior to the breakout could be an extended multiple top pattern, it doesn't matter. What matters is that there has been a breakout from a pattern. Column 5 is the initial breakout column.

- This first breakout should be between 1 and 3 boxes. See column 5.

- The price must then pullback into the pattern as in column 6.

- The pullback must not generate a reverse signal.

- It must then turn around and break out beyond the previous breakout column as in column 7.

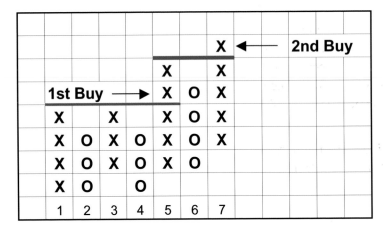

Figure 3-24: 3-box bullish catapult showing the breakout and pullback

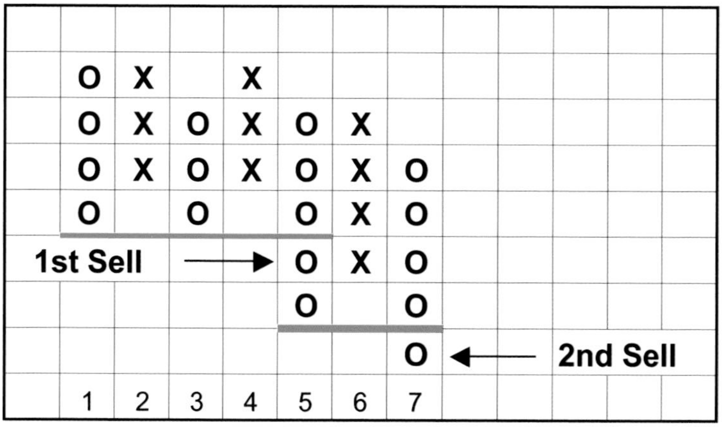

O	X		X							
O	X	O	X	O	X					
O	X	O	X	O	X	O				
O		O		O	X	O				
1st Sell		→		O	X	O				
				O		O				
						O	←	**2nd Sell**		
1	2	3	4	5	6	7				

Figure 3-25: 3-box bearish catapult showing the breakout and pullback

Once again, as you can see, the 3-box catapult is just a variation of the basic patterns discussed earlier. The bullish catapult has a triple-top breakout, followed by a pullback and then a double-top breakout. It is the pullback into the pattern and the subsequent breakout that makes it stronger. The converse applies to bearish catapult patterns. It is a triple-bottom breakout, followed by a pullback and a double-bottom breakout.

The essence of the catapult pattern, and why it is so strong, is one of reassertion. There has been reassertion on the part of the bulls in the case of a bullish catapult, or the bears in the case of the bearish catapult. Having been pushed back after the first breakout, they are strong enough to reassert their position and drive the price past the previous resistance or support level, leading to another breakout. This is highly significant and signals the next big move in the price.

3-box catapults can be continuation or reversal patterns. There is no distinction between the two types in 3-box reversal charts but there are differences in 1-box charts, as you will see on page 138.

1-box catapult patterns

Whereas the definition of catapult is narrow in 3-box charts, and only applies when there is a breakout, then a pullback followed by a second breakout, the 1-box catapult definition is far wider. You have already seen that a continuation 3-box double-top is a semi-catapult in a 1-box chart. In fact the name, semi-catapult applies to any continuation pattern in 1-box analysis. For example, a continuation triple-top in a 3-box chart is a semi-catapult in a 1-box chart.

If a semi-catapult breaks out but fails to advance, and instead the price falls back below the catapult point, it is called a 'false catapult' which is the same as the half-way situation with the 3-box catapult. If, after the pullback into the pattern, the price then breaks out again, the false catapult becomes a larger full semi-catapult, as shown in Figure 3-26.

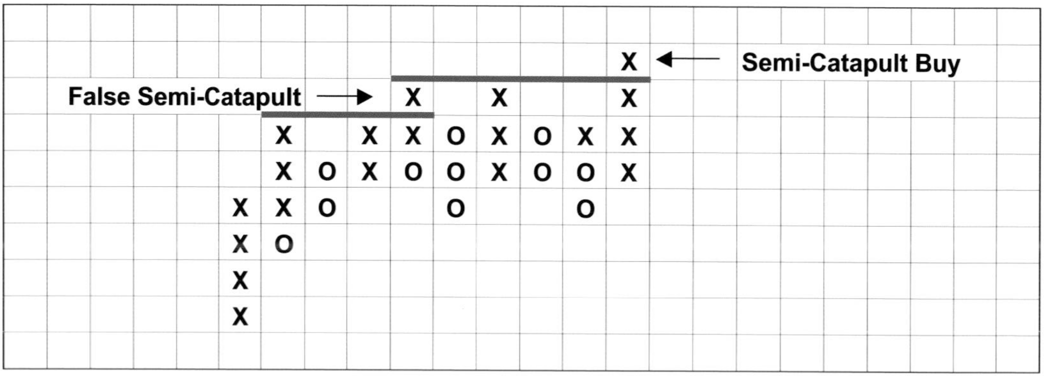

									X	← Semi-Catapult Buy
False Semi-Catapult →				X		X		X		
	X		X	X	O	X	O	X	X	
	X	O	X	O	O	X	O	O	X	
X	X	O			O			O		
X	O									
X										
X										

Figure 3-26: 1-box false semi-catapult

When discussing reversal catapults, the terminology becomes slightly confusing. A reversal pattern in a 1-box chart is actually called a fulcrum, which was discussed on page 120. The point at which the fulcrum is complete, and breakout occurs, is called the Full or True catapult. This is the point at which the price has exceeded the high of the pattern. It sounds as if a 1-box fulcrum is different from a 3-box catapult, but if the 1-box fulcrum has a false catapult point part-way through, it is equivalent to a 3-box catapult.

Figure 3-27 shows a 1-box reversal bullish fulcrum, with a false catapult buy part-way through and a full catapult buy at the end. Figure 3-28 shows the equivalent 3-box reversal bullish catapult. The same sequence of prices was used in both diagrams. Most students of Point and Figure know the 3-box catapult but are unfamiliar with the 1-box fulcrum version. The 3-box version is a condensed version of the 1-box chart.

Both charts can be inverted to show sell signals from tops, rather than buy signals from bottoms.

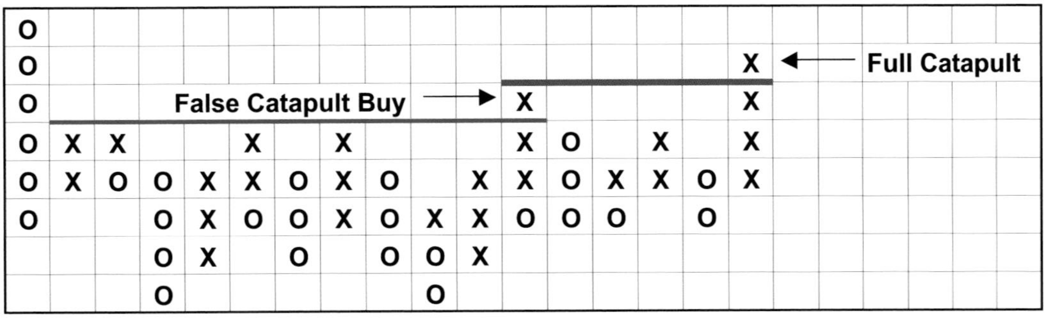

```
O
O                                          X  ← Full Catapult
O        False Catapult Buy  ──►  X        X
O  X  X        X     X           X  O   X  X
O  X  O  O  X  X  O  X  O     X  X  O  X  X  O  X
O        O  X  O  O  X  O  X  X  O  O  O        O
O  X        O           O  O  X
O        O              O
```

Figure 3-27: 1-box bullish fulcrum with false catapult

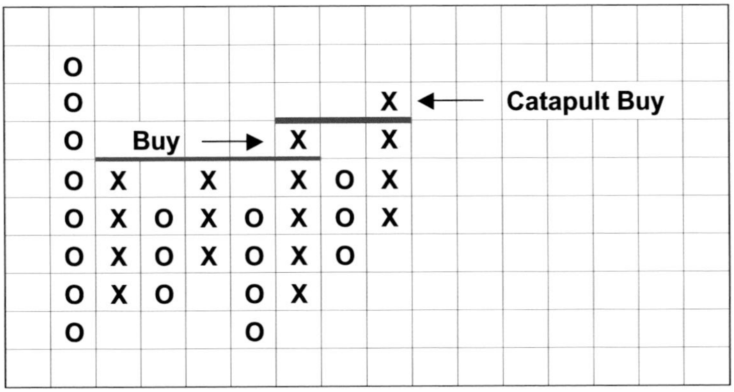

```
O
O                    X  ← Catapult Buy
O     Buy  ──►  X    X
O  X        X       X  O  X
O  X  O  X  O  X  O  X
O  X  O  X  O  X  O
O  X  O     O  X
O        O
```

Figure 3-28: 3-box bullish catapult

Note that all the semi-catapults and fulcrums shown so far are bullish. Bearish patterns are the inverse and work in the same way. There will, of course, be many variations in the patterns. The key thing is to understand the make-up of the pattern in order to recognise the variations.

With 3-box catapults, there is always an initial breakout of a triple-top, followed by a retracement into the pattern, which does not give a reverse signal, followed by another breakout to a new level. With 1-box false fulcrums and false semi-catapults, there is a move in the middle with creates the false catapult, then the price retraces into the pattern before breaking out in the same direction.

Chart 3-4 of BT Group plc shows a number of different catapults, two of which were successful (A & B) and one which failed (C).

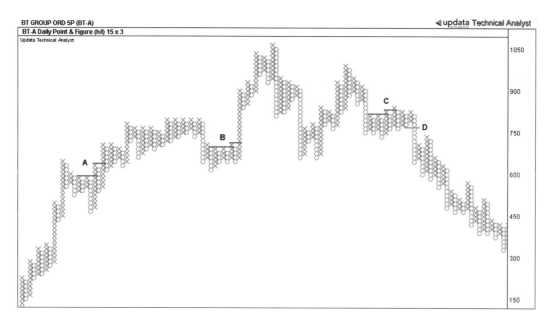

Chart 3-4: 15 x 3 (h/l) of BT Group plc showing two successful catapults (A&B) and one failed (C)

Catapult A in Chart 3-4 is a typical triple-top breakout of 3 Xs with a pullback right into the middle of the pattern. Notice that the pullback column of Os does not go below any previous column of Os in the pattern. After the pullback, a double-top breakout completes the pattern.

Catapult B also forms to the textbook fashion, and results in an explosive move.

Catapult C is an example of a failed catapult. It has all the ingredients of a successful catapult: there is the initial triple-top breakout, followed by a pullback into the pattern and then a double-top breakout. After the double-top, there is another pullback into the pattern and one could be forgiven for thinking that a compound catapult could be developing. Two failed attempts at reaching the high of the pattern result in a long column of Os against the pattern and a subsequent double-bottom breakdown at point D. This is called a trap and is discussed in the next section.

Catapults can take on many forms. Chart 3-5 opposite shows a multiple catapult in the Land Securities plc chart. There is a triple-top breakout at point A, followed by a pullback into the pattern. A second attempt is made to breakout again but it is repulsed twice, forming another triple-top. A second breakout does occur from the second triple-top at point B, followed by another pullback into the pattern. Finally, at point C a double-top breakout occurs, completing a complex catapult pattern.

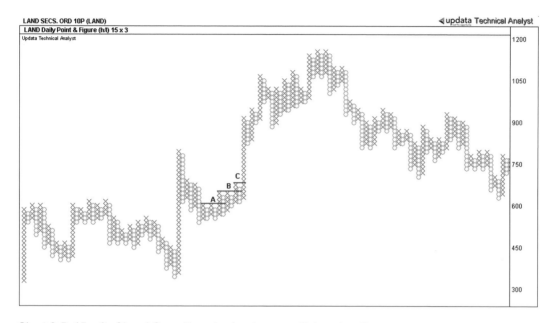

Chart 3-5: 15 x 3 of Land Securities plc showing a multiple catapult

Remember that catapult patterns show up differently in 3-box and 1-box charts. Chart 3-6 is a 10 x 3 Point and Figure of Alliance UniChem plc. Pattern A is a perfect bullish catapult, showing the initial triple-top breakout, then the pullback and finally the double-top breakout to complete the pattern. Chart 3-7 is a 10 x 1 Point and Figure of Alliance UniChem. Pattern A is the same section of data and demonstrates well what a bullish catapult looks like in a 1-box reversal chart. The 1-box chart gives much more detail of the way the pattern has evolved.

Sometimes the 3-box chart doesn't show the pattern at all. Pattern B in Chart 3-6 is a series of double-top buy signals, not a particularly powerful pattern; however, in the 1-box Chart 3-7 it shows a continuation or semi-catapult quite clearly.

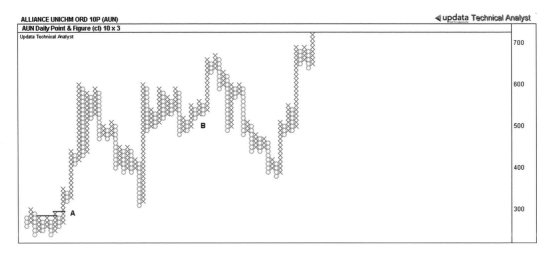

Chart 3-6: 10 x 3 of Alliance UniChem plc showing a catapult at A but not at B

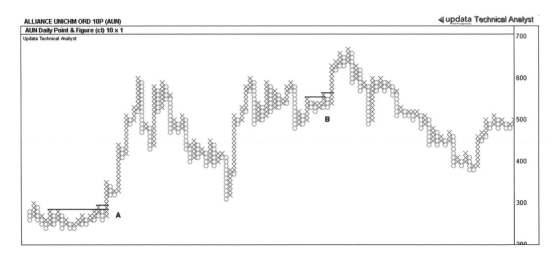

Chart 3-7: 10 x 1 of Alliance UniChem plc 10 x 1 showing a catapult at A and a semi-catapult at B

Terminology clarification

Because the terminology covered so far can be confusing, the summary below should help you to familiarise yourself with it.

- A continuation 3-box double-top/bottom is equivalent to a 1-box semi-catapult.

- A reversal 3-box double-top/bottom is equivalent to a 1-box fulcrum.

- A continuation 3-box triple-top/bottom is equivalent to a 1-box semi-catapult.

- A reversal 3-box triple-top/bottom is equivalent to a 1-box fulcrum.

- A continuation 3-box catapult is equivalent to a 1-box semi-catapult with a false catapult part-way through.

- A reversal 3-box catapult is equivalent to a 1-box fulcrum with a false catapult part-way through.

1-box and 3-box patterns

There are essentially only two 1-box patterns: semi-catapult, if the pattern is a continuation pattern; and fulcrum if it is a reversal pattern. Within these two pattern types there are hundreds of variations.

With 3-box charts there are many more defined patterns. Because 3-box charts have been researched more than 1-box charts, many of the 3-box patterns have been given names.

The rest of this chapter will concentrate on the 3-box variations. Where possible, however, the 1-box translation of the defined 3-box pattern is shown.

Traps

A trap is a pattern which looks like one of those discussed so far, and which breaks out as expected, but then reverses back into the pattern and breaks out the other side. There is no way to avoid them. They will occur and you will be caught. The important thing to note is the point at which you should realise that your initial signal has failed. You cannot assume that any pullback into the pattern after a breakout is a failure, because that's exactly what a 3-box catapult is. In fact, traps are really just failed catapults. The first clue to any failure is a double signal in the opposite direction. Remember, when discussing catapults, it was noted that there should not be an opposite signal. If this does occur, it becomes a trap.

Traps don't have to occur from triple patterns; a simple double pattern can fail and become a trap particularly if they occur during strong trends. There is no distinction between traps in 3-box as opposed to 1-box charts, other than the patterns will be wider in 1-box charts. They are however much harder to see in 1-box charts. The traps discussed below are the 3-box variant.

Bull trap

If you act on a triple-top buy signal and the price then pulls back into the pattern, you must remain in the position because a 3-box catapult may be building. In fact, you should remain with your initial signal until there is a double-bottom sell signal, as shown in Figure 3-29.

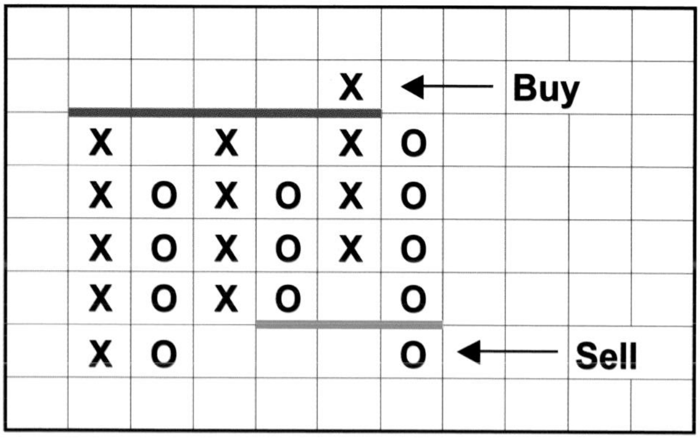

Figure 3-29: Bull trap: triple-top buy becomes double-bottom sell

Bull traps take on many guises. The essential ingredient is that there has been a top (double or triple) buy signal, which has been reversed into a double-bottom sell signal. The important thing is not to pre-empt the sell signal because you may be in the middle of a strong, bullish, 3-box catapult pattern. If you panic during the pullback into the pattern and close your position, you will have lost the advantage gained by buying at the first breakout, if the pattern does turn into a 3-box catapult. So, you have to sell on the opposite side of the pattern, losing an amount equivalent to the depth of the pattern.

Bear trap

A bear trap is the opposite of a bull trap. There must be a bottom sell signal, which is then reversed into a top buy signal, as shown in Figure 3-30 opposite.

O	X				X	←	**Buy**	
O	X	O	X		X			
O	X	O	X	O	X			
O	X	O	X	O	X			
O		O		O	X			
					O	←	**Sell**	

Figure 3-30: Bear trap: triple-bottom sell becomes double-top buy

Trading traps

By their very definition, traps are there to ensnare you, so there is no easy way to trade them without the benefit of hindsight. The assumption is that the first signal is taken. The opposite signal on the other side of the pattern needs to be taken as well, and a loss equivalent to the depth of the pattern is incurred. Can you predict if the pattern is going to turn out to be a trap? The answer is 'no'. It is most likely that the last signal in a bull trend will be a trap, but how do you know that it is the last signal at the time? You could ignore any buy signal in an extended trend, but that would mean missing some good moves if a trap does not emerge. The only way to trade a trap is to grit your teeth and take every signal in the hope that the trap does not turn into a broadening formation, discussed on page 147.

Chart 3-8 (overleaf) of the FTSE All Share Index shows a number of examples of traps.

Trap A is a compound trap. During the strong uptrend, the price gives a double-top buy signal, signalling a further advance. It is, however, reversed by the next column of Os giving a double-bottom sell signal, thus closing the position. The next signal is a strong triple-top buy signal. It is again reversed by a double-bottom sell signal eventually leading to a fall. In fact trap A turns into a broadening formation which is discussed in the next section.

Trap B starts with a triple-top buy signal, one of the strongest, most bullish signals you can get. The price runs up and back down again, giving a double-bottom sell signal. Trap B is also a high pole, discussed on page 155.

Trap C is another strong triple-top buy signal which on first glance could be the start of a new uptrend. After the triple-top, there is a pullback into the pattern, setting it up for a bullish catapult, but a new double-top buy does not occur; instead, a double-bottom sell signal cancels any notion of the pattern being bullish.

Trap D is another triple-top buy, which leads to some consolidation at a higher level, and another double-top buy. Two buy signals followed so closely by one another is a bullish sign.

However, a double-bottom sell shortly after that cancels the bullishness and a number of double-bottom sells confirms the bull trap.

Trap E is a double-top buy being reversed into a double-bottom sell. The initial double-top buy is such a weak signal, and is in a downtrend, that it is unlikely it would have been taken.

Chart 3-8: 20 x 3 of FTSE All Share Index showing traps

Trap F starts with a continuation double-top buy signal, which worked a number of times during the strong uptrend. It is cancelled by a double-bottom sell in the next column, which in turn is cancelled by a double-top buy signal, which leads to a strong advance. Again, this is more of a broadening formation. Some of these traps, namely C, D and E, could have been avoided by trading with the trend. The others are painful traps from which there is little escape. You can see that ignoring the reverse signal can lead to actual losses or a loss of profit.

Shakeouts

Closely related to traps is the shakeout. The difference between the two is that a shakeout occurs at the start of a new trend, usually a bull trend. The trend starts, a new bull trend is established, but then there is a double or triple-bottom sell. It was Earl Blumenthal in his book, *Chart for profit Point and Figure Trading*, who first suggested that the first sell in a bull trend should be ignored. Far from being a sign of weakness, it is actually a sign of strength. The bulls push the price until it is overbought and then stop buying, allowing selling pressure to take the price down below the previous O column low. The first occurrence of this should be ignored unless it falls and breaks below the trend line. The shakeout bottom, or mini-bottom, becomes an important part of the chart when assessing Point and Figure counts, discussed on page 207.

Shakeouts are double-bottom sells in 3-box charts or fulcrums in 1-box charts. When they reverse back up again, they provide the opportunity for a new trend line to be established. This should be read in conjunction with the section on trend lines on page 176. Pattern F in Chart 3-8 is an example of a shakeout – the first sell signal in a new bull trend.

The question remains whether shakeouts can occur in downtrends, and whether the first buy in a downtrend should be ignored. They do, there is one in Chart 3-8, in the 4th column after the all time high. Normally however all buy signals in a downtrend are ignored except to close short positions.

Broadening patterns

The logical progression from bull and bear traps is the broadening pattern, because it starts off as a double or triple-top (or bottom) pattern which turns into a bull or bear trap, where the initial signal is reversed by an opposite signal, which is in turn reversed by another signal in the direction of the initial one. The problem is that confidence is usually shaken. It could also be termed a 'whipsaw' pattern because if you take every single signal you will be whipsawed out and in again.

The broadening patterns described above are the 3-box version. The 1-box version starts with a continuation semi-catapult signal. The semi-catapult is part of a larger fulcrum which reverses the signal, and which in turn is part of a larger semi-catapult that reverses the signal again.

You will hear some Point and Figure practitioners say that a broadening pattern within an uptrend is very bullish, but that is with hindsight. It may indeed turn out to be very bullish, but, at the time, you have no idea that it will. Remember it starts off as a double or triple-top, which is reversed by a double-bottom sell, which in turn is reversed by a double-top buy signal (see Figure 3-31). Bullish indeed, but the likelihood of taking the final buy signal after being whipsawed is small. In fact, it may not be the final signal. Another reversal into the pattern may occur and another sell signal generated, until the final buy signal comes.

Pattern A in Chart 3-8 is an example of a broadening pattern which did not lead to a good up move; in fact it led to a severe correction, so do not assume all broadening patterns will be bullish.

Pattern F in Chart 3-8 is also a small broadening pattern that did eventually lead to a strong advance.

Point and Figure chartists hate broadening patterns and usually 'bail out' after the first reversal signal never to return. In order to benefit from a broadening pattern, you have to ignore some signals. The first signal in a broadening pattern in an uptrend, like the one in Figure 3-31, is a buy signal. You may already be long, but if you are not, you would buy especially if it is a triple-top breakout like this one. The next signal is a sell. The question you will have to ask yourself is, would you ignore the sell signal? It is unlikely and any longs you have would be closed out. With no position open, the next buy signal is easier to take and you would go long again. If that is the final signal from the pattern, you would remain long, but what would you do if the price turns round and gives another sell from the bottom of the pattern? You could ignore it, but that could lead to bigger losses. You could take it and be whipsawed out of your trade again, incurring another loss. If the price turns round and breaks out above the pattern again, how confident would you be to take a third buy signal from the same pattern? The simple fact is that there is no easy answer. Either you move on to another instrument after the first whipsaw, or you take every buy and sell signal in succession, incurring losses each time, on the basis that when the price does run from the signal, you make up for any losses incurred during the whipsawing action. But this strategy will only work if you trade the long as well as the short side, so you profit from a fall, should the final break be to the downside. If you are merely closing out longs each time there is a sell, losses will be incurred and no profit will be gained if the final sell does lead to a big down move as it does in pattern A in Chart 3-8.

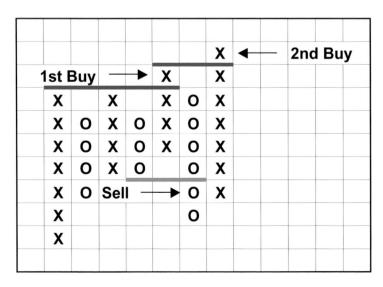

Figure 3-31: Broadening pattern in an uptrend

Broadening patterns don't have to start with a buy signal; they can start with a sell, as shown in Figure 3-32. The same dilemma applies: which, if any, signals do you take and which do you ignore?

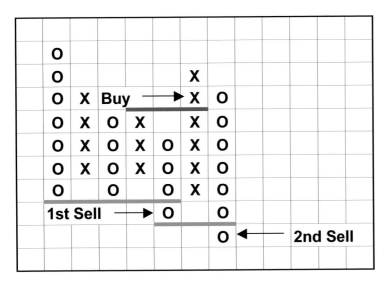

Figure 3-32: Broadening pattern in a downtrend

1-box broadening patterns

Broadening patterns in 1-box charts start with a continuation semi-catapult buy (or sell), which is reversed into a reversal fulcrum, which in turn is reversed and becomes a larger semi-catapult with a false catapult part-way through. Once again, this does not occur in such a defined way as the 3-box version.

Bullish and bearish patterns that reverse

Traditionally, these are 3-box patterns and are called bearish signal reversed, or bullish signal reversed, which is a confusing name. They should probably be called bearish pattern reversed and bullish pattern reversed. It's because bearish and bullish pattern reversed patterns are essentially bearish or bullish trends, which turn in the opposite direction and generate a buy or sell, respectively. Bar chart analysts will recognise them as flag patterns, which occur against the prevailing trend. Unlike flags in bar chart analysis, however, these bullish and bearish patterns reversed can be either trend reversal patterns or continuation patterns, the difference being the trend of the pattern prior to reversing. In continuation patterns, the trend of the 'flag' is against the prevailing trend. In top and bottom patterns, the trend of the 'flag' is with the prevailing trend. Once again they are more visible and defined in 3-box charts, although they can be spotted in 1-box charts, as you will see.

Bearish pattern reversed

The bearish pattern reversed is a series of X/O columns with consecutive lower highs and lower lows, indicating bearish downtrend behaviour. A column of Xs then breaks above the high of the previous column of Xs and the pattern, and trend, is reversed. Some writers specify that there must be 7 columns in the pattern in order to qualify. Some specify the exact make-up of the columns. Both are too rigid. It is better to observe that there is a potential pattern in the making, understanding that it may not look just like one in a book, and then wait for the signal. As with most Point and Figure patterns, there is one essential ingredient that defines the pattern. In this case, it is that there must be a series of lower highs and lower lows, the trend of which is eventually broken by a double-top buy signal. Remember what lower highs and lower lows means: it means repeat double-bottom sell signals but no double-top buy signal until the one that breaks the pattern. Furthermore, there should be no strict specification as to the number of these columns, nor that each high and low must be only 1 box lower than the previous column. Point and Figure patterns should not be learnt by heart, but rather fully understood so that any variation in the pattern can be catered for. You will know by now that the greater the number of columns, the greater the potential from the breakout, the reason being that complacency has set in and those who have confidently taken positions with the trend are shocked when it suddenly reverses leading to short covering and position altering.

Remember, however, that at the end of the pattern the buy signal may never come. The pattern may give repeat sell signals and lead to a significant fall. What is powerful about these patterns is that they take time to build and, as they do, you can start to see what is forming. The pattern, however, is only confirmed when the final signal – buy, in this case – is generated.

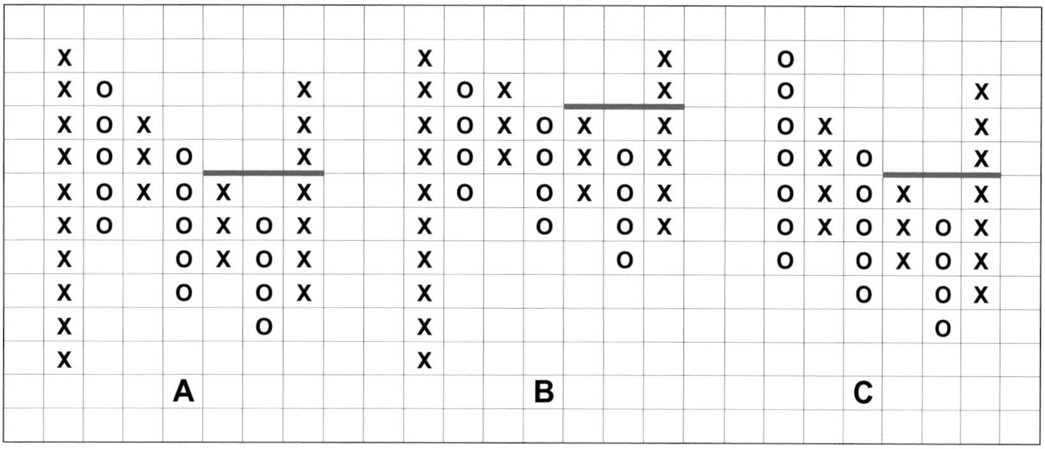

Pattern A

X						
X	O					
X	O	X				
X	O	X	O			X
X	O	X	O	X		X
X	O		O	X	O	X
X			O	X	O	X
X			O		O	X
X					O	
X						

Pattern B

X						X
X	O	X				X
X	O	X	O	X		X
X	O	X	O	X	O	X
X	O		O	X	O	X
X			O		O	X
X					O	
X						
X						
X						

Pattern C

O					
O					X
O	X				X
O	X	O			X
O	X	O	X		X
O	X	O	X	O	X
O	X	O	X	O	X
O		O	X	O	X
		O		O	X
				O	

Figure 3-33: Examples of bearish pattern reversed

Figure 3-33 shows three variations of the bearish pattern reversed; there will be others. Pattern A is a typical continuation bearish pattern reversed. The price rises into the pattern and is rebuffed by a column of Os. The second column of Xs rises short of the previous X column and is turned back by a column of Os that goes to a new low, giving a close long positions sell signal. The subsequent column of Xs falls short of the previous, and the new column of Os makes a lower low, giving a repeat sell signal. The action is bearish. The bulls cannot reach previous levels and the bears are reaching new low levels. Finally, a new column of Xs rises past the previous column of Xs and gives a double-top buy signal. The buy signal is good and should be acted on. The reason is that the bulls have been repulsed a few times but have finally gained enough power to push through the bearish resistance and make the first new high. The shock to the bears results in short covering and a significant move, especially in the case of a continuation pattern.

Pattern B is another example of a continuation bearish pattern reversed. The downtrend within the pattern is not as sharp as that in pattern A, but the pattern is still valid and the buy signal at the end should be taken. Pattern C is a reversal pattern, rather than a continuous. A column of Os descends into the pattern. A column of Xs rises against this but a new column of Os forms and makes a new low issuing a repeat sell signal in the overall downtrend. The next column of Xs fails to reach the level of the previous X column and another new low is made by the next column of Os. It is typical bear market action of lower highs and lower lows. Then a column of Xs manages to get above the previous column of Xs, breaking the pattern of lower highs and a buy signal is issued. The buy signal should be taken as it generally means the end of the downtrend.

Bullish pattern reversed

Bullish pattern reversed is the exact opposite of the bearish described above. Instead of a series of lower highs and lower lows, there is a series of higher highs and higher lows which eventually reverse with a sell signal. This is the essential ingredient that defines the pattern.

Figure 3-34 shows three variations of the bullish pattern reversed. They are the inverse of the bearish patterns shown on the previous page. Patterns D and E are continuation patterns, and pattern F is a reversal pattern. In each case, a sell, reversing the bullishness of the pattern, is issued at the end.

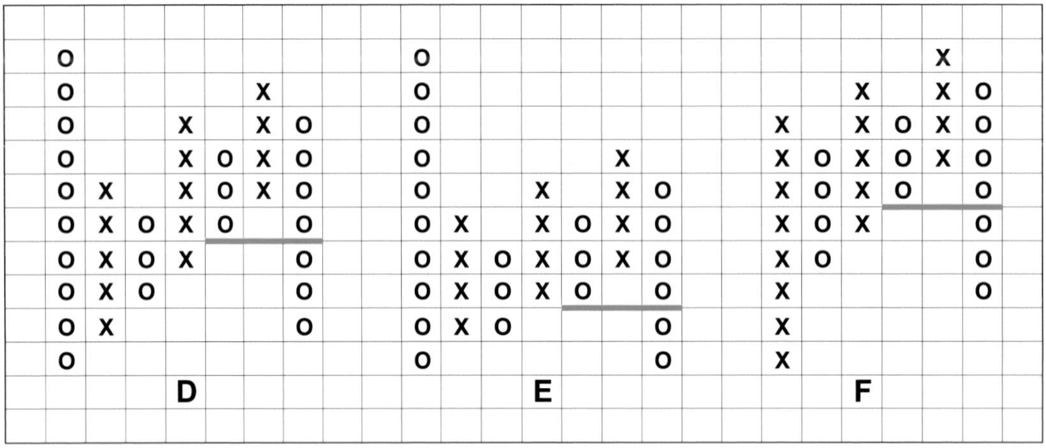

```
O                       O                           X
O           X           O                       X   X O
O     X     X O         O                   X   X O X O
O     X O X O           O               X   X O X O X O
O X   X O X O           O           X   X O X O X O ___ O
O X O X O ___ O         O X     X O X O X O X ___   O
O X O X       O         O X O X O X O X O X O       O
O X O         O         O X O X O ___ O   X         O
O X           O         O X O         O   X
O                       O             O   X
      D                       E                 F
```

Figure 3-34: Examples of bullish pattern reversed

Bullish and bearish pattern reversed patterns are not that common but they tend to be reliable. For the obvious reason that the final buy or sell signal is with the prevailing trend, continuation patterns are more reliable than top or bottom patterns. Acting on the buy signal in pattern C, or the sell signal in pattern F, is far more risky than the buy in patterns A, B, D and E. Of course, some of these patterns will fail but, by this stage, you will have realised that no pattern works every time.

You may be thinking by now that there are too many exceptions or that you can easily get caught out. Of course, all techniques have a failure rate. That is the reason for having stops in place. These will be discussed later. One advantage of Point and Figure charts is that you know if a pattern has failed early on. Furthermore, you will see when trend is discussed that this can dramatically reduce the chance of being caught out by failed patterns.

Perfect examples of any pattern are usually hard to find, but there could be no better example than the continuation bearish pattern reversed that occurred in the Dow Jones Industrial Average during 2004. Chart 3-9 opposite shows 100 x 3 Point and Figure of the Dow. The circled pattern A is a typical continuation bearish pattern reversed. Notice that it has 9 columns. The pattern has taken the Dow to a new local high. If you were applying a strict 7 column rule, you would have ignored this pattern. The simple fact is that it is rare to find an exact textbook pattern; you must be prepared to look for variations that still tell the same story and lead to the same result. Pattern B is one such example. It is a continuation bullish pattern reversed; it is not exactly the same as the textbook, but it has the essential ingredients – higher highs and higher lows which are then reversed with a sell signal. The last X column didn't make a new high but that doesn't invalidate the pattern, in fact if anything it shows the inherent weakness in the pattern reinforcing the expectation of a sell signal.

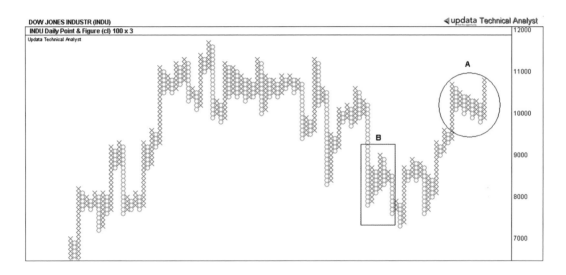

Chart 3-9: 100 x 3 of Dow Jones Industrial Average 100 x 3 showing bullish and bearish patterns reversed

Comparing 3-box and 1-box charts

As usual, the patterns tend to be more compact and neat in 3-box charts. They are much harder to spot in 1-box charts because the 'flag' is not so clear-cut as Chart 3-10 shows. However, if you know what you are looking for – a series of higher highs and higher lows, or lower lows and lower highs – then they should be easy enough to spot.

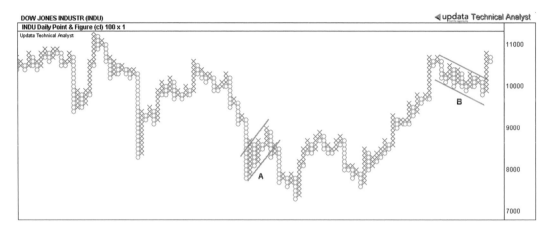

Chart 3-10: 100 x 1 of Dow Jones Industrial Average 100 x 1 showing bullish and bearish patterns reversed

Chart 3-11 is a 0.01 x 3 Point and Figure of Cable (USD/GBP). Pattern A is a perfect example of a bearish pattern reversed. There is some discussion to be had as to whether it is a continuation in a flat trend or a bottom pattern, but it doesn't actually matter. There are 13 columns in the pattern. On the same chart, pattern B can be considered as well. It fits the essential ingredient of lower highs and lower lows, although one of the lows was at the same level as the previous. Although variation patterns should be treated with suspicion, they should always be observed as potential patterns. In the case of pattern B, the buy signal at the end of the pattern was very profitable.

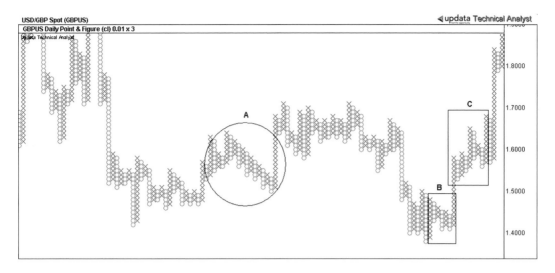

Chart 3-11: 0.01 x 3 of Cable (USD/GBP) showing bullish and bearish patterns reversed

As stated earlier, patterns sometimes fail. One advantage of Point and Figure is that it does tell you when the pattern has failed. Pattern C in Chart 3-11 is a potential bullish pattern reversed. There is a series of higher highs and higher lows. There is the final double-bottom sell in the 8th column and the pattern is complete. The sell is, however, cancelled in the next column by a double-top buy and the pattern has failed.

Poles

Poles are also a 3-box pattern although, as you will see, they can be translated into 1-box patterns. They are different from other patterns discussed so far in that they are reversal patterns, never continuation. A pole is a long column of Xs or Os with a column of Os or Xs alongside it. Although poles are reversal patterns, not every pole you see will work as such. There are specific conditions which must apply before the pole can be considered as a reversal. High poles were first identified by Earl Blumenthal in his book, *Chart for Profit: Point and Figure Trading*. Low poles were introduced by Michael Burke subsequently. Both authors are proponents of the 3-box reversal method and, for this reason, poles are essentially 3-box chart patterns. It is, however, possible to see them on 1-box charts, as you will see below.

For a pole to occur there should be some sideways consolidation prior to the pole. Usually there is further sideways consolidation on the other side of the pole before the pattern breaks. The pole is an opportunity to enter a trade before the pattern is complete.

Poles occur when price breaks above (or below) previous price action and a long column of Xs or Os is created. This breakout column must exceed previous highs or lows by at least 3 boxes; this is what Blumenthal specifies but this may not be enough. The less the number of boxes, the greater the chance of a failure, so you should be looking for more than 5 boxes in height for poles to be effective. The reason has to do with the psychological make-up of the pattern discussed below. After the initial breakout column, the very next column must be an opposing column of Os or Xs in the opposite direction, adjacent to the breakout column. This column must retrace the previous breakout column by more than 50% for a pole to be in the making; so if the breakout column was 10 Xs, the pole will be made after the 5th O in the next column.

Poles can occur in uptrends or downtrends. High poles indicate near-term weakness and low poles indicate near-term strength.

As with all Point and Figure patterns, it is important to consider what is going on in the minds of the participants. Considering the high pole in Figure 3-35, there is a long breakout column of Xs showing strong demand and buyers prepared to pay up to get the stock. At some stage that demand ceases and the column of Xs comes to an end. All participants expect there to be a small correction of perhaps 3 Os to bring the price back, before demand comes back in again, but that doesn't happen. The next column of Os is as determined as the previous column of Xs. Sellers, who are now receiving higher prices, push the price back, trying to find new buyers, but the buyers are not forthcoming because all the available buyers were 'sucked' into the initial breakout column, so the price continues to fall, effectively cancelling out the column of Xs. The bulls that bid up the stock, especially those who bought in at the top of the column of Xs, will be totally shocked. Many, already showing losses, will close their positions, which removes the bulls from the market and adds to the list of sellers. It is the shock reverse column of Os that makes the high pole such an important reversal pattern. It is as if the buyers have been slapped in the face. After the high pole is complete there is usually, although not always, an unwinding of positions that takes place resulting in some sideways movement in a tight range before a complete breakdown of the pattern takes place.

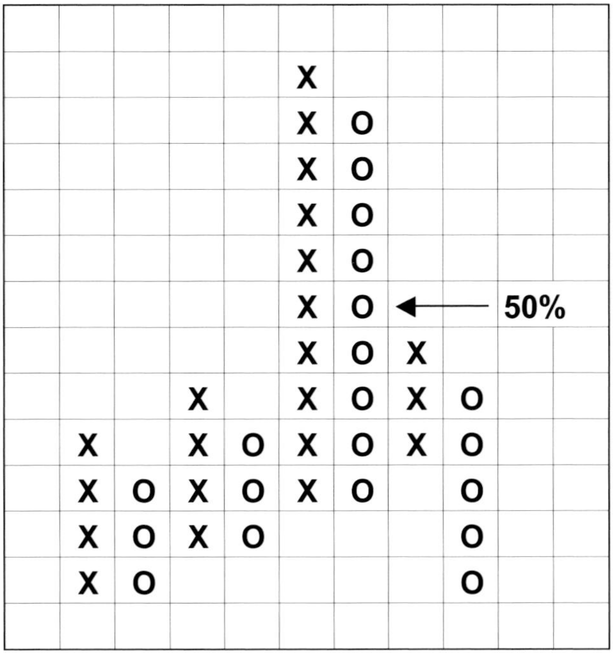

				X				
				X	O			
				X	O			
				X	O			
				X	O			
				X	O			← 50%
				X	O	X		
		X		X	O	X	O	
X		X	O	X	O	X	O	
X	O	X	O	X	O		O	
X	O	X	O				O	
X	O						O	

Figure 3-35: High pole

The converse is true for the low pole in Figure 3-36. Bears, which may include short sellers, push the price down aggressively. They will then expect some demand to come in to push the price up a touch to allow them to start selling again. The bulls, however, use the lower prices to accumulate stock, and are so keen that they push the price right back to the start of the bear move, wiping out any advantage the short sellers had gained. In fact, sellers covering shorts will contribute to the rise as well. As with the high pole, there is some unwinding that takes place before there is a breakout to higher levels, as the bulls continue to demand stock and short sellers are cautious about selling.

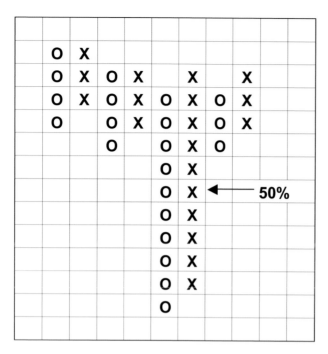

Figure 3-36: Low pole

The main issue with poles is the complete reversal of sentiment and the shock and disbelief it gives those caught on the wrong side of the move.

Trading strategy with poles

Most patterns should not be anticipated. The final signal from a pattern may never come, so it is best to wait for it before acting. High and low poles are different. It is possible to act while the pattern is being formed. The common strategy with a high pole is to sell when the reversal column of Os retraces 50% of the X column length. This is fine in theory, but, in the heat of the moment, it is quite a difficult strategy to follow, especially if you have been involved in buying during the X column. The tendency instead is to wait for further columns to build before selling on a double-bottom breakdown. There is nothing wrong with waiting, but early action does allow extra gains.

If you do take the early signal at the 50% retracement, consider what is the risk in doing so. The risk is that the column of Os does not continue down but instead turns round into a column of Xs. This would cancel the high pole and the pattern would have to be re-assessed. The risk from the first sell point is the number of boxes that make up your reversal on the chart you are using – 3 Xs if it's a 3-box chart, 1 if it's a 1-box chart. The reason is that if the down-column of Os does not continue uninterrupted, then it is no longer a high pole.

The risk is also related to your trading style. If your initial sell is simply a close of a long position that you had taken during the breakout column of Xs, you are at less risk than a sell which opens up a short position. A sell at the 50% retracement to close your long position leaves you neutral to assess the pattern to see what builds from it and so the simple reversal of the column of Xs would not trigger a buy signal. In this case, you must wait for the next double-top or double-bottom buy or sell signal to open a new position.

However, if your sell at the 50% retracement was a short, then the simple reversal of the column of Xs should be taken as a buy to close a short position. Figure 3-37 shows the situation.

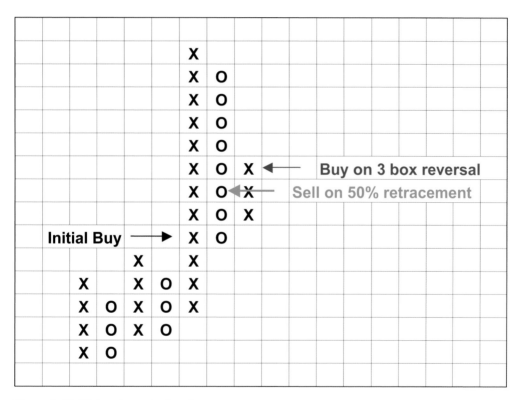

Figure 3-37: High pole early signal

Poles are one of the most effective, yet most dangerous, patterns. They are so clear in their formation and so clear in their completion but they often fail to provide the expected move.

Chart 3-12 below is a 25 x 3 of the Dow Jones Industrial Average. After a nearly 1000 point uptrend, the price consolidated for three columns and then broke out upwards again by 11 Xs setting up the basis for a high pole. In the next column, the price fell by more than the length of the rise, confirming a high pole. Whether you exited on the 50% retracement or whether you exited on the double-bottom sell signal, the expectation would have been for a reasonable correction. Instead the price fell and set up a low pole bottom, leading to a double-top buy signal. This is quite a common occurrence. A high pole followed immediately by a low pole, as in this example, is very bullish and less common, while a low pole followed immediately by a high pole is very bearish. It's really a special case of a broadening formation.

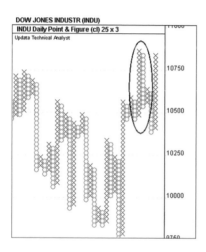

Chart 3-12: 25 x 3 of the Dow Jones Industrial Average showing a high pole

Poles in 1-box reversal charts

Nothing has ever been written about poles in 1-box reversal charts. Awareness of the pattern didn't exist when De Villiers, & Taylor and Wheelan were writing about 1-box charts, so they have only ever been discussed in relation to 3-box charts. At first sight, it is less likely that you will ever see a long unbroken column of Xs or Os in a 1-box reversal chart, but that is not the way to look at it. In a 3-box reversal chart, the price could reverse by up to 2 boxes without interrupting the unbroken column, so it is really the reversal that is preventing you from seeing the interplay as the column builds. But that is exactly the purpose of 3-box charts – to filter out any countermoves of less than 3 boxes. With 1-box charts, however, every reversal is shown. This means that a column interrupted by a step back of one or two boxes can, for the purposes of a pole, still be considered as an 'unbroken' column, because if it was on a 3-box chart it would be.

Figure 3-38 shows a high pole using a 1-box reversal chart. Compare it with Figure 3-35 on page 157, which is constructed with the same data. You can see that the advance shown by the blue line is uninterrupted by a reversal of 3 or more boxes, as is the decline shown by the red line. It is, therefore, a high pole, but perhaps not as easy to spot as it would have been in a 3-box chart.

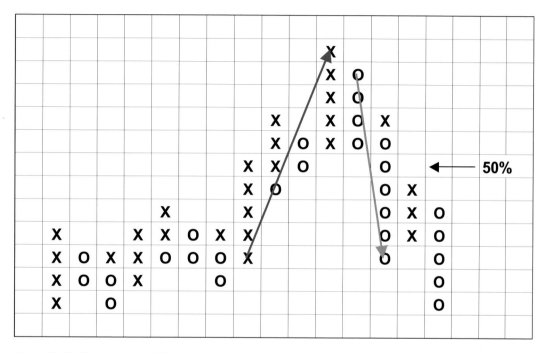

Figure 3-38: High pole in a 1-box reversal chart

The example given here will not always be the case. Sometimes the initial move and the adjacent correction are so severe that even on a 1-box reversal chart there is no step-back.

Chart 3-13 is a 0.5(½) x 3 of Whirlpool Corp. As you can see, there are a number of poles, both high and low, marked on the chart. Whilst looking at them, consider also Chart 3-14 which is a 0.5 x 1 of Whirlpool. When comparing the charts you will be able to see how poles show up on 1-box charts compared to 3-box charts. In the case of each pattern described below, try to put yourself in the position of a participant. This will give you a better understanding of the psychology that goes to create the patterns.

Pattern A is an unusual high pole. Normally, high poles occur at the end of uptrends. This one has occurred part-way through a downtrend. Consider the make-up of the participants. After a severe downtrend, there is some congestion, then a long column of Xs shows confident buying by the bulls. The bears take advantage of the higher prices to push the price down again leaving the bulls shocked. The triple-bottom sell completes the pattern.

Pattern B is a low pole. There is some congestion prior to the long column of Os down to the bottom. Notice that the column of Os in the 1-box reversal chart is interrupted by a step-back of two Xs. This does not, however, invalidate the pole in the 1-box reversal chart. The adjacent column of Xs back up again completes the low pole. So strong was the move, that even on a 1-box chart there was no step-back.

Pattern C is a high pole. Once again, there is congestion prior to the long breakout column of Xs, which is followed by a retracement column of Os. The 1-box reversal chart shows that the breakout column of Xs had a number of one-step-backs during the building of the column. This does not invalidate the pole in the 1-box chart.

Pattern D is a low pole with only a small congestion before the long O column down. Remember, bears and short sellers will be euphoric, but then the adjacent column of Xs changes everything. What is interesting is that the pole in the 1-box chart is identical. There are no one-step pauses during the O or X column.

Pattern E is a very long high pole taking the price to new highs. Bulls riding this X column will also believe that there are higher prices to come. Although they will expect a small, perhaps a 3 box, retracement, they will not be prepared for complete retracement of the X column by the next column of Os. This strong retracement shows that the bears are in control and not the bulls. In the 1-box chart, the retracement column of Os has two one-step-backs during its construction.

Pattern F is a low pole that looks very different on the 1-box chart. In fact looking at the 1-box chart on its own, you could be forgiven for missing it completely. The long column of Os in the 3-box chart consists of a number of one and two-steps-back in the 1-box chart. This does not invalidate the pattern. The adjacent retracement X column also has a step-back in the 1-box chart.

Chart 3-13: 0.5 x 3 of Whirlpool plc showing high poles and low poles in 3-box charts

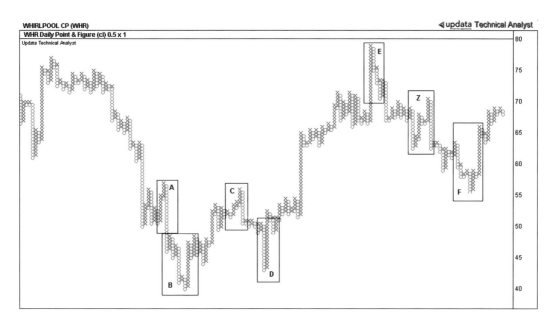

Chart 3-14: 0.5 x 1 of Whirlpool plc showing high poles and low poles in 1-box charts

Poles are easier to spot in 3-box charts. If you are using 1-box charts for your analysis, the above gives you a clue what a pole looks like. It may be better, however, to switch to a 3-box chart if you are in any doubt.

Opposing poles

You will sometimes see opposing poles occurring within a few columns of one another; such as high pole A followed by low pole B or high pole C followed by low pole D. When this happens, the strength of the second pole in the sequence is considerably enhanced, allowing you to act on an early signal with more confidence. The area marked Z in Chart 3-13 and Chart 3-14 is an example of a low pole followed by what could be regarded as a marginal high pole. Under normal circumstances the high pole on its own barely fulfils the conditions for a pole, but it is enhanced by the presence of a low pole preceding it.

Congestion analysis

The reading of Point and Figure charts is enhanced by the width of any pattern. The more columns that occur within a range, the more information you can glean from the pattern. Congestion occurs when the bulls and bears are not confident enough to engage in too much buying or selling pressure. Congestion areas tend to occur after a strong advance or decline. It is the time that profits are taken and positions are reversed after the rise or decline into the area, and it is a time for adjusting to the new price level after the strong move. Adjustments by the bulls and bears to their positions leads to a number of small changes in direction, resulting in a number of columns being formed. The market is, in effect, neutral at this point.

Congestion is a good time to take new positions as well, provided that there is sufficient evidence as to the future direction. The key to congestion analysis is to identify whether accumulation or distribution is taking place. Accumulation and distribution are identified by where the majority of the price action is taking place. Activity towards the bottom of a congestion area indicates strong support and the probability that the move out of the area will be to the upside. The reason is that if there is activity towards the bottom of the range – lots of small column changes – it shows buyers using every opportunity to open new positions.

Conversely, activity towards the top side of the pattern indicates strong resistance and that the break from the pattern will be to the downside. This activity shows profit taking, because sellers are taking every opportunity to close their positions or, indeed, open short positions.

One of the benefits of the 1-box reversal chart is that you will see congestion patterns that are not apparent on the condensed 3-box charts. The analysis of the chart within the congestion area can give an indication as to the probable direction of any breakout. This is virtually impossible with 3-box charts based on end-of-day data.

Congestion patterns are simply just a combination of the basic Point and Figure patterns discussed so far. They may take months or just a few hours to form. If you can use the action within a congestion area to predict the direction of the breakout, you can open low-risk trades before the breakout occurs. Although this is seen to be against the Point and Figure rule that you buy or sell on breakouts, it is a low risk way to trade.

Some congestion areas tell you nothing, some, like the fulcrum, can tell you an enormous amount.

The fulcrum

You will already be familiar with the 1-box fulcrum as was discussed in the context of reversal patterns in 1-box charts. It can be a fairly small pattern but in its larger form, it is the most important of all congestion area patterns. It was De Villiers who coined the term fulcrum and went to great lengths to explain it by using the analogy of leverage in the subject of mechanics. The fulcrum occurs when the forces of demand and supply are balanced.

Fulcrums can occur at bottoms as well as tops, as is the case with all Point and Figure patterns. It is less likely that you will see a fulcrum if you use end-of-day data and 3-box reversal charts. They are far more apparent when using tick data or 1-box reversal charts with end-of-day data, but that doesn't mean you shouldn't look for them. In fact, if you do see one in a 3-box chart it is of very high significance. Fulcrums may be regarded as the head and shoulders pattern of the Point and Figure world, although some attribute that honour to the poles discussed in the previous section. The reason is that, like head and shoulders patterns, fulcrums are where the stock changes hands and positions are re-assessed.

The fulcrum takes on many guises. De Villiers listed three types, while Wheelan listed eight fulcrum tops and eight fulcrum bottoms. It is pointless listing them all, but to assist identification there are some essential components for a fulcrum bottom:

- There must be a downward move or downtrend into the congestion area. This means that there are more Os than Xs and the columns of Os are longer than the columns of Xs. The downtrend is often within a clear channel.

- The downtrend must be broken by substantial sideways activity. Sideways activity means that the columns of Xs and Os become shorter and similar in length. This is caused by position adjustment or simply exhaustion. This sideways activity takes the price action out of the downtrend channel.

- There is usually, although unfortunately not always, a half-hearted mid-pattern rally usually into resistance. This is caused by a number of factors such as short covering by bears who have ridden the downtrend and believe it to be over and short-term buying by day traders looking for a quick profit from an oversold situation, but the essential thing is that no group is buying to establish a long-term position. The sharpness of the mid-pattern rally is caused by the lack of sellers.

- Lows should be re-tested again because, after the mid-pattern rally, there is no continued buying pressure: the short coverers have covered their shorts and the day traders have taken their short-term profits.

- There will be further sideways congestion after the price has come back into the region of the lows and further position adjustment is undertaken.

- Once all the position adjustment has taken place and all the shorts are covered, bulls start taking their positions, the columns of Xs start to lengthen and more Xs than Os appear as an uptrend starts.

- At this time one or more double-top or semi-catapult formations begin to occur as demand exceeds supply and the bulls push the price through resistance levels.

- Finally the price breaks above the pattern mid-point, a full catapult in 1-box reversal terms, and the fulcrum pattern is complete.

- There is no time limit on the completion of the fulcrum.

Figure 3-39 shows a typical fulcrum bottom. There is a downward move into the congestion area, often, though not always, a downtrend channel. The price action moves across and out of the channel as it consolidates sideways. There is a weak rally, which is rebuffed, and the price descends into the support at the lows. It is during this sideways stage that bulls are accumulating at the lower levels. This is followed by a more determined rally which leads to a catapult buy signal, where the X exceeds the highest X within the congestion area.

Figure 3-39 is a 1-box reversal chart and that is why the fulcrum can be seen. Figure 3-40 on the other hand, is a 3-box chart using the same data. The resultant pattern is just a double-top buy signal. It won't always be the case, but this really highlights the importance of using 1-box reversal charts.

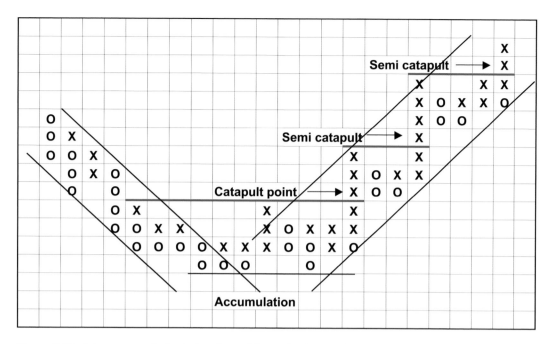

Figure 3-39: 1-box reversal chart showing a fulcrum bottom pattern

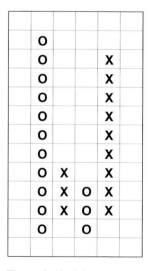

Figure 3-40: 3-box reversal chart with fulcrum pattern not apparent

Fulcrums are really just a combination of the basic patterns discussed earlier. Within the fulcrum, there will be double and triple-tops, semi-catapults, traps and other false signals that may be ignored by looking left in the pattern. Furthermore, fulcrums, like other patterns, have many variations. Sometimes there will be two mid-pattern rallies; sometimes there is no rally at all; some will have V bottoms; some will have typical double-bottom shapes; some will have flat bottoms. Some will be compound patterns, which are fulcrums within fulcrums, but they are all essentially the same because the forces that create them are always the same.

The fulcrum described above is a fulcrum bottom, while fulcrum tops are the inverse. Remember however, the psychology is different at tops and bottoms. Long position holders are less desperate to close long positions when they are on the wrong side of the market, whereas holders of shorts will cover quickly when the market goes against them. This means that you are more likely to see sharp mid-pattern rallies in a fulcrum bottom than you are to see sharp mid-pattern declines in a fulcrum top. Figure 3-41 is an example of a fulcrum top. The sideways consolidation at the top is the distribution phase, where profits are taken and positions are unwound. The pattern is completed by the catapult sell signal followed by a number of semi-catapult sells.

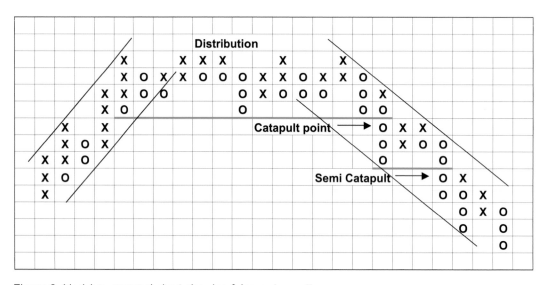

Figure 3-41: 1-box reversal chart showing fulcrum top pattern

Strength and weakness in fulcrum patterns

Not every fulcrum will be a reliable reversal pattern. Some may fail after the breakout catapult and become continuation patterns. Weakness in the fulcrum is indicated when, after the catapult, the price does not keep going, but instead forms another sideways pattern with a sloping top in the case of fulcrum bottoms, and a sloping bottom in the case of fulcrum tops. Figure 3-42 shows the same fulcrum as shown in Figure 3-39, but instead of continuing to rise after the catapult it consolidates in a negative way around the breakout point. This points to weakness and the strong possibility that the fulcrum has failed. The width of the pattern after the catapult is what determines the extent of the failure. If the width, as it is in Figure

3-42, is greater or equal to the height of the original congestion, the likelihood is that the price will break below the lowest point in the fulcrum.

What this means is that, after the catapult point in a fulcrum, the price must continue to show strength otherwise the breakout of the fulcrum is false and a complete reversal is possible. For the fulcrum to be effective, there must be a series of double-tops or semi-catapults in the uptrend out of the pattern as seen in Figure 3-39.

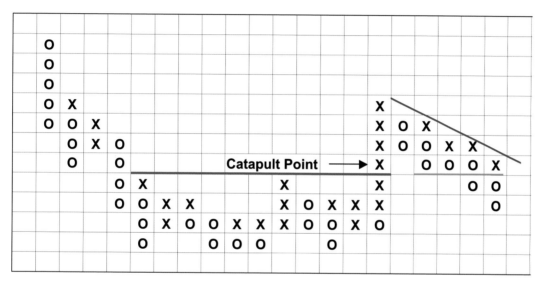

Figure 3-42: 1-box reversal chart showing weakness in a fulcrum pattern

The row (or rows) with the most filled in boxes controls the bullishness or bearishness of the fulcrum pattern. You will see later that this is also used for establishing targets from the pattern. The reason these rows are important is because they are at the level which the price has passed through most often in the pattern and where most of the battle for control has taken place. They provide the pivot or anchor about which the pattern is balanced. If the rows are towards the base of the fulcrum, it indicates strength in the base and a likely break to the upside. If they are towards the top, it indicates strength at the top and a likely break towards the downside. Often they are simply in the middle of the pattern giving no clues at all.

Weakness within a fulcrum is indicated by mid-pattern rallies caused by short covering, in the case of bottoms, and mid-pattern declines caused by profit taking, in the case of tops. If you are able to use these clues to assess on which side, top or bottom, the strength or weakness lies, you can start to take positions within the fulcrum pattern.

Considering fulcrum bottoms, you should wait for the mid-pattern rally during a fulcrum bottom and then look to take a position as close to the previous lows of the pattern as possible, provided there is more price action at the lows. Some traders prefer not to 'fish' for the bottom, instead they wait until the price has come back to within an O of the previous bottom after the mid-pattern rally, and then take a long position on the first reversal of 2 Xs back up again. Why 2 Xs? Because, if you are using a 1-box chart, 1 X could just be one-step-back in a downtrend, and you would not want to commit to a long position on the basis of a one-step-back alone, so you must wait for at least 2 Xs. In a 3-box chart, it will be 3 Xs. It may sound high risk, but in fact it is low risk, because at the same time you would place a stop one box below the low of the pattern, so your risk is two or three boxes at most. The reason for waiting for a reaction back off the low is that you don't actually know it is a low until after the fact. The price may print a box below the previous lows. If it does, you need to see that it can recover from that position.

Figure 3-43 shows a fulcrum bottom. Notice that the strength is towards the low because that is where you find the row with the most filled in boxes. After the mid-pattern rally, the price goes below the previous lows of the pattern. Anyone taking a position on the previous lows would have been stopped out immediately. After the new low has been made, a long position is taken after the second X in the new column of Xs and a stop placed one box below the low. Of course, this strategy is not always possible. Firstly, there may not be a mid-pattern rally. Even if there is, the price may not get back down to the lows and so you will not be alerted to take a long position.

Contrast this with taking a position at the full catapult point. Your stop would still be one box below the low of the pattern. If the pattern fails, as it did in Figure 3-42, then your risk is the height of the fulcrum pattern, which is 6 boxes.

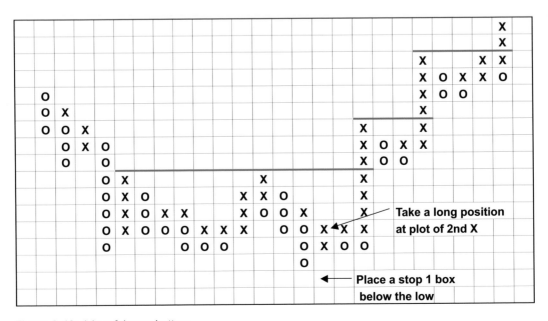

Figure 3-43: 1-box fulcrum bottom

Chart 3-15 is a 1 x 1 tick Point and Figure chart of the S&P 500 Index. This is a very short-term chart for short-term traders. It shows a number of fulcrums of different type, some successful, some not so.

The first half of pattern A contains a number of continuation semi-catapults. This is the first requirement for an inverse fulcrum: a strong move into the highs. At this stage there is no clue that it will be an inverse fulcrum. After the highs, however, the downward sloping top gives it the look of a V-shaped inverse fulcrum. The balance of the pattern is around the centre line.

Pattern B is another V-shaped inverse fulcrum. Notice the X breaking to a new high on the middle of the pattern, giving a semi-catapult continuation buy signal. Again this is part of the uptrend taking the price into the fulcrum. Notice that the balance of the pattern is towards the top indicating strength at the top. Notice the downward sloping top in the second half of the pattern.

Pattern C is a small flat top and bottom fulcrum. With an evenly balanced pattern like this, it is impossible to predict which way it will break.

Pattern D starts off with a number of continuation semi-catapults as the uptrend takes the price into the pattern. A sharp decline mid-pattern shows profit taking; however, the price rises to new highs again. It is interesting to note that within the large fulcrum pattern D, a smaller fulcrum has built with a catapult point on the break below the blue line at point 'x'. This would be an opportunity to take a short with a stop one box above the high of the pattern. Pattern D's fulcrum point at the lower blue line 'y', completes the pattern.

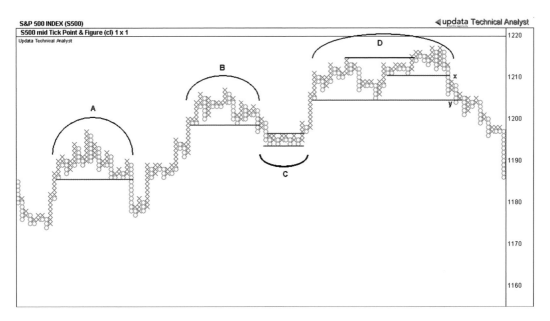

Chart 3-15: 1 x 1 tick chart of S&P 500 Index showing fulcrum tops and bottoms

You have seen that fulcrums don't fit the textbook patterns perfectly. The deeper the fulcrum, the more necessary it is to take positions within the pattern.

Fulcrums are much more common in intra-day charts, but you will find them in end-of-day charts as well.

Chart 3-16 below is a 15 x 1 of Whitbread plc. There are two clear fulcrum patterns, both of which are compound fulcrum bottoms, which means they start off as small fulcrums that fail but then become part of a larger pattern.

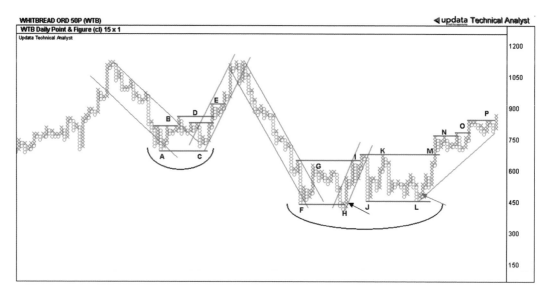

Chart 3-16: 15 x 1 of Whitbread plc showing fulcrums and semi-catapults

The first pattern starts with the downtrend to point A. The price trades sideways, breaking the downtrend line and resistance at point B. It continues to trade sideways, eventually falling back to point C. At this stage, it can be seen that a large fulcrum is in the making and it is possible to open a low risk buy on the first 2 box reaction from point C, although some traders prefer to wait until the lows are matched. The price rallies back up again, breaking through a semi-catapult and finally through a new fulcrum catapult point at D, where longs should be added to. Notice the continuation semi-catapult at point E re-confirming the completed fulcrum and the continuing uptrend. Notice also the very clear trend channel into the fulcrum, then the sideways movement out of the channel and the clear trend channel out again.

The second pattern starts with a very bearish tight downtrend channel to point F. The price rallies to point G, moving out of the channel. It falls back to point H, suggesting that a bullish fulcrum is in the making. The trend channel has been broken by sideways action, and there has been a rally in the pattern which has aborted and gone back to re-test the lows. Notice that the price goes below the previous low, which demonstrates the danger of taking a long position at the lows. A long position can, however, be taken on the completion of the 2nd X marked with an arrowhead, with a stop one box below the low at point H. A new, tight uptrend develops and takes the price up to the pattern highs and, after a minor pullback, through the catapult point at I. The trend does not continue, and instead the price breaks sharply down through the uptrend line and falls to point J, then rallies again to newly established resistance at point K. This now has the makings of another smaller fulcrum making up a much larger one. The price makes its way down to point L at exactly the same level as point J, triggering another early buy alert on the 2nd X up from the low, which is shown at the arrow head. At point M, a second catapult point is breached. Another long could be taken, but the trader has two longs already from point H and L. As expected, after a successful catapult point, the price makes a semi-catapult at point N, then another at point O and another at point P, in almost textbook fashion.

So that you can see what these patterns look like in a 3-box chart, Chart 3-17 is a 15 x 3 chart of Whitbread plc. The chart is labelled with the same letters used in Chart 3-16, so that you can compare it with the 1-box chart.

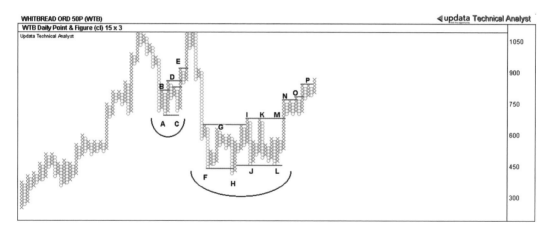

Chart 3-17: 15 x 3 of Whitbread plc showing fulcrums and catapults

The patterns are narrower, obviously, but you can still see the fulcrums and catapults as they develop.

The fulcrums chosen in these examples have deliberately been difficult ones because it is important that you get used to the fact that they seldom look like textbook examples.

Fulcrums are fundamental to Point and Figure analysis, and they come in all shapes and sizes.

Chart 3-18 is a 0.5 x 1 of Xerox Corp. There are three clear fulcrums: a fulcrum top marked A, a small fulcrum bottom marked B and an excellent example of a fulcrum bottom marked C, which shows a number of semi-catapults in the trend out of the pattern.

Chart 3-18: 0.5 x 1 of Xerox Corp. showing fulcrums

Final word on patterns

The patterns discussed so far are an illustration of the more common formations you will find in Point and Figure charts. In 3-box charts they are all made up of double-top and double-bottom patterns. You can 'take them apart' by reverting to a 1-box chart where the pattern may become clearer. Double and triple-tops and bottoms become semi-catapults and fulcrums in 1-box charts. In all cases, it is the reassertion of control that you must look for. How important is it that an X has broken above the previous X or previous 10 Xs? How important is the double-bottom sell? The only way you can answer these questions is to look left on the chart and decide where there is a more important level than the one currently being breached. This was clearly illustrated in the examples in Figure 3-15 and Figure 3-16.

2-box reversal charts

Nothing, in the preceding pages on patterns, has been said about 2-box charts, but all the patterns described, which apply to 3-box charts, apply equally to 2-box charts in the same way. 2-box charts, however, are more sensitive than 3-box charts and so the congestion areas are wider. You are less likely to see poles and more likely to see fulcrums.

Signals with the trend or against the trend

You have learnt that Point and Figure signals start with double-tops and bottoms in 3-box charts and with semi-catapults in 1-box charts. You have also learnt that these are weaker than triple-tops and bottoms, but many double-tops and bottoms are good reliable signals. Although we will look at this in more detail in the section on trend lines, it is worth stressing that when assessing signals, the prior trend is important.

In a strong downtrend, for example, double-bottom sell signals are much more reliable than double-top buy signals. Each sell can be taken but a double-top buy should be treated with suspicion until there is more evidence of a trend reversal.

Figure 3-44 shows the price in a strong downtrend. Each double-bottom sell signal is good for acting on. However, the double-top buy signal should be used only for closing out short positions and not for going long until more price movement confirms the end of the downtrend.

You can dramatically improve your success rate just by taking clear signals with the prevailing trend.

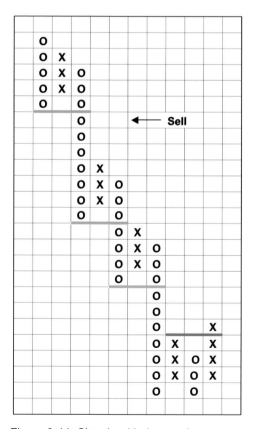

Figure 3-44: Signals with the trend

The converse is true for strong uptrends, where double-top buys can be relied on and double-bottom sells treated with suspicion.

It is worth noting at this point that generally prices can only rise if there is an increase in demand, but prices are well capable of falling due to a simple lack of buyers with no real increase in supply.

Trend lines on Point and Figure charts

Trend lines play an important, if not an essential, part in Point and Figure analysis. They bring Point and Figure charts alive. There is, however, a subtle difference between trend lines drawn on line or bar charts and those drawn on Point and Figure charts. With line and bar charts, trend lines show the line at which there is constant rate of change. This is because line and bar charts show price versus time. The trend line on a bar chart therefore shows constant change in price per unit time. With Point and Figure charts, however, there is no time. Instead, the x-axis shows the number of columns, which is the number of times the price has reversed. So, a trend line on a Point and Figure chart shows constant price change per reversal.

In the Figure 3-45, the price rose from 100 to 230 (the shaded box) and, in doing so, it reversed its price direction ten times. Therefore, the rate at which the price has risen is 130/10 = 13 points per reversal. As you will see, this figure is important because if it is less than the value of one box, it indicates that the trend has weakened. For the moment, however the illustration shows that the trend line is the rate at which the 'change in price per reversal' is constant.

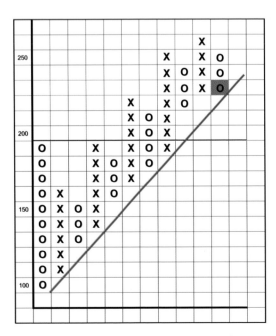

Figure 3-45: Rate of price rise per reversal

Trend lines on Point and Figure charts are drawn in exactly the same way as they are on bar or line charts. Uptrend lines connect higher lows and downtrend lines connect lower highs. Chart 3-19 shows a 10 x 1 chart of the S&P 500 Index. The downtrend line connects lower highs and the uptrend line connects higher lows.

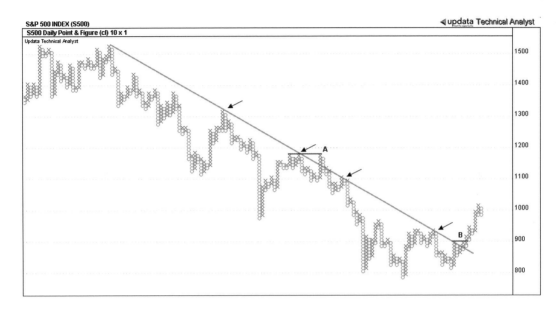

Chart 3-19: 10 x 1 of the S&P 500 Index showing trend line breaks

Trend line breaks

In Point and Figure analysis, signals are generated by double-top and double-bottom signals in 3-box charts, and by catapults and semi-catapults in 1-box charts. These have to be taken into account when assessing trend line breaks and the validity of the trend line. At point A in Chart 3-19, the downtrend line from the top was breached, but there was no Point and Figure signal at the time. This allows the trend line to be continued through the data. Notice how many times the price touches the line (shown by the arrows), increasing its validity. The break at point B however, is accompanied by a semi-catapult buy signal, confirming the break.

Here are some guidelines for breaks of a downtrend:

• If, at the time the break occurs, there is also a double-top (or wider), a catapult or a semi-catapult buy signal, as shown at point B in Chart 3-19, then the break is valid and should be acted on. The break at point A is invalid.

- If, at the time of the break, there is no Point and Figure signal, look to see if one occurred just prior to the break. 'Just prior to' means that the signal must have occurred within an X or two of the trend line break. This still makes the break at point A an invalid break.

- If, at the time of the break, there is no Point and Figure signal and no signal prior to the break of the trend line, then take any Point and Figure signal that occurs after the break. Point A remains an invalid break.

- If, at the time of the break, there is no Point and Figure signal, no signal prior to the break of the trend line and no Point and Figure signal after the break, then it is much more difficult to assess the break. Point A in Chart 3-19 is a good example. In a case like this, you must look to see if a wider pattern has been breached. Has there been a breakout of an extended top, or a catapult or fulcrum pattern? If you look left at point A you will see two columns of Xs at the same height as the X at point A. If at point A another X had printed, there would have been a catapult breakout and that would have made the break of the trend line valid. In the case of Point A as it exists, this did not occur and it remains an invalid break.

The converse of the above applies in the case of breaches of an uptrend. As you become more familiar with Point and Figure charts, so you will be able to modify these rules according to your trading strategy.

Bullish support and bearish resistance lines

Subjective trend lines (those which you decide on yourself) like those in Chart 3-19 on page 177 can be used to good effect, but one of the great advantages of Point and Figure charts is that you can also draw objective trend lines. The objectivity means that you do not need to decide on the angle of the trend line: it is already established. Because of the 'square' nature of Point and Figure charts, it is possible to draw 45° trend lines, something which is impossible on bar or line charts because of the aspect ratio. Bar and line charts have no fixed aspect ratio – the ratio of the height of the chart to its width. If this is not constant, trend lines at fixed angles cannot be drawn because the angle changes as the aspect ratio changes. With Point and Figure charts, the aspect ratio is a constant 1:1 because they are constructed on a squared grid. To maintain a 45° trend, therefore, and the price action above the trend line, the price must rise by more squares up than squares sideways. Squares up or down are created by the price rising or falling by the box size and squares across are created by the price oscillating without any direction. The latter tends to occur during periods of distribution at the end of an uptrend, or accumulation at the end of a downtrend.

Bullish support lines are rising trend lines drawn at 45° from an important low. Bearish resistance lines are falling trend lines drawn at 45° from an important high.

45° lines are not drawn just for the sake of it. They have an important meaning. They show the rate at which the price is rising or falling by one box every time a new column is formed, in other words, every time the price changes direction. They therefore demarcate the line at which price is considered to be in a bull or a bear trend and hence the last level of support or resistance to a trend change. Although they can be placed on 1-box charts, bullish and bearish 45° lines are essentially a 3-box tool.

Rationale for bullish and bearish 45° trend lines

The rationale for the importance of the bullish support line at 45° is that, if the price cannot maintain a rise of at least the value of 1 box every time it makes a reversal, it can no longer be considered to be in a bull trend. This is because the 45° line is drawn diagonally through the imaginary corners of the boxes, meaning that speed or trend of the line is 1:1, or 1 box up and 1 box across. If this doesn't sound that onerous, then you probably haven't thought carefully about what is required to maintain that 45° trend.

Remember how a 3-box chart is constructed. A reversal means the price must change direction by at least the value of 3 boxes. This means that no column can have less than 3 boxes. If the price rises by 3 boxes and then falls by 3 boxes, the trend is horizontal. In order, therefore, to maintain a 45° trend, the O marking the bottom of each alternate column must be 2 boxes higher than the O at the bottom of the previous column of Os. To do this, the price must rise by 2 boxes more than the reversal. This means that to maintain a 45° trend in a 3-box reversal chart, the price must rise by 5 boxes each time it reverses by 3.

The thought that Point and Figure analysts regard the most important trend in Point and Figure charts to be constructed using 5 boxes up and 3 down will certainly make any Elliottician[13], who has picked up this book in error, much more interested in Point and Figure charts.

Figure 3-46 shows three possible trends on a 3-box reversal chart. The first is the condition where each reversal is 3 boxes. The trend is, therefore, horizontal. The second is where the price rises by 4 boxes before reversing by 3. This results in a trend that is described as 1 box up and 2 boxes across or 22.5°. The third is the 45° trend that can only occur when the price rises by 5 boxes before reversing by 3. The trend is described as 1 box up for every 1 box across or 45°.

---

[13] An Elliottician is a follower of Elliott Wave theory which is based around the observation that prices move up in five waves and down in three and are related by Fibonacci Ratios, of which 5 by 3 is one.

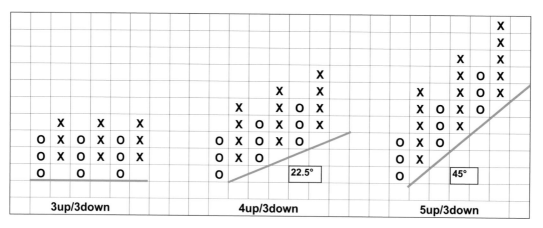

Figure 3-46: 3 possible trend angles on 3-box reversal charts

So, although the 45° trend is one box up and 1 box across, in order to comply with the trend the price must rise 5 boxes for every reversal of 3 boxes. Any rise of less than 5 will result in a correction of 3 boxes breaching the 45° trend line. So, what sounded like a mild condition turns out to be a fairly strong condition. To maintain a 45° uptrend, each upthrust must be at least 5 boxes worth. It is this that makes the 45° line so important.

The converse is true for bear trends. Bearish resistance lines at 45° demarcate the line at which the price is falling by 1 box every time it changes direction. If the price is below that line, then it is falling by more than 1 box and that would be considered as being a bear trend. This means that the price must thrust down by at least 5 Os each time. If it does not do this, the bearish resistance line is at risk.

Obviously, in both cases, an initial thrust of *more than* 5 boxes takes the price away from the 45° trend line, which means that the next thrust does not have to be as strong to maintain the 45° trend.

Changing the reversal from 3-box to 1-, 2- or 5-box has an effect on the interpretation and strength of the 45° lines. In each case, to maintain the 45° trend, the thrust column must be 2 boxes longer than the reversal column. So, in a 1-box reversal chart, the thrust column must contain 3 boxes, in a 2-box chart, it must contain 4, and in a 5-box chart, it must contain 7. This means that the 45° trend line has varying importance, depending on the reversal you use. For instance, a 45° trend line breach in a 5-box reversal chart has greater implications than in a 1-box reversal chart.

Where to draw bullish support and bearish resistance lines

Bullish support lines are drawn at 45° up from a known important low point. They are drawn by taking a diagonal through the corners of the square below the low of the lowest column of Os. The advantage is that as soon as a bottom is made, and a column of Os reverses to a column of Xs, the bullish support line can be drawn. There is no need to wait for a further reaction to give a second touch point, none is needed. Bearish resistance lines are drawn at 45° down from an important high point in the same way, by drawing a diagonal through the corners of the square above the highest column of Xs.

Figure 3-47 shows an idealised chart with bullish support and bearish resistance lines to illustrate the point. Immediately when column 2 is drawn, the blue bullish support line, can be drawn at 45° from the low. Notice that the line goes through the diagonal corners of the boxes. Columns 3 to 12 show the price well above the bullish support line indicating that it is rising by more than one box every time it changes direction. In column 13, the price is on the 45° line, which means it is rising by one box per reversal. In column 15, the bullish support line is broken as the price penetrates below it. This means that the price is no longer rising by one box per reversal.

As with all Point and Figure patterns, it is only when the double-bottom sell signal is given, and an O goes below the red support line in column 15, that the bull trend is clearly over. Once this happens, however and the price has moved into a bear trend, a bearish resistance 45° line may be drawn from the high in column 14. (This is the red trend line in the diagram.) Columns 15 to 23 show the price well below the bearish resistance line indicating that it is falling by more than one box every time it changes direction. This is typical bear market action. In columns 24 and 25, the price is on the bearish resistance line, meaning that it is falling at one box per reversal. In column 26, the price breaks above the bearish resistance line and confirms the break with a triple-top buy above the blue resistance line.

Whilst this pattern is idealised, it is an extremely common scenario in real-life charts, and one that you will see played out repeatedly.

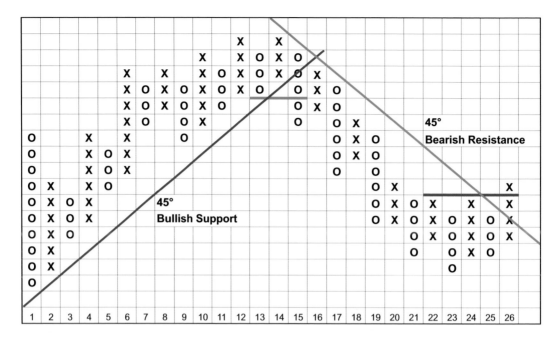

Figure 3-47: Drawing 45° bullish support and bearish resistance lines

45° trend line drawing rules

A 45° uptrend line remains intact until broken with a double-bottom sell signal. Once this happens and a trend reversal is indicated, you must draw a 45° downtrend line. You do this by finding the highest top which allows an unbroken downtrend line to be drawn. You can see this in Chart 3-22 on page 186 where trend line 1 is broken immediately after a double-bottom sell signal. Trend line 2 is then drawn from the highest top that yields an unbroken downtrend line. Take note also of the trend line break guidelines on page 177.

The converse is true for downtrend lines. A 45° downtrend line remains intact until broken with a double-top buy signal. Once this happens, you must draw a 45° uptrend line. You do this by finding the lowest bottom which allows an unbroken uptrend line to be drawn. You can see this in Chart 3-22 on page 186 when trend line 2 is broken it coincides with a double-top buy signal. Trend line 3 is then drawn from the lowest bottom that yields a new unbroken uptrend line.

The important thing is that the new, or latest, trend line must be drawn from a high or a low, which yields a new trend line that has no breaks. In most cases, this will be the top of the pattern immediately preceding the break of the uptrend or the bottom of a pattern immediately preceding the break of a downtrend.

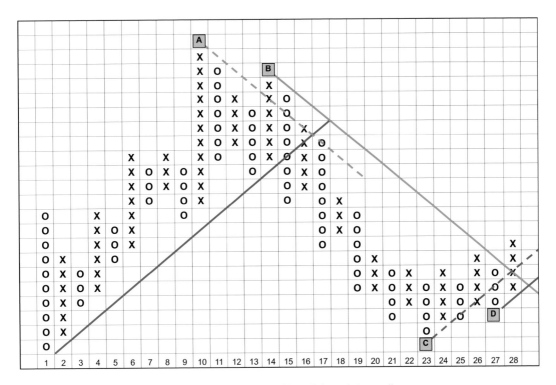

Figure 3-48: Where to draw 45° bullish support and bearish resistance lines

The blue bullish support line in Figure 3-48 is broken with a double-bottom sell signal in column 15. This means a new red bearish resistance line must be drawn. Although the top at point A is higher, a new bearish resistance, shown dashed in red, cannot be drawn from the top because it is penetrated in column 14, prior to the break of the uptrend. The new bearish resistance line must, therefore, be drawn from the top at point B.

The bearish resistance line is broken with a double-top buy signal in column 28. The new bullish support line, shown dashed in blue, cannot be drawn from the low at point C because it is penetrated in column 27. The bearish resistance line is, therefore, drawn at point D.

Implications of different box reversals on 45° trend lines

Although early authors on Point and Figure charts used trend lines, 45° lines were not used until Cohen's work in 1947. Until then, trend lines were drawn subjectively to follow trends. What was different between early works and Cohen's was the fact that Cohen completely ignored 1-box reversal charts in favour of 3-box charts. He also abandoned tick Point and Figure charts and used the daily high/low method (explained in chapter 2) exclusively to construct his charts.

1-box reversal charts have many more minor reversals than 3-box charts, making the patterns three or four times wider; consequently, the 45° lines are constantly breached. Chart 3-20 is a 50 x 1 daily Point and Figure chart of the FTSE 100 Index using end-of-day close prices. Notice how many times the 45° lines are breached. Every time this happens, another 45° line must be drawn, parallel to the first, but from the new high and low. The numbers on the chart show the sequence in which the 45° trend lines have been drawn. This is not to say that you should not use 45° trend lines on 1-box charts, but rather, if you do, you should be aware that there will be many breaches and the 45° lines will have to be constantly redrawn. This is not a problem. In fact, 45° lines can alert you to trend changes much sooner than subjective lines do. Black line AA is the subjective downtrend line. Notice how much later the end of the trend breach occurs, compared to the breach of 45° line 9.

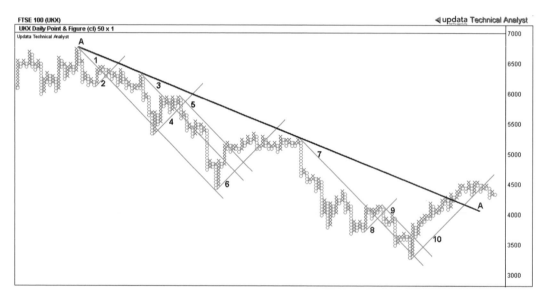

Chart 3-20: 50 x 1 of the FTSE 100 Index showing the drawing of 45° trend lines

Instead of 1-box close charts, Cohen used 3-box charts based on high and low, but these also result in many breaches of the 45° lines. Chart 3-21 shows a 20 year history of a 50 x 3 Point and Figure of the FTSE 100 Index using daily high/low data. The chart has had to be reduced in size to show all the 45° lines from the start, and these are numbered as they would have been drawn. The breaches are not a problem per se, provided you understand that once there is a breach you have to adjust the bullish and/or bearish lines again. Some would argue that it is not the high/low that is the problem, but that the box size is too small. Certainly, moving to a 100 point box would eliminate all the breaches, but in doing so would make the chart far too insensitive to price changes.

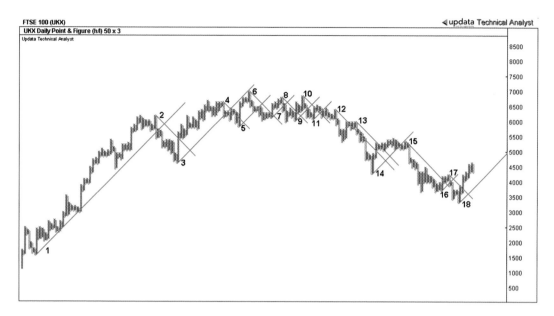

Chart 3-21: 50 x 3 (h/l) of the FTSE 100 Index showing the drawing of 45° trend lines

Chart 3-22 shows a 50 x 3 of the FTSE 100 Index using end-of-day close. As you can see, the 45° lines are much more reliable when using close-only data and are therefore recommended. In fact, the whole chart is covered with only five trend lines and only once has an adjustment had to be made. When Point and Figure analysis is discussed in chapter 5 you will see that each instrument has its own character and you must alter the view to extract the most valuable information from the chart.

The important thing to note is the implication of changing the construction method. Tick charts provide wider patterns than daily charts. 1-box reversal charts provide wider patterns than 3-box charts. Daily high/low charts provide wider patterns than daily close-only charts and a combination of tick data and 1-box reversal provides even wider patterns.

The essential thing to remember is that although the definition of bull trend or bear trend is unchanged, the time horizon changes when you change the sensitivity of the chart. Chart 3-21 above shows a number of minor bull and bear trends, whereas Chart 3-22 shows only the major bull and bear trends.

Chart 3-22: 50 x 3 (cl) of the FTSE 100 Index showing the drawing of 45° trend lines

45° lines and log scaled charts

The issue of trend lines on log scaled charts is always a point of contention, not only for Point and Figure analysts, but also for Technical Analysts in general. Some will argue fiercely that they are only valid on log charts, others will say arithmetic. The fact is that some prices rise and fall arithmetically and some do so exponentially. There is no right or wrong way. The only way to tell is to draw both log and arithmetic charts and draw the lines on both.

Chart 3-23 shows the FTSE 100 Index again but this time using a 1% box size instead of 50 points. The bullish support and bearish resistance lines are shown as before. The breaks of trend are at slightly different points but it is clear where they are.

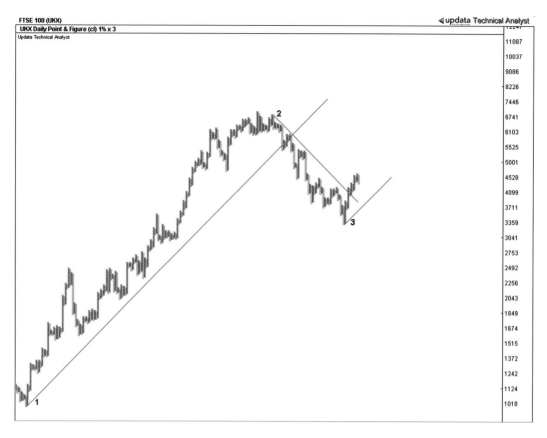

FTSE 100 (UKX)

UKX Daily Point & Figure (cl) 1% x 3

Updata Technical Analyst

Chart 3-23: 1% x 3 (cl) of the FTSE 100 Index showing the drawing of 45° trend lines

From a long-term perspective, you would have been long of the UK market from August 1984 to July 2001. You would then have been out or short until July 2003 and long again from then on. Few other techniques would have been so unambiguous over the 20 years.

Changing the time horizon of 45° trend lines

You will read a good deal about time horizons for Point and Figure charts in this book, and may question how that is possible when Point and Figure charts don't have time in their construction. Time horizon is not the same as time-scale. Point and Figure charts don't have a time-scale, but they certainly have a time horizon. Remember, Point and Figure charts filter price movement, so the time horizon of a Point and Figure chart can be altered in a number of ways.

45° trend lines drawn from tops and bottoms define the bull or bear trend for the chart being studied. You will learn later that varying the box size changes the time horizon of the chart and so the 45° trend lines will then show longer- or shorter-term bull and bear trends, depending on whether the box size is increased or decreased.

You may also view support and resistance over different time horizons by drawing internal 45° trend lines closer to the price action. Each reaction low during an uptrend, or each reaction high during a downtrend may be used to draw further 45° lines, called internal 45° lines, which then provide additional support levels. The reason and logic behind this is that although bull and bear trends on the chart are defined by the 45° line from bottoms and tops, during any trend there will be reactions (corrections) where the price is forced towards the 45° line but stops short of it. The question is, why does it stop short? The answer is that there is support, in the case of an uptrend, or resistance, in the case of a downtrend, at that point. This being the case, we can project that support and resistance forward at 45° because we know that the limit to the trend is one box per reversal. These internal 45° lines don't show the main bull and bear trends, but rather support and resistance during uptrends and downtrends, which when broken may result in a correction to the next 45° line.

The S&P 500 Index in Chart 3-24 shows how these internal 45° lines are drawn. The lines are numbered in the order they are drawn.

Line 1 is the main 45° bullish support line from the bottom. Notice that the price moved well away from it during the strong bull trend, rendering it useless for intermediate support. At the first reaction, therefore, internal 45° line 2 may be drawn closer to the action, then line 3 when there is another reaction, then line 4 and finally line 5. Each of these internal 45° lines demarcates a level at which support may be found in the future. The further these internal lines are away from the main 45° line 1, the shorter-term they are.

The first time support is found is at point A on line 5, where the price rallied away very strongly. This means the reaction at the start of line 5 has had some influence on the price in the future. However, this is a short-term trend, which may not last long. Line 5 is eventually broken and the price falls to point B on line 4. Line 4 now becomes the shortest-term trend until the price falls back to allow line 6 to be drawn. Line 6 did provide some support around the top where the price oscillated above and below the line, before falling to points C and D on line 4, making line 4 an important internal trend line showing the intermediate trend. A break of line 4 must be considered an important break because it has had two important thrusts from it at points B and C.

Line 4 is broken strongly with a double-bottom sell at point D. Support should now be sought on line 3. It should be remembered that line 3 has not been reinforced by any previous reactions and so is not expected to provide significant support. Furthermore, line 3 was not drawn from a mini-bottom, but rather just a corrective column of Os. A mini-bottom occurs when the price makes an intermediate low, as it did at points 5 and 6, for example. Points 3 and 4 are not mini-bottoms. 45° lines drawn from mini-bottoms have more significance.

Line 2 also provides no support at all for a strongly falling price, leaving the last level of support as line 1, the main bullish 45° support line from the chart low. Although the main bull trend has not been broken, a tentative main bearish resistance line 7 can be drawn. In addition, an internal 45° downtrend line 8 can also be drawn.

Notice how the price falls to point E, picking up support on the main bullish 45° support line 1, although there is actually a break of line 1 because there has been a double-bottom sell signal. Notice too that it rallies to point F, where the price meets resistance on two fronts, from internal uptrend line 2 and internal downtrend line 8. The second touch here reinforces line 8 as an important internal 45° downtrend line.

As you would expect, the main bullish support line 1 provides support again at point G, but this is only temporary and the price breaks through with a double-bottom sell. With no more support left, the price is unambiguously in a downtrend and the main 45° bearish resistance line is line 7. The price remains in a bear trend until, firstly, line 8 is broken and, shortly after that line 7. Once this happens, a new bullish 45° support line 9 may be drawn. As is normal in strong bull trends, the price rallies away from the line, and, on the first reaction, internal 45° line 10 may be drawn. Notice that the price soon finds support near internal line 10 at point H. Because the price did not actually touch line 10, a new internal 45° line 11 can be drawn from the reaction low at point H.

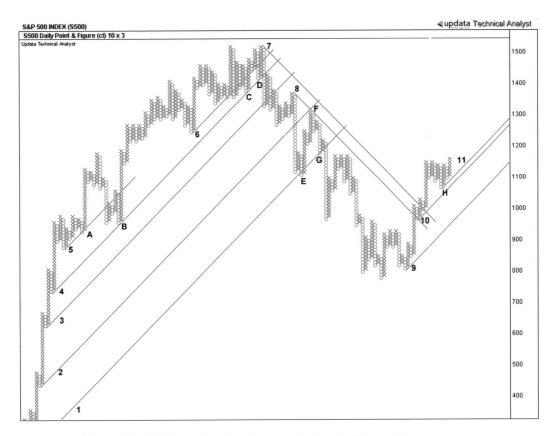

Chart 3-24: 10 x 3 S&P 500 Index showing drawing of internal 45° trend lines

Now that you have become more familiar with the way that main and internal 45° lines are drawn, you will notice that there are other lines that could have been drawn on the chart. Draw them yourself to familiarise yourself with them.

When drawing these internal or shorter-term 45° lines, it is just as well to note that they are stronger if drawn off an actual reaction high or low, rather than just a single reversal column. This means that those drawn off mini-bottoms or mini-tops are more important than those drawn from a corrective column. For example, trend line 8 is drawn from a mini-top, whereas trend line 3 is drawn from a corrective column. If a trend line is drawn from a corrective column, like trend line 4, and it provides support to a mini-bottom like point B, the trend line is regarded as if it had been started from a mini-bottom. The converse applies to mini-tops.

Parallel trend lines

Channels are important. Prices tend to move up and down within channels, and so lines parallel to the trend, but on the opposite side of the price action, which delineate trend channels are important for understanding the strength of the trend. In an uptrend, these lines offer resistance to the price and in a downtrend they offer support. If the price fails to reach the upper channel in an uptrend, this is a sign of weakness. Conversely, if they fail to reach the lower channel in a downtrend it is a sign of strength.

In Point and Figure analysis, the parallel line to the uptrend bullish support line is called the bullish resistance line. The parallel to the downtrend bearish resistance line is called the bearish support line.

When using line and bar charts, these parallel lines are usually drawn by studying the chart and placing the line in the most obvious place. Much has been written about how these lines should be drawn on Point and Figure charts; it is difficult to reconcile the strict rules that must be applied when a parallel line is drawn.

Any trend line, whether up or down, can be enhanced by the drawing of a parallel line on the other side of the price action. That is not in dispute, but what is, is the matter of where these parallel lines should be drawn. Rules that cannot always be followed are difficult to accept.

In his 1996 book, Carroll Aby suggests that once a bullish support line is drawn, the analyst should place the parallel on top of the highest X in the column to the right of a large column of Os. If that line is broken then locate the next column of Os to the left and repeat the procedure. It is good to have a guideline like this, but sometimes no such wall exists or if it does exist, the column of Os may be short, forcing the parallel line through the price action. There is nothing wrong with adopting this approach but you must be flexible. By all means, look left and, if there is a significant column of Os, then place the parallel line on the highest X to the right of the column of Os. However, if you look further left and see a more obvious one, then use that instead.

Chart 3-25 shows a 10 x 3 Point and Figure chart of the S&P 500 Index. Red line 1 is the 45° bullish support line from the October 1998 low. Dashed blue line P11 is the parallel bullish resistance line drawn from point A, according to Aby's rule. The rule is to locate a wall of Os and place the parallel on the top of the column of Xs to the right of the column of Os. You can see immediately that there is little point in drawing it there, because it gets breached by the first column of Xs off the low.

So, line P12 is drawn by moving left to find the next possible long column of Os, and the parallel is from point B, the top of the next column of Xs. You can see that line P12 is also breached by the first column of Xs off the low. If this is the case, then perhaps the best way to draw parallels is to move left until a sensible starting point is found. Then if that gets breached, reassess the parallel line. By 'sensible starting point', consider what the parallel is there for. It is an upper channel resistance line in a bull trend and a lower channel support line in a bear trend, so it should be drawn where early resistance or support is seen.

Parallel line P13 is one such line drawn from the high at point C. You can see that it had already provided resistance at the start, at point D, and continued to do so at points E, F and G. In fact, it proved to be a very effective bullish resistance line. Failure of the price to maintain touches on this line can be regarded as a weakening of the bull trend, as happened when the top was being made.

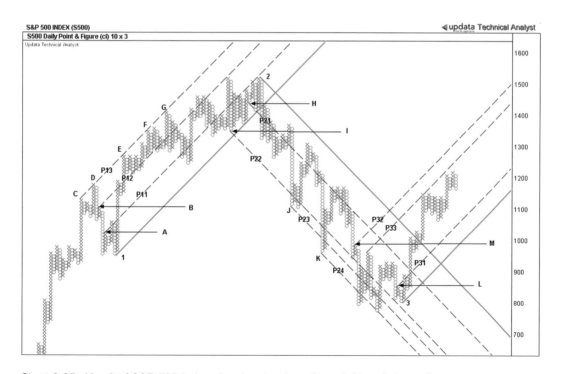

Chart 3-25: 10 x 3 of S&P 500 Index showing drawing of parallel trend channels

Bearish resistance line 2 shows the 45° downtrend. Parallel P21 is the first parallel (bearish support line) to be drawn according to the rule for downtrends. That is, find a wall of Xs and place the parallel on the lowest O in the column to the right of the column of Xs, at point H. Parallel P21 is breached by the long column of Os after the top.

The next parallel, P22, may be drawn according to the rule from point I. P22 is breached at point J, from where a new parallel P23 may be drawn. As the market fall becomes steeper, P23 is breached at point K and another parallel, P24, can be drawn, using the support at K as the point of contact. Further steep falls result in P24 being breached as well. Parallels need to be adjusted as the price rises or falls. It is important to remember that if your parallel is breached, it means that the price is accelerating. In the chart above, the uptrend is orderly and within the channel; however, the downtrend is steeper than the initial channel predicted and so new channel lines have had to be drawn to contend with it. The action of having to reassess the parallels shows the bearish nature of the market. Parallels are less likely to be continually breached in uptrends and more likely in downtrends.

Bullish support line 3 in Chart 3-25 shows the 45° trend from the low. Once again applying the parallel rule leads to parallel line P31 from point L, which serves no useful purpose. Applying the rule again results in parallel P32 from point M which has not yet been tested. Parallel P33, however, drawn subjectively is a better bullish resistance line for the time being. The drawing of 45° trend lines as parallels is so easy with modern software that it is simple to test a number before deciding which is best.

Parallels are not as important as the trend lines themselves. They can be used to assess the limits to the uptrend or downtrend. Breaches of significant parallels tend to indicate that the price is overbought (in an uptrend) or oversold (in a downtrend) and result in a reaction in the opposite direction.

Summary of the use of 45° bullish support and bearish resistance trend lines

45° trend lines are called bullish support and bearish resistance lines. The rules for the type of Point and Figure charts to be used with them are:

- For the definition of major bull and bear trends, 3-box reversal daily close data should be used.

- For the definition of major as well as intermediate bull and bear trends, 3-box reversal daily high/low data should be used.

- For the definition of minor bull and bear trends, 1-box reversal close only or high/low data should be used.

- For the definition of short-term as well as minor bull and bear trends, 1-box tick data should be used.

- Any other interval data can be used for varying degrees of short-term trends.

Remember 45° trend lines alternate. The price is either subject to an uptrend line (bullish support) or a downtrend line (bearish resistance). Only once the bullish support line is broken, can the bearish resistance line be drawn, and only once the bearish resistance line is broken can a new bullish support line be drawn. This means that the price is in either a bull trend or a bear trend. It can't be in both at the same time. However, you will often see charts with both bull and bear to show how one has been breached, as you will see in the example on page 194.

Trend lines and signal rules

Trend lines, whether subjective or at 45°, can affect the validity and strength of any Point and Figure buy or sell signal and, therefore, play an important part in Point and Figure analysis. The rules are:

- Point and Figure buy signals generated above an uptrend line can be considered good for opening a long or adding to an existing position.

- Point and Figure sell signals generated above an uptrend line should be used to close or reduce a long position, but should not be used for going short.

- Point and Figure sell signals generated below any downtrend line can be considered good for opening a short or adding to existing shorts.

- Point and Figure buy signals generated below a downtrend line should be used to close an open short position but should not be used for going long.

Of course, these rules can be broken by experienced traders who are aware of the risks involved. The rules, therefore, can be adjusted according to personal trading strategy and whether the position is long- or short-term. Trend lines can also be combined with congestion pattern analysis to enhance the signals generated by the patterns.

For example, a long-term investor may sell a portion of the holding when a sell signal is generated above an uptrend line and consider selling the whole holding only if the trend line is broken. Alternatively, the investor may ignore simple buy and sell signals, waiting rather for a compound pattern like a catapult or fulcrum to develop. There is a risk in doing this, as the compound pattern may not develop at all. A short-term trader, on the other hand, may take all simple signals and may sell the whole position on a sell signal above the trend line but wait for a trend line break to go short.

Exercise in drawing 45° trend lines on a log scale chart

This exercise is intended to show the process of drawing trend lines; it is not a trading exercise. Chart 3-30 of British Airways plc on page 199 has been split up into sections so that the process of drawing trend lines can be followed. The lines are numbered in the order in which they were drawn, so you can see the procedure. Try to follow the logic of each line as it is drawn.

Referring to Chart 3-26, the first line to be drawn is bearish resistance line 1. Notice that it is breached at the same time as an extended triple-top buy signal is given at point A, which is a valid breach. Remember, 45° trend lines alternate and so bullish support line 2 can be drawn. The price then falls back to bullish support line 2. Notice that it positions itself for a double-bottom sell signal but nothing comes of it. The bullish support line 2 holds and is the new uptrend. Line 2 is breached at point B, but because there is no double-bottom sell, the breach is ignored. It is breached again at point C combined with a double-bottom sell and the bull trend is over. Bearish resistance line 3 can now be drawn.

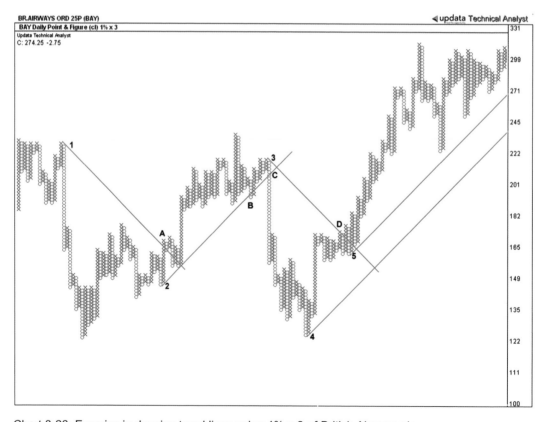

Chart 3-26: Exercise in drawing trend lines using 1% x 3 of British Airways plc

Line 3 is breached with a double-top buy at point D and, although the price fell back, the buy signal was not cancelled because the column of Os did not fall below the previous column of Os.

The breach of bearish resistance line 3 allows new bullish support line 4 to be drawn. Line 4 is well away from the price action and so, because the price consolidated at point 5 an intermediate/internal 45° bullish support line 5 can also be drawn. This allows a shorter-term trend to be followed.

The exercise follows on in Chart 3-27. This shows trend line 5 being broken at the same time as there is a double-bottom sell signal at point E. Notice how much earlier you would receive the signal than if you had waited for the break of trend line 4. This shows the advantage of drawing internal 45° lines closer to the price action as the trend matures. Whilst these lines do not define the major bull and bear trends, they show the important shorter-term trends.

On the break of trend line 5, the price continues to fall and breaks the main bullish support line 4 at point F, also with a double-bottom sell signal. This indicates the end of the bull trend and allows new bearish resistance line 6 to be drawn. You may ask why line 6 is not drawn from the high to the left. The reason is that the 45° line from the high (shown in light red) is breached at point 6. Although this is not a valid breach, it is customary to re-position the 45° line.

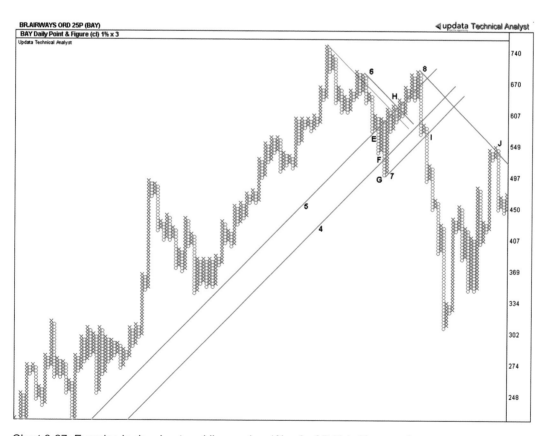

Chart 3-27: Exercise in drawing trend lines using 1% x 3 of British Airways plc

New bearish resistance line 6 is breached at point H, with a double-top buy signal allowing a new bullish support line 7 to be drawn from point G, indicating a resumption of the bull trend.

Line 7 does not survive very long when it is broken at point I with a double-bottom sell. This is the last possible support from any 45° bullish support line. No others can be drawn, and so a main bear trend is in place. Bearish resistance line 8 can now be drawn.

The breach of bearish resistance line 8, which just occurs at point J, is accompanied by a double-top buy signal at point J. This is a valid breach that turns out to be false and the downtrend resumes. You must accept that, as in all analysis, there will be the occasional false signal.

The process continues with Chart 3-28, where bearish resistance line 8 is finally breached with a double-top buy at point K. This means that bullish support line 9 can be drawn from the low. Line 9 is breached at point L resulting in a new bearish resistance line 10. The breach of line 10 does not occur with a double-top break; however the 4th rule[14] of trend line breaks states that: "*If, at the time of the break, there is no Point and Figure signal, no signal prior to the break of the trend line and no Point and Figure signal after the break, then you must look to see if a wider pattern has been breached.*" The wider pattern encompasses the top at point K. Although this is a little obscure, if you think about it, resistance has been broken at that level.

---

[14] See these rules on page 177-178.

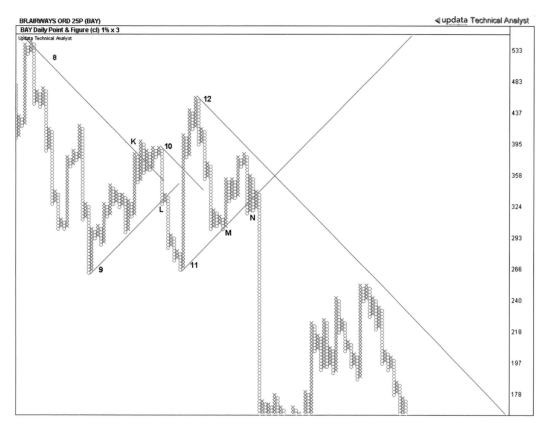

Chart 3-28: Exercise in drawing trend lines using 1% x 3 of British Airways plc

Notice how the price finds support on the bullish support line 11 at point M. The first break at point N is a valid break because there is a multiple-bottom sell just after the break. With the bull trend over, new bearish resistance line 12 can be drawn from the high.

Chart 3-29 completes the run of charts. The sharp rally to point O provides further resistance to the up move and shorter-term bearish resistance line 13 can be drawn from point O. The next rally to point P provides another opportunity to draw bearish line 14 closer to the price action. The price breaks line 14 at point Q, which is not a valid break. It finds resistance at point R on line 13, reinforcing the importance of line 13. In reality, line 13 is a better bearish resistance line than line 12. Line 13 is broken at point S with a double-top buy and line 12 offers no resistance to the advance.

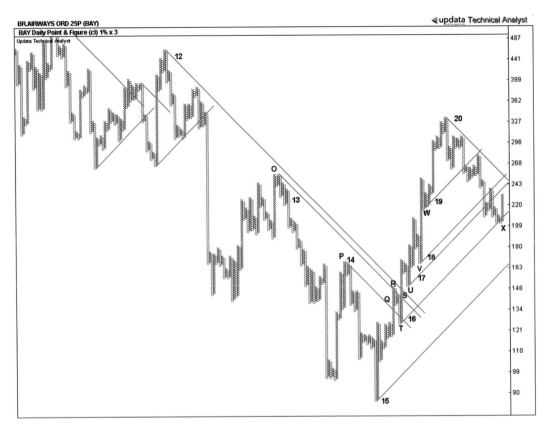

Chart 3-29: Exercise in drawing trend lines using 1% x 3 of British Airways plc

With the breaks of these bearish lines, new bullish support line 15 can be drawn. Notice that because it is so far from the price action, additional shorter-term internal lines (16 at point T, 17 at point U, 18 at point V and 19 at point W) may be drawn during the advance. The purpose is to assess any support above the bullish support line. As soon as line W breaks, new tentative (tentative, because the chart is still ruled by bullish support line 15) bearish resistance line 20 can be drawn. The price finds no support on line 18 or 17, but does find support at point X on line 16. This support reinforces the strength and importance of shorter-term internal bullish support line 16, which should be noted for the future.

Chart 3-30 shows the summary of all the trend lines discussed and drawn in this exercise. The Xs and Os have had to be reduced in size to show the whole chart, but you can still see the trends.

Chart 3-30: 1% x 3 of British Airways plc showing the procedure for drawing trend lines

45° or subjective – which do you draw?

The question remains, do you use 45° trend lines or subjective trend lines? The answer is not easy. Obviously, 45° objective lines are important in Point and Figure analysis, but there will be times when a subjective trend is so obvious that it should be drawn as well. This is much more likely in 1-box reversal charts where the widths of the patterns do not allow effective use of 45° lines, but subjective lines are just as useful in many conditions on 3-box chart as Chart 3-31 shows. It is the same chart of British Airways plc used in the previous exercise. Notice how the blue subjective trend lines work better than the objective 45° lines in marking out the trend.

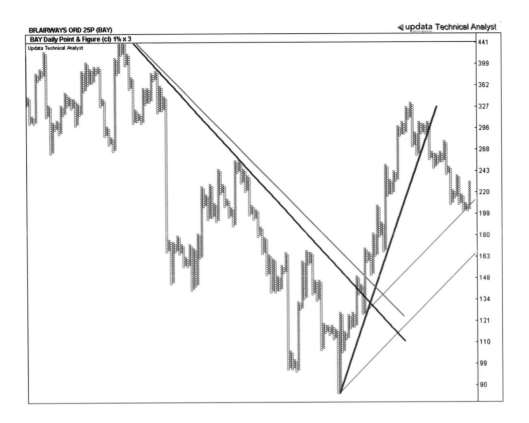

Chart 3-31: 1% x 3 of British Airways plc comparing subjective trend lines with 45° lines

There is an important difference in the way that objective 45° lines and subjective lines are drawn. All that 45° lines need is a bottom or a top; that is to say, all they need is a column of Xs which is reversed into a column of Os (for a top) or a column of Os which is reversed into a column of Xs (for a bottom). This means that 45° lines can be drawn immediately the top or bottom has been made. Subjective trend lines, on the other hand, require a reaction point after the trend has started. The subjective line is then drawn from the top or bottom to the reaction point, which means they cannot be established as soon as 45° lines can.

You will find that subjective trend lines will be used almost exclusively on 1-box reversal charts and on 3-box reversal charts using high and low in their construction. This is illustrated by the charts opposite of the FTSE 100 Index.

Chart 3-32 is a 50 x 3 Point and Figure chart of the FTSE 100 Index constructed using daily high/low data. The red trend lines are standard 45° lines and the blue are subjective trends. This is a good example, where both methods can be used. Both the blue uptrend and downtrend lines describe the price trend better than any of the 45° lines. The subjective lines show the main trends and the 45° lines show the intermediate trends.

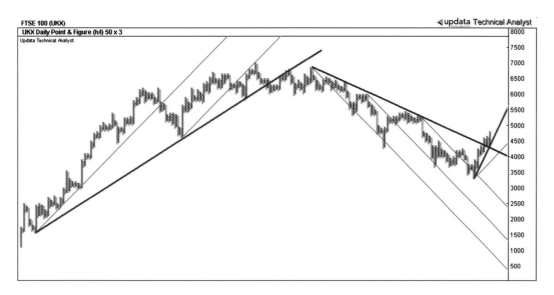

Chart 3-32: 50 x 3 (h/l) of the FTSE 100 Index comparing subjective trend lines with 45° lines

Chart 3-33 below is also a 50 x 3 of the FTSE 100 Index but is constructed with close only data. In this case, the red 45° lines have been excellent in describing the price trend. Only the last uptrend may be better described by the blue subjective trend line.

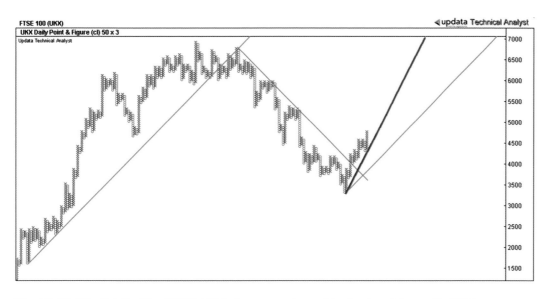

Chart 3-33: 50 x 3 (cl) of the FTSE 100 Index comparing subjective trend lines with 45° lines

Chart 3-34 below is a 50 x 1 Point and Figure chart of the FTSE 100 Index. In order to show all the price history, it has had to be further reduced in size. By definition, the use of 1-box reversal means wider congestion patterns and, therefore, more breaches of 45° trend lines. The blue subjective uptrend line, that starts on the left, has picked up all the major turning points during the uptrend and is, therefore, far more useful than a number of 45° lines have been in this case.

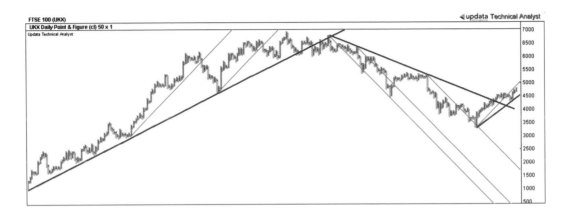

Chart 3-34: 50 x 1 (cl) of the FTSE 100 Index comparing subjective trend lines with 45° lines

So, the rule is use both, and always be aware and look out for trends that are not at 45°.

Trend line summary

Trend is everything. Never analyse a Point and Figure chart without carefully considering the trend using trend lines. Trends enhance the signals from Point and Figure charts. A break of a trend line puts you on an alert to look for the next Point and Figure signal. Without trend lines, Point and Figure charts lose much of their meaning.

- 45° trend lines are most important when analysing 3-box reversal charts.
- 45° trend lines apply on other reversals but are less likely to be of benefit on 1-box charts.
- 1-box charts require normal subjective trend lines connecting higher lows or lower highs.
- Internal 45° trend lines change the time horizon of the trend.
- Breaks of trend lines are valid only if the break is combined with a Point and Figure signal.
- Parallel trend channels are important for showing the strength of the trend.
- Touches of the upper channel in an uptrend indicate the price is overbought.
- Touches of the lower channel in a downtrend indicate the price is oversold.

Understanding Point and Figure charts summary

This chapter has covered many aspects of Point and Figure charts. Below is a brief summary of what you should remember:

- Point and Figure charts show the demand and supply: demand pushes up a column of Xs, supply pushes down a column of Os.

- When demand overcomes supply, and an X breaks above the previous column of Xs, a basic Point and Figure buy signal is generated. When supply overcomes demand, and an O breaks below the previous column of Os, a basic Point and Figure sell signal is generated.

- All Point and Figure patterns and signals are based on these basic patterns in various combinations.

- The wider the pattern, or the more times a level is challenged, the stronger the buy or sell signal from the pattern.

- Point and Figure patterns can be continuation, as well as reversal, patterns.

- The ability to breakout, be forced back and then breakout again is a strong sign.

- Patterns vary according to the reversal size used.

- 1-box patterns:

  - Less rigid formations than 3-box patterns.
  - Fall essentially into two categories: semi-catapult and fulcrum.
  - Semi-catapults are continuation patterns.
  - Fulcrums are reversal patterns.
  - A breakout from either pattern is called the catapult point.
  - A false breakout from either pattern, and pullback into it, is called a false catapult.
  - A successful breakout from a fulcrum is called a true or full catapult.

- 3-box and other box patterns:

  - More rigid and recognisable formations than those in 1-box charts.
  - Easier to categorise and name.
  - All decompose into either of the 1-box chart patterns.

- Not every buy and sell signal should be taken, as it could be part of a larger, more complex pattern.

- Learn when to ignore signals.

- Always look left to see additional support or resistance.

- Sloping bottoms make patterns more bullish, sloping tops make patterns more bearish, whereas sloping tops and bottoms indicate uncertainty.

- Sideways movement or congestion is an important part of Point and Figure analysis and indicates accumulation at bottoms and distribution at tops.

- Congestion patterns are a combination of a number basic Point and Figure patterns.

- Analysis of congestion helps to predict the likely breakout direction.

- Trend lines are vital to Point and Figure analysis and no Point and Figure chart should be drawn without them.

- Trend lines at 45° provide an objective way of establishing trends in 3-box charts.

- Taking note of the trend enhances standard Point and Figure signals.

Chapter 4

Projecting Price Targets

One of the biggest advantages of Point and Figure charts is 'the count', as it is called, which is the ability to project price targets from the chart. As with 45° trend lines, these counts are objective. They are potential targets that give the analyst an idea as to how far the price can go. It is important to stress the word 'potential'. These targets are a rough estimate. It would be naïve to expect them to be anything else. Sometimes the price may reach the target with pinpoint accuracy; sometimes it will be some way off. However, the bonus is that not reaching a target, or indeed exceeding a target, does give the analyst additional information about the price action and this will be discussed.

Unfortunately, Point and Figure counts are also one of the most abused techniques, because it is alluring to 'know' a price target, and computers have made it all too easy to place counts on charts at points where perhaps there should be none. Whilst it is an excellent and satisfying technique, it is just as well to note that there are rules which should be followed.

Two methods are used to establish price targets: horizontal and vertical counts. 3-box reversal charts allow both vertical and horizontal counts, whereas 1-box charts allow horizontal only. The horizontal counting method is different for 1-box and 3-box reversal charts, although, as you will see, the 1-box method can be used with 3-box charts, but has fallen out of favour. It is rare to use any other box reversal charts for counting, but there is nothing to prevent it. When counting was first developed by Thomas Sexsmith nearly 100 years ago, no mention was made of vertical counts. Counts on 1-box and 3-box charts were horizontal counts only.

Counts on 1-box reversal charts

It is not possible to conduct vertical counts on 1-box reversal charts, because, as you have seen earlier, columns can contain both Xs and Os, so only horizontal counts are possible. These horizontal counts are not quite as effective as counts on 3-box charts, partly because the counting method is not as precise. The logic behind the count is that the width of the pattern determines the extent of the subsequent move, and the area where most of the action has taken place is the level at which the count is taken. This is the pivot or anchor point, about which the pattern balances.

It is important to remember that if a 1-box chart is plotted incorrectly, as discussed on page 62 in chapter 2, the width of the pattern will be twice what it is meant to be; consequently, the count will be double and, therefore, wrong.

One advantage of horizontal counts on 1-box charts, however, is that they can be used effectively for counting across any congestion pattern, including continuation patterns. Every pattern yields a valid upside as well as a downside count. Once obtained, you must decide at the time the breakout occurs whether it is the upside or the downside that is activated.

There are a number of rules associated with 1-box counts so it is important that you understand them, because 1-box counting is subjective even if you have a computer. You have to be sure you are counting the right part of the pattern. There are a number of ways to establish the width of any pattern, all of which are valid.

How to establish a horizontal count on 1-box reversal charts

Step 1 – Look for a congestion pattern

You must look for a congestion pattern, which could be a top, a bottom, or a continuation pattern. At the time of counting, you may not actually know what it is. It is only when the price breaks out of the pattern that you will. It is for this reason that every pattern yields valid upside, as well as downside, counts up until the breakout.

Step 2 – Measure the width of the congestion pattern using the following rules:

There are four methods used to measure the width of the pattern in no particular order.

Method 1

Count the number of columns in the row that has the most filled boxes, that is to say the row with the most Xs and Os. This is where most of the price action has taken place and, therefore, where the strongest part of the pattern is. It is the level that has been crossed the most times and can be regarded as the anchor point for the pattern. The number of boxes in the row is counted from the far left to the far right of the pattern, including any empty boxes that do not have an X or O. You are, therefore, measuring the total width of the pattern based on the width of the row you have chosen. The logic is that the more times a price level is passed through within the congestion pattern, the more important that price becomes in defining the width of the pattern. Please note that the row with the most filled in boxes is not necessarily the longest row in the pattern. You are not counting the longest row; you are counting the length of the row that has the most activity within the pattern.

Method 2

Count the width of each row within the pattern and divide by the number of rows to give the average row width, rounded up to a full box size. The trigger row is taken to be the row in the middle of the pattern. This was the method introduced by Thomas Sexsmith and preferred by De Villiers and Taylor.

Method 3

If the pattern has 'walls', that is to say a clear column entering the pattern and a clear column exiting the pattern, then count the number of columns in the pattern at the level of the start of the right-hand wall across to, and including ,the left hand wall. This is the method preferred by Alexander Wheelan. Very often, this row will coincide with the row chosen by method 1.

<u>Method 4</u>

Count the width of the pattern (number of columns) at the breakout or catapult point. This will either be the width between the entry and exit walls at the catapult point, or, if none exist, it will be the width of the pattern one row below the catapult point.

This may seem unnecessarily complicated and ambiguous. If all four rules are employed on the same pattern, it is likely that you will obtain four different counts. This appears to be a bigger issue than it is, because the way the horizontal count is calculated means that the four counts will be within one or two boxes of each other, and you will recall that counts are an approximation anyway. You will also find that most 1-box congestion patterns are much shallower than their 3-box counterparts. You will find that some of the methods coincide at the same row anyway; for example, the most Xs and Os row may also be the middle row of the pattern, as well as the start of the breakout column. It is not suggested that you use all four methods on each pattern but rather choose one method, considering the pattern as follows:

- From experience, counting the width of the row with the most filled in boxes (method 1) is the best method.

- If the pattern has walls, then choose method 3 because this fixes the width of the pattern.

- If you are prepared to wait until the pattern breaks out, then choose method 4.

- If the pattern does not have walls but has a number of rows with the same number of Xs and Os, choose method 2.

If the pattern is shallow, as most 1-box patterns are, it will not make much difference which method you use.

Step 3 – Project the count up and down by an equal number of boxes

- Multiply the number of columns calculated in step 2 by the box size (the value of each X and O).

- Add this number to the value of the box in the row from which the count was taken, to achieve an upside target.

- Also subtract this number from the value of the box in the row from which the count was taken, to achieve a downside target.

- If the pattern has already broken out then you will already know the direction, so only the target in the direction of the breakout is valid.

Figure 4-1 shows a number of 1-box horizontal counts on a 10 x 1 chart. Each box is 10 points and the reversal is 1 box.

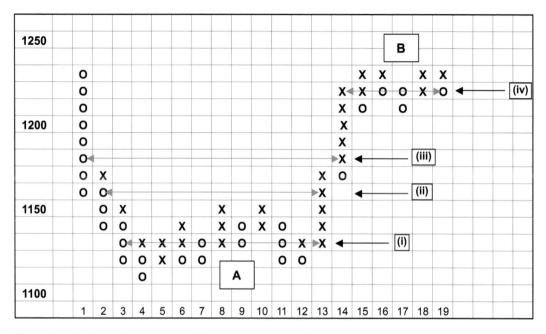

Figure 4-1: Horizontal counts on a 1-box reversal chart showing rows that may be counted

There are two patterns in the chart. Pattern A is a bottom fulcrum from which three counts may be obtained by measuring the width of the rows marked (i), (ii) and (iii). Note that rows (ii) and (iii) are the rows below the catapult point. Pattern B is a congestion pattern that has not yet broken out, so could be either a fulcrum top or a semi-catapult continuation pattern. The count is obtained by measuring the width of row (iv).

Remember, there are a number of different methods, some more important than others. Remember also that every pattern gives an upside as well as a downside count if the pattern has not broken out conclusively.

Count (i) – using method 1 or method 3

Two methods may be employed to obtain a count at row (i) from pattern A. Which method you choose depends at what stage you count the pattern. If you wait until the pattern breaks out, you will know the direction of the breakout and you can see the pattern has clear-cut walls in columns 3 and 13. In this case, you would use method 3.

If, however, you decide to obtain a target before the breakout, you will not know the direction, nor will you be able to see the right-hand wall. In this case, you would use Method 1, which is the row marked (i), with the most filled in Xs and Os. From this, you will obtain an upside as well as a downside count.

In this example, however, methods 1 and 3 give the same width of pattern.

- Upside target = (number of columns in the row at the count level) x (box size) + the level at which the count is taken

  - Method 3 – The count row is at the base of the exit column, so count the number of columns across the pattern until you reach the column entering the pattern. In this case it is from 13 back to column 3, which is 11 columns.

  - Method 1 – The count row is the row in the pattern that has the most Xs and Os. It does not have to be the longest row. This is also 11 columns.

- The box size is 10.

- The level at which the count is made is row (i) at 1130.

- Upside target for method 1 and 3 is (11 x 10) + 1130 = 1240

- Downside target for method 1 is 1130 – (11x10) = 1020

Count (ii) – using method 4

Count (ii) may only be taken after the catapult point and is done so by measuring the width of the pattern at the catapult point. Because by this stage the pattern has broken out, only the upside count can be taken.

- Target = (the number of columns from the far left to far right of the pattern taken at the row at the catapult point) x (box size) + the level at the catapult point

- The row for count (ii) goes from column 2 to column 13, which means there are 12 columns in the row.

- The box size is 10.

- The level at which the count is taken is 1160.

- Target = (12 x 10) + 1160 = 1280

Count (iii) – using method 4

Notice that there are actually two catapult points in pattern A. The second one at count (iii) is for a wider pattern. This often happens as a smaller pattern breaks out and forms a second wider pattern. Count (iii) is taken at the level of the second breakout.

- Target = (the number of columns from the far left to far right of the pattern taken at the catapult point) x (box size) + the level at the catapult point

- The row for count (iii) goes from column 1 to column 14, which means there are 14 columns in the row.

- The box size is 10.

- The level at which the count is taken is 1180.

- Target = (14 x 10) + 1180 = 1320

As you have seen, pattern A has produced four counts, two of which are the same. A pattern often does this. If the targets are near to each other, then it gives you a better target area to aim at. If they are very different, it is possible that once the first target is reached, the price will go on to the next target. In the case of Figure 4-1, the area is between 1240 and 1320 with a mid-count of 1290, which is the most likely target.

Although pattern A initially produced a downside count as well, this was negated once the pattern broke to the upside.

Figure 4-1 has another congestion area, pattern B, around the 1220 level. The pattern could be a fulcrum top or a continuation semi-catapult. When counting a target from this pattern, therefore, you must calculate an upside as well as a downside target, because at this stage it could turn into either.

Count (iv) – using Method 1 or Method 2

In this case, there is clearly a row that has the most filled in Xs and Os, and this is the row that should be used. It also happens to be in the middle of the pattern, which means the pattern is evenly balanced.

- Upside target = (number of columns in the row at the count level) x (box size) + the level at which the count is taken

- Downside target = the level at which the count is taken – (number of columns in the row at the count level) x (box size)

- The row for count (iv) runs from column 14 to column 19, which means there are 6 columns in the row.

- The box size is 10.

- The level at which the count is taken is 1220.

- Upside target = (6 x 10) + 1220 = 1280

- Downside target = 1220 – (6 x 10) = 1160

As you have seen, targets may be obtained from every congestion pattern in a 1-box reversal chart. The essence of the method is identifying which row represents the pattern, then calculating and projecting the target from that row. There has been some discussion about the importance of each row within a pattern and four methods have been put forward. Two of the methods, 3 and 4, may only be used once the congestion pattern has broken out and indicated its direction. Methods 1 and 2, on the other hand, may be used before the pattern has indicated its direction and consequently they yield counts in both directions.

In the case of methods 3 and 4, the row at which the count is taken is easy to reconcile. It is either the breakout row or it is the row at the start of the breakout column. In the case of methods 1 and 2, the row is the one which is the most important. Method 1 states that the row that has the most price action is the most important row. This is logical and easily reconciled. Method 2 states that an average row length should be taken and then the middle row should be used. This is less logical.

As to which method is best, it is impossible to say, other than to reiterate that the differences in the targets are so slight as not to be of importance. A checklist has already been given as to which method to use first.

1-box counts were designed initially for tick charts, that is to say charts constructed from the ticker where every price during the day is recorded. This is the most common application, but they may be used on any other time-frame including daily charts.

Chart 4-1 is a 1 x 1 tick Point and Figure of the NASDAQ Composite Index. The price is in a downtrend and breaks out sideways, an indication that some congestion is taking place. Whenever there is congestion, there is an opportunity to obtain a count. At this stage, the direction from the congestion is uncertain. It could be a bottom or a continuation pattern, which seems the most likely. For this reason, the best count to take is along the row with the most filled in Xs and Os. The row marked on the chart has 14 Xs and Os, which is the greatest number in any row in the pattern. It should be noted that although this is also the longest row, it does not have to be.

Since the direction is uncertain, a downside as well as an upside count should be established from the pattern, giving two targets, 1892 or 1930. The pattern is quite evenly balanced, with support at the bottom and resistance at the top, so the break could occur in either direction.

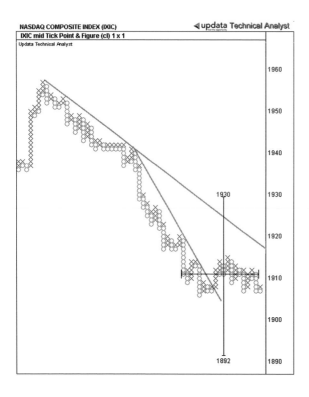

Chart 4-1: 1 x 1 tick chart of the NASDAQ Composite Index showing 1-box horizontal counts

Chart 4-2 shows the congestion pattern becoming wider. Notice that the action appears to be towards the base of the pattern, indicating strength at the base and suggesting now that the price will break to the upside, but the direction is still unknown. What is interesting, however, is that although the pattern width is increasing, the count is exactly the same, because there is no other row which has more filled in Xs and Os.

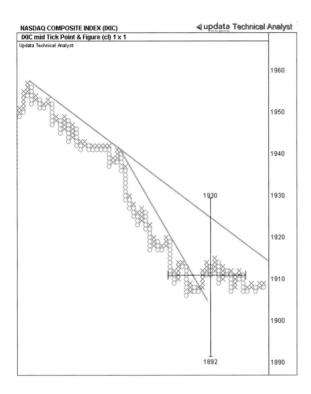

Chart 4-2: 1 x 1 tick chart of the NASDAQ Composite Index showing 1-box horizontal counts

Chart 4-3 shows the congestion pattern eventually breaking out to the upside, at the same time as breaking the downtrend line, indicating that it is a bottom pattern rather than a continuation pattern in the overall downtrend. Because of this, the downside 1892 count should be removed from the chart. Furthermore, because there is now a pattern with a wall of Os entering it and a wall of Xs exiting, it is possible to establish another upside count at the base of the exit wall. The count gives a target of 1928, which is only 2 points away from the already established 1930 count. Both counts are valid.

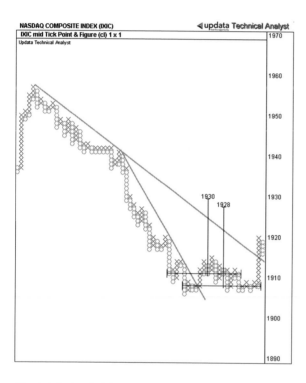

Chart 4-3: 1 x 1 tick chart of the NASDAQ Composite Index showing 1-box horizontal counts

Chart 4-4 shows the completed pattern. Notice that after the mid-pattern rally, which looked like a breakout, the price returned to support at the base, shown by the lower blue line. This is typical fulcrum action. The pattern continues to build around the centre, allowing another count to be established. Remember, to find the correct row to count, you must find the row with the most filled in Xs and Os and once you have, you must count all the squares in the row including those that are blank. There are 22 Xs and Os in the row marked A. There are actually 42 squares in the row, giving a target of 1955 (1913+42). There is nothing to stop you establishing a downside count at the same time if you think there is still a possibility that this congestion is a continuation pattern. This gives a target of 1871 (not shown).

Eventually a column of Xs leads the breakout of the pattern above the upper blue resistance line. Another count may be established at the base of the breakout column, marked B, giving a target of 1981.

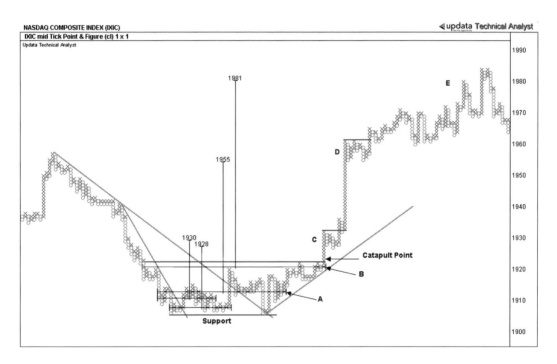

Chart 4-4: 1 x 1 tick chart of the NASDAQ Composite Index showing 1-box horizontal counts

Another count could be established at the catapult point but this would yield a count only 1 point different from the 1981 count.

All the counts on the chart are valid. The 1928 and 1930 counts are achieved when the price consolidates and forms a semi-catapult marked C. The 1955 count is achieved at the semi-catapult marked D, and the 1981 count is the top of the move at point E.

Tick charts are not restricted to 1-point box sizes. Chart 4-5 is a 2 x 1 Point and Figure chart of the NASDAQ Composite. A number of horizontal counts have been placed on the chart. In each case, the count has been taken at the row with the most filled in Xs and Os and, in each case, upside and downside counts have been established because, at the time of counting, the direction was uncertain. Notice how often the counts were achieved within a few points. The main thing about the counts is that they give you some idea of the potential upside or downside, should the pattern break out. Once the breakout does occur, the opposing count is removed.

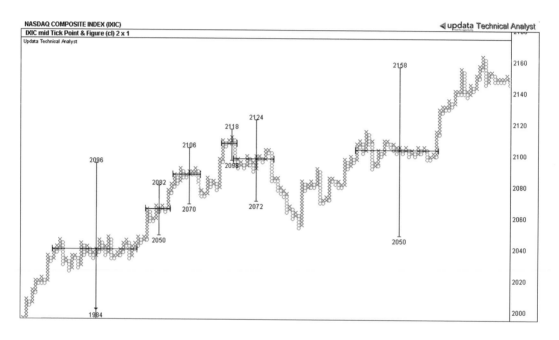

Chart 4-5: 2 x 1 tick chart of the NASDAQ Composite Index showing 1-box horizontal counts

Horizontal counts are not restricted to tick charts. They may be established and applied to any time-frame including daily charts, as Chart 4-6 of eBay Inc. shows. The large base pattern breaks out sideways from the downtrend, indicating that accumulation is starting to take place. A small fulcrum bottom, marked A, is formed, yielding a target of 39 counted across the row with the most Xs and Os. The target was not achieved, indicating that bearish sentiment is prevailing. The price continued to trade sideways, creating a far bigger congestion pattern, B. Notice the small fulcrum top within the larger pattern yielding a downside target of 22, which was achieved. Pattern B eventually becomes so wide that a downside count cannot be taken. (See page 241 for more details on impossible counts.) The pattern does yield an upside count of 113, across the row with the most filled in Xs and Os. This target coincides with the price at the top of the strong uptrend in eBay.

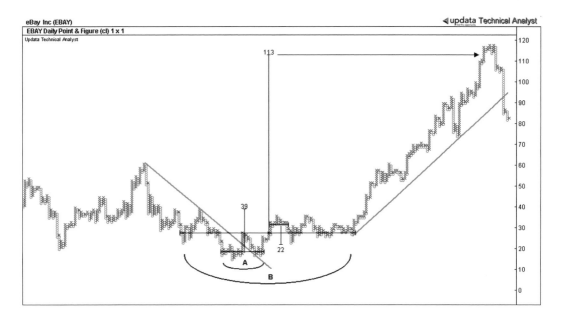

Chart 4-6: 1 x 1 daily chart of eBay Inc. showing the establishment and achievement of 1-box horizontal counts

Large congestion tops on daily charts also provide an opportunity for downside 1-box counts as the 50 x 1 Point and Figure chart of the FTSE 100 Index in Chart 4-7 shows. Within the large top marked B, there is a smaller top marked A, which has a wall of Xs entering it and a wall of Os leaving it. The count for the smaller top A is taken at the start of the exit column and yields an accurate target of 4750. The larger top B also has a column of Xs entering it and the same columns of Os exiting it. The count is taken along the same row and yields another accurate count of 3200.

Pattern C is an excellent example of distribution taking place after a rally during the downtrend. There is a clear wall entering and exiting, making the count easy to establish. Once again, it yields an accurate target of 3800.

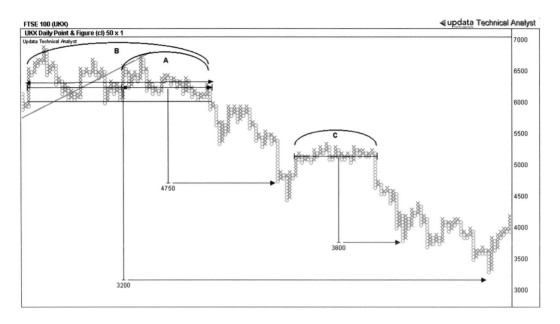

Chart 4-7: 50 x 1 daily chart of the FTSE 100 Index showing the establishment and achievement of 1-box counts

Summary of 1-box counts

1-box counts may be used to count continuation, as well as reversal patterns. The basis of the count is the width of the pattern determined by a number of methods, all of which yield a similar target. Although 1-box charts, and hence 1-box counts, tend to be used mainly for short-term charts using tick data, they may also be used with daily data and can count longer-term targets, although this is where 3-box counts take over.

Counts on 3-box reversal charts

Not only are counts on 3-box reversal charts more popular, but also they are less ambiguous and easier to use than those on 1-box charts. 3-box charts lend themselves to two counting methods, vertical and horizontal, because of the way the chart is constructed. The asymmetric filter against the trend means that 3-box reversal charts tend to have longer columns of Xs and Os than 1-box charts, thereby allowing vertical counts for which 1-box charts are not suitable.

It is important to note at this stage, that 3-box counts cannot give an upside and a downside target from the same pattern. Only one direction is possible and is triggered on a breakout of the pattern, which is explained shortly.

Vertical counts on 3-box reversal charts

The vertical count did not exist until A.W. Cohen first introduced it in 1948. It has become more popular because there are more opportunities on a chart to use it. The vertical count measures the length of a column of Xs or Os and projects it by 3 times that length. That is the easy part; however, choosing the correct column to count is important, so careful note must be made of the following guidelines. Vertical counts may only be established from the following columns:

- The first move up off a bottom; in other words, the first column of Xs after a bottom has been made.

- The first move down off a top; in other words, the first column of Os after a top has been made.

- The second move off a bottom if the second column is part of the bottom pattern, namely that the bottom is made up of either two Os at the same level, or two Os where the second O is only one box higher than the first and if the first column of Xs is a short column.

- The second move off a top if the second column is part of the top pattern, namely that the top is made up of either two Xs at the same level, or two Xs where the second X is only one box lower than the first, and if the first column of Os is a short column.

- Any other significant X or O column. This is not a licence to count every column you see. 'Other significant column' means either an intermediate mini-top or mini-bottom during an uptrend or downtrend, or a breakout column from a congestion area.

At this point it is important to understand that only these column types may be used to establish vertical counts. No other column should be counted, as this devalues the method and results in too many counts, giving a false impression as to the count's effectiveness.

How to establish upside targets using the vertical count method on 3-box charts

Step 1 – Choose a column of Xs considering the rules above

- The most important count is one from an important bottom. Look for an important bottom at the end of a downtrend where a column of Os has reversed into a column of Xs.

- The column of Xs should be the first rising column from the bottom.

- The column of Xs must be a completed column. This means that the length of the column of Xs must be fixed by the creation of a new column of Os to the right of it.

- If, however, you have already counted from the bottom, then there are three other counts you may consider:

    - Look for a second column of Xs off the bottom, but only if the first column of Xs is a short column.

    or

    - Look for an intermediate mini-bottom during an uptrend. The mini-bottom must have a 'tail' of Os. A simple 3-box pullback during an uptrend is not enough to trigger a count and is where most students make a mistake. The reason is that there must be some bearish action, which has been overcome by bullish action to increase the validity of the count. For example, a simple double-bottom sell would be sufficient to do this. As above, the column of Xs which you are counting must be complete and its length fixed by a new column of Os to the right of it.

    or

    - Look for any significant X column breakout. This could be a column of Xs that breaks out of a sideways congestion, or any other X column that changes the look of the chart. As above, the column length must be terminated so that the count is fixed.

Step 2 – Count the number of Xs in the column and calculate the count

- Once the column has been chosen, and its length fixed by the emergence of a new column in the opposite direction, count the number of Xs in the column.

- Multiply the number of Xs by the box size (the value of each X and O).

- Multiply this product by the reversal, which is 3.

- Add this total to the value of the lowest O in the column of Os immediately to the left of the counting column.

- You now have the upside target, which you may mark on the chart.

Figure 4-2 is a 5 x 3 Point and Figure chart showing three upside vertical counts. Each box is 5 points and the reversal is 3 boxes.

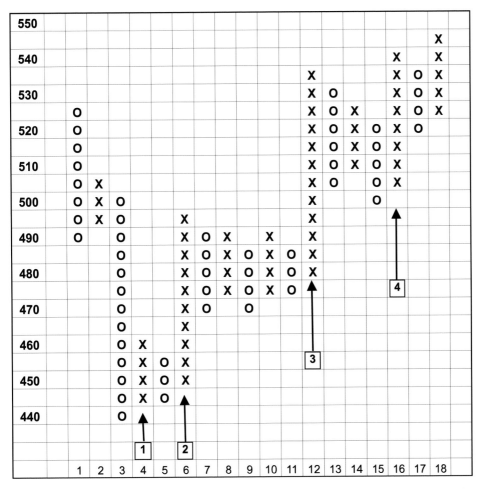

Figure 4-2: Vertical upside counts on a 3-box reversal chart showing columns that may be counted

Count 1

The price falls to a low in column 3. Column 4 is the first column of Xs off the bottom. This allows count 1 to be established, once a reversal of 3 Os has been plotted in column 5 as follows:

• Target = (number of Xs in column 4) x (box size) x (reversal) + lowest low in column 3.

• There are 4 Xs in column 4, the box size is 5 and the reversal is 3.

- The value of the lowest O in column 3 is 440.

- Target = (4 x 5 x 3) + 440 = 500

Count 2

You may count the second column off a bottom if the first column is short. Count 2, therefore, utilises column 6 as follows:

- Target = (number of Xs in the column 6) x (box size) x (reversal) + Lowest low in column 5

- There are 10 Xs in the column 6, the box size is 5 and the reversal is 3.

- The value of the lowest O in previous column 5 is 445.

- Target = (10 x 5 x 3) + 445 = 595

Count 3

To establish any additional count on the chart, you must find a significant column according to the rules detailed on page 221. The price spends a number of columns consolidating sideways after the move off the bottom but finally breaks out of the congestion area in column 12. Column 12 changes the look of the chart and is, therefore, a significant column. It is a column that has changed the look of the chart, so count 3 can be established as follows:

- Target = (number of Xs in the column 12) x (box size) x (reversal) + lowest low in column 11

- There are 12 Xs in the column 12, the box size is 5 and the reversal is 3.

- The value of the lowest O in column 11 is 475.

- Target = (12 x 5 x 3) + 475 = 655

Do not assume that there will always be a third or fourth count. If they are not obvious, they don't exist.

Note regarding vertical breakout counts

Some practitioners state that all vertical upside counts should use the bottom of the pattern as the anchor and that this is the value that should be added to. This is incorrect and illogical. Using the low of the pattern for all counts out of the pattern is self-defeating because there may be no direct relationship between the breakout column and the pattern low. Patterns where vertical counts are used are usually deep, making the connection between the low column and any column other than the adjacent columns spurious. For example, there is no direct link between column 12 and the low in column 3. If the low of the pattern had been used for count 3, the target would have been 620 instead of 655. This may seem trivial, but consider what would be the case if the breakout in column 12 had only been five Xs. This would have yielded a target almost identical to count 2, inferring that the sideways congestion after the bottom had no effect on the target from the breakout in column 12. This contradicts the thinking on horizontal counts, which suggests that the width of the pattern does influence the count. So, in all cases, the low that is added to the count is the low of the preceding O column.

<u>Count 4</u>

Having counted the first move off the bottom, and the second move off the bottom, as well as the breakout column, the only other possible count is a mini-bottom during the uptrend – not simply a pause, but an actual bottom. This occurs in column 15, so the first move off the mini-bottom is therefore column 16, and must be counted as follows:

- Target = (number of Xs in the column 16) x (box size) x (reversal) + lowest low in column 15

- There are 8 Xs in the column 16, the box size is 5 and the reversal is 3.

- The value of the lowest O in column 15 is 500.

- Target = (8 x 5 x 3) + 500 = 620

These four counts are the only valid counts in the chart in Figure 4-2. Do not be tempted to count any other columns. Yes, you can establish 'targets' off any other column, but they won't add anything to the counts obtained in the proper way and they will confuse the overall picture.

How to establish downside targets using the vertical count method on 3-box charts

The downside count is the inverse of the upside count, but it is just as well to go through it here so there is no doubt.

<u>Step 1 – Choose a column of Os considering the rules above</u>

- The most important count is one from an important top. Look for an important top at the end of an uptrend, where a column of Xs has reversed into a column of Os.

- The column of Os should be the first falling column from the top.

- The column of Os must be a completed column. This means that the length of the column of Os must be fixed by the creation of a new column of Xs.

- If you have already counted from the top, then there are three other counts you may carry out:

  - Look for a second column of Os off the top, but only if the first column of Os is a short column.

  or

  - Look for a mini-top during a downtrend. The mini-top must have a peak of Xs, after a double-top buy signal. A simple 3-box rally during a downtrend is not enough to trigger a count. The reason is that there must have been some bullish action that has been overcome to increase the validity of the count. As above, the column of Os must be complete and its length fixed by a new column of Xs.

  or

  - Look for any significant O column breakout. This could be a column of Os that breaks out of a sideways congestion, or any other O column that changes the look of the chart. As above, the column length must be terminated so that the count is fixed.

Step 2 – Count the number of Os in the column and calculate the count

- Once the column has been chosen and its length fixed, count the number of Os in the column.

- Multiply the number of Os by the box size (the value of each X and O).

- Multiply this product by the reversal, which is 3.

- Subtract this total from the value of the highest X in the column of Xs immediately to the left of the counting column.

- You now have the downside target, which you may mark on the chart.

Although downside counts are really just the inverse of upside counts, it is important to have a reference example so that no misunderstanding exists. Figure 4-3 shows three downside vertical counts. Once again, the chart is a 5 x 3 Point and Figure chart. Each box is 5 points and the reversal is three boxes.

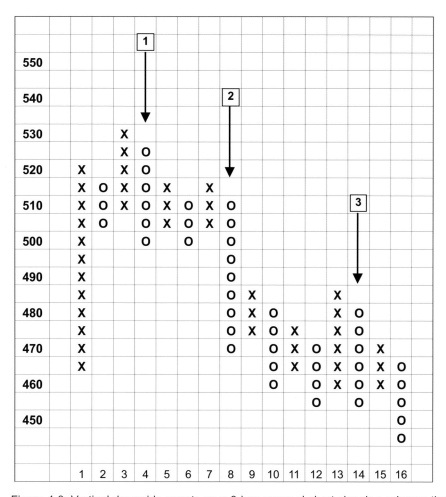

Figure 4-3: Vertical downside counts on a 3-box reversal chart showing columns that may be counted

Count 1

The price rises to a high in column 3 so column 4 is the first column of Os off the top. This allows count 1 to be established as follows:

- Target = Highest high in column 3 - (number of Os in the column 4) x (box size) x (reversal)

- There are 6 Os in the column 4, the box size is 5 and the reversal is 3.

- The value of the highest X in column 3 is 530.

- Target = 530 - (6 x 5 x 3) = 440

Count 2

Once again, to establish any additional counts you must find a significant column according to the rules detailed on page 221. The price consolidates sideways but finally breaks out of the congestion area in column 8, which is a significant column because it has changed the look of the chart. Count 2 may, therefore, be established as follows:

- Target = Highest high in column 7 - (number of Os in column 8) x (box size) x (reversal)
- There are 9 Os in column 8, the box size is 5 and the reversal is 3.
- The value of the highest X in column 7 is 515.
- Target = 515 - (9 x 5 x 3) = 380

It is important to remind you of the note regarding vertical breakout counts made on page 224. The high that the count is subtracted from is the high of the preceding X column, which is 515 in this case. It is not the high of the overall pattern.

Count 3

The third type of column that can be counted is a mini-top during the downtrend. This occurred in column 13, so the first move off the mini-top in column 14 must be counted as follows:

- Target = Highest high in column 13 - (number of Os in the column 14) x (box size) x (reversal)
- There are 6 Os in column 14, the box size is 5 and the reversal is 3.
- The value of the highest X in column 13 is 485.
- Target = 485 - (6 x 5 x 3) = 395

Vertical count establishment and activation

It is important to note that there are two stages to the vertical count. There is the establishment stage and the activation stage. The establishment stage occurs when the length of the column being counted is fixed by the addition of a new column in the opposite direction. The count can then be performed and a target established.

The count and the target cannot, however, be considered active until there has been a break above the highest X in the counting column (in the case of an upside count), or a break below the lowest O in the counting column (in the case of a downside count).

This point was illustrated in Figure 4-2 on page 223. Column 4 is the first column of Xs off the bottom. Its length is fixed by the addition of a column of Os in column 5. A target of 500 may be calculated, but it cannot be considered active, in other words, it should not be relied on until there is a break above the highest X in column 4. That occurs with a double-top buy in column 6. Then, and only then, can you start looking for the 500 target to be achieved.

The same occurs with count 2 (target 595) in Figure 4-2 on page 223, which is activated only when column 12 breaks above column 6 at the 500 level. Count 3 is activated by column 16 and count 4 by column 18. You will find that some established targets can take many columns before they are activated. A count cannot be considered to have failed if it has not yet been activated, unless of course it has been negated, which is explained under the heading of 'Negating a count' on page 238.

It is important to note, though, that not all counts will be activated. On a number of occasions you will see counts established, but not activated. Chart 4-8 below is a 1% x 3 of Avis Europe plc. A count of 507 is established off the mini-bottom. Notice, however, that the count was not activated by a new column of Xs breaking above the top of the count column, above the blue horizontal line shown.

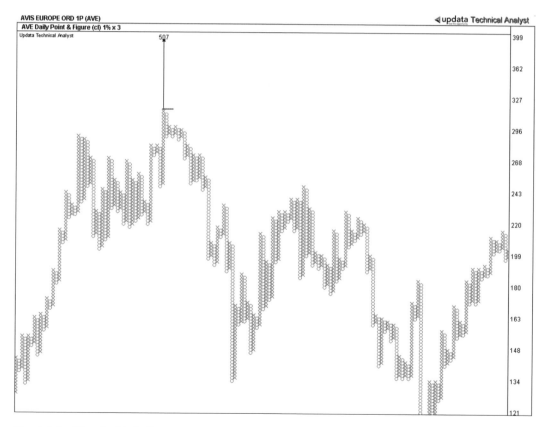

Chart 4-8: 1% x 3 of Avis Europe plc showing a count being established but not activated

Activation does not have to be the next column of Xs, but it must be within the same pattern.

The logic of the vertical count

As you have seen, the vertical count is taken on an upthrust or a downthrust column. The logic is that the greater the buying demand off a bottom or selling supply off a top, the stronger the participants creating the column. The analogy is throwing a ball: the harder or faster the arm is moved, the further the ball will go, overcoming any resistance. The greater the enthusiasm of the bulls in reversing the downtrend, the stronger they will remain during the uptrend as latecomers get on the trend expecting higher and higher prices. The converse is true for downtrends. The greater the move off a top, the more confident the bears become and the more shocked the bulls are at the change in trend, causing them to keep away.

It is no good, however, having just one thrust which could catch the other side off-guard; it is important that there is a reaction against the first thrust column, followed by a reassertion of the trend by at least a double-top/bottom breakout, and that is why the activation of the count is separately important.

Horizontal counts on 3-box reversal charts

Although only one method of 3-box horizontal counts is really used today, there are, in fact, two methods. The original method was devised by Thomas Sexsmith, a colleague of De Villers and Taylor. It is along the same lines as that used for 1-box horizontal counts described earlier, which was also devised by Sexsmith. In the interests of thoroughness, and in order not to disrupt the flow of the text, this method is discussed briefly at the end of this chapter.

The other method that is in common usage today is the method introduced by Cohen. 3-box horizontal counts can only be used when there is a wide congestion area, and when that congestion area is a top or a bottom. The prerequisite is that there must be a move into the top or bottom pattern, then a consolidation phase and a move out in the opposite direction. Some Point and Figure analysts, including this author, do not believe that continuation patterns can be counted on 3-box charts using this method. If you wish to do this, you should use the original De Villiers & Taylor method described on page 252.

In the Cohen method, the horizontal count measures the width of any congestion top or bottom pattern and projects it by 3 times that width. Although not as popular as vertical counts, horizontal counts do yield worthwhile targets and should be used whenever possible, especially where they confirm vertical counts. Conditions for establishing a horizontal count are:

- There must be a top or bottom pattern.

- There must be a move into the pattern.

- There must be some sideways consolidation.

- There must be a move out of the pattern in the opposite direction, so the column type leaving the pattern is opposite to that entering the pattern.

- The width of the congestion determines the extent of the move.

How to establish upside targets using the horizontal count method on 3-box charts

Step 1 – Look for a congestion pattern bottom

- Look for any bottom patterns at the end of a downtrend that have the shape of a U, V or W.

- The shape of the pattern is not so important, but it must have walls.

- There must be a column of Os entering it and a column of Xs leaving it.

- Between the entry and exit columns, there must be some consolidation or congestion.

Step 2 – Count the number of columns in the pattern

- Once the entry and exit columns have been chosen, count the number of columns across the pattern, including the entry column of Os and the exit column of Xs.

- Multiply the number of columns by the box size (the value of each X and O).

- Multiply this value by the reversal, which is 3.

- Add this total to the value of the lowest O in the pattern.

- You now have the upside target, which you may mark on the chart.

Figure 4-4 overleaf shows four upside horizontal counts. For ease of calculation, the chart is once again a 5 x 3 Point and Figure chart. Each box is 5 points and the reversal is 3 boxes.

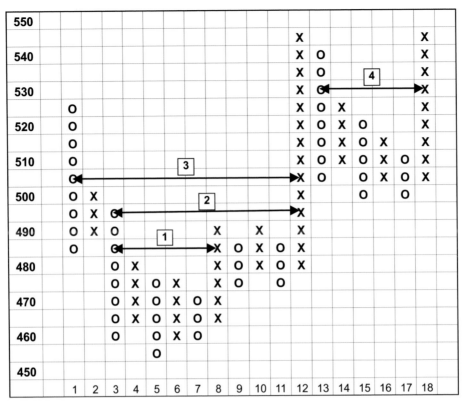

Figure 4-4: Horizontal upside counts on a 3-box reversal chart showing rows that may be counted

Count 1

Column 3 is a wall of Os entering the bottom pattern, and column 8 is the wall of Xs leaving it. Between the two walls, there is some congestion. This allows count 1 to be established as follows:

- Target = (number of columns in the pattern) x (box size) x (reversal) + lowest low between columns 3 and 8

- There are 6 columns between the walls (including the walls), the box size is 5 and the reversal is 3.

- The value of the lowest O in the pattern is in column 5, which is 455.

- Target = (6 x 5 x 3) + 455 = 545

Very often, a bottom pattern has two or more parts to it. A smaller bottom pattern is often contained within a larger bottom pattern that develops at a later stage. This allows more than one count to be established from a single bottom. In the example in Figure 4-4, there are actually two additional counts.

Count 2

Notice that a smaller bottom pattern (count 1) bounded by columns 3 and 8 is contained in a larger bottom pattern bounded by columns 3 and 12. This allows count 2 to be established. Before doing the calculation, you can see that the target will be greater because the pattern is wider.

- Target = (number of columns in the larger pattern) x (box size) x (reversal) + lowest low between columns 3 and 12

- There are 10 columns between the walls (including the walls), the box size is 5 and the reversal is 3.

- The value of the lowest O in the pattern is still in column 5, which is 455.

- Target = (10 x 5 x 3) + 455 = 605

Count 3

In Figure 4-4 there is actually an even larger bottom pattern bounded by columns 1 and 12. This allows a third count to be established. The target will be greater than counts 1 or 2.

- Target = (number of columns in the larger pattern) x (box size) x (reversal) + lowest low between columns 1 and 12

- There are 12 columns between the walls (including the walls), the box size is 5 and the reversal is 3.

- The value of the lowest O in the pattern is still in column 5, which is 455.

- Target = (12 x 5 x 3) + 455 = 635

It is important to keep a look out for multiple counts from within the same bottom. As the bottom builds and the congestion area increases so additional, higher targets may be established. Do not, however, assume that there will always be a second or third count. If they are not obvious, then none exists.

Count 4

As stated before, using the Cohen horizontal method for counting continuation patterns is not recommended, so you may well ask why count 4 is being considered. It is a consolidation pattern contained within a continuation pattern, so in this instance it can be counted. In the same way that vertical counts may be established from mini-bottoms during an uptrend, so horizontal counts may be established from them as well. There is a move into the mini-bottom in column 13. There is some congestion during which a bottom is made, and there is a move out of the pattern in column 18.

The target is calculated as follows:

- Target = (number of columns in the mini-bottom pattern) x (box size) x (reversal) + lowest low between columns 13 and 18

- There are 6 columns between the walls (including the walls), the box size is 5 and the reversal is 3.

- The value of the lowest O in the pattern is in columns 15 and 17, which is 500.

- Target = (6 x 5 x 3) + 500 = 590

These four horizontal targets are the only ones available from the chart in Figure 4-4.

How to establish downside targets using the horizontal count method on 3-box charts

Step 1 – The first step is to look for a congestion pattern top

- Look for any inverted U, V or W-shaped top at the end of an uptrend.

- There must be a column of Xs entering it and a column of Os leaving it.

- Between the entry and exit columns, there must be some consolidation or congestion.

Step 2 – Count the number of columns in the pattern

- Once the entry and exit columns have been chosen, count the number of columns across the pattern including the entry column of Xs and the exit column of Os.

- Multiply the number of columns by the box size (the value of each X and O).

- Multiply this product by the reversal, which is 3.

- Subtract this total from the value of the highest X in the pattern.

- You now have the downside target.

Figure 4-5 shows three downside horizontal counts. The chart is also a 5 x 3 Point and Figure chart opposite.

Count 1

Column 3 is a wall of Xs entering the top pattern. There is some congestion in columns 4, 5, 6 and 7, then there is a wall of Os leaving the pattern in column 8. Count 1 may be established for this pattern.

- Target = Highest high between columns 3 and 8 - (number of columns in the top pattern) x (box size) x (reversal)

- There are 6 columns between the walls (including the walls), the box size is 5 and the reversal is 3.

- The value of the highest X in the pattern is 545.

- Target = 545 - (6 x 5 x 3) = 455

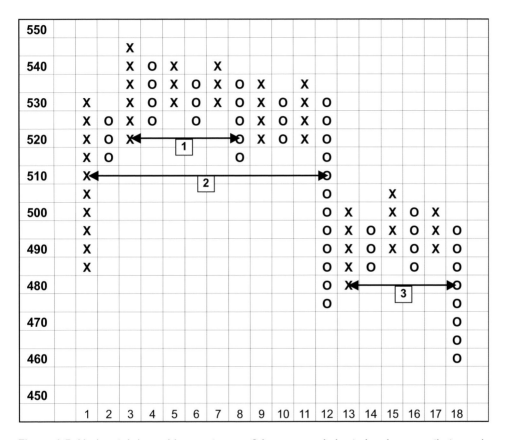

Figure 4-5: Horizontal downside counts on a 3-box reversal chart showing rows that may be counted

Count 2

As with the upside count example, there may be more than one count available from the pattern as it becomes wider. Column 1 is a wall of Xs entering the top pattern. There is congestion in columns 2 to 11 before there is a wall of Os leaving the pattern in column 12. Count 2 may be established for this pattern.

- Target = Highest high between columns 1 and 12 - (number of columns in the top pattern) x (box size) x (reversal)

- There are 12 columns between the walls (including the walls), the box size is 5 and the reversal is 3.

- The value of the highest X in the pattern is 545.

- Target = 545 - (12 x 5 x 3) = 365

Count 3

You will see that count 3 may be established from a mini-top during the downtrend. The mini-top pattern is created by the column of Xs in column 13 entering the pattern and the column of Os in column 18 leaving it. The count is established as follows:

- Target = Highest high between columns 13 and 18 - (number of columns in the mini-top pattern) x (box size) x (reversal)

- There are 6 columns between the walls (including the walls), the box size is 5 and the reversal is 3.

- The value of the highest X in the mini-top pattern is 505.

- Target = 505 - (6 x 5 x 3) = 415

Horizontal count stage

Horizontal counts don't have two separate stages like vertical counts. The establishment and activation stage occur at the same time, when the entry column is matched by an exit column after some congestion. In the case of a bottom pattern, the exit column must rise above the highest X in the pattern so that there is a clear row running between the entry and exit columns. The width of the pattern is then fixed, the count can then be calculated, the target established and activated. The arrows marking the width of each count in the previous figures are placed at the point in the column where the count is established and activated.

In the case of a top pattern, the exit column must fall below the lowest O in the pattern so that there is a clear row running between the entry and exit columns.

The logic of the horizontal count

To understand the logic of the horizontal count, you must consider why congestion areas develop. They are a summary of the battle for supremacy by the bulls and the bears, neither wishing to progress too far. It is like a pressure cooker. When the lid blows, the contents are expelled with force. The distance it travels will depend on the pressure built up inside. It is similar with congestion patterns in Point and Figure charts. The longer the battle for supremacy, in other words the more columns built up by opposing sides taking contrary positions, the stronger the resultant move when one side is overcome.

Things you should know about Point and Figure counts

Chart 4-9 below is a 5 x 3 Point and Figure chart of Barclays plc, showing a number of counts. Don't concern yourself by the large number of them, some are invalid. The chart is referred to in the following paragraphs to illustrate a number of points about vertical and horizontal counts. Although the chart below is a 3-box reversal chart, the points made in the following paragraphs apply equally to counts on 1-box charts.

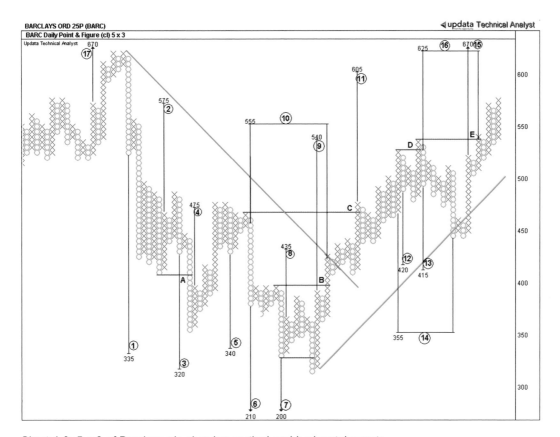

Chart 4-9: 5 x 3 of Barclays plc showing vertical and horizontal counts

Targets have no time-scale

Perhaps the hardest thing for non-Point and Figure chartists to come to terms with, is that having been given a target, there is no time-scale for its achievement. Even an experienced Point and Figure analyst struggles with this. The fact is that Point and Figure charts have no time-scale, so it is impossible to calculate when a target – vertical or horizontal – will be reached. It is futile to attempt to do so. Simply accept that it is the situation.

Nearest counts must be achieved first

Those of a bullish disposition will be tempted to seek out the highest possible count just as those of a bearish disposition will seek the lowest target. Before doing so, consider the logic. On the upside, lower targets have to be achieved before a higher count can be considered. If a lower target is not achieved, then the achievement of the higher count is obviously impossible. Counting is a progressive tool. By all means, select counts that cluster around a target, but do not select one that is double the next target. Its presence on the chart will give you a distorted view of the future. In Chart 4-9, count 15 of 670 may be established to show the strength of the chart, but should not be relied on or even quoted until counts 11 of 605 and 16 of 625 have been achieved. It is pointless relying on count 14 until vertical counts 12 and 13 have been achieved. In fact, they never were.

Clustering of counts

You have already been advised to avoid trying to count every column; however, there will be times when a number of valid counts, both vertical and horizontal, may be obtained from the same area of the chart. Normally when there is a horizontal count, there will be a vertical count from the breakout column. Any clustering of these multiple targets reinforces the likelihood of that particular target being achieved. Vertical count 9 of 540 and horizontal count 10 of 555 in Chart 4-9 show clustering, as do vertical counts 1, 3 and 5 to the downside. Counts 11 and 16 of 605 and 625 do as well. Often, three separate targets come in within a few percent of one another.

Remember, however, that although counts may be clustered, this does not mean that they will definitely be achieved. Counts 6 and 7, and 12 and 13, are good examples. Clustering of counts means that if the price does look like it is heading in that direction, then it is likely to stop somewhere within the clustering area. Clustering does not assure the count, it simply increases the likelihood that a target within the cluster area will be achieved.

Negating a count

Not all counts will be achieved, so there has to be a process for removing them from your analysis. A vertical upside count is negated when the price falls below the low that anchored the count. Conversely, a downside count is negated when the price rises above the top that anchored it.

Count 2 of 575 in Chart 4-9 is negated when the price falls through point A, opposite the bottom, or anchor, of the count. Count 2 should, therefore, be removed from the chart. Count 7 is negated at point B. Count 6 is negated at point C. Counts 12 and 13 are negated at points D and E respectively. Once a count is negated, it should be removed to avoid confusion.

Horizontal counts are negated in the same way. A downside horizontal count is negated when the price rises above the top of the pattern encompassing the count. An upside horizontal count is negated when the price falls below the bottom of the pattern. Horizontal downside count 14 is negated when the price rises above the level at point E.

Negation of a count shows weakness in the direction of the count. It shows that the determined bulls or bears that caused the count to be established and activated in the first place are not strong enough to follow it through. Understanding the negation of counts is closely related to the ideas in the following section on opposing counts.

Opposing counts

It is often the case that you will have an upside and a downside count working against one another. Do not feel that your analysis is weak. Downside count 1 is established from the top. Thereafter, the price falls and consolidates around the 450 level. Eventually it makes a bottom from where upside count 2 can be established and activated. The chart is now under the influence of two counts. Although count 1 is the most important, count 2 must be taken note of as it may be achieved if the trend has changed. The discussion on trend lines in the next section will help you to assess the likelihood of count 2 being achieved.

Once counts 1, 3 and 5 have been achieved, the chart comes under the influence of counts 6 and 7. These cluster around the 200 to 210 area and look distinctly possible, especially after count 8 is negated. Then another bottom is made and count 9 is activated. The chart is now under the influence of bearish counts 6 and 7, but, at the same time, there is an upside count 9 pulling in the other direction. Knowing when one side is pulling stronger than the other then becomes important. Initially counts 6 and 7 are the strongest, but as the bottom develops and the move from count 9 is extended, so count 7 is negated, which is a weakening of the bear side. It is a downside count that has not been achieved and has had to be cancelled; count 6 remains dominant though. Further development at the bottom results in the establishment of count 10, which is activated at the same time as the bearish resistance line is broken. Counts 9 and 10 now become the more likely targets, with count 6 looking doubtful. Remember that count 6 remains valid, however, so there are still valid upside and downside counts working against one another. This remains the case until count 6 is negated at point C.

Combining counts with trend lines

The validity of counts is enhanced by the use of trend lines, especially 45° trend lines. An upside count is more likely to be achieved if it occurs when the count column is above a 45° bullish support line. A downside count is more likely to be achieved if it occurs below a 45° bearish resistance line. Counts established against the prevailing trend should always be viewed with suspicion. They can, however, be useful because their achievement or non-achievement does explain more about the underlying nature of the trend in place. Count 2 of

575 is below the bearish resistance line and so should be considered a speculative target, unless the chart pattern changes sufficiently to indicate that a major bottom has been made. What does happen, in fact, is a weak rally that reverses well short of the count, thus reinforcing the bearish nature of the trend. Further reinforcement of the bearish trend occurs when count 2 is eventually negated.

A similar situation occurs with count 8. A possible bottom is made around the cluster target of 320/335/340, generated from counts 1, 3 and 5. Count 8 is established and then triggered, but what occurs is a weak rally, which fails to follow-through, and the count is eventually negated, reinforcing the downtrend. At this stage, counts 6 and 7 become the most likely downside targets. See the next section on unfulfilled counts for more information about this situation.

Some countertrend counts are achieved, but these also provide more information about the chart. A countertrend target which falls short of the prevailing downtrend line, but which is then achieved, reinforces the prevailing trend. It means that there is sufficient power for a countertrend rally, but not enough to challenge the downtrend. During any trend, there will be countertrend rallies, or countertrend corrections. If targets from these fall short of the trend line, and are achieved, it reinforces the strength of that trend line. Count 4 is a countertrend count, which has a target short of the bearish resistance line. The fact that the count was achieved indicates that the bear trend is more powerful than the bottom from which the count 4 rally occurred.

Unfulfilled counts

The previous sections hinted at this. By definition, there will most likely be at least one upside and one downside count that will not be achieved on most charts. The reason is that as the trend matures, so new counts are established. The likelihood of a count near the end of a trend not being achieved is increased. It is not always the case, but, when it does happen, it is a clear indication that the trend is coming to an end.

Downside counts 6 and 7 in Chart 4-9 are examples of counts that were never achieved. At the time they were established, the downtrend in place was strong and there was no indication that these counts were not going to be achieved. Then a possible bottom was made and count 9 established first, followed by count 10. At the same time, count 7 was negated. Count 10 became active at the same time that the bearish resistance line was broken. The conclusion is that it is now highly unlikely that downside count 6 will be achieved. This non-achievement is further evidence that the bear trend is over.

Non-achievement is also common in uptrends, as count 17 on the far left of the chart shows. It is a valid upside count, which was not achieved. You would not know this at the time, however, but the establishment and activation of count 1, cancelling count 17, confirms that a new bear trend is being established.

Improbable and impossible counts

Always be on the look out for counts that are impossible or improbable. Impossible counts are easier to spot because they give a figure that is impossible. This can only happen with downside counts and occurs when the downside count yields a value less than 0. Most software makes the target 0. Of course, a count of zero could mean that the company is going out of business but it is more likely that the column you took the count from is invalid.

Chart 4-10 shows a 2 x 3 of Alizyme plc. The count from the top produces a target of zero. Of course, there is a possibility that the company could go out of business, but what is more likely is that your box size is too big or the column cannot be used for the count. Often, if this happens, the next column can be used, in this case yielding a target of 22, which was achieved almost exactly.

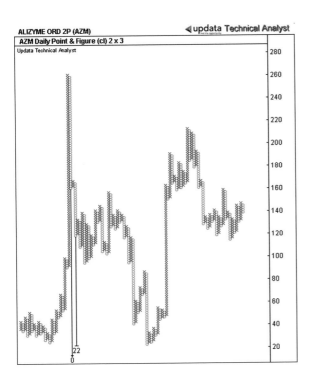

Chart 4-10: 2 x 3 of Alizyme plc showing impossible and improbable counts

Improbable counts are another matter. The probability that a count will not be reached is a subjective interpretation and should, therefore, be treated with caution. Many improbable counts have been achieved. Xerox Corp. in Chart 4-11 is a good example, using a 0.5 x 3 chart. When the price was around 50, it broke down out of a large fulcrum top allowing a horizontal downside target to be calculated. The target came out as 3. Anyone looking at the chart at the time, with the price at 50, may well have thought that this was an improbable count. In fact, within 18 months it had fallen to 4.5, only 1.5 points from that target.

You will not know at the time whether the count will be achieved, but you must look at the chart for signs. The signs are that a large top has been made at the same time an important 45° trend line has been broken. The top pattern yields a horizontal target of 3, the breakout column yields a vertical target of 15.5 (not shown). Both are so far from the current price, that it is difficult to justify remaining long. It doesn't matter whether they are achieved with any accuracy. The point is that they are less than half the current price. Once you have no long positions, it is much easier to follow the price down and make decisions during the downtrend about where the price will stop. The bottom pattern between 20 and 25 looked like it would halt the downtrend but that quickly faded and, when it did, the target of 15.5 and then 3 became more likely.

Chart 4-11: 0.5 x 3 of Xerox Corp. showing an improbable count being achieved

Counts on different time horizons

Remember that changing the box size has the same effect as changing the time horizon. If you want a short-term count, then reduce the box size. If you want a long-term count, then increase the box size. Sometimes the counts from a different box size will be within a few points of one another, but often you will see a different perspective too.

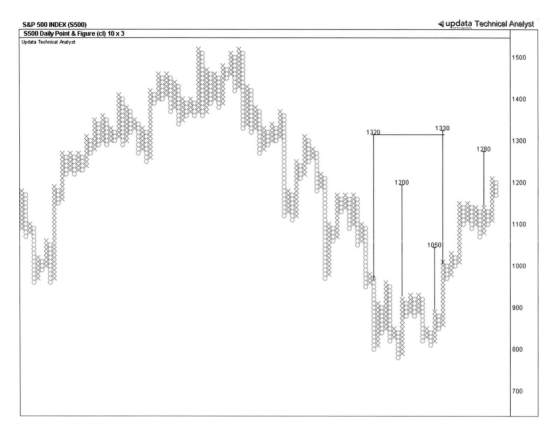

Chart 4-12: 10 x 3 of the S&P 500 Index showing vertical and horizontal counts

Chart 4-12 shows a 10 x 3 of the S&P 500 Index. The first bottom in October 2002 yields a vertical count of 1200, which, at the time of writing, had just been achieved. A further count off the March 2003 bottom yields 1050, which was also achieved. Only three other counts are possible: the large horizontal count of 1320 from the bottom; a vertical count of 1330 from the breakout column; and the minor vertical count of 1280 from the mini-bottom, three columns from the end. Note, however, that no count targeted the important resistance at 1150.

Chart 4-13 is a 5 x 3 of the S&P 500 Index, half the size of the box in Chart 4-12. Reducing the box size to 5 has exposed more detail and many more counts can be established. The two bottoms yielded almost identical counts of 1080 and 1075, and then two mini-bottoms during the uptrend yielded two identical counts of 1150, which is where major resistance was encountered.

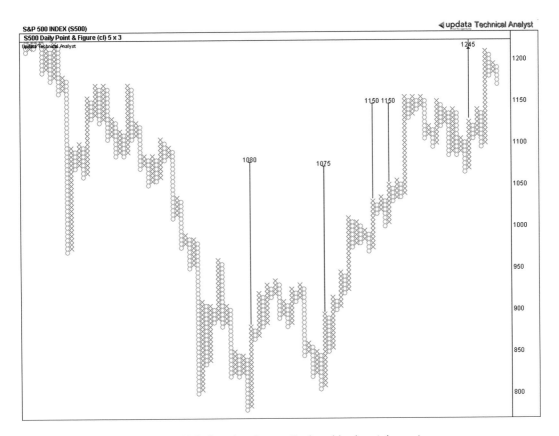

Chart 4-13: 5 x 3 of the S&P 500 Index showing vertical and horizontal counts

It is always worth looking at counts on various box size charts, as you may see something not apparent on the box size chart you normally use.

A short-term trader will use intra-day charts of 1-box and 3-box reversal to give intra-day counts. Chart 4-14 shows a 1 x 3 tick chart of the FTSE 100 Index covering 28th January 2005 to 15th February 2005. Notice how, as the price rises in a strong uptrend, short-term vertical (marked with V) and horizontal (marked with H) counts are established, activated and achieved. Notice too that any downside counts (not shown) are not achieved.

Chart 4-14: 1 x 3 (tick) of the FTSE 100 Index showing achievement of vertical and horizontal counts

Good counter or bad counter

Counts do not work well on some instruments; on others, it is uncanny how accurate they are. It has nothing to do with the instrument type, but rather the characteristic of the particular instrument. The advantage of charts, however, is that you can go back into the past and perform a number of counts to see whether they have worked or not. If they have been fairly accurate, the chances are that the current counts will be. If they have failed a number of times, it is likely that the current counts will fail.

The important thing to remember is that counting is just a tool. If used irresponsibly it will be a hindrance rather than a benefit. You must observe the patterns as well as the trends and, if you do, the counts will benefit you. What you will find, if you persevere, is that the counts will be incredibly useful in your overall analysis.

You will learn to spot instruments that don't count well. It is to do with the way they trade. Either they have long columns of Xs and Os next to one another, yielding outlandish counts, or they have short columns next to one another, yielding small counts. Either way, it is the matching of column lengths that is the first thing to notice. If this happens, it means the price is not trending in a true Point and Figure fashion. It means that the bulls take hold and the bears take it back and vice versa. Point and Figure relies on a move from the one camp, a weakish response from the latter and a reassertion by the former. Without this, some of the value of the Point and Figure charts is lost and part of that loss is the accuracy of targets from the chart. Instruments that have traded sideways over a long time tend to be bad counters as Chart 4-15 of Bradford and Bingley plc shows. A selection of past counts indicates that targets are unlikely to be met and should therefore be treated with caution.

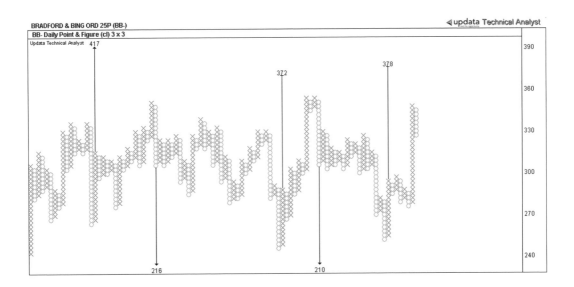

Chart 4-15: 3 x 3 of Bradford and Bingley plc showing a example of a bad counting chart

Counts on close or high/low charts

There is no evidence to suggest that counts are more accurate on close or high/low charts. Chart 4-9 of Barclays plc discussed on 237 is a close only chart. Compare this with Chart 4-16 overleaf, which is the same 5 x 3 box and reversal, but is constructed with high/low data. All relevant counts have been placed on the chart. You can see some are the same, some are very different. Because high/low charts have wider congestion patterns there are more horizontal counts. Using high/low data increases the volatility of the chart, so there will be less longer-term vertical counts because the columns will be shorter. Some readers will want to know whether it is best to use close or high/low charts. Unfortunately, it is not possible to say. Some instruments will perform better with close, some better with high/low. It is the same problem with deciding on log or arithmetic. It is best to apply the rule in the previous paragraph. Draw both the close and the high/low charts, perform the counts and see which type of chart has worked best in the past. If you feel uncomfortable about either of them, do not use the chart.

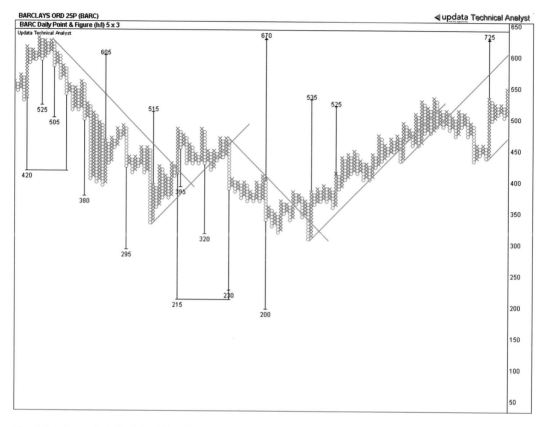

Chart 4-16: 5 x 3 daily (hl) of Barclays plc showing counts on a high/low constructed chart

Counts on other box reversal charts

Counting tends to be conducted on 1-box and 3-box charts only. It is rare to see them used on 5-box charts because the counts tend to be too long-term and often transpire to be completely wrong. The columns on 5-box charts are very long because the price has to reverse by 5 boxes to change columns. Vertical counts, therefore, yield improbable counts and are best ignored. You will recall that near-term counts must be achieved before the far-term counts can be considered. With 5-box charts, you will not obtain any near-term counts. Horizontal counts tend to be better because the 5-box reversal makes congestion patterns narrower, and this makes up for the fact that the width must be multiplied by 5.

The vertical count formula does not work very well on 2-box charts either. Vertical counts always fall short of the correct target, because the column is only projected by twice its length instead of 3 times. As with 5-box charts, however, horizontal counts can be used on 2-box charts and do produce reasonable results. This is because there are more columns and so the width of the congestion patterns is greater. As explained already, it is best to try a number of earlier counts to see whether the counts have been accurately achieved in the past.

Counts on log scale charts

As if it weren't enough to contend with vertical and horizontal counts, and then two methods of conducting horizontal counts, mention also needs to be made of counts on log scale Point and Figure charts. A log scale Point and Figure chart, as you have seen, is a chart where the box size is set to a percentage of the price and, therefore, varies exponentially as the price rises. This means that you cannot use an arithmetic calculation method. Whilst it is inadvisable to draw log scale Point and Figure charts by hand, and therefore calculate the counts by hand, there will be those who wish to do this.

Consider what is important when calculating a count. The three parameters you use to calculate the target are the box size, the reversal and the number of boxes in the column or across the pattern, which are multiplied together and added to, or subtracted from, a base price to give the target. In the case of log scale Point and Figure charts, however, the box is a percentage change in price. It means that every X in a column of Xs is slightly larger, by the percentage, than the previous. If the box size is 1% then each box will be 1.01 times larger than the previous one as the price rises. So, a 3-box reversal would not simply be formed by a 3% move, but by a 3.03% up or a 2.97% down.

To obtain a target on a log scale chart, therefore, you must proceed as follows:

- Count the number of boxes in the vertical column in the case of a vertical count, or across a pattern in the case of a horizontal count.

- Multiply the number of boxes by the reversal and by the natural log[15] (ln) of the box size. This gives the extension, which is either added to or subtracted from the anchor point.

- Take the ln of the anchor point (the high or low to which the count is anchored).

- For upside counts, add the extension to the ln of the anchor point. For downside counts subtract the extension from the log of the anchor point.

- Finally, take the exponential (e) of this figure to give the target.

Chart 4-17 overleaf is a 1% x 3 Point and Figure of the S&P 500 Index. A number of counts have been shown.

---

[15] The natural log (ln) is the preferred method of logging data.

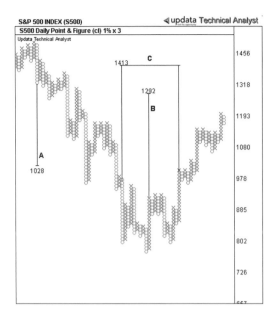

Chart 4-17: 1% x 3 of the S&P 500 Index showing counts on a log scaled chart

Vertical count A

- There are 13 Os in the column. The box size is 1.01.

- The extension is ln(1.01) x 13 x 3 = 0.388063

- The highest X in the previous column is 1515.41.

- The target is the exponential of ln(1515.41) - 0.388063 which is
  $e^{(7.323441-0.388063)} = 1028.01$

Vertical count B

- There are 17 Xs in the column.

- The extension is ln(1.01) x 17 x 3 = 0.507467

- The lowest O in the previous column is 778.03.

- The target is the exponential of ln(778.03) + 0.507467 which
  is $e^{(6.656765+0.507467)} = 1292.36$

Horizontal count C

* There are 20 columns in the pattern.

* The extension is $\ln(1.01) \times 20 \times 3 = 0.597020$

* The lowest O in the pattern is 778.03.

* The target is the exponential of $\ln(778.03) + 0.597467$ which is $e^{(6.656765+0.597467)} = 1413.44$

Accuracy of counts on log scale charts

Log scale counts tend to overstate both the downside and upside targets as you can see by comparing log scale Chart 4-17 and arithmetic Chart 4-18.

Chart 4-18: 10 x 3 of the S&P 500 Index showing counts on an arithmetic chart

The difference is normally so small as not to make much difference. The reason is that the extensions are compounded by 1% per box. You should understand that you will never estimate the same targets or, in fact, retracements if you change from arithmetic to log and vice versa. Every aspect of the chart is different, including trend lines. This applies not only to Point and Figure, but all other chart types as well.

This should not prevent you from using one method over the other. In any case, it's not really a true test, because it is impossible to draw an arithmetic and a log scaled chart which are the same. In this example, one is 10 points and the other is 1%. There will only be one place on the chart, at the 1000 level, where the box size is identical. So, accept that counts on log scale Point and Figure charts will be different. The suggestion made earlier applies: try a few counts on past data and see how accurate they have been.

De Villiers and Taylor 3-box horizontal counts

The De Villiers and Taylor method of 3-box horizontal counts was devised by Thomas Sexsmith. It is not really mentioned any more, but that does not mean that you can't use it. Unlike the Cohen method, it is very effective for counting targets from continuation patterns.

It uses the same logic as the 1-box horizontal count discussed on page 207, the only difference being that the total is multiplied by 3 before adding it to the row at which the count is taken. So in a 10 x 3 chart, if the counting row had 12 squares, the total would be the number of squares times the box size times the reversal, 12 x 10 x 3. It seems that this method of 3-box horizontal counting fell into disuse once Cohen's book was published. Its use was discontinued because 3-box patterns are deeper and so it was quite time consuming to find the row with the most filled in Xs and Os.

Risk and reward

There are two questions that every trader must ask and then answer before placing a trade: 'What do I do if I am wrong?' and 'How do I know I am wrong?' The first is easy to answer: you must close your position. Many people are unable to answer the second question, and if it remains unanswered, the first becomes redundant. At the time you make the decision to trade, you must look to see what would make you close that trade. Some traders use a simple trailing stop loss, but Point and Figure charts allow you to be more specific, based on signals you can see in the charts – normally a double-bottom (top) or a breakout from the other side of a compound pattern. Once you have decided what would 'cancel' your position, resulting in a loss, you know the risk of placing the trade. That is one side of the equation, because there is a potential reward as well and estimating this is an important part of the process of making the decision to trade. This is where Point and Figure counts, discussed earlier in this chapter, come in.

In fact, combining the risk and the reward creates the misnamed[16] risk-reward ratio. Point and Figure charts are ideally suited to computing these ratios because there is always a clear-cut entry and clear-cut exit point. For this reason, the risk-reward ratio is more suited to 3-box reversal charts rather than 1-box, because in 1-box charts the signals, although effective, are not quite so clear-cut.

The risk-reward ratio is the ratio of the potential gain from any trade, derived from the Point and Figure count, to the possible loss if the trade goes wrong and the price goes in the opposite direction, derived from Point and Figure double-top and double-bottom signals.

Risk-reward ratio from vertical counts on 3-box charts

You will recall that there are two stages to the vertical count – the establishment and the activation. The risk-reward ratio can only be computed once the count has been established and the activation column is in the process of being built.

Figure 4-6 shows a typical bottom. After the first column of Xs in column 2 off the low, the establishment stage takes place when the length of the column of Xs is fixed by the reversal of a column of Os in column 3. At this stage the vertical target can be established and the reward calculated. The reward is the difference between the vertical target and the price at the breakout above the highest X in the counting column of Xs.

The length of the correction column of Os in column 3 is fixed by a reversal of a column of Xs in column 4. At this stage, the risk may be calculated. The risk is the difference between the price at the breakout above the highest X in the counting column – above the blue line – and the value of the O below the correction column of Os – below the red line. The calculation is as follows:

The vertical target is the number of Xs in column 2 multiplied by the box size, multiplied by the reversal, added to the low in column 1.

Vertical target = (7 x 1 x 3) + 20 = 41

The reward is the vertical target minus the price at the double-top breakout above the blue line, marked A.

Reward = 41 – 28 = 13

The risk is the price at the double-top breakout minus the price at which the first double-bottom sell would appear on the chart if the price went against the trade – below the red line in Figure 4-6, marked B.

Risk 1 = 28 – 22 = 6

Risk-reward ratio 1 = Reward/Risk = 13/6 = 2.17

---

[16] The ratio is called risk-reward, but in fact it is actually reward divided by risk.

This means that the potential reward for every actual point of risk is 2.17 points. Although it is a matter of personal preference, governed by your time horizon, a good risk-reward ratio is around 3 or greater. Short-term traders will accept lower risk-reward ratios that are sufficiently greater than, say, 1.0 to 1.5

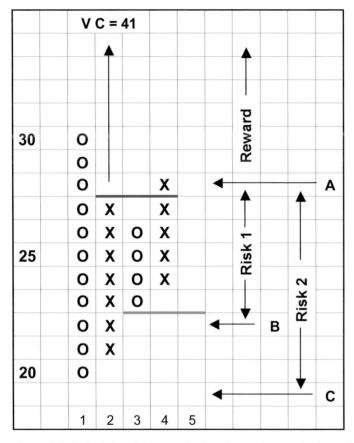

Figure 4-6: Calculating risk-reward ratios from 3-box vertical counts

You can see that the risk is governed by the length of the corrective column of Os (in column 3) after the initial X column off the low (in column 2). The longer the corrective column of Os, the greater the risk of taking the trade at the breakout.

Although the reward is fixed, the risk may be adjusted by looking for support levels lower down in the pattern. Often two or three risk-reward ratios may be calculated from the same count. For example, risk could be established at the box below the lowest O in the pattern, at 19, marked C in the example in Figure 4-6.

The calculation is as follows:

Reward remains the same at 13.

Risk 2 = 28 – 19 = 9

Risk-reward ratio 2 = 13/9 = 1.44

Risk-reward ratio from horizontal counts on 3-box charts

Not as common, and not as easy to calculate, are risk-reward ratios from horizontal counts. The problem with horizontal counts is not the reward but the risk, because the exit from the pattern can be quite complex. Although it is customary to place the stop below the lowest low in the pattern, this results in increased risk levels. It is, therefore, best to study the pattern and determine subjectively where your stop should be placed.

Figure 4-7 is a typical bottom pattern from which a horizontal count may be established.

Risk level 1 is the price at which the first double-bottom sell would appear on the chart if the price went against the trade (below the red line in Figure 4-7, marked B), whereas risk level 2 is the row below the low of the pattern, marked C.

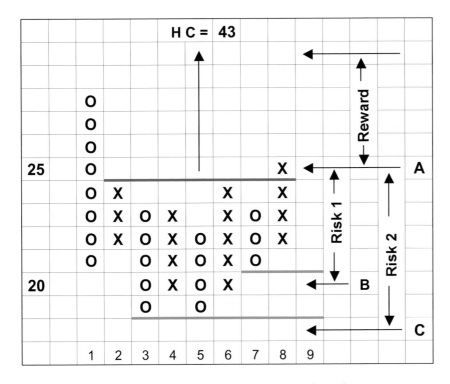

Figure 4-7: Calculating risk-reward ratios from 3-box horizontal counts

The horizontal target = (8 x 1 x 3) + 19 = 43

The breakout row is at 25, marked A.

The reward = 43 - 25 = 18

Risk 1 = 25 – 20 = 5

Risk 2 = 25 – 18 = 7

Risk-reward ratio 1 = 18/5 = 3.60

Risk-reward ratio 2 = 18/7 = 2.57

You therefore have two risk-reward ratios to work with and may allocate your trade accordingly.

Chart 4-19 is a 10 x 3 Point and Figure of Whitbread plc. The horizontal count across the base pattern yields a target of 1320. The level at the breakout is 690. The reward is, therefore, 630 points (1320-690).

There are two possible risk levels. The level for establishing risk 1 is the price at which the first double-bottom sell would appear on the chart if the price went against the trade; at 520 on the chart risk level 2 is the row below the low of the right-hand side of the pattern, at 450. In Chart 4-19 you will notice that there is a lower risk level below the low of the whole pattern at 410; however, the use of risk 2 negates the need for using the risk 3 level, which is why it is not shown. Normally, however, the low of the whole pattern would be the greatest risk level.

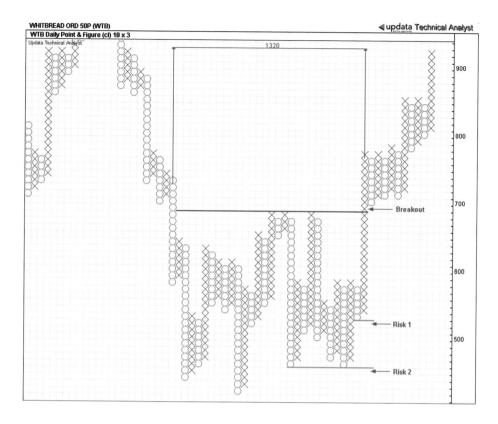

Chart 4-19: 10 x 3 of Whitbread plc showing risk-reward ratios from 3-box horizontal counts

Risk 1 is 690 – 520 = 170

Risk 2 is 690 – 450 = 240

Risk-reward ratio 1 = 630/170 = 3.71

Risk-reward ratio 2 = 630/240 = 2.63

In both cases, the risk-reward ratio is at an acceptable level, making the trade attractive. Remember, however, that it is based on the count. If you are not sensible when establishing the count, your risk-reward ratios will be misleading. Always base the risk-reward ratios on the most conservative count.

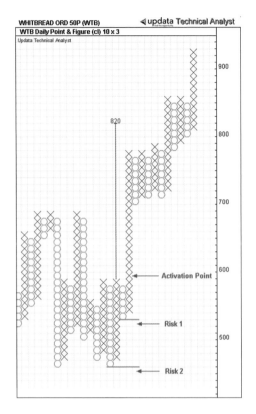

Chart 4-20: 10 x 3 of Whitbread plc showing risk-reward ratios from 3-box vertical counts

Often there is a vertical count from the same pattern. The horizontal target shown in Chart 4-19 was 1320, whereas the vertical target in Chart 4-20 is only 820. The activation point is at 590, making the reward 230 points.

There are two risk levels at 520 and 450 making risk 1, 70 and risk 2, 140.

Risk-reward ratio 1 = 230/70 = 3.29

Risk-reward ratio 2 = 230/140 = 1.64

Risk-reward ratio 1 is confirming the ratios from the horizontal count, but risk-reward ratio 2 is on the low side. This means that a stop below the low of the pattern is unacceptable for a target based on the vertical count only, but, since the horizontal count yields a greater target and hence a more favourable risk-reward ratio, the trade can be considered on the basis of a stop below the low of the pattern.

Risk-reward ratio from horizontal counts on 1-box charts

As you will have realised by now, 1-box charts are more subjective than 3-box charts, so the placement of counts and stops is not as clear-cut and, consequently, risk-reward ratios are more difficult to obtain. However, if you follow some basic rules they are possible.

You will recall that there are a number of ways to conduct a horizontal count. When calculating risk-reward ratios, it is the count across the row which acts as the balancing point of the pattern that is important. This is the row with the most filled in boxes. A break below this level after the pattern has broken out and given a buy signal, is your level of risk. The second level of risk is the row below the low of the pattern. The reward is the horizontal count target minus the value at the breakout of the pattern.

Figure 4-8 is a typical fulcrum pattern from which a horizontal count may be established.

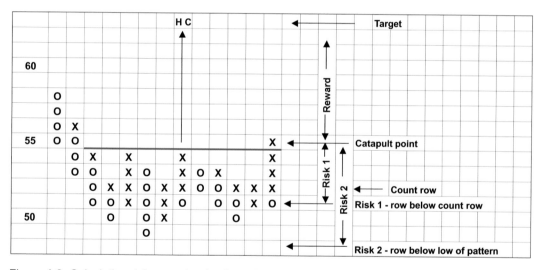

Figure 4-8: Calculating risk-reward ratios from 1-box horizontal counts from fulcrums

The horizontal target across the row with most filled in boxes = $(11 \times 1 \times 1) + 52 = 63$

The catapult point is at 55.

The reward = $63 - 55 = 8$

There are two levels of risk. Risk 1 is the row below the pivot row: the row with most filled in boxes. Risk 2 is the row one box below the low of the whole pattern.

Risk 1 = $55 - 51 = 4$

Risk 2 = $55 - 48 = 7$

Risk-reward ratio 1 = 8/4 = 2.00

Risk-reward ratio 2 = 8/7 = 1.14

Risk-reward ratio 1 is acceptable, but if you intend taking the trade based on a stop below the low of the pattern it is not, based on risk-reward ratio 2. Stops below the low of the pattern in 1-box charts are usually too far away.

Figure 4-9 is a typical 1-box continuation semi-catapult.

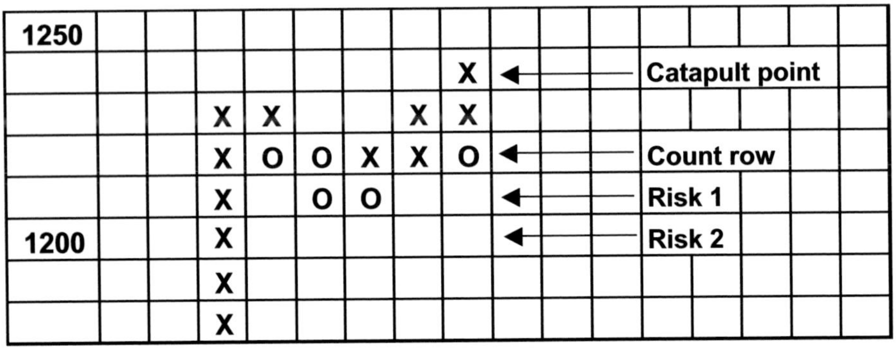

1250																	
								X	◄————	Catapult point							
			X	X			X	X									
			X	O	O	X	X	O	◄————	Count row							
			X		O	O			◄————	Risk 1							
1200			X						◄————	Risk 2							
			X														
			X														

Figure 4-9: Calculating risk-reward ratios from 1-box horizontal counts from semi-catapults

The horizontal target across the row with most filled in boxes = (6 x 10 x 1) + 1220 = 1280

The catapult point is at 1240.

The reward = 1280 – 1240 = 40

Again, there are two levels of risk: one below the pivot row and one below the low of the semi-catapult.

Risk 1 = 1240 – 1210 = 30

Risk 2 = 1240 – 1200 = 40

Risk-reward ratio 1 = 40/30 = 1.33

Risk-reward ratio 2 = 40/40 = 1.00

The risk-reward ratios from semi-catapults are characteristically low, but remember that these are continuation patterns where, unlike reversal fulcrums, the likelihood of a reversal is low. Consequently, a low risk-reward ratio might be considered acceptable. It would not be if the pattern were a reversal pattern.

Chart 4-21 is a 20 x 1 Point and Figure of Whitbread plc. It shows a horizontal count of 1160 out of fulcrum pattern A and 960 from continuation semi-catapult B.

The catapult point of fulcrum A is 700. The reward, is therefore, 460 points (1160-700).

Risk 1 is the row below the counting row at 540 and risk 2 is the row below the low of the pattern at 400, making the two risks 160 and 300, respectively.

Risk-reward ratio 1 = 460/160 = 2.88

Risk-reward ratio 2 = 460/300 = 1.53

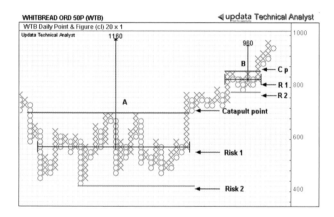

Chart 4-21: 20 x 1 of Whitbread plc showing risk-reward ratios from 1-box horizontal counts

The catapult point of semi-catapult B is 860. The reward is, therefore, 100 points (960-860).

Risk 1 is the row below the counting row at 800 and risk 2 is the row below the low of the pattern at 760, making the two risks 60 and 100, respectively.

Risk-reward ratio 1 = 100/60 = 1.67

Risk-reward ratio 2 = 100/100 = 1.00

Risk-reward ratios on shorts

All the risk-reward ratios shown have assumed long trades. You may establish them in exactly the same way for downside counts and short trades.

Risk-reward ratios in aiding the placement of stops

The placement of stops is vital for good trading, making the calculation of risk-reward ratios useful in determining where to place your stops. Having calculated the various risk-reward ratios from a pattern based on a number of different stop levels, you may then look at the risk-reward ratios achieved and place your stop according to the risk-reward ratio you feel comfortable with.

Finally

Risk-reward ratios are calculated to help you decide whether or not to take the trade. The reward is established from the count, the risk from where you will close the trade, should it go wrong. Once the trade has been entered, however, the ratio itself is no longer of interest. Of course, the count still applies and the risk remains the same until a new stop can be placed at a higher level, but knowing the risk-reward ratio does not affect the way you manage the trade. What is important is that if the decision to trade has been based on a particular risk-reward ratio, then the level of that risk must be the level at which you close a bad trade. It is foolish to assess a trade based on a risk-reward ratio and then ignore the signal to close a trade that goes wrong.

From one target there is one level of reward, but there may be a number of levels of risk. In the examples above, risk-reward ratio 1 is calculated using the risk from the first double-bottom sell signal. You may decide that this will not be your exit point and, if that is the case, you should not use risk-reward ratio 1 to determine your level of risk. Very often, the first double-bottom sell is too close to have your stop. Looking left in the pattern will tell you whether there is a better level lower down to use.

In practice, risk-reward ratios are just a guide, but it is good practice to always calculate them. Many traders will use trailing stops to protect an open position, but very few, it seems, have a reliable method for arriving at the reward, and hence the risk-reward ratio. This is yet another advantage of Point and Figure charts. Of course, risk-reward ratios may be arrived at in a number of ways. You may use the Point and Figure count and combine that with a money management stop rather than a Point and Figure sell signal.

Other ways of projecting targets

Although the Point and Figure counts discussed so far are unique to Point and Figure charting, they are not the only way to project targets. It may seem out of place to have a section on Fibonacci[17] retracements in a chapter on counts but it is not: the two are inextricably linked. Prices often retrace previous moves by key Fibonacci levels and often these levels match the targets from vertical and horizontal counts. The most common Fibonacci retracement levels are 23.6%, 38.2%, 50%, 61.8% and 78.6%.

Fibonacci retracements

Fibonacci retracements are used to establish the possible 'bounce' levels of a correction against a previous trend. A bounce level is the amount of the previous trend – up or down – that is retraced by the price during the correction. They provide possible support or resistance levels, which are calculated on Fibonacci ratios rather than observation of previous congestion areas, although they often coincide with these.

Chart 4-22 is the same 10 x 3 Point and Figure chart of Whitbread plc used earlier. Some of the Fibonacci retracement levels of the trend from A to B are shown. Once the top at B has been made, the vertical height between A and B is divided into the Fibonacci ratios or percentage retracement levels. For example, a retracement back to the level of A is a 100% retracement. The price will not always retrace to every Fibonacci level. The levels are potential target areas – in this case, potential support levels. Notice that the 23.6% retracement level provides the initial support at point C. The 38.2% level provides no support at all and is, therefore, not shown on the chart. Do not assume that every Fibonacci retracement level will provide support, and do not assume that the price will stop exactly at every level. Fibonacci levels are target areas rather that exact target levels. The 50% level provides the strongest support at point D. Notice that this coincides with the previous bottom on the chart to the left. The price tests the 50% retracement level a second time at point E, before rising to point F, level with point B.

After reaching point F, the price falls, finding support again on the 50% retracement level at point G. It eventually falls through this level and finds support on the 78.6% level at point H. Notice that the 61.8% level (not shown) provides no support at all, but the 78.6% level is tested a second time at point I. You will often find that if one Fibonacci level has held, the next will not.

---

[17] Leonardo of Pisa, more commonly known by his nickname, Fibonacci, a 13th century mathematician, discovered a number series, 1, 1, 2, 3, 5, 8 etc., where the next number in the series is the sum of the previous two. What is important about these numbers is that eventually the ratio between any two consecutive numbers is the golden ratio, 0.618. This ratio, as well as many derivations of it, are widely used in Technical Analysis.

Within Chart 4-22 there are smaller trends, which have Fibonacci retracement levels associated with them. The rise from E to F can also be defined by retracements of the fall from B to D and is shown in detail in Chart 4-23; the fall from F to H is defined by retracements of the move from E to F and is shown in detail in Chart 4-24. The incomplete rise from point I is defined by retracements of the move from F to I and is shown in detail in Chart 4-25.

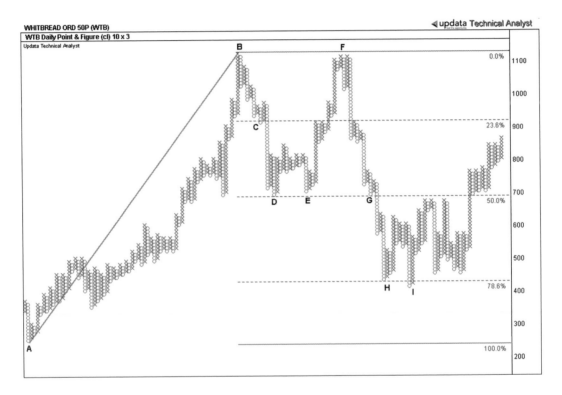

Chart 4-22: 10 x 3 of Whitbread plc showing Fibonacci retracement levels

Chart 4-23 shows the retracements of the trend from B to D. The 23.6% level provides resistance to the uptrend at point a. The price then rises to encounter resistance from the 38.2% level at point b. The 50% level at point c provides the strongest resistance, but the 61.8% also provides enough resistance to cause the price to pause at point d. The price then rises to point F, which is almost 100% retracement of the B to D trend. Notice that, in this case, the 78.6% level (not shown) provided no resistance at all.

Chart 4-23: 10 x 3 of Whitbread plc showing Fibonacci retracement levels

Chart 4-24 shows the retracements of the trend from E to F. The 23.6%, 38.2% and 50% levels provide no support at all. The 61.8% level does however provide support at point e, as does the 100% retracement level at point f. The price then falls to point g, which is a retracement of 161.8%.

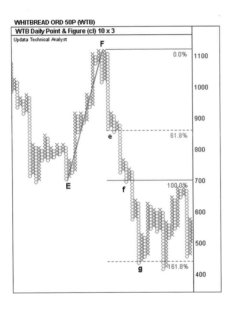

Chart 4-24: 10 x 3 of Whitbread plc showing Fibonacci retracement levels

Chart 4-25 shows the retracements of the trend from F to I. The 23.6% level (not shown) provides no resistance, but the 38.2% does at point a, as does the 50% at point b and 61.8% at point c. Notice that the target of 870 from the vertical count off the low at point I matches the 61.8% level. 78.6% is the next Fibonacci level that has not been reached.

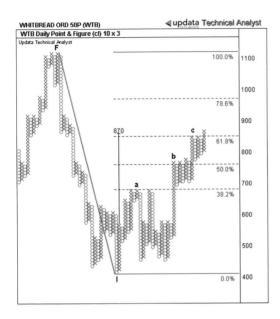

Chart 4-25: 10 x 3 of Whitbread plc showing Fibonacci retracement levels

As with counts, retracement levels are target areas, which may or may not provide support or resistance to the price. It is customary to draw all the levels but then remove those which have had no effect, as has been done in the charts above.

Summary

You have seen the benefits and the pitfalls of counting. You have also seen, how counts help with the general analysis of the chart. It is almost impossible to conduct Point and Figure analysis without establishing counts, just as it is impossible without trend lines. Counts and trend lines go hand in hand and either confirm or contradict one another. Confirmation gives confidence to your analysis. Contradiction casts doubt, which requires further investigation and a search for more evidence.

Counts assist in determining the strength, and the possible decay, of trends. This is because, in bull trends, upside counts are usually exceeded, and, in bear trends, downside counts are usually exceeded. In fact, the degree to which they are exceeded goes some way to explaining the underlying strength of the bull or bear trend. Conversely, in a bull trend downside counts are not usually achieved and in bear trends upside counts are not usually achieved. A downside count which is not achieved during a bull trend reinforces the trend, as does an upside count which is exceeded.

The corollary of this is perhaps more important. In any bull trend, there will always be one upside count that is not achieved. This is normally the last count undertaken in the trend, but does not have to be. A count not being achieved is evidence that a bull trend is coming to an end, but you will not know that this is the case until you see a top pattern taking place. The degree or size of the top pattern is dependent on the size of the trend that precedes it. When an upside count is not achieved, it indicates a decay in the bull trend and provides evidence of an end to the trend.

The same occurs in bear trends. There will always be one downside count that is not achieved, normally the last count conducted in the trend, which gives evidence for the end of the bear trend.

As you have seen, you will often have counts working against one another. You will have the upside count that has not been achieved working against a new downside count, or a downside count that has not been achieved working against a new upside count. Do not concern yourself with this; it is quite normal when a trend is changing. The count that 'wins' defines and reinforces the change in trend. At some stage, however, a count will be negated or cancelled as explained on page 238.

To summarise, therefore:

- Counting yields potential price targets.

- There are two counting methods, vertical and horizontal.

- 1-box reversal charts allow horizontal counts only.

- 3-box reversal charts allow vertical and horizontal counts.

- The horizontal counting method is different on 1-box and 3-box charts.

- 3-box reversal charts are more suited to longer-term counts.

- 1-box reversal counts tend to be shorter-term.

- There can be upside and downside counts working against one another.

- There is no time-scale for the achievement of a count.

- There is no rule as to whether counts are better on close only or high/low charts.

- Vertical upside counts are negated when the price breaks below the bottom of the counting column.

- Vertical downside counts are negated when the price breaks above the top of the counting column.

- Horizontal upside counts are negated when the price breaks down through the low of the pattern.

- Horizontal downside counts are negated when the price breaks up through the high of the pattern.

- In bull trends, upside targets tend to be exceeded and downside counts are not achieved.

- In bear markets, downside targets tend to be exceeded and upside counts are not achieved.

- The achievement or non-achievement of counts gives clues as to the state of the trend.

- Counts should be combined with trend line analysis.

- Counts are approximate and a guideline. The targets given are potential targets.

- The more counts that coincide or cluster at a particular target, the stronger the target is.

- Counts give unambiguous targets. They may not be right but they are unambiguous.

- Counts work well on some charts but not on others.

- Counts reinforce support and resistance levels.

- Don't keep adding new counts to your chart just because you feel bullish or bearish. There is no point in finding a count that yields, say, 865 if the price has not yet achieved an earlier count of 620.

- Counts on log scale Point and Figure charts are also possible. Their calculation leads to them overstating the targets achieved from arithmetic charts.

- Counts, combined with standard Point and Figure sell signals, mean that risk-reward ratios may be determined each time a count is established.

- Fibonacci retracements of a prior trend may also be used to establish targets.

Chapter 5

Analysing Point and Figure Charts

When faced with analysing a Point and Figure chart, there are a number of thought processes you need to go through. This chapter takes you through those processes so that you can make the decisions that affect the look and feel of the Point and Figure chart that you draw, using two stock indices: the NASDAQ Composite Index and the FTSE 100 Index.

Before you draw your Point and Figure chart you must decide what data you intend to use and then what box and reversal size, because this affects the look of the chart and any subsequent analysis. To do this you need to consider a number of things:

- Are you taking a long-, medium- or a short-term view?

- Do you wish to use 1-box, 3-box or any other reversal chart?

- What sort of price moves do you wish to isolate?

- How sensitive do you wish to make the Point and Figure chart?

- Do you wish to expose or hide the instrument's volatility?

- What is the range of the past prices?

- What drawdowns are you prepared to accept before a reversal is indicated?

Even knowing the answers to these questions, an experienced Point and Figure analyst may still not instantly know what to choose and will, therefore, draw a 'tester' chart first. Looking at the tester chart helps you to decide what adjustments to make to show more or less sensitivity.

The reversal size

The first decision you should make is the reversal, that is the number of boxes required to change from a column of Xs to a column of Os or vice versa. Remember, changing the reversal changes the look of the chart completely. Refer to the 10 x 1 and 10 x 3 charts constructed in chapter 2. Remember, also, that the reversal relates to column changes. The smaller the reversal, the more column changes will occur. Increasing the column changes can give you more information but it can also introduce more volatility and noise into the chart.

A medium-term trader – someone who expects to hold for 1 to 6 months – would certainly use a 3-box as well as a 1-box reversal chart. Medium-term traders are concerned with remaining within the trend and not being coaxed out by small countertrend moves, both of which 3-box charts are good for. In fact, 3-box reversal charts are the first port of call for all newcomers to Point and Figure and are highly recommended. That is not to say that a medium-term trader would not use a 1-box chart, some would because they are also useful. In fact, as you will discover, it is wise to look at a number of different Point and Figure charts at the same time. Chart 5-1 shows a 3-box reversal chart of the S&P 500 Index and Chart 5-2 shows a 1-box reversal chart. The letters A-B show the trend since March 2003 for reference.

S&P 500 INDEX (S500)
S500 Daily Point & Figure (cl) 10 x 3
Updata Technical Analyst

Chart 5-1: 10 x 3 of the S&P 500 Index showing a 3-box reversal chart

Notice how the 3-box chart is a condensed version of the 1-box chart. Both charts are however, useful to the medium-term trader. The 1-box chart contains information and patterns that are not visible in the 3-box chart. In fact, essentially, you can regard 1-box and 3-box charts as being two completely different methods of charting. Not only is their construction different, but, as you will see, their interpretation is different as well.

Chart 5-2: 10 x 1 of the S&P 500 Index showing a 1-box reversal chart

What about the short-term trader? The short-term trader will hold until any minor trend change occurs because they tend to be trading on margin and cannot afford to accept drawdowns. The length of the hold period ranges from hours to a few weeks. Short-term traders should always include a 1-box reversal chart as well as a 3-box chart, perhaps even a 2-box chart. The 1-box chart is essential for seeing support and resistance levels, and where most of the price activity is taking place. Ideally, this should be drawn using tick data, where every trade is recorded and plotted. But the short-term trader also needs to know the trend, so 3-box charts, which condense the price movement and give more emphasis to the prevailing trend by the asymmetric filter, are used as well.

The following two charts show the FTSE 100 Index 1 x 1 (Chart 5-3) and 1 x 3 (Chart 5-4) using tick data. The first thing you should notice is that the 1 x 1 chart has many more changes from X to O and O to X. There is nothing wrong with this; in fact, it gives you a lot of information about the trading taking place. The consequence, however, is that the chart shows a fraction of the time period that is shown in the 1 x 3 chart. Actually, this is not strictly true. It is just that because the Xs and Os are a physical size, it is not possible to show them all at one time without making them very small. Chart 5-5 is the same 1 x 1 chart but the Xs and Os have been reduced in size so that all the trading over the period can been seen.

Chart 5-3: 1 x 1 tick chart of the FTSE 100 Index

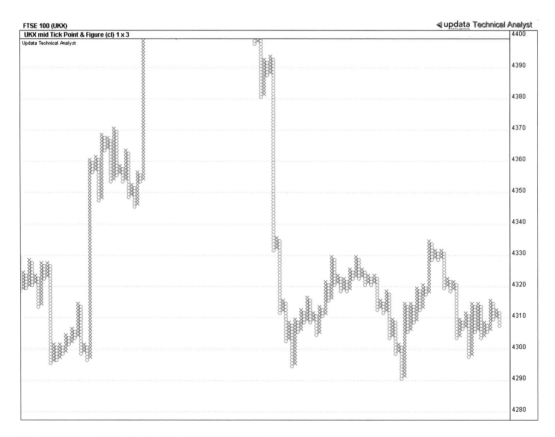

Chart 5-4: 1 x 3 tick chart of the FTSE 100 Index

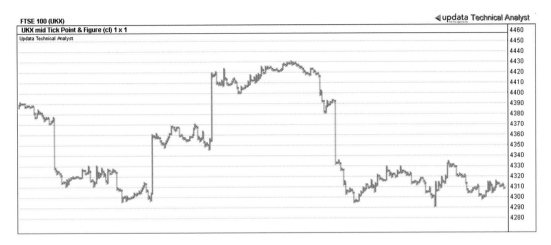

Chart 5-5: 1 x 3 tick chart of the FTSE 100 Index

The important thing is to notice the difference between the 1 x 1 and 1 x 3 charts. Each shows the same range of prices but in a different way. A short-term trader really needs both. If you are a short-term trader and feel uncomfortable with 1-box charts, then 2-box is a good alternative. It is not as sensitive as a 1-box chart and not as coarse as a 3-box chart.

Long-term investors will almost certainly use 3-box reversal charts and may also use 5-box charts to show the long-term trend, although the use of 5-box charts is rare. A long-term investor will never use 1-box charts.

To summarise, therefore, short- and medium-term traders should use both 1-box and 3-box charts. Long-term investors should use 3-box charts, and possibly 5-box. 2-box charts are a good alternative for anyone who does not wish to use 1-box charts. If you are going to use 1-box charts, then you must ensure they are drawn correctly and that they can have both an X and an O in the same column.

Choosing the correct box size

Having decided on the reversal, the next thing to decide on is the box size. Choosing the correct box size is vital for good Point and Figure analysis and it is not as difficult as it sounds. It does need to be logically thought through, although some make it out to be a bigger issue than it is. It requires a complete understanding of what the Point and Figure chart represents and what it is that you are trying to extract from the chart. There are, of course, rules of thumb to do this, but having to rely completely on a rule of thumb demonstrates a lack of understanding as to what the Point and Figure chart is showing you.

To choose the box size, you must again consider your time horizon. This may sound strange when it is known that Point and Figure charts don't take any account of time, but altering the box size increases or decreases the sensitivity of the chart and hence has the effect of altering the time horizon of the chart. You have seen this already with the reversal size. For example, a medium-term trader of the FTSE 100 Index may decide that a 50 point or 25 point box size would be about the right sensitivity, but a day-trader would find them impossible to use. The thinking is as follows:

A 50 x 3 Point and Figure chart (Chart 5-6 opposite) means that every 50 point movement in the direction of the trend is plotted and every reversal of 150 (3 x 50) is plotted. Anything below these values is ignored. With the index at around 4500, that is a reasonable record of the medium trend. Furthermore, a 150 point, or 3% reversal is not an unreasonable amount for a medium-term trader to bear before a column change is signalled. It is, however, totally unacceptable for a short-term trader.

You will learn later that it is best to use at least two, preferably three, different Point and Figure charts when doing your analysis. In drawing more than one, you will see things in one that you may not see in another. Using more than one chart helps to refine your timing. Where the longer-term chart may have generated a buy signal, the shorter-term chart may be signalling a small correction, allowing you to wait for the short-term chart to signal a resumption of the uptrend.

Chart 5-6: 50 x 3 of the FTSE 100 Index

Chart 5-7 is a 25 x 3 chart of the FTSE 100 Index. The uptrend move from point A to B, shown on both charts, demonstrates the difference. In the 50 x 3, the move from A to B has taken place in 6 up legs; in the 25 x 3, it has taken 16. The reason, obviously, is that the 25 x 3 chart plots 25 point moves in the direction of the trend and 75 point moves against the trend.

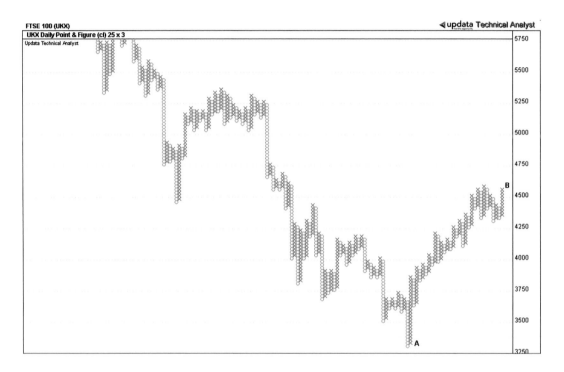

Chart 5-7: 25 x 3 of the FTSE 100 Index

The 25 x 3 chart does give more information than the 50 x 3, but do not assume that you can simply keep reducing the box size to gain more and more information. There will be a point when the chart becomes unreadable. 'Unreadable' is a subjective condition, but the more you use a Point and Figure chart, the easier you will find it.

Chart 5-8 shows a 5 x 3 chart. Points A and B are shown again – the Xs and Os have been reduced in size to show the same area as that in Chart 5-7. You need to look at the chart and decide whether it is showing too much volatility. The test is to look at adjacent columns. If the columns of Xs and Os are long, uninterrupted columns, which they are in the 5 x 3 chart, then the chart is of little use, even if your time horizon demands that you need to be looking at 5 point movements in the direction of the trend and 15 point reversals against the trend. A 5 x 3 of the FTSE 100 Index is far too sensitive for a medium-term trader. No medium-term trader would be interested in 5 point movements in the direction of the trend of the last column and 15 points moves against, but 5 x 3 is most useful to the short-term trader.

Chart 5-8: 5 x 3 of the FTSE 100 Index

You will have noticed that all the above charts are constructed using the end-of-day close price rather than the daily high or low. It is argued that the reason for using high/low charts is that they cater for the trading range, which close only charts ignore. That is true, but that is only of importance if intra-day data is not available. Remember high/low daily charts still take only one price per day, according to a set of rules which determine whether the high or the low should be used. So, in constructing a daily chart with high/low data, you take the high or the low, but not both, and consequently you take no account of whether the price hit the high or the low first. You will also recall that there is a flaw in the construction rules when the high and low produce a new box as well as a reversal, but only one can be used. That is not to say that you should ignore high/low charts. They do add an extra dimension to Point and Figure construction and analysis. Sometimes daily high/low charts will show patterns like the W-shaped bottom (circled) in Chart 5-9 that cannot be seen in daily close only charts, as demonstrated by the circled area in close only 5 x 3 Chart 5-8 and high/low Chart 5-9.

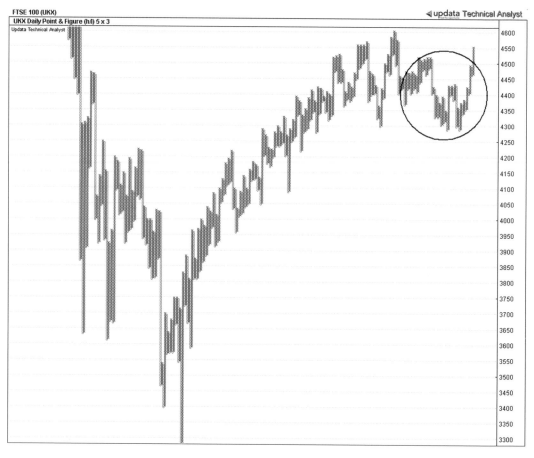

Chart 5-9: 5 x 3 (h/l) of the FTSE 100 Index

What looks like nothing more than a decline and rise in the daily close only Chart 5-8 shows up as a W formation bottom followed by a double-top breakout in Chart 5-9. From this, a horizontal as well as a vertical count may be obtained.

Daily high/low charts are fine if you do not have access to intra-day data; however, if you do, you are far better off drawing your chart using the close price at the end of every hour, instead of the high or low at the end of the day. So there comes a point when the short-term trader can no longer operate on daily data, and a single price per day and a switch to intra-day data is required.

Chart 5-8 and Chart 5-9 are constructed by taking one price per day at the end of the day. Although Chart 5-9 shows more information, it is really just a proxy for using intra-day data. Most importantly, it takes no account of the order in which the high and low occurred, and, in fact, only takes the high or the low – not both. Short-term traders need to know what is going on during the day. They need to know how the instrument has traded, where the intra-day support and resistance levels are and in what order highs and lows were hit, hence the use of intra-day data.

Choosing your data time series

The original Point and Figure charts were constructed using tick data, but, as tick data was difficult to obtain, many Point and Figure chartists started using the price at the end of the day. Data is not limited to tick and end-of-day; there are other time series such as weekly, as well as a number of intra-day interval data series, such as hourly, 15 minute, 5 minute etc., where the price is summarised into hourly, 15 minute or 5 minute high, low and close.

The use of weekly data is unusual, however, even when taking a long-term view. Taking only one price per week to construct your Point and Figure chart leaves out a lot of important information. The purpose of using weekly data is to avoid minor, often false, Point and Figure signals, but if you draw a weekly Point and Figure chart and keep the box size the same, you will get many of the same false signals that are present in the daily Point and Figure chart. You are, therefore, better off increasing the box size of your daily chart than switching to weekly. At least that way, your chart is constructed with five data points per week instead of only one.

Moving to intra-day data where more than one data point is taken per day widens the choice considerably, because not only are you able to choose different box sizes, but also different time series. For example, a 5 x 3 using hourly data allows 8 prices per day to be taken into account in the construction. Using 5 minute data allows 96 price changes to be used. What happens is that charts that were not helpful with daily data become readable again when intra-day intervals are used. The column lengths shorten because the thrusts are not uninterrupted.

The circled area in the daily 5 x 3 Chart 5-9 is shown in the hourly 5 x 3 Chart 5-10. Notice immediately how much more information you obtain from the chart, even more than the daily high/low Chart 5-9. The chart has a good 'look and feel' about it. Where the daily high/low chart showed a double-top breakout, the hourly chart shows a triple-top breakout, which indicates that three attempts, not two, were made at breaking out.

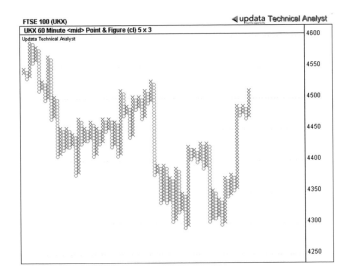

Chart 5-10: 5 x 3 (60 minute) of the FTSE 100 Index

Remember that a close only hourly chart may not pick up the actual high and low of the day, because the price may not close at either of these extremes at the end of each hour. You could, therefore, draw your hourly chart using the end of hour high or low as shown in Chart 5-11. As you can see there is even more detail.

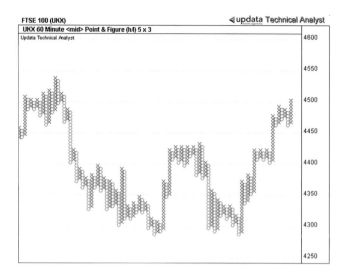

Chart 5-11: 5 x 3 (h/l) (60 minute) of the FTSE 100 Index

You don't have to stop there; a shorter-term view may be obtained by moving to 1 minute and eventually, tick data to extract as much information as you require.

Log scale charts

Don't forget that you may also use a percentage box size, which provides a log scale chart. There is no rule to follow as to whether an arithmetic points box size is better than a logarithmic percentage box size, except to say that log scale provides no benefit when shorter-term charts are being considered. This is because the change in logarithmic box size from one level to the next is not significant.

When using percentage boxes, however, you should always start with 1% for the medium-term, 0.5% for the shorter-term and 2% for the longer-term on daily charts. With intra-day charts, you should start with a 0.1% box size, except tick charts, which should always use an arithmetic box size. This is discussed in more detail below.

Summary

To summarise, therefore, only *you* can decide the data series as well as the box and reversal size you require. Both the box size and the reversal are dependent on what it is you wish to extract from the chart.

- Decide on the reversal first. Short-term traders use 1-box and 3-box reversal charts. Medium-term traders use 3-box, and perhaps 1-box, reversal charts. Long-term investors use 3-box, and perhaps 5-box, reversal charts

- Next is the box size. Decide whether you require log or arithmetic charts. Draw both if you are not sure.

  - If you intend to use an arithmetic scale, start with a box size which is 1% of the latest price. Round up the box size to one of the standard sizes, which are: 1, 2, 3, 5, 10, 15, 20, 25, 50, 100, 250, 500 etc. If you are looking at currencies or low priced shares, you would use 0.5, 0.25 0.2, 0.1, 0.05, 0.025 etc. If you are looking at an instrument that trades in narrow range, then choose 1% of the trading range and round up the box size. The box size for bonds, for example, is best estimated based on the range rather than the last price. In both cases, do not use odd sizes such as 13 or 23, or any number between the standard sizes.

  - If you intend to use a log scale, start with a box size of 1%.

- Draw the chart and study it. Decide whether you are able to extract sufficient information from the chart.

- Always decrease and increase the box size by one or two sizes to see if you get more information or a clearer picture from the changed box size.

- You will nearly always need at least two, perhaps three, different Point and Figure charts to perform the analysis you need. Never assume one is enough.

- As you go shorter-term, so you will need to move to intra-day data.

Analysis of 3-box reversal charts

The purpose of this section is to talk you through the analysis of a 3-box chart example, so you may understand the thought process you need to go through when analysing any instrument using the 3-box method. Although it is similar for medium-term and short-term, an example of both is shown. In fact, what follows is a medium-term analysis, which then goes shorter and shorter-term so you can see how more information is exposed.

The FTSE 100 Index is chosen as the instrument for no other reason than that many watch this index and it has had a number of major trends. What is said below may be applied to any index, stock, commodity, future, currency etc. It is not the fact that it is the FTSE 100 Index that is important, but that it is the analysis of an instrument. The name could easily have been removed from the chart, but has been left to avoid suspicions that the data has been contrived. When following through the analysis, try to do it sequentially; try to place yourself in the position you would be at the time, *without* looking at the subsequent history to the right of your position on the chart. If necessary, place a blank sheet over the chart to hide any information to the right.

It is August 1998. Chart 5-12 is a 50 x 3 close only Point and Figure chart of the FTSE 100 Index at that time. A 50 point box is chosen because it is around 1% of the current price rounded to the next sensible box size.

When faced with a chart like this, the first thing to do always is to 'carve' it up into bullish and bearish sections using 45° bullish support and bearish resistance lines. In fact, there are no bearish lines in this example, but that is not always the case. Trend line 1 is drawn at 45° from the 1987 low. The first thing to notice is how the line was touched twice at points A and B thus reinforcing its strength as the main bullish support line. Notice the look of the chart – the long columns of Xs and short columns of Os. This is typical bull market action. The further away from the 45° support line, the longer the columns of Xs have to be. Notice also, the vertical count of 4000 from the first move off the 1987 low was exceeded and, in fact, the price did not even pause at that target. This is further evidence of a strong bull trend. Remember achieving and exceeding targets is bull trend action. Notice that the count 3200 off the mini-bottom was also exceeded. An internal 45° bullish support line, 2, may then be drawn from the first reaction point above the main 45° bullish support line. This provides additional shorter-term support.

Notice the potential high pole just above point 2. This is an example where the price makes a high pole, but there is no follow-through. Some traders sell on a 50% retracement of the column of Xs by the column of Os. Some wait for a subsequent double-bottom sell. Either way, the double-top buy after the high pole must be taken to either re-open a closed position or add to an existing holding. The price continues to rise with one double-top after another. Each is an 'add to position' signal, which is one of the great advantages of Point and Figure charts. Each time the supply and demand come into equilibrium, re-assessment of the trend takes place and a new double-top buy, in this case, confirms and strengthens the trend.

At point C, the first double-bottom sell signal is issued and a mini-top is made. After the strong trend that preceded it, it would be wise to take some profits on this signal, although it is important to stress that, although the double-top and bottom signals are the basis for 3-box Point and Figure analysis, you should not take every single one, but in this case looking left provides no support.

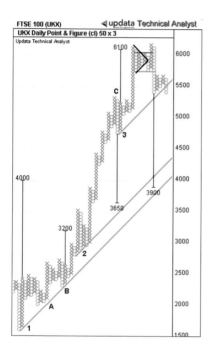

Chart 5-12: 1st chart analysing the 50 x 3 of the FTSE 100 Index

The mini-top at C allows a downside vertical count of 3650 to be established, but notice that, although it was established, the count is never activated – further evidence of bull trend action. The reaction point following this top allows internal 45° trend line 3 to be drawn. At the same time, a new upside vertical count of 6100 can be established and activated from the mini-bottom at point 3. The risk-reward ratio of this count is 3.4, based on a stop at 5000. Calculating the risk-reward ratio helps you to decide where to place your stop.

This 6100 count is achieved almost exactly and some sideways congestion takes place. Notice what happens. The length of columns of Xs and Os start to balance one another out and a small triangle, marked in black, is formed around the 6000 level. If this happens after an uptrend, it indicates that distribution is taking place. Some would say that stock is being transferred from strong holders to weak holders. It could be either a top or a continuation pattern; it is impossible to say which at this stage. Remember, you do not have any information to the right of this pattern at the time. The odds, however, favour a continuation because the price is in a strong uptrend.

However, a double-bottom sell signal is generated from the triangle and although it is not an important sell signal because the price is in such a strong uptrend, it is just as well to weigh up the evidence. There has been the strongest of uptrends; the upside count has been achieved with no other count pointing higher; a triangle has formed which has broken down, but looking left you can see support one box below, which may cause you to hold off selling until that level is broken. This is an example where not every double column signal has to be taken.

What follows is a triple-top buy signal with the price breaking above the blue horizontal line. It is a strong signal and it would be wrong to ignore it, but if you are already holding you may not add to existing but rather simply continue to hold, the reason being that there is no new target to aim for at this stage. It could be the continuation of the bull trend. The price, however, turns back again, pulling back into the pattern and setting up for a possible bullish catapult. That does not happen; instead, a multiple-bottom sell signal is generated, indicating that all long positions should be liquidated even though the price is still above the internal 45° trend line. In fact, what you have seen take place is a typical broadening pattern as discussed on page 147. These often occur at tops, where a continuation of trend buy signal is given which is then reversed.

The price falls and consolidates just above trend line 3. At this stage, you have no idea whether it will continue down or turn around from the support it has found. A downside vertical count of 3900 may now be established from the top, although not yet activated. What follows is an attempt to form a double-top buy which does not materialise; instead, the price registers another double-bottom sell breaking down from an ascending triangle, at the same time breaking internal trend line 3. All medium-term positions should be closed, although the price is still above the main bullish support line 1. With the patterns that preceded the break of the trend line, and a downside count which is over 1000 points away from the current price, there is now no reason to remain long.

The analysis continues using Chart 5-13 on page 292. Once the 45° uptrend line 3 is broken, internal bearish resistance line 4 may be drawn. The price is in a short-term downtrend defined by this line. Notice how the columns of Os are now longer than the columns of Xs, indicating the most significant bear trend action for some time.

What happens next is that the price falls towards 45° trend line 2 and forms a small bottom, and then thrusts back up, touching downtrend line 4. It pulls back and then re-asserts itself, breaking the bearish line 4 at the same time as giving a double-top buy signal. It is an indication to go long again. Notice that the downside count of 3900, which looked possible, has not been achieved – further evidence of a continuing bull market. Remember, achieving and exceeding upside counts, as well as the non-achievement of downside counts, provides evidence of bull market action.

From the upthrust column, a new upside vertical target of 7400 may be established. This is a good example of where you count the second column if the first is very short. In this case, the second column is a chart-changing column. Everything now looks in place for a bull run to 7400. The risk-reward ratio is a very favourable 7.0. To track the progress and provide internal support, 45° trend line 5 may be drawn from the reaction point at the break of trend line 4. Notice how the price rises within a channel contained by trend line 3 providing resistance, and trend line 4, providing support. It would make sense to decide to close some long positions on a breach of this channel. The price does eventually breach the channel at point D, giving a double-bottom sell signal, however all it does is come back to support on long-time established internal 45° trend line 2. At the same time, a new downside count of 4800 may be established from point D.

The price pushes away strongly from trend line 2, cancelling the new downside count, which reaffirms bull trend status, and at the same time giving a new double-bottom buy signal and breaking a small 45° downtrend line (not shown) from point D. It is a signal to go long again. At the same time a new vertical upside count of 8900 may be established. But notice the 8900 count is never activated because the price did not exceed the high of the counting column. For bulls, that is a worrying sign. Here is an upside count which has not been activated, providing some early evidence of bearishness.

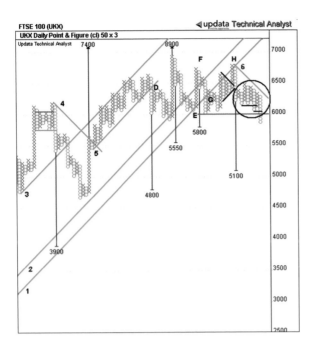

Chart 5-13: 2nd chart analysing the 50 x 3 of the FTSE 100 Index

The price turns, giving a double-bottom sell signal which may be ignored as no trend line has been broken, but then, after bouncing on trend line 2, gives another sell signal while breaking trend line 2, which must now be taken. It finds support on the main bullish support line 1 at point E. A mini-top has also been made and a downside count of 5550 is established and activated. So instead of an upside count being activated, a downside count has been. The date is February 2000. It is the first time that the bullish support line has been tested since 1992. Once again, the price thrusts away from the main bullish support line reinforcing its importance. Once again, a new upside count (not shown) may be established. Once again, the count is not activated.

It is just as well to stop and weigh up the evidence. The price has bounced off the long-term bullish support line, confirming the bull trend is still in place. Two thrusts have produced good vertical counts, but neither has been activated. There is an active downside count of 5550 running against the 7400 upside count. The columns of Xs are no longer dominating; they are beginning to balance out with the columns of Os. Clearly, the price is trading sideways within a range which indicates distribution when the prior trend is up. The bull market is still intact, but, where there was no bearish evidence before, there is some now.

The price rises away from the bullish support line with a double-top buy signal. Once again, you would take out long positions. It makes another mini-top at F, giving another sell signal as well as another downside vertical count of 5800. As a medium-term trader, you have seen two long trades go wrong, which is a worrying sign of a change in the characteristic of the chart.

The price approaches the main bullish support line again and, without pausing, breaks through. There is no double-bottom sell signal on the break, so you would do nothing until the next one, which occurs a few columns later. Even with all the evidence switching from bullish to bearish, it is still possible not to be completely bearish. What may be forming is a large continuation pattern with strong support at the 6000 level – shown by the blue horizontal line – before the ascent to the 7400 target.

It is just as well to make a comment about the 7400 count. There will always be one upside count that will not be achieved during a bull trend, just as there will be at least one downside count in a downtrend that will not be achieved. That is not to say that you know this is one now, but it is always worth remembering it. As a count begins to look less likely – which is the case with the 7400 count now – so you must begin to assume it will be the one count that will not be achieved.

Notice how the price hugs the underneath of the bullish support line 1 as it rises to point H. Although there are double-top buy signals during this phase, you would not take them as the price is below the bullish support line. Notice that as the price rises underneath the bullish support line, it also forms a small bullish continuation triangle, where the move into the triangle equals the move out to point H, where it makes another mini-top. Another downside count of 5100 may be established and activated. Notice how the columns of Os are beginning to dominate, indicating increasing bear trend action.

With bullish support line 1 being conclusively broken, new bearish resistance line 6 may be drawn from point H. The evidence is swinging more towards a bear trend now. Remember, however, it is not all to do with trend lines and counts. You must always look for patterns and one of the most powerful patterns in Point and Figure analysis exists in its inverted form. The circled area shows a bearish or inverted catapult. Anyone still holding longs must certainly close everything once the price makes its second double-bottom breakout of the inverted catapult. Because this occurs below the main downtrend line, you may even start opening short positions. It is now the strongest piece of evidence in favour of the bearish side.

Finally, if you still had any bullishness left at the beginning of March 2001, the price broke down below the 6000 level, below the blue support line. Look at the chart now. Can you see any evidence that the bull trend still exists? Weigh up the evidence for yourself, and if you can still see a bull trend, read on………

Flipping charts

Now is a good time to introduce a technique every Technical Analyst should use. The technique is: when in doubt, flip your charts upside down. If you don't have software that will do it, simply print out the chart, turn it over vertically so the chart is turned upside down and the unprinted side of the paper is facing you. Hold it up to the light and look at the chart through the paper. You will be amazed at what you see. Flipping your chart removes any in-built bias that you have. If you are an eternal bull, it removes your bullish nature; if you always see the bear side, it removes your bearish nature. Although you are consciously aware that the chart is upside down, your sub-conscious does not and forces you to analyse it as if it is what you are seeing.

Chart 5-14 is the FTSE 100 Index flipped upside down. Notice that the advantage of software doing it is that it will change round the columns of Xs and Os as well. Notice the main downtrend line was broken half way through the 'basing' pattern. Notice also the break above the blue resistance line. But, most of all, notice the very bullish catapult buy signal, circled. What you are looking at is a very bullish recovery out of a long downtrend. Would you buy it? Then remember that what you are looking at is a very bullish chart, which is actually upside down and that can only mean one thing. What you are really looking at is a very bearish chart when it is turned the right way up!

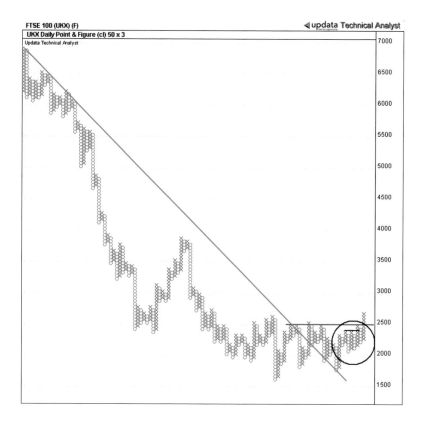

Chart 5-14: Flipped 50 x 3 chart of the FTSE 100 Index

Having decided that your flipped Chart 5-14 looks bullish, you have to see Chart 5-13 as bearish.

The analysis (the right way up) continues with Chart 5-15. The price falls, uninterrupted by any 150 point rally, to point I. In fact, it took nearly a month to do so, giving you more than enough time to close all longs. In the process, it achieved both the 5100 and 5550 downside counts. This is an important point. It is the first time since 1984 that a downside count on the 50 x 3 chart has been achieved. Remember, the achievement of downside counts is more evidence of bear trend action. Not only is the price below the bearish resistance line, but also downside counts are being achieved. It now makes it more likely that the final 7400 upside count will not be achieved, but that can only be confirmed when the price breaks below 4650, the level at which the count was taken.

A new vertical downside count may now be established from the breakaway column, yielding a downside target of 3450. The count is not yet active. A small bottom is made at point I, allowing an upside vertical count of 6400 to be established and activated. The risk-reward ratio for the 6400 count is only 2.2, which is on the low side and may make you suspicious. The double-top buy generated should be used to close any short positions, but under no circumstances should any long positions be taken out as you are below the bearish resistance line. A new tentative 45° uptrend line 7 can be drawn from point I. The line provides you with support for the small uptrend, which, if broken, re-confirms the downtrend.

The price rises from this bottom up to the blue resistance line. The blue resistance line at the 6000 level was initially the support line for the top pattern. Remember how support, once broken, becomes resistance. The price makes four attempts at breaking above this blue resistance level. The last attempt was met by the additional resistance from downtrend line 6. The resistance is now very strong. A break above the resistance line would confirm the resumption of the uptrend. Bulls would have been praying for this to happen here.

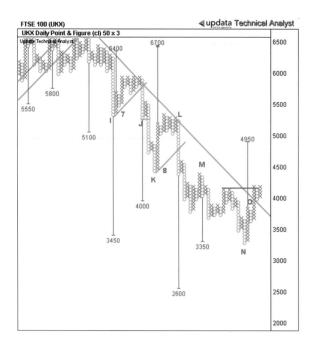

Chart 5-15: 3rd chart analysing the 50 x 3 of the FTSE 100 Index

The price is poised either to give a very strong buy signal if it breaks above the quadruple-top, or to be resisted and continue the downtrend. To break above, all it needs to do is rise by 50 points. The conflict is eventually resolved when internal uptrend line 7 is broken with a double-bottom sell signal, so further short positions may be taken out on the break.

There are a number of things to notice in relation to counts. A new vertical downside count of 4000 is activated. The previous upside count of 6400 is cancelled because the price falls below point I and the downside count of 5100 from the top is achieved. All these add up to confirmation of the bear trend. The additional double-bottom sell at point J reasserts the downtrend and allows additional short positions to be taken out. During this down move another very significant thing occurs; the last active upside count of the bull trend, 7400, is finally cancelled because the price has fallen below the low of the count column. There is nothing bullish left in the chart.

The price makes a bottom at point K and rallies sharply, allowing another vertical upside count of 6700 to be established and activated by the next X column. The double-top buy signal should once again be used to close any shorts. You cannot take long positions below the main bearish resistance line. New tentative 45° uptrend line 8 may be drawn from point K. The price runs into resistance from the downtrend line at point L. A double-top buy signal and a break of the downtrend would signal a new uptrend but it doesn't occur. Instead, the price turns down again and breaks uptrend line 8 and cancels the upside count of 6700, because it falls below the point at which the 6700 count was taken. Another downside count using the break away column may be established, giving 2600 as the target. It is important to pause and think about this target. There are already two active downside counts, of 4000 and 3450. Only once these counts have been achieved can you seriously consider the lower count of 2600.

Count 4000 is achieved as the price falls further and the bear trend strengthens. Notice the long columns of Os and short columns of Xs confirm bear trend action and move the action well away from the main downtrend line. Then what happens is that the price starts to trend sideways. The column lengths start equalling one another. Sideways movement after a downtrend shows accumulation. It may, however, just be profit taking before a continuation of the downtrend, so no action should be taken. The price is still well below the bearish resistance line.

A mini-top is made at point M, allowing another downside vertical target of 3350 to be established. Notice that there are two downside counts targeting 3350 and 3450, indicating that this is what the price is aiming for. Both counts are achieved at point N, leaving one remaining downside count of 2600 outstanding. Remember what was said earlier: there will always be one count at the end of a trend which is not achieved. There is no evidence to suggest that 2600 will be that count at this stage, however.

From point N, the price has a strong rally and a new vertical upside count of 4950 can be established, which is then activated. With the previous history of these vertical upside counts not being achieved, there is little hope that 4950 will be achieved, especially as the price is below the main bearish resistance line and there is a 2600 downside count waiting to be achieved. The price continues to rise, however, and breaks the bearish resistance line at point O which is a significant break but not a valid Point and Figure break. It is, therefore, not a signal to go long, although all shorts should now be closed.

Look left on the chart and note that the price has also broken horizontal resistance offered by the blue resistance line. It then corrects back below the resistance and stops above the downtrend line, before rising again. The pattern is beginning to look interesting. It is a good time to weigh up the evidence.

- The bear trend line has been broken.

- The price has been pushed back down to the break but there is enough demand to push it back up again and is sitting on a possible double-top buy.

- The price has broken through horizontal resistance, been forced back and then broken above it again.

- All downside counts, except 2600, have been achieved.

- The price has spent some time moving sideways in a range after a long downtrend, indicating accumulation.

- There is an upside target of 4950 from the bottom where downside targets were achieved.

The conclusion must be that the evidence is in favour of a new bull trend and all that is required to confirm this, is a double-top buy signal. The price does just that. It gives a double-top buy and breaks above another important resistance line shown in blue. See Chart 5-16 opposite.

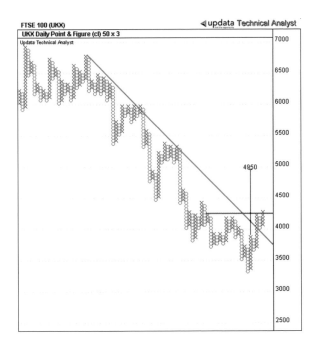

Chart 5-16: 4th chart analysing the 50 x 3 of the FTSE 100 Index

But even with this evidence, you may still feel bearish. You may not be able to see a bottom. You may see it as a pause within a downtrend. If you have a bearish bias, then flipping the chart is the only way to resolve your dilemma. It removes your sub-conscious bias.

Chart 5-17 is the flipped chart. Does it look like it is making a top? If so, then you believe that the price is actually making a bottom. If, however, you think the flipped chart is simply a continuation pattern that will go higher, then you believe that the actual price will go lower. Flipping the chart can really make it so much clearer.

Chart 5-17: Flipped version of chart 5-16

Chart 5-18 shows the chart the right way up again. Now that the main downtrend has been broken, new main 45° uptrend bullish support line 9 may be drawn from the low at point N. This is your new bull trend, remembering that there is still a downside count hanging over you, but remembering as well that there will always be one downside count that will not be achieved. At this stage, you don't really know, but there is no doubt that, for the time being, the trend is up again.

In addition to the main bullish support line, internal 45° trend lines 10 and 11 should be drawn from reaction points to give additional support levels. Notice how trend line 11 provided support to the price at point P.

Notice the structure of the new trend. The columns of Xs are longer than the columns of Os. Columns of Xs are breaking out of double-tops, giving repeat buy signals, but Os are not even reaching the levels of the previous Os, until at point P there is a double-bottom sell signal. It is customary to ignore the first double-bottom sell in any new bull trend as this tends to be caused by profit taking by early adopters of the trend. It is a shakeout of weak holders. However, if you feel comfortable taking the sell, then by all means close any longs at this stage and wait for the next double-top buy signal. The fact that, after the double-bottom sell, the price found support on a trend line and turned back up again confirming the bullish nature of the trend. Then a triple-top buy signal occurs, reasserting the uptrend. Remember a triple-top means that the buyers tried three times to break the sellers' resistance and eventually managed to do so. It is just as well to note that the triple-top pattern took a year to form. Although it takes no part in the analysis, that is a year of frustration for bulls and bears. After breaking the triple-top, the price then went on uninterrupted to achieve and exceed the 4950 target set nearly two years previously. This target was established at a time when few would have believed it possible.

Chart 5-18: 5th chart analysing the 50 x 3 of the FTSE 100 Index

This is the first upside count to be achieved since the 6100 count in 1998. This confirms the new bull trend and lessens the likelihood that the downside target of 2600 will be achieved, although the 2600 count is still valid. Notice that the 4950 target also coincided with horizontal resistance from previous congestion, showing that it is vital to 'look left' when doing your analysis. Additional resistance lines drawn by looking left are also shown in Chart 5-18. You must always be aware that these exist, as it is likely they will provide some resistance that may also coincide with other counts in the future.

Taking a shorter-term view

There comes a time when the chart you are looking at can give no more information until further patterns develop. That is the case with the 50 x 3 chart of the FTSE 100 Index. The last long column of Xs from the mini-bottom will eventually be used to obtain the next upside target, but that can only be done after the price corrects by 150 points or more to generate a column of Os and fix the length of the column of Xs. It is at this stage that you need to reduce the box size to extract more information from the chart by taking a shorter-term view. In fact, a good Point and Figure analyst should have a different box size chart available all the time anyway, because it gives a different time horizon.

Chart 5-19 shows the 25 x 3 chart of the FTSE 100 Index. Work your way through it from the left with the knowledge to have gained from the 50 x 3 chart, drawing trend lines first, then counts. Notice the fulcrum top pattern, marked A, which could have been a continuation of a new uptrend, but turned out to be a top instead. At the time, the pattern looked bullish and short-term long positions could be taken out on the double and triple-top buy signals. You would remain long while the price remained above short-term 45° trend line 1 and above the blue support line. However, longs would be liquidated on the break of the trend line at point B and shorts taken out on the break of the support line at point C. Remember that all the time this was happening, the price was still below the bearish resistance line in the 50 x 3 chart. In the 25 x 3 chart, the trend lines are shorter-term.

New 45° bearish resistance line 2 may now be drawn, confirming the continuation of the downtrend. The fulcrum top allows two counts to be extracted: a horizontal count of 3250 and a vertical count from the breakout column of 3450. Notice how similar these are. Notice too, that the 3450 count matches the 3450 count taken from a completely different place on the 50 x 3 chart. This gives considerable weight to the target area, as so many counts are homing in on it.

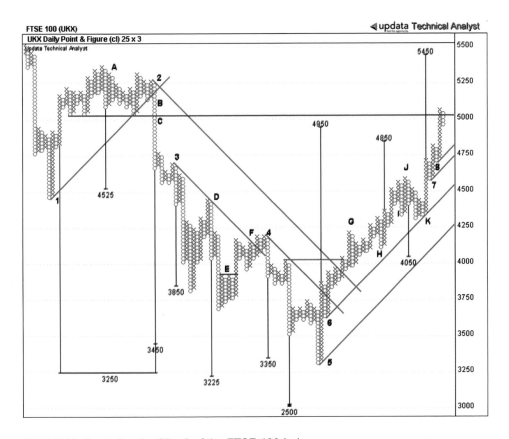

Chart 5-19: Analysing the 25 x 3 of the FTSE 100 Index

A mini-top allows internal downtrend line 3 to be drawn, as well as a new intermediate downside target of 3850 to be established. Notice how that target was achieved within a few columns, confirming the bearish nature. The price rises and bounces off trend line 3 at point D, allowing another downside target of 3225 to be established from the mini-top. There is now overwhelming evidence that the target area is around 3200 to 3400. Targets are not exact; they give you a rough idea of how far the price will go.

The triple-top buy at point E indicates that shorts should be closed. Remember the rules suggested when trend lines were discussed: because the triple-top buy occurs below downtrend lines, long positions should not be taken out. The price breaks through trend line 3 at point F. Depending on your time horizon, you may take long positions on this break, noting that the price is still below the main downtrend line 2. If you are in any doubt about what to do, you should look at a more sensitive chart. The price does not follow-through; instead, it creates yet another mini-top, yielding a downside count of 3350. If the message hasn't got through yet, it should now, because another count comes within the 3200 to 3400 target area. It would now be wise to ignore any signals to go long until these downside targets have been achieved or a main downtrend line has been broken.

Another mini-top yields a target of 2500. Note that this is only 100 points from the 2600 target hanging over the 50 x 3 chart, which was taken from a completely different part of the chart.

Eventually, the predicted target area of 3200 to 3400 is reached and the sharp rise from it – the longest column of Xs on the chart – breaks trend line 4 and the main downtrend line 2 a few columns later, allowing new bullish support line 5 to be drawn. All short positions should now be closed and long positions taken out, because there is a sequence of double-top buys before and after the break of downtrend line 2. At the same time, a new vertical count of 4950 can be established. Internal trend line 6 may be drawn at the reaction point as well. Notice how it provided support at point K. Notice, too, that the price is now above the point at which the 2500 downside count was taken – shown by the red horizontal line – thus cancelling the count. On the 25 x 3, there are no unfulfilled downside counts – a significant point. Notice the mini-top at point G, allowed the establishment of a downside count (not shown), which was never activated. All these occurrences contribute to a bullish viewpoint.

As the trend matures, new double-top buys are generated, allowing new long positions to be taken out. Eventually, a double-bottom sell is generated at point H, but, because this is the first of the new bull trend, it can be ignored unless it matures and breaks trend line 6. What does occur is a mini-bottom allowing an intermediate upside vertical count of 4850 to be established and activated. The uptrend continues and a second double-bottom sell occurs at point I. It is a minor sell because it is above an internal trend line; however short-term traders may wish to take profits and wait to see what happens. What does happen is another double-top buy at point J, which does not follow-through and which yields a loss when closed on stop at the double-bottom sell. A mini-top is created, yielding a downside target of 4050.

It is just as well to note here that whereas many believe you should take every double-top buy, and every double-bottom sell signal, it is not the case. A certain amount of subjectivity is required by considering two things. Always look left to see if there is additional support or resistance, which makes the double signal weak, and always consider the position of the signal in relation to the 45° trend lines.

The price falls from the mini-top at point J to support on trend line 6 at point K, where it makes a mini-bottom yielding a new upside target of 5450. At the same time, the downside count of 4050 is negated, adding more weight to the bullish evidence.

So, that is the position at the time of writing. The first vertical count off the bottom has been achieved, with the next target at 5450. It is not possible to say whether that target will be achieved, but if the price does get into that area, it will also face resistance from the horizontal resistance line at 5350, shown on the 50 x 3 Chart 5-18. At the present time, the current trend is up. New internal trend lines 7 and 8 will give you indications of any deterioration in that trend. The price has reversed by 4 boxes, or 100 points, which is to be expected after such a steep uptrend.

The advantage of Point and Figure, however, is that you can continue to 'drill down', exposing more information by reducing the box size. Remember, you are still looking at the same set of daily data.

Chart 5-20 is now a 10 x 3 of the FTSE 100 Index, exposing more information about the recent uptrend.

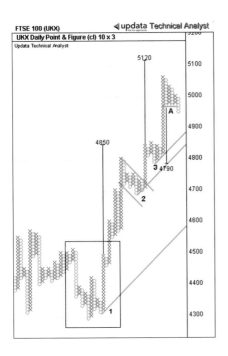

Chart 5-20: Analysing the 10 x 3 of the FTSE 100 Index

Notice how accurately the 4850 count was achieved and how the price paused afterwards, indicating profit taking. The next target from the 10 x 3 chart is 5120. Internal 45° trend lines 2 and 3 may be drawn to show additional support in the uptrend. Notice the bearish pattern reversed – or flag – prior to the bottom at point 2. The first double-bottom sell within this pattern would be ignored because it is the first in the trend; the second would, however, be taken. The double-top buy signal emerging from bearish pattern reversed (flag) is an important signal and should be taken.

It is likely that the double-bottom signal at point 3 would be ignored and instead notice taken of trend line 2. The final triple-bottom sell signal at point A is a signal to stop buying and take short-term profits. If the bull trend is in place, then the downside target of 4790 will not be achieved. To achieve it, both internal lines 2 and 3 will have to be broken.

If you are a medium-term bull waiting to take out long positions, then you will be watching the shorter-term Point and Figure chart, perhaps this 10 x 3 chart, for the next buy signal. At the moment, it is telling you to hold off. Short-term charts like this can really help longer-term investors with their timing.

Changing time-frames

The analysis does not have to stop here. As stated earlier, you may continue to shorten your time horizon by reducing the box size on your daily charts, but there will come a time when switching to intra-day data exposes even more information.

Chart 5-21 is a 5 x 3 Point and Figure chart using hourly data, that is the close price at the end of every hour, thereby using 8 prices per day to construct the chart. This is a short-term chart, but you treat it just like any other chart. The analysis is the same, no matter what data the chart uses. The bull and bear trends are simply mini bull and bear trends within larger bull and bear trends.

The chart shows the section outlined in Chart 5-20 above but much more clearly. Notice 45° trend line 1 being broken by the breakout out column from the W pattern, indicating a new mini bull trend and allowing 45° trend line 2 to be drawn. The W pattern has clear entry and exit walls, so a horizontal count may be established, yielding a target of 4710. In addition, two vertical counts may be taken from the two bottoms, yielding 4680 and 4520.

Internal 45° trend line 3 may be drawn as well. The price rises and forms a triple-top pattern where there is a double-bottom sell, which, being the first in the new trend, can be ignored.

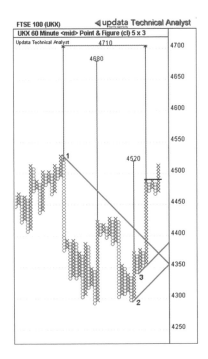

Chart 5-21: 1st chart analysing the 5 x 3 hourly chart of the FTSE 100 Index

Chart 5-22 shows the price continuing to rise and to achieve and exceed the 4520 target. Another internal trend line 4 may be drawn from the mini-bottom and a new vertical count taken on the first move off the mini-bottom, yielding 4765. Notice the bullish catapult at point A.

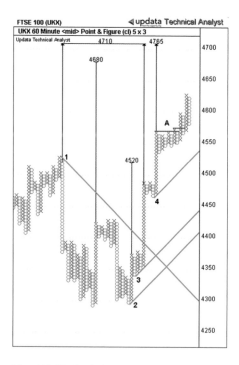

Chart 5-22: 2nd chart analysing the 5 x 3 hourly chart of the FTSE 100 Index

The price continues to rise and thrusts a new column of Xs above the price action, followed by an adjacent column of Os. This could be a high pole in the making. Either you close longs during the 50% retracement by the column of Os, or you wait for a double-bottom sell signal to occur.

Chart 5-23 shows the chart to the end of the data at the time of writing. You should try to analyse it sequentially, without looking right. The first thing to notice is that the double-bottom sell does occur and the high pole completes. The price falls and sets up a low pole that stops short of trend line 4. The occurrence of a high pole followed immediately by a low pole is bullish, and the first double-top buy signal after the low pole must be taken. Another vertical count of 4720 may be taken off the low pole. There are now three counts targeting the 4680 to 4720 area. When this happens, you must take note that the area is significant.

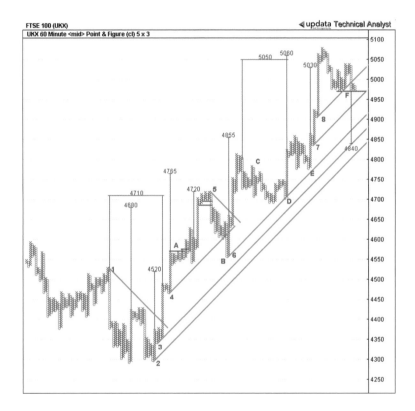

Chart 5-23: 3rd chart analysing the 5 x 3 hourly chart of the FTSE 100 Index

A small top forms in the 4720 target area at point 5. There is a triple-bottom sell signal, but looking left shows there is still support one row below, so it is advisable to ignore the triple-bottom. However, the price falls through the second support line and the top pattern is complete, giving a short-term sell signal, albeit above the internal bullish trend lines. If a target is hit and a sell signal occurs, it is advisable for a short-term trader to take profits and wait for the next clear entry signal. Remember, once you have decided to act, you must wait for a standard Point and Figure signal before doing so.

45° downtrend line 5 may now be drawn from the top. The price falls and breaks internal trend line 4, forming a low pole at point B, which yields a new upside count of 4855. The count is activated and breaks up through downtrend line 5, signalling you to go long. At this point, new internal 45° uptrend line 6 may be drawn.

In the area marked C, the price trends sideways, indicating distribution. There are no clear-cut signals. The price continues sideways and finds support at point D on internal 45° line 6. The thrust away from that support is bullish and confirms the strength of trend line 6. Two counts can be established from the pattern marked C: a horizontal count of 5050 and a vertical count of 5060. Notice how close these two targets are. Often a vertical and horizontal target from the same pattern will coincide, meaning the pattern is square; the length of the thrust column off the bottom is the same as the number of columns in the pattern.

Once again, the price comes close to trend line 6 at point E before rising sharply again and generating another vertical count of 5030. You now have three counts within 30 points of each other, indicating that the area 5030 to 5060 is an important target area and any sign of a top there, such as a double-bottom sell, should be taken as a signal to close long positions.

When there is a vertical rise like this, additional internal 45° lines become important for support and are shown as lines 7 and 8. The position at the end of the data is that the target area has been reached. Some short-term traders would close longs on that basis alone, others will wait for a clear sell signal that would be a break of trend line 8. Trend line 8 does indeed break and the price finds support on the blue support line F. A break below the support points to a possible target of 4850.

It is possible to take your analysis even shorter-term by reducing the intra-day time-frame of the data. Chart 5-24 is a 5 x 3 using tick data, which is the traditional and best way to draw Point and Figure charts. The chart is constructed using every price in the order it is received during the day. It is ideal for short-term analysis and should be used wherever possible, as it shows the intra-day support and resistance better than any other Point and Figure chart. When 1-box reversal analysis is discussed below, you will see the value of using 1 x 1 tick charts.

If you are unable to obtain tick data, then a chart constructed with 1 minute high/low data will suffice.

Chart 5-24 starts in the immediate area of point E in Chart 5-23. Comparing the two charts, you can see how much more detail there is in Chart 5-24.

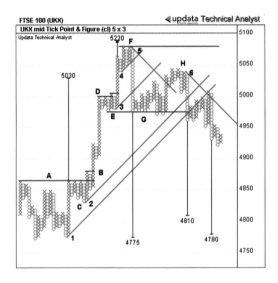

Chart 5-24: Analysing the 5 x 3 tick chart of the FTSE 100 Index

There is a clear W formation bottom with resistance shown by the blue line marked A. The price hits the resistance, forming a quadruple top, which eventually breaks out and pulls back into the pattern, setting up for a bullish catapult. Remember that this means at least a triple-top breakout by a few boxes, a pullback into the pattern and a subsequent breakout. The catapult is confirmed by the subsequent double-top buy signal at point B. Although all patterns can fail, and the catapult is no exception, it is a strong signal to buy and should not be ignored. There is a vertical count of 5030 from the first move off the bottom. New internal 45° trend line 2 may also be drawn from the low of the catapult at point C. The price rises strongly and forms another bullish catapult at point D. Note that, while doing this, a double-bottom sell is given. It is a signal to take some profits but not to liquidate your whole position or to go short against the prevailing trend.

The catapult does in fact break out, allowing another vertical count of 5220 to be established. The previous vertical target of 5030 is reached and exceeded, confirming the bull trend. New internal 45° trend line 3 may be drawn from the low of the catapult at point E. This is now your support level.

The price continues to be bullish up to point F, when it turns down, breaking a small internal trend line 4, at the same time giving a double-bottom sell signal. It then breaks internal trend line 3. New 45° downtrend line 5 may be drawn from the top. The price falls to point G, finding support from the line running below the catapult pattern to the left. At the same time, the 5220 vertical count, set just above this level, is cancelled and a new downside count of 4775 is established.

The price rises to break the small downtrend line 5. The break is followed by a double-top buy signal. If you take this signal you must be aware of the resistance from the horizontal line from point F. The rally runs out of steam and the price turns down again, allowing new 45° downtrend line 6 to be drawn from point H and a new vertical downside count of 4810 to be established. Notice how the lengths of the columns of Xs and Os are changing to a more bearish nature. The fall from point H breaks two 45° uptrend lines, including the main one from the bottom. It then rises up underneath the uptrend line 1 to encounter resistance from the small bearish resistance line 6 before forming a top, yielding a new downside target of 4780. This is the position at the time of writing.

That is the end of the 3-box analysis. Some of the main points will be summarised at the end of this chapter. What you must remember when 'drilling down', is that although you are looking at shorter and shorter-term charts, particularly when you switch to intra-day data, you must not forget your own personal time horizon. If you are a medium-term trader and are looking at a tick or other short-term chart, you are doing so to give yourself more information about your medium-term trades, not to make you trade short-term. Medium-term traders can, and should, use tick or at least 1 minute charts to help to fine-tune their timing.

Analysis using 1-box reversal charts

The analysis of 1-box reversal charts is different from 3-box charts in a number of aspects. The first is that 45° trend lines have little validity, so most trend lines are drawn subjectively. The second is that, as you have read earlier, the double-top and bottom signals in the 3-box sense have no validity. You are looking instead for semi-catapults as continuation patterns, and catapults from fulcrums as reversal patterns. Vertical counts are not possible either, and horizontal counts tend to give a shorter-term view. So why use 1-box charts at all?

1-box charts really tell you much more about what is going on. You will, however, have to practise with 1-box charts to familiarise yourself with them. 1-box charts are not a substitute for 3-box charts – they complement them. Early adopters of the Point and Figure method used 1-box charts as well as 3-box charts. The 3-box charts gave them the longer-term view, but that does not mean you cannot use 1-box charts for medium- to long-term analysis. Once again, try to follow the process sequentially. If necessary, cover up the right-hand side of the chart.

Chart 5-25 shows a log scale 2% x 1 chart of the NASDAQ Composite Index. Once again, it is not the choice of the instrument that is important; any instrument could have been chosen, as the analysis is the same. A log scale chart is chosen to show you that the analysis of log scale charts is the same as arithmetic charts. It is customary with medium-term 1-box charts to start with a box size larger than you would have used on a 3-box chart, hence the 2% box size. This means every box change with, or against, the trend is 2%.

The first thing you will notice is that the chart is constructed using the traditional Point method of Xs only rather than Xs and Os. Although this was mentioned earlier, it has not been used until now, because knowing whether a box had an X or an O was important for your understanding of construction and pattern analysis. The preferred way to analyse a 1-box reversal chart, is however, with Xs only because it is not important to know whether a box has an O or an X. It may not seem to be the case now, but the removal of the Os does make the chart easier to read. There is also no reason to identify them with colour, which is why black Xs have been used. Drawing 1-box charts on a squared grid helps analysis too. Finally, for convention and ease of articulation, all trend lines are drawn in red, all horizontal resistance lines indicating breakouts or potential breakouts from catapults and semi-catapults are drawn in blue and all horizontal support lines are drawn in red. Signals to buy and sell come from ordinary breaks of trend lines as well as breaks from catapults and semi-catapults.

The chart starts with the November 1990 low. You must analyse the chart from the left sequentially, referring to the text as you do, otherwise you will not understand why certain lines have been drawn.

During the rise from the low, notice the one-step-back as well as the semi-catapult continuation buy signal marked A. Notice the upward sloping bottom in the semi-catapult, showing bullish tendency. Once the semi-catapult completes by breaking out, you may draw your first trend line, 1, touching the base of the semi-catapult. The price continues to rise to point E, where it falls back to trend line 1, and breaks it. Uptrend lines are broken because the speed of the price rise has slowed and the price is moving sideways rather than up. In 1-box terms, it is a signal to close longs. What happens next is what helps you decide whether to open shorts. The price continues down, making new lows, but only a break below red support line B would complete a small fulcrum top and signal an opportunity to open shorts. However, notice support line B1 below. The presence of this indicates that you should be cautious when opening shorts. The price breaks B but not B1; instead, it continues to trade sideways. Notice the short columns containing 2 boxes. This is distribution and profit taking place. Once that has completed, only the presence of strong new buyers can make it rise. Look to see where most of the price action is taking place as this can give you a clue as to the next move out of the pattern. In this case, the pivot or balancing row of the pattern, where the most Xs occur, is near the low. This is the level where you would take the horizontal count. Remember that all 1-box reversal counts can be up, as well as down counts. You would normally establish both if you are unsure of the direction at the time. From now on, however, only the activated one will be drawn to avoid cluttering the chart.

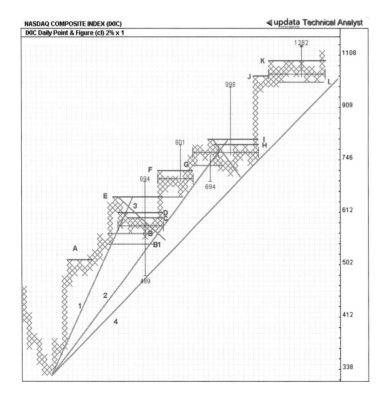

Chart 5-25: 1st chart analysing the 2% x 1 of the NASDAQ Composite Index

There are three possible catapult points out of the fulcrum pattern to the upside, marked with three blue resistance lines, C, D and E. The first buy signal comes from the break of C. It is a weak signal because you will be aware of line D as well, but short-term traders can start taking long positions on breaks of these lines, with stops below the pivot row of the pattern. Once the price breaks C, the horizontal count of 694 becomes active and new uptrend line 2 may be drawn to the right side low of the pattern. The price reaches the 694 target and starts to trade sideways again. Once again, this is distribution caused by profit taking. It finds support on previous resistance line E, as is often the case as the price 'climbs the steps', and on trend line 2 which is a bullish sign. The next semi-catapult point is resistance line F, with a horizontal target taken at the row with the most Xs of 801.

The 801 target is reached and again there is some sideways congestion, eventually breaking trend line 2. This is a sell signal to close longs. What then forms is a small inverted fulcrum that completes with the break below the red line marked G. This is a signal to open shorts, because not only has the main uptrend line 2 been broken, but also there has been a catapult sell signal. However, because the downside target is 694, only 2 boxes, or 4%, below where you open the short, you may decide not to take the trade. Furthermore, your stop would have to be either one row above the count row or above the pattern high, resistance line I, which is 6 boxes, or 12%, above your open level, making the risk-reward ratio most unfavourable. Whatever you decide, the price is in a downtrend, shown by the new downtrend line.

The price continues down and makes a low, but then immediately runs back up again breaking the downtrend line, and encounters resistance from horizontal line H. The position is now neutral. There are sellers at line H, but there is no level that can be called the buying level at this stage. Notice, however, that when the price falls again, it does not get down to the previous lows. This means buyers have moved up their buying level and is typical bullish fulcrum action; the right side of the pattern is upward sloping. The catapult point for the fulcrum is line I; however, a break of line H may be used to open early long positions.

The price breaks both line I and line H, enabling you to establish a horizontal count of 998 across the row with the most Xs. Notice that this is not actually the longest row in the pattern. At the same time, new uptrend line 4 may be drawn from the low, touching the right-hand side of the bullish fulcrum. The price then runs uninterrupted up to the target of 998. This means that at no time did it retrace by 2% or more. Notice that, as the target is reached, there is sideways activity as profits are taken and distribution takes place. A small semi-catapult at J then takes the price higher. In fact, the target out of the semi-catapult (not shown) takes the price to point K. After a move of this magnitude, profit taking is to be expected and so the price trades sideways again as stock is passed from old holders to new holders. Once again, you must look for clues as to where the weakness is in the pattern and where the pivot or pattern anchor point is. The pattern is only four boxes high, locked between support line L and resistance line K. The pivot of the pattern switches between rows 2 and 3, giving no clues at all, but then the price breaks through the resistance at line K, allowing another upside count of 1282 to be established.

Look left on the chart. It is very bullish. There have been three uptrends and only two small downtrends that lasted only a few columns.

The analysis continues with Chart 5-26. The price pulls back after the break and hits the 1282 target in a one column thrust. It then retraces the rise without giving any signal. It trades sideways at the lower level, eventually finding support on uptrend line 4, from which it rises again. Resistance line M is the semi-catapult point for the next move. You are still long waiting for new entry points. Because there have been no breaks of any uptrend, there have been no sell signals. The price breaks resistance line M and pulls back below it again, finding further support on uptrend line 4. Another semi-catapult line may be drawn at point N. When the price breaks this, a new horizontal count may be established from the pattern beneath it across the row with the most Xs. This yields a target of 1572. Once again, the target is hit and exceeded by a few boxes, confirming the strength of the uptrend. Further sideways action sees the price set up for another semi-catapult at resistance line O.

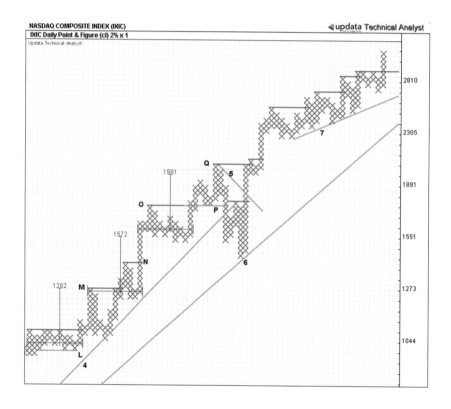

Chart 5-26: 2nd chart analysing the 2% x 1 of the NASDAQ Composite Index

When it does break above line O, another horizontal count may be established, yielding a target of 1981. Again, the target is exceeded. The price then forms an inverted fulcrum, breaking down through catapult point P as well as breaking uptrend line 4, a well-established and last remaining uptrend line at the time. All longs should, therefore, be closed and shorts taken out. At the same time a new downtrend line 5 may be drawn. The price falls by 10 boxes from the catapult line, then rallies with a catapult and breaks the downtrend line 5. Shorts must be closed – probably for a loss. Longs will only be taken out on the break of line Q. New uptrend line 6 may now be drawn from the bottom to the recent low.

After breaking above line Q, the price continues to rise in steps, forming a number of small semi-catapults shown by the blue unlabelled resistance lines. Notice that a new angle trend is emerging, allowing you to place another trend line, 7, on your chart.

The action carries on in Chart 5-27. After breaking through semi-catapult R, the price runs up strongly making another semi-catapult at S. The base of this catapult allows a sharper uptrend line 8 to be drawn, reflecting a change in trend angle. Although horizontal counts are not shown, they have all been exceeded, confirming very strong bull trend action. The price hits a high at point T, but then makes a small inverted fulcrum with the catapult point at U, coinciding with a break of trend line 8. Longs should be closed but shorts should not be taken out because the price is still subject to the main uptrend line 6. A downside target of 4289 may, however, be established from the inverted fulcrum which takes the price down to a continuation semi-catapult at point V. A tentative sharp downtrend line, 9, may be drawn, touching the right side of the semi-catapult once it completes.

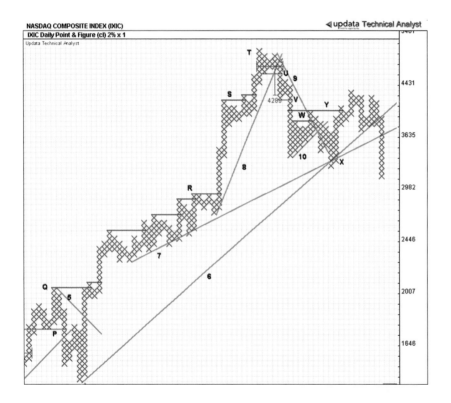

Chart 5-27: 3rd chart analysing the 2% x 1 of the NASDAQ Composite Index

A bullish fulcrum with a catapult point at W forms beneath the downtrend line 9. Although names are not important, it is called a recoil fulcrum, which tends to occur after a steep fall in price. It is a strong pattern and once the breakout occurs it should not be ignored, especially as the downtrend line is broken at the same time. When a fulcrum has a clear pattern of rising bottoms on the exit, new uptrend line 10 must be drawn. In this case, the recoil fulcrum fails to prove any strength and the price falls below trend line 10 stopping you out, but you can learn from this; a pattern that usually works has failed. It is worth keeping that in mind when assessing the overall picture.

The price falls back, finding support on main uptrend line 6 and internal line 7. You are now looking for another catapult point to give you an entry signal. Line Y provides the signal to go long again. Again, the pattern doesn't yield much and the price falls back, bouncing on and then breaking the main bullish trend line 6. The whole picture is changing. There are now two bullish fulcrum patterns that have failed and yielded losses.

The time has come to view the bigger picture. Chart 5-28 shows the progress since the 1990 low. Look at it carefully.

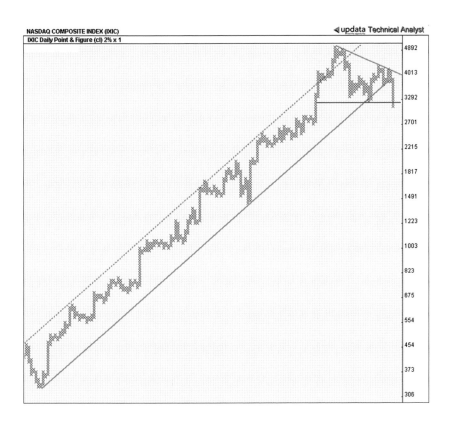

Chart 5-28: NASDAQ Composite Index from 1990 to 2000

Notice the clear uptrend channel. Notice how the price breaks out of the upper resistance, but then breaks back inside the channel. Notice the second top being made which is lower than the first. Can you see the large inverted fulcrum with the catapult point at the blue horizontal line? It is a textbook example of a fulcrum top. Notice how the top of the pattern slopes down showing sellers coming in at lower and lower levels. Can you see anything bullish in the chart? If you can, it means you have a bullish bias – the most common affliction that traders suffer from in a long bull run.

You already know the cure, it was discussed on page 294. When in doubt, flip your chart upside down. Chart 5-29 shows the same chart turned upside down. Does it look bullish or bearish to you? Can you see the break of the downtrend as well as the classic fulcrum bottom formation and the break above the catapult point at the blue line? There is no doubt you would see this as the beginning of a new uptrend and would want to buy the index. If that is the case, then you are seeing an important top being made on the normal chart. It cannot be stressed enough. Flipping your charts upside down exposes you to a whole new dimension of analysis.

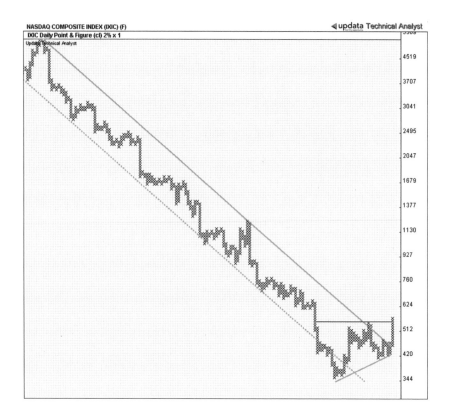

Chart 5-29: NASDAQ Composite Index from 1990 to 2000 flipped upside down

The analysis continues with Chart 5-30. The break below the catapult point of the fulcrum is a signal to open short positions because this occurred below the main uptrend line. New downtrend line 11 may now be drawn touching the right-hand side of the inverse fulcrum. At the same time, a horizontal downside count of 2049 may be established from the fulcrum across the row with the most Xs, which also happens to be the row at the top of the breakout column. Notice how the price pulls back up again after the break in a small potential bullish recoil fulcrum pattern marked (a), but does not break above its catapult point to activate it. Instead, it continues lower, forming a number of inverted semi-catapults reinforcing the downtrend. A small bullish fulcrum at point (b) signals you to close shorts and wait for the next indication. Remember, you cannot open longs below the downtrend line 11.

The price turns down again signalling another opportunity to open shorts when the semi-catapult marked (c) is activated. Although not shown, horizontal downside counts from each semi-catapult are exceeded. The price then forms another small bullish fulcrum at (d), signalling the closure of shorts again. This does not lead anywhere either and the price continues down, forming a larger inverted fulcrum/semi-catapult at (e) which yields a horizontal downside target of 2053. The top of this pattern allows new internal downtrend lines 12 and 13 to be drawn. The price continues lower and eventually forms another small bullish fulcrum below line 13. Shorts must again be closed, but no longs must be opened. The price breaks above trend line 12 at point (f), but longs should still not be opened because you are still below the main bearish downtrend line 11.

A large inverted fulcrum forms with its catapult point at (g), which, when broken, is a signal to open shorts again. A horizontal downside target of 1526 may be established from the row at the top of the breakout column and new downtrend line 14 may be drawn, touching the right-hand side of the fulcrum.

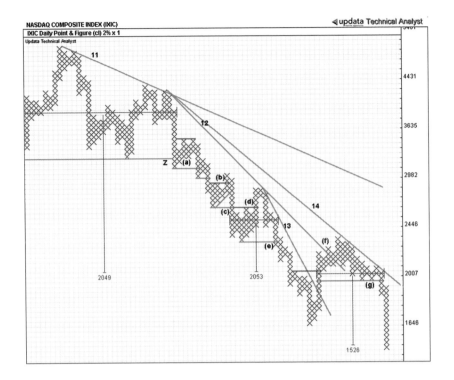

Chart 5-30: 4th chart analysing the 2% x 1 of the NASDAQ Composite Index

The analysis continues with Chart 5-31. The 1526 target is achieved and the price rallies strongly, breaking through internal trend line 14, but meets resistance at the blue horizontal line from where it forms another inverted fulcrum with catapult point at (h). Trend line 15, drawn from the same origin as trend line 14, becomes the new internal downtrend line. Notice, however, that although the price is falling and rallying, the bearish pattern of lower highs and lower lows is maintained. Notice also that there is no accumulation taking place. This occurs when, after a down move, the price trades sideways. That is not yet happening. The only sideways trading that is occurring is after the sharp uptrends, which indicates distribution.

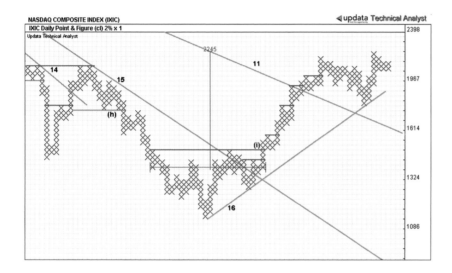

Chart 5-31: 5th chart analysing the 2% x 1 of the NASDAQ Composite Index

Notice that something starts to change in the chart. Downtrend line 15 is not broken by a sharp rally; instead it is broken after some considerable sideways congestion which begins to form a bullish fulcrum with a catapult point at (i). If you can't see it, flip your chart upside down again.

A break above catapult point (i) completing the fulcrum would result in all shorts being closed. The upside target taken at the bottom of the breakout column yields a count of 2245, making the risk-reward ratio favourable for longs even though the price is still below the main downtrend. As the price rises out of the fulcrum, notice that, in textbook fashion, there is a series of semi-catapults indicated by the blue horizontal resistance lines, eventually breaking the main downtrend line 11 from the top. At this stage a new uptrend line 16 may be drawn touching the rising bottom on the right side of the fulcrum bottom. As the price approaches the target of 2245, it begins to trade sideways, indicating profit taking and distribution. It corrects back and touches the new uptrend line, reinforcing it as the new main trend.

A break below trend line 16 would put the chart back into a bear trend.

Taking a shorter-term view

As with 3-box charts, you may change your time horizon by simply changing the box size of the chart. Chart 5-32 shows the result of halving the box size to 1%. The section shown is from the 2002 bottom to the present. Notice how more trends are exposed, making it easier for the shorter-term trader to find short-term opportunities. Notice how a potential inverted fulcrum with potential catapult at A, not visible on the 2% chart, is exposed on the 1% chart.

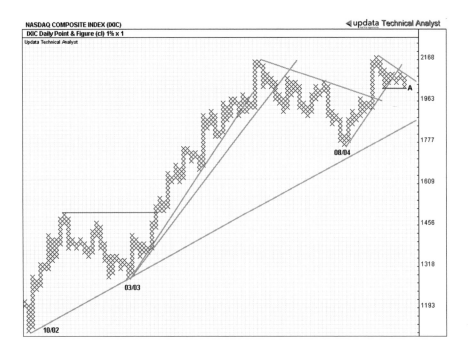

Chart 5-32: Analysing the 1% x 1 of the NASDAQ Composite Index

1-box charts actually thrive on intra-day, especially tick or 1 minute data, which is where they originally came from. Once you move to intra-day data, however, you should use arithmetic points box sizes rather than log. The reason is that you are no longer taking a general view and at this level each round number can be psychologically important for market participants. You are interested in the actual prices recorded because these are the prices that are being dealt by the participants and it is their behaviour you wish to assess. Although it is recommended for all intra-day time-frames, it is essential for tick charts.

Chart 5-33 is a 10 x 1 Point chart using hourly data, showing the section of the chart from the August 2004 low. Notice how trends become much clearer: fulcrums and semi-catapults become more visible for the short-term trader. The potential inverted fulcrum that was barely visible in Chart 5-32 is now clear and well formed in the hourly Chart 5-33.

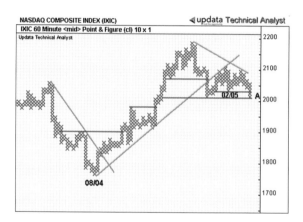

Chart 5-33: 10 x 1 hourly chart of the NASDAQ Composite Index

Finally, Chart 5-34 is a 1 x 1 using tick data, showing every price change from the February 2005 low. Compare it with the hourly Chart 5-33. Notice how much more detail the tick chart shows. Every 1 point change in price is plotted. It is an essential chart for the short-term trader because no other chart shows what is actually happening in the sequence as it occurs. Fulcrums and semi-catapults are clearly visible, as are the internal trend lines. It is worth spending the time going through the analysis yourself.

Chart 5-34: 1 x 1 tick chart of the NASDAQ Composite Index

That is the analysis of 1-box reversal charts. Although they were the original type of Point and Figure chart, they have been ignored by many newcomers to Point and Figure analysis. If you want to trade using Point and Figure, then it is essential that you get used to using 1-box charts.

Analysis of 2-box charts

The analysis of 2-box reversal charts, as you might expect, is a cross between 3-box and 1-box analysis. 45° trend lines are not as important as they are in 3-box charts. Trend lines on 2-box charts are best drawn subjectively as they are on 1-box charts. Although you will see double-top and double-bottom signals, these are of less importance and should not be acted on. It is the wider patterns that look more like fulcrums and semi-catapults that are important.

As with 3-box charts, the lengths of the columns in 2-box charts inform you about the price action's bullishness or bearishness. Consequently, it is important to distinguish between columns of Os and columns of Xs.

Vertical counts are available on 2-box charts and have a similar accuracy factor to those on 3-box charts, but they are shorter-term counts. Congestion areas are wider, making horizontal counts more available in 2-box charts than they are in 3-box charts.

2-box charts have an advantage over 1-box charts in that they have the asymmetric filter, meaning that a 2% x 2 chart requires 4% to change columns.

For reference purposes, three log scale 2% charts of the NASDAQ Composite Index are shown below. Chart 5-35 is a 2% x 1, Chart 5-36 is a 2% x 2 and Chart 5-37 is a 2% x 3. Study them to familiarise yourself with the differences.

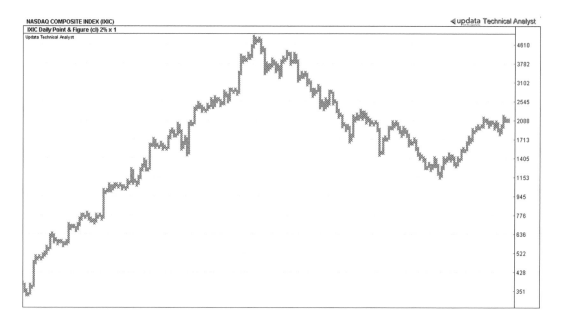

Chart 5-35: 2% x 1 of the NASDAQ Composite Index

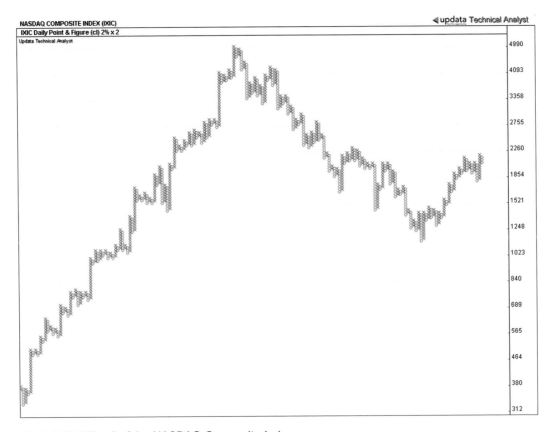

Chart 5-36: 2% x 2 of the NASDAQ Composite Index

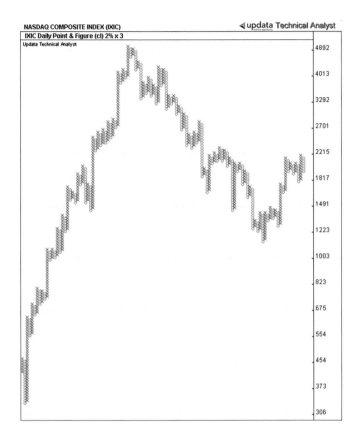

Chart 5-37: 2% x 3 of the NASDAQ Composite Index

Stops in Point and Figure analysis

You will recall that there are two questions you must ask yourself and then answer before placing a trade: 'What do I do if I am wrong?' and 'How do I know I am wrong?' The answer to the second question relates to the level at which you no longer believe the signal to be valid. There are two ways to handle this.

The Point and Figure way is to look at the pattern that made you take the signal in the first place and ask yourself what would have to change to make the signal invalid. The answer is easy in 3-box reversal charts because a double-bottom sell after any buy signal is your stop to close the long, and a double-top buy after any sell signal is your stop to close your short. You will recall, however, that in most cases it is best to look left in the pattern to determine where your stop will be placed, which is often not on the first double signal in the opposite direction, but rather a row or two away from it.

In 1-box reversal charts, if the pattern is a bullish semi-catapult or fulcrum, there are two places to position your stop, depending on the depth of the pattern. If the pattern is shallow, perhaps 2 to 4 boxes deep, as many semi-catapults are, then the stop should be placed one box below the low of the pattern. If the pattern is deep, as most fulcrums are, then the stop should be placed one box below the pivot or anchor point of the pattern in the case of a fulcrum bottom, or one box above in the case of a fulcrum top. Remember the pivot row is the row at which your horizontal count is taken, that is to say the row with most filled in boxes.

In all cases, the risk-reward ratio should be determined as this will affect whether you take the trade, and, if you do, where you place your stop.

Standard percentage stop losses

Good money management is the key to successful trading, whether you use Point and Figure or some other method to generate entry signals for you. Consequently, a simple percentage trailing stop loss, based on the volatility of the instrument, is used by many as the exit stop. The advantage is that all you have to do is look for entry signals based on your knowledge of Point and Figure charts, and then use a trailing stop to exit the trade. The disadvantage is that, after exiting on the break of a trailing stop, there may not be an opportunity to re-enter the trade.

Stop losses the Point and Figure way

If you think about it, Point and Figure already has a trailing stop mechanism built into it if you use log scale charts. A 2% x 3 log scale chart means that the price must fall by 3 boxes or 6% from the last plotted box to trigger a column of Os. So, by adjusting your box size and your reversal, you can have an inbuilt stop loss. If you wanted a 10% stop loss, you would need to use a 2% x 5 or a 1% x 10 or a 3.3% x 3 chart. The problem is that charts with odd sized box sizes and reversals like these are no good for entry signals, so you must operate two charts. If your chosen stop is 10%, then you should use your standard 2% x 3 or 1% x 3 chart to obtain your entry signals and once you are in the trade, you switch to a 2% x 5 or 3.3% x 3 chart to wait for the exit on the first appearance of a column of Os.

Some may argue that this is a rather roundabout way of running a trailing stop, but the two methods are not quite the same. The simple trailing stop method subtracts 10% from the highest price reached and uses that as the stop level. No regard is taken of any Point and Figure rules. With Point and Figure however, you will recall that once a box has been plotted, the price which achieved it is forgotten and all measurements for reversals are taken from the value of the last box plotted. So, a 10% reversal or the appearance of the column of Os is based on a reversal from the last X plotted. It is a less 'noisy' way of using a stop loss.

The method you choose is up to you. The very fact that you have chosen a way of exiting a trade means that you are one giant step down the road to success.

Early entry points

You will have seen that Point and Figure analysis is based on breakouts, because only at this time has the equilibrium been broken in favour of either the bulls or the bears. Many regard this as the low-risk way to trade but if you look at the risk-reward ratios, you will see that they are relatively unfavourable if calculated on the breakout, because in deep patterns the stop is a long way away.

The low-risk trade is, therefore, the one opened on the opposite side of the pattern to the breakout. Many regard this as high-risk, but actually, your risk-reward ratio is more than double that if you had entered on the breakout. This is because your stop is placed below the low of the pattern, in the case of a bottom pattern, and above the high in the case of a top, making the difference between your entry point and your stop very small.

Therefore, it is important to assess the strength of the pattern, so that you can prejudge the direction of the break. Once you are able to do that, you may take positions on the opposite side of the pattern to the potential break with a close stop. If the pattern does break in the direction you predicted, you have a 'free ride' from your entry point to the breakout point. If it doesn't, and goes the other way, you stop out for a small loss. Of course, trades taken at the breakout are likely to be more successful than those taken within the pattern.

Summary of Point and Figure analysis

It is not possible to cover every possible combination of patterns and trend lines, but you should have noticed the following:

•   The analysis of 3-box charts is different from 1-box charts.

•   Changing the box size has the effect of changing your time horizon, not the time-frame.

•   The smaller the box size, the shorter the time horizon.

•   Changing the reversal also affects the time horizon but to a lesser extent.

•   The use of 3-box, 2-box and 1-box charts is not mutually exclusive.

•   It is essential that you have more than one Point and Figure chart available for analysis with different box sizes and/or different reversals, so that you obtain a view from a number of different time horizons.

•   In the 3-box analysis, all the trend lines, including the internal lines, were drawn at 45°. This is the most effective and objective way of defining the trends and subsequent support and resistance levels. That is not to say that subjective lines at any angle cannot be used; they can, but are more difficult to place. There will be times when a subjective line touching more than two points is stronger than a series of 45° lines.

•   In 1-box analysis, although 45° lines may be used, it is better and more reliable to use subjective lines joining higher lows for uptrends and lower highs for downtrends. These lines tend to be drawn touching the right-hand sides of semi-catapults.

•   Trends are the most important aspect of any chart and should always be placed on the chart first.

•   Do not assume that every double-top buy and double-bottom sell in a 3-box should be taken. Always look left on the chart to see whether there is a more complex formation with resistance at a higher level or support at a lower level.

•   The more complex the pattern, the more important it becomes.

•   In 3-box analysis, always look at the relative column lengths. Longer columns of Xs indicate bull trends. Longer columns of Os indicate bear trends.

•   Look for changes in the chart's characteristic. The occurrence of a long column of Os during a bull trend is a warning of an imminent trend reversal, as is a long column of Xs during a bear trend.

•   If the preceding trend is an uptrend, and columns of Xs become shorter while the columns of Os become longer to eventually balance one another out, a top is being made. The converse is true for bottoms.

- In 1-box charts, the presence of sideways congestion is the main area of analysis. It means that there is either accumulation or distribution taking place; distribution if the preceding trend is up, accumulation if the preceding trend is down. Point and Figure, especially 1-box, shows this better than any other chart because sideways congestion can only happen through trading and not the passage of time.

- Vertical and horizontal counts should always be used, not only to establish targets, but also to provide evidence for and against the underlying trend.

- The weighing up of evidence for and against the trend, using targets, trends and columns lengths, should be undertaken constantly.

- Double-top and bottom signals become less important as box size is reduced

- The placing of stops is vital for good Point and Figure analysis and three methods are available: a stop placed by observing the pattern that generated the entry signal; simple percentage trailing stop losses; or stop losses based on a Point and Figure column change.

Chapter 6

Point and Figure Charts of Indicators

The Point and Figure method is really just another way of charting data, just as line and bar charts are. There is, therefore, no reason why they cannot be used for charts other than pure price charts, such as calculated lines, called indicators.

In theory, there is no limit to the indicators that can be drawn using the Point and Figure method. In practice, however, it is wise to consider what the benefits are of doing so. Point and Figure charts are very good at showing trends because a column of Xs represents an uptrend and a column of Os represents a downtrend. They are also good at showing reactions against the trend and reassertion of the trend. Their sensitivity can be altered to hide or expose minor fluctuations and these fluctuations create congestion patterns which give the analyst more information about the movement. This means Point and Figure charts do not work well on data that has already been smoothed. For example, a Point and Figure of a moving average of the price data is no more useful than drawing a Point and Figure of the price. In fact, it does not give much detail at all as Chart 6-1 shows. The chart is a 50 x 3 Point and Figure of the 20 day moving average of the FTSE 100 Index. The average has removed so much of the countertrend noise that the chart reveals nothing important. Compare it with other charts of the FTSE 100 Index shown previously. Obviously as the period of the average is reduced, so the Point and Figure reveals more information, but no more information than the price itself. For this reason, Point and Figure charts of moving averages are not recommended.

The implication, therefore, is that Point and Figure charts should not be drawn of any smoothed indicator. Indicators that are smoothed by using one or other averaging technique means the resultant Point and Figure chart will not be of much use. MACD[18] and slow stochastic[19] are examples of smoothed indicators. That leaves three types of indicator which can be drawn using the Point and Figure method.

- Relative strength[20] against another instrument

- Cumulative lines such as on-balance volume.[21]

- Oscillators such as RSI[22] and momentum.[23]

Some are in common use, some are not.

---

[18] MACD, or Moving Average Convergence Divergence is a calculated indicator which plots the difference between two moving averages.

[19] Stochastic is a calculated indicator which looks at the relationship of the price high, low and close over selected periods and creates an indicator from the observations.

[20] Relative strength is an indicator created by dividing the price of one instrument (usually a share) by the price of another (usually an index). It is either plotted in its raw form or indexed to start at 100, which is the preferred method when Point and Figure is used.

[21] On-balance volume is a cumulative line constructed by adding or subtracting the period's volume based on whether the price has risen or fallen.

[22] RSI is a weighted, velocity index with a fixed scale ranging between 0 and 100. Although it has averaging in its calculation, the resultant line is not smoothed.

[23] Momentum is a rate of change indicator measuring the percentage change in price from the period a pre-determined number of periods ago.

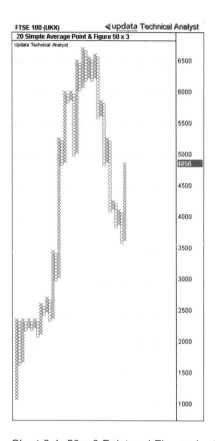

Chart 6-1: 50 x 3 Point and Figure chart of the 20 day moving average of the FTSE 100 Index

Point and Figure of relative strength

One of the best and most important indicator charts to be drawn using the Point and Figure method is relative strength. The reason is that, unlike many other indicators, the relative strength scaling is mostly irrelevant. What is important is trend, and Point and Figure shows and defines trend better than any other chart. You will recall that the most important trend in 3-box Point and Figure charts is the 45° trend. The 45° trend lines define the main up and downtrends objectively. You recall, the essence of the 45° trend is that to maintain the price action above the trend, the price must rise by more squares than it moves sideways. In relative strength terms this means that the relative strength ratio must rise by more squares than it moves sideways. More squares sideways indicates that the numerator instrument is no longer performing better than the denominator instrument.

The reason this is important is that fund managers who are benchmarked to an index must try to accumulate shares that have rising relative strength charts and dispose of those with falling relative strength charts. This is easy to do in theory but not quite so easy in practice, using the traditional relative strength line chart. The reason is that trend is not quite so defined when a line chart is used.

It is worth noting at this stage that relative strength shows relative performance, not absolute performance. A rising relative strength trend does not mean that the stock (numerator) is rising, it simply means that the stock is performing better than the index (denominator). It could mean that the stock is falling but not by as much as the index; or it could mean that the stock is trading sideways but the index is falling; or it could mean that they are both rising but the stock is rising more than the index. The converse applies with a falling relative strength trend.

When drawing Point and Figure charts of relative strength, scaling becomes an issue because relative strength is a ratio of the price of one instrument to the price of another and therefore has very small or very large numbers. The preferred method, therefore, is to normalise the relative strength data before plotting the chart, by dividing each relative strength value by the first relative strength value in the series and then multiplying by 100. This makes construction easier and has the additional benefit that all relative strength charts become directly comparable. If the last value of the normalised relative strength chart is 145, this means that the stock has outperformed the benchmark – or denominator – by 45% since the base date. If another relative strength chart shows 163, you can immediately see that it has performed better than the first stock. Of course, if the relative strength chart shows a value of 87, it means the stock has underperformed the benchmark by 13%. This gives a whole new dimension to benchmarking because it allows you to set your benchmark date at one which may be relevant – for example, the start of the year.

It is important to understand, however, that the relative strength chart is exactly the same shape whether you normalise it or not, and is analysed in exactly the same way. It is far more difficult to choose a box size when using a raw relative strength chart, because the ratio could be in thousandths.

Point and Figure charts of relative strength are analysed in exactly the same way as Point and Figure charts of price. The relative strength rising above the 45° line is a signal to continue to accumulate the stock at times when the price registers buy signals. Once the relative strength falls to, and breaks, the 45° trend line, it is a time to stop buying and start selling at the most opportune time by looking at the price chart for sell signals.

Before drawing a Point and Figure of relative strength you have to consider the box size and the reversal. You will find that, in general, log scale relative strength charts using a 1% box size are the most effective and show 45° trends better than arithmetic charts. Furthermore, if you are analysing a group of stocks against the same benchmark, you need the relative strength charts to be directly comparable with regard to the time horizon – remember the box size adjusts your time horizon.

Chart 6-2 is a 1% x 3 Point and Figure of the relative strength of BAA plc against the FTSE 100 Index and Chart 6-3 is a 1% x 3 Point and Figure of BAA plc's price.

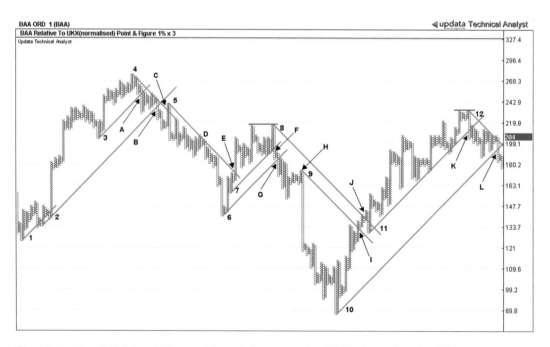

Chart 6-2: 1% x 3 Point and Figure of the relative strength of BAA plc against the FTSE 100 Index

Trend line 1 in Chart 6-2 is the relative strength bullish support line from the relative strength low, meaning that long positions in BAA plc may be accumulated while the relative strength stays above the 45° line. There is an early invalid break below trend line 1 which allows new bullish support line 2 to be drawn. Notice that the relative strength rises away from the bullish support line showing strong relative strength, which in turn means that BAA plc is outperforming the FTSE 100 Index by a wide margin. The reaction halfway up the trend allows internal 45° line 3 to be drawn. This is a shorter-term line which gives early warnings of trend deterioration. This occurs at point A when the internal 45° trend breaks, signalling that any accumulation of the stock should cease for the moment. Breaks of internal lines do not signify disposal: they are an early warning and any buying should cease. The point at which this occurs on the price chart is shown by point A1 in Chart 6-3. A tentative downtrend 45° line, 4, can be drawn on the relative strength chart, which acts as resistance to any up move. This leads the major 45° uptrend line 2 to be broken at point B. This indicates that you should find opportunities to start disposing of BAA plc and replacing it with another stock which has relative strength in an uptrend. Point B1 in the price chart shows the point at which the relative strength broke its uptrend. You should use any strength to sell BAA plc.

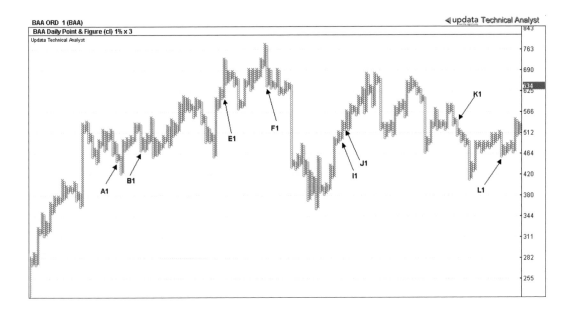

Chart 6-3: 1% x 3 Point and Figure chart of BAA plc

Downtrend line 4 is now the valid 45° bearish resistance line on the relative strength Chart 6-2. The breach at point C is not a valid trend line break because there is no Point and Figure signal on the break. It does, however, allow the bearish resistance line to be adjusted to line 5. While the relative strength remains below line 5, you must continue to dispose of any holdings in BAA plc. Depending on your trading style, shorts may be considered as well. The strength of line 5 is reinforced by the test at point D, which failed to breach it. Finally, at point E, the bearish resistance line 5 is breached, signalling that BAA plc can be accumulated again when a buy signal emerges on the price chart. The point at which the relative strength trend changes is shown on the price chart by point E1. You can see that there is no buy signal at this stage. In fact, the price shows some weakness and a buy doesn't emerge until the double-top buy ten columns further on. A new relative strength bullish support line 6 may now be drawn. Internal line 7 may also be drawn to show the shorter-term support. The relative strength remains above line 7 but eventually breaks at point F. Notice that prior to breaking it met resistance forming two tops at the same level. This was the first sign that any relative strength was failing. At this stage, accumulation of the stock should cease. Shortly after this, bullish line 6 breaks as well, indicating that BAA plc should be disposed of as sell signals emerge from the price chart. Point F1 shows the area on the price chart where the relative strength chart bullish support line broke down. A double-bottom, then a triple-bottom sell signal is generated on the price chart.

The new bearish resistance line is now line 8. Below this line the stock should be disposed of whether or not it is rising. The reaction at point H on the relative strength chart, and failure to reach bearish resistance line 8, allows internal 45° line 9 to be drawn for the shorter-term view. Downtrend line 9 eventually breaks at point I, shown on the price chart as point I1. From this point, no more selling of the stock should take place. Eventually, the main bearish resistance line 8 is broken at point J, which is point J1 on the price chart. From this point the stock can again be accumulated on any buy signals on the price chart.

With the break on downtrend line 8, new bullish support line 10 may be drawn from the bottom. At the same time, internal 45° line 11 may be drawn from the reaction low at the break. The relative strength remains above this line for over two years, during which time the FTSE 100 Index declined but BAA plc went sideways. This is a good example of a rising relative strength line not necessarily meaning that the price is rising. The breach of the internal trend line 11 at point K indicates that any accumulation should cease from point K1 on the price chart. Notice that the relative strength again ran into resistance just prior to the break, creating a M-shaped top pattern.

As usual, the breach of the internal trend line 11 allows a tentative downtrend bearish resistance line 12 to be drawn. Notice how the relative strength line rises up to this new bearish resistance line but cannot break through. Instead it goes on to break the main bullish support line 10 at point L, which is point L1 on the price chart. At this point, BAA plc should be disposed of whenever there is a sell signal. Notice how the price continues to rise but the relative strength continues to fall, showing that BAA plc is performing worse than the market.

This example has shown just one relative strength chart where the same stock is accumulated and disposed of each time the relative strength trend changes. In reality, there will be many relative strength charts turning negative or positive, so having disposed of one stock, another may be accumulated when its relative strength turns positive.

Although trend lines play an important part in relative strength analysis, normal Point and Figure pattern signals apply as well. Trends are most important because the trend of the relative strength chart tells you whether the stock is performing better or worse than the index.

Most Point and Figure of relative strength analysts use 3-box reversal charts but 1-box charts are effective too. Remember, however, that 45° trend lines are not as important on 1-box charts; subjective trend lines are used instead. Chart 6-4 and Chart 6-5 follow on from one another and show a 1% x 1 relative strength Point and Figure of BAA plc against the FTSE 100 Index. Notice that although the trend lines are not at 45° they are still very effective at showing the relative strength trends.

Chart 6-4: 1% x 1 Point and Figure chart of the relative strength of BAA plc against the FTSE 100 Index (chart 1 of 2)

Chart 6-5: 1% x 1 Point and Figure chart of the relative strength of BAA plc against the FTSE 100 Index (chart 2 of 2)

Although you have seen the advantages of using Point and Figure charts of relative strength, the main disadvantage is that they cannot be lined up with the price chart, the reason being that the column reversals do not occur at the same times. They have to be read independently. That is a disadvantage that extends to all Point and Figure charts of other indicators.

Using Point and Figure counts on relative strength charts

Point and Figure counts can be used on Point and Figure charts of relative strength, but remember the numbers don't really mean anything. It is the levels that you are looking for. You will recall, when counts were discussed in chapter 5, that they are potential targets, the achievement or non-achievement of which gives you more information about the quality of the trend. You will also recall that some charts do not count well, so you should always check past counts. Counts work on log as well as arithmetic scaled Point and Figure charts of relative strength. The following examples, however, are arithmetic charts so it is easier for you to evaluate the counts yourself.

Chart 6-6 is a relative strength chart of Carnival plc against the FTSE All Share Index. It has provided an excellent vertical and horizontal count. The likelihood of other counts being achieved is increased by the accuracy of these.

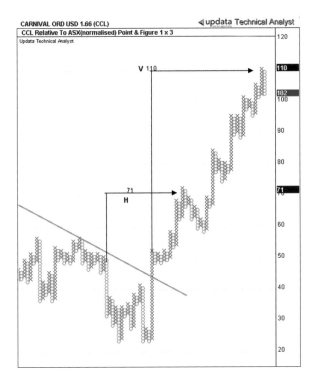

Chart 6-6: Showing counts on the 1 x 3 chart of the relative strength of Carnival plc against the FTSE All Share Index

The relative strength chart of Cairn Energy plc against the FTSE ALL Share Index, shown in Chart 6-7, has also generated some accurate vertical and horizontal counts. Note the downside vertical count of 1120 has been exceeded, indicating further downside of the relative strength to come. Remember, when a count is exceeded, this indicates a strong trend in the direction of the count.

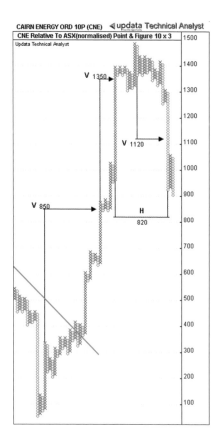

Chart 6-7: Showing counts on the 10 x 3 chart of the relative strength of Cairn Energy plc against the FTSE All Share Index

So remember to always check past counts to see how accurate they have been. If they have, then new counts are likely to be as well. Always consider the trend when assessing counts. Downside counts in an uptrend are unlikely to be achieved, as are upside counts in a downtrend. Remember, too, that counts will give you some idea of where the relative strength trend will pause. That is all they can do. It's a major advantage of Point and Figure charts of relative strength; no other chart is able to give you an estimate as to where relative strength is headed.

Point and Figure of on-balance volume

Point and Figure charts don't show volume but volume may be incorporated by drawing Point and Figure charts of on-balance volume (OBV). It lends itself to the Point and Figure representation because it is a cumulative line where the values that are used to construct the line have no meaning. As with relative strength, the main analysis of OBV is the trend. A rising trend in an OBV chart indicates accumulation, whereas a falling trend indicates distribution. OBV shows the presence of informed buyers and sellers. It can show accumulation taking place prior to a price rise and distribution prior to a price fall. The rationale behind it is that high volume combined with a price move indicates powerful informed investors taking positions. For this reason, it can show the presence of trading on sensitive information.

The biggest problem with Point and Figure of OBV is that it can have large values, depending on the volume of the share in question. This makes choosing a box size extremely difficult. Unfortunately, using log scale OBV charts does not help because percentage changes in OBV have no meaning. The best method of approximating a box size is to use an arithmetic box size which is 1% of the range of OBV values instead of 1% of the latest value. This will give you a sensible Point and Figure chart which may require some adjustment after first viewing.

Chart 6-8 is a 3-box reversal Point and Figure chart of the OBV of BG Group plc. Point and Figure charts of OBV are analysed and interpreted in exactly the same way as any other Point and Figure chart. Notice the downtrend being broken by a very strong X column rise, marked A on the chart. This is the beginning of a new uptrend in OBV and strong accumulation. Chart 6-9 shows the price line chart of BG Group plc. The point at which the buy signal is given on the OBV chart is shown by point A1 on the line chart. The OBV enhances any price move.

Notice the vertical count of 1750000 from the breakout column was achieved almost exactly, at which point the OBV gave a triple-bottom sell, the first sell signal during the entire uptrend. With accumulation coming to an end, profits must be taken. The OBV proceeded to consolidate sideways within a large triangle pattern. The breakout with a triple-top buy signal from the triangle occurs at point B on the OBV chart. This is shown on the price line chart by point B1. Note also, that this occurs before the price itself has broken out, creating another good buying opportunity. Vertical and horizontal counts are available from the pattern. The vertical count is exceeded, indicating a strong trend. The horizontal count has not yet been achieved. Notice that in the case of both the uptrends started at points A and B, there is no double-bottom sell signal given during the trend. A series of double-top buys is a signal to add to long positions.

Experienced OBV followers will be able to ascertain the likely consequences on a share price with such a potential rise in OBV.

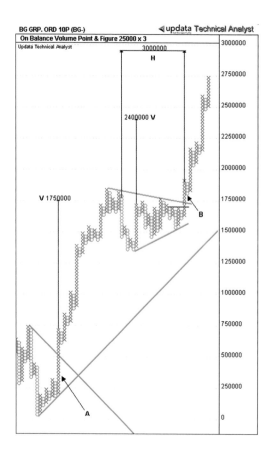

Chart 6-8: 25000 x 3 Point and Figure chart of the on-balance volume of BG Group plc

Chart 6-9: Price line chart of BG Group plc

Point and Figure of oscillators

In theory any oscillator may be drawn as a Point and Figure chart. As stated earlier, smoothed oscillators such as MACD should, however, be avoided, as the lack of minor trend changes results in long columns of Xs and Os which render the Point and Figure chart useless. Remember, Point and Figure charts thrive on reversals. Oscillators such as momentum, overbought/oversold, commodity channel Index and RSI do work well in Point and Figure format, but there is, in fact no limit to the indicators that can be drawn using Point and Figure charts rather than line charts.

It is important not to lose sight of the reason for drawing a Point and Figure chart, rather than a line chart, of the oscillator. It is to benefit from the filter, as well as the clear signals, that Point and Figure charts offer. Chart 6-10 shows a 1 x 3 Point and Figure chart of the 14 day RSI of IBM Corp. The centre window shows a line chart of the same RSI and the lower window shows the price line. The charts have been lined up so as to match approximately, although remember the line charts are governed by a date scale whereas the Point and Figure chart is not.

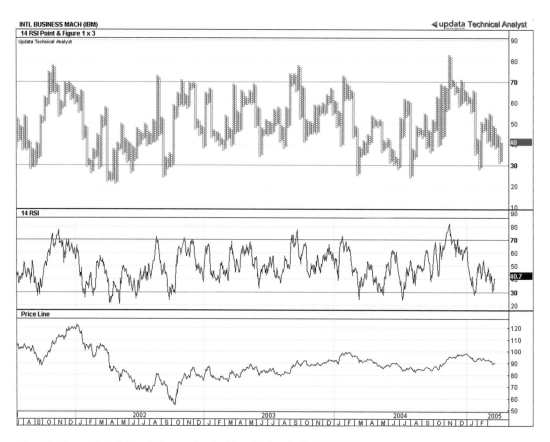

Chart 6-10: 1 x 3 Point and Figure chart of the 14 day RSI of IBM Corp, with line charts of RSI and price

A full explanation of Wilder's RSI indicator cannot be undertaken here, and you are referred to the many excellent texts, such as that by Wilder himself, as well as John Murphy, listed in the reference section at the end of this book. But here it is shown that RSI can be drawn as a Point and Figure chart. Notice that the Point and Figure version removes some of the noise from the RSI line chart. This is because any change less than 1 point in the direction of the column and 3 points against are ignored, making the Point and Figure version easier to read.

It has not been found that counts are of any use. This is due to the fact that RSI is within a fixed scale range. Divergence is, however, easier to spot because the chart ignores decimals.

If you currently use RSI as one of your indicators, then it is suggested that you try drawing it as a Point and Figure. With what you have learnt so far about Point and Figure analysis, it is likely that you will find that it enhances your analysis.

Summary

Point and Figure is a method for representing any series of numbers. Most often those are prices, but Point and Figure charts can also be drawn of any calculated line which can then be subjected to all the power of Point and Figure analysis.

- Smoothed indicators should be avoided because Point and Figure thrives on volatility.

- The most common indicator to be represented as a Point and Figure chart is relative strength.

- Point and Figure works well with any cumulative line, such as OBV.

- Oscillators which are not smoothed also benefit from Point and Figure representation.

- Trends show up better when an indicator is drawn as a Point and Figure.

- Point and Figure counts can be used to calculate targets for the indicator, although they do not work with fixed scale indicators.

- The value of the count used on indicators is not important, rather it is the level that the count projects.

Chapter 7

Optimisation of Point and Figure Charts

Before discussing the optimisation of Point and Figure charts, it is worth discussing optimisation in general, as it is a subject that requires clarification.

The case for and against optimisation

Optimisation of technical indicators and chart signals has its devotees and its detractors. Optimisation in technical analysis is the testing of various entry and exit conditions, as well as calculation parameters, in order to determine which combination has yielded the best results. The emphasis is on the past tense, but it is a wide remit. It can be helpful, but a hindrance as well. It is only helpful when the analyst undertaking optimisation understands the chart or indicator that is being optimised.

It is important, when considering optimisation, to look at it from a Technical Analyst's, rather than a statistician's, point of view. In doing so, you need to stop and think for a moment what Technical Analysis is. Technical Analysis is the study of price through the use of charts. It is the study of the past in the belief that it can tell you something about the future. It is the understanding that patterns in price and indicator charts repeat. That is what chart reading is all about. Technical Analysts look for 'things' in the chart that have proved reliable in the past – such as shapes, patterns, indicator movement and so on – on the premise that they will occur in the future and will, therefore, assist the analyst in making decisions. If you look back and inspect a chart and notice that every time there is a particular pattern, the result is a significant price rise, or that every time there is another pattern type, there is a sharp fall, this is just mental optimisation – optimisation by inspection; looking at past history and applying what you have learnt to current data. Every time you look at a chart you are, in effect, mentally optimising it.

But optimisation goes further than that. Some charts can be altered by altering the parameters that are used to draw them. Point and Figure is an example of this. You have seen that the look of the chart can be completely altered by changing the box size and the reversal.

Optimisation takes a set of data and then works out what would have been the best way to have analysed it, with the benefit of hindsight. If those results are then applied to the same set of data you will have, by definition, fitted the curve. Some may argue that you should optimise one section of data, then test the results of the optimisation on a different section and finally apply it to a third section, but that would be said without an understanding of the market and market charts. Market data is not just a series of numbers. Technical Analysts understand that price data has 'life', and that there is a relationship between past data and future data because the data is created by human market participants. Whereas some will go to lengths to eliminate any sign of autocorrelation, and work on data that has had its 'life' removed, Technical Analysts yearn for autocorrelation.[24] They want, and believe, that past prices have an influence on future prices because the same human beings who set the prices in the past will also be setting them in the future.

---

[24] Autocorrelation describes a condition where data points in a time series are not independent of each other.

Technical Analysts understand the market and market charts. They understand that market charts are created by price data and that the price data is created by human beings who have human traits, such as following trends and behaviour pattern repetition. They understand that these human market participants are subject to human emotions, which affect the price and consequently the charts. If today's price were independent of tomorrow's, Technical Analysis would be worthless. Technicians realise that each instrument has different characteristics and so understanding the movement of one, does not mean that another is understood. They understand that the characteristics of the price movement are different, depending on whether the price is in an uptrend, downtrend or sideways trend.

Whether you agree with optimisation or not, it is worth considering the side-benefits that may stem from an optimisation exercise. Optimisation is such a wide subject that it cannot be given full treatment here; only a dedicated text with thousands of tests and examples can do it any true justice. What follows are simply guidelines for you to follow, should you wish to embark on an optimisation exercise of Point and Figure charts.

Approaching Point and Figure optimisation

When you draw a Point and Figure chart, you have to decide what box size and reversal you wish to use. After doing so, you may look at the chart and decide you have chosen incorrectly and change the parameters again. This is, in effect, mental optimisation through the process of trial and error. It is the way a skilled Point and Figure analyst operates.

While deciding on the best box size and reversal, you also have to decide what constitutes a buy and what constitutes a sell signal. Is it better to wait for a triple-top buy and a triple-bottom sell? What if these never occur? These are the sorts of questions that mathematical optimisation can answer. To do this, you have to decide what you want to achieve. The assumption is that profit is the motive, so you could take a section of data and then test a range of parameters and conditions which generate buy and sell signals to mathematically decide which set of signals gives the greatest profit.

The input parameters of any Point and Figure optimisation are:

- Reversal size – 1, 2, 3, or 5 etc.

- Box size – arithmetic points size or log percentage size.

- Construction using end of period close or end of period high/low.

- Entry signals – normal Point and Figure signals such as double-top, triple-top, catapult, and simple column change.

- Exit signals – normal Point and Figure signals such as double-bottom, triple-bottom, catapult, and simple column change or other exit signals which are not Point and Figure related, such as stop loss.

- Waiting period or signal delay.[25]

- Data under consideration.

- Dealing costs.

- Long or short.

A full optimisation would have to take every combination of these parameters: run through the data to find the best box and reversal which yielded the greatest profit; find which entry and exit signals achieved this, at the same time working out whether the Point and Figure chart should be constructed with close or high/low data. Before plunging headlong into a complex optimisation using all these parameters, you need to stop and consider a few things. Ground rules have to be laid.

---

[25] Signal delay is the waiting period after a signal has been generated to see if the signal remains in place. If after the waiting period, the signal is still in place, it is acted on. The purpose of the signal delay is to avoid whipsaws. The disadvantage is that it introduces a lag to the signal.

Entry and exit signals must be unambiguous, which is seen as a great advantage of 3-box reversal Point and Figure charts. 1-box charts, you will recall, are much more subjective in their interpretation and their signals are not quite so clear-cut. For example, a double-top buy on a 3-box chart could be a complex semi-catapult on a 1-box chart. The first ground rule, therefore, is that all optimisations should be calculated on 3-box reversal charts. Although 5-box reversal charts can also be used, they are too long-term to be of interest. Although double-top and bottom signals work with 2-box charts, it is felt that they also rely on bigger patterns and so will produce too many signals.

Having fixed the reversal at 3-box, the first optimisation, therefore, could be to test a range of box sizes, testing various entry and exit signals, but this also presents a problem. You will recall that if you use a points box size, there will be times when it is not suitable because the price has either risen or fallen significantly from the area where the box size was determined. This means that long-term optimisations cannot be conducted using a fixed points box size. This should be reserved for instruments with a history of a narrow trading range. Log scale percentage box sizes, on the other hand, adjust the box size at every price level. It is, therefore, advisable to use a range of percentage box sizes rather than points. The number of permutations is significantly reduced if the test has a fixed reversal size and the need to test arithmetic points box sizes is eliminated.

There is no way to tell whether close only or high/low data is best for the Point and Figure construction, so it is best to include the choice in the optimisation. What about signals? You will have learnt that triple-tops and bottoms are more important than double-tops and bottoms, but you must understand that there is a big difference between entry signals and exit signals. There is no problem waiting for a rare entry signal to occur. If it doesn't occur, you do not enter the trade and no loss is incurred. That is not the case with exit signals. A rare exit signal that may never occur will keep you in an unprofitable trade without any chance of exiting. Exit signals must be guaranteed, which means that triple-bottom exit signals on longs, and triple-top exit signals on shorts, cannot be considered in the optimisation. The same applies to the powerful catapult pattern, which cannot be relied upon to provide an exit for a trade. It is the reason why trailing stop loss is included as an exit condition, because it is a guaranteed exit. So, more input parameters may be eliminated by thinking about the optimisation before entering into it. Exit conditions should be limited to double-bottom (or double-top for shorts), as well as a range of percentage trailing stop losses.

The next parameters to consider are signal delay and data. Some analysts and traders dismiss the idea of a signal delay out of hand, because, administratively speaking, it is difficult to implement. It is difficult to have the procedures in place to receive a signal one day but act perhaps two days later. As this widens the field of research, no account has been taken of signal delay in the optimisations conducted.

Data, too, provides a point for some discussion and argument. The idea that you should divide your data set into three equal sets, to optimise on the first, test on the second and apply the conditions to the third, is unrealistic. It may work with trend-less statistical data, but it will not work with data from the markets. As discussed in the introduction to this chapter, market data has trend. What worked best in an uptrend may well not work best in a downtrend. It means that to optimise effectively you must decide whether the current trend is up or down and how long it will continue. Of course, if you knew the answer to that, you would not need to optimise. The section on consistency and adaptability below discusses the issue of data in greater depth.

Dealing costs must also be considered. If you operate your optimisation with no dealing costs, then there is no cost in taking a trade that results in 0.1% profit. This means that your most profitable situation may be dozens of small profit trades which add up to a high overall profit, when in fact, with dealing costs, those same trades would have all been unprofitable. The dealing costs you use in your optimisation are there to avoid small trades. Throughout the optimisations conducted, a 1.5 % commission on the price is applied on entry and exit. Prices dealt are always the middle price of the period. You could make your optimisations more onerous, and perhaps more realistic, by buying at the high and selling at the low.

Test parameters

Throughout all the optimisations undertaken, the following test parameters were used:

- 3-box reversal charts only.

- Log scale charts only.

- Box size range from 0.5% to 5%, stepping up 0.1% at a time. This means that 0.5% will be tested, then 0.6%, then 0.7% and so on.

- Test using close only and the high/low construction methods.

- Entry and exit signals. Buy on first occurrence of a double-top buy signal. Ignore any subsequent double-top buys. Sell on first occurrence of a double-bottom sell. Ignore all subsequent double-bottom sells, until the next double-top buy starts the process again.

- Data. This is discussed in the data consistency and adaptability section below.

Data consistency and adaptability

The data under consideration is seen to be the most difficult issue when optimisation is considered, not only how the data is arranged, but also the number of data points. The number of data points relates to your time horizon. The more data you take into account with your optimisation, the longer your time horizon is. Conversely, the less data, the shorter the time horizon. The reason is that if the optimisation exercise has less data to work with, it needs to adjust the parameters to extract the greatest profit from a small amount of data. The longer the data series, the more compromises are made to satisfy all the different characteristics within the data series.

For the results of the optimisation to be useful, they must be consistent as time passes, otherwise what worked best in the past can be of no use in the future. At the same time, they must be adaptable, so that, as new data becomes available, the parameters adjust by small amounts to account for the new information. Consistency and adaptability means that the results adjust slowly as time passes. It is, therefore, unlikely that you will achieve this by selecting a period of 250 days, 5 years ago, and then another 250 days, 5 years later. The results of the two optimisations will most likely be entirely different because the two sections of data are independent of one another. The lack of data overlap means that the parameters have not been able to adapt to changes in the data's characteristics as time passes.

Amazon.com Inc is a share that has risen as well as fallen over the last seven years, making it an ideal candidate to conduct an optimisation. Table 7-1 below shows the results of optimisations undertaken on Amazon.com Inc, a year at a time, without any overlapping of the data series. In each case, January-to-January data was used. Notice the consistency in the results for the first two years. This means that if the parameters found by optimising year 1 were used in year 2, they would have achieved the best result in year 2 as well.

Year	Date range	Box x Reversal
1	1998-1999	2.2% x 3
2	1999-2000	2.4% x 3
3	2000-2001	1.0% x 3
4	2001-2002	1.0% x 3
5	2002-2003	1.1% x 3
6	2003-2004	1.9% x 3
7	2004-2005	0.9% x 3

Table 7-1: Optimised box size for 3-box reversal charts for Amazon.com Inc– one year sections of data

The problem is that if you had used those same parameters in year 3, you would have suffered, because the box size has halved. It then remained consistent for years 3, 4 and 5, then in year 6 the box size doubled again. It halved again in year 7. There is no consistency because there is no adaptability. To achieve this, therefore, there must be an overlap of data so that the parameters can change as new data becomes available. Overlapping the data will explain how the 'jump' from 2.4% to 1.0% occurred.

In fact, it is easy to see why it changed by observing Chart 7-1 opposite. The section outlined in black is the year January 2000 to January 2001. It is obvious that the characteristic of the chart has changed completely and those parameters determined prior to the outlined section are unlikely to work during it. This illustrates the problem of optimising market data.

Chart 7-1: 2.4% x 3 chart of Amazon.com Inc

The answer to this is to move your year forward by a small number of data points at a time. So, instead of optimising a year from January 1999 to January 2000 and then January 2000 to January 2001 with no overlap as shown in Table 7-1, the optimisation shown in Table 7-2 is conducted by moving forward by a month at a time. So, the period January 1999 to January 2000 is optimised, then February 1999 to February 2000, then March 1999 to March 2000 and so on until the year January 2000 to January 2001 is reached. In this way, the data used for each optimisation is still only a year, but 11 months of the previous optimisation's data is used to perform each new one.

Optimisation no.	Date range	Best Box x Reversal	2nd Best Box x Reversal	3rd Best Box x Reversal	4th Best Box x Reversal	9th Best Box x Reversal
1	01/99 - 01/00	2.4% x 3	2.5% x 3	1.7% x 3	1.6% x 3	
2	02/99 - 02/00	1.7% x 3	1.8% x 3	2.4% x 3	2.0% x 3	
3	03/99 - 03/00	1.7% x 3	1.8% x 3	2.4% x 3	1.0% x 3	
4	04/99 - 04/00	1.7% x 3	1.6% x 3	1.8% x 3	1.0% x 3	
5	05/99 - 05/00	1.0% x 3	1.7% x 3	1.6% x 3	1.8% x 3	2.1% x 3
6	06/99 - 06/00	2.1% x 3	0.9% x 3	1.6% x 3	1.3% x 3	
7	07/99 - 07/00	1.0% x 3	0.9% x 3	2.1% x 3	1.3% x 3	
8	08/99 - 08/00	1.0% x 3	0.5% x 3	0.9% x 3	2.5% x 3 H/L	
9	09/99 - 09/00	1.0% x 3	0.9% x 3	0.5% x 3	0.9% x 3 H/L	
10	10/99 - 10/00	1.0% x 3	0.5% x 3	0.9% x 3	2.5% x 3 H/L	
11	11/99 - 11/00	1.0% x 3	0.5% x 3	2.5% x 3 H/L	0.6% x 3	
12	12/99 - 12/00	1.0% x 3	2.5% x 3 H/L	0.5% x 3	2.2% x 3 H/L	
13	01/00 - 01/01	1.0% x 3	0.5% x 3	0.6% x 3	2.1% x 3	

Table 7-2: Optimised box size for reversal for Amazon.com Inc – stepping forward one month at a time

The table also shows the top four results in each case because often the difference in profit between these is so slight that any one of them could be used. Notice in the first optimisation, 2.4% was best and 1.7% was 3rd best. In the second optimisation, 1.7% moved from 3rd to 1st, and 2.4% moved from 1st to 3rd. This is adaptability. The parameters are adjusting to the new data, allowing the parameters to change slowly as time passes. The only one that seems out of place is 2.1% in the 6th optimisation. In this case, 2.1% was the 9th best in the 5th optimisation, making it still acceptable. This will occur occasionally at the chart's change over point when the chart's trend has finally changed. In the Amazon.com Inc chart, it occurs in the year that ends with the column breaking down from the large top pattern.

Notice also that 1% proved to be the best box size from the seventh optimisation onwards, indicating consistency. The purpose of this exercise was to demonstrate that taking independent sections of data and expecting the parameters to remain constant is not the case. Optimisations should be conducted regularly, perhaps every week, every month or even every day, including the latest data. Many reading this will throw up their arms in horror and dismiss the technique as curve fitting. Indeed it is, but is it not important to adjust your parameters by using the latest data? There is one proviso, however: you must exclude any unrealised profit or loss resulting from an open position. This means that only data to the left of the last open position signal is used to determine the profit or loss that in turn determines the best set of parameters to use. Those parameters will, by definition, be the best possible 'guess' for the near future.

Finally, it is significant to note that in all the optimisations, the close only method proved best although the high/low method started to appear in the rankings towards the end. From this you may reach the conclusion to use the close only rather than the high/low construction method.

Alternative exits

Having decided on the method with which optimisations should be undertaken, it is possible to conduct larger optimisations and introduce an alternative exit strategy. The optimisations conducted so far have assumed an exit on the first double-bottom sell after a double-top buy, but it is possible that there is a better exit. Trailing stop loss is thought by many to be the best exit strategy, no matter what the entry signal is.

Optimisation of FTSE 100 constituents for longs

Table 7-3 shows the results of an optimisation conducted on the FTSE 100 constituents using data from January 1998 to the present day. Those with less data history have been excluded.

Code	Entry: Double-top Exit: Double-bottom Box x Rev.	Entry: Double-top Exit: Double-bottom or stop loss Box x Rev.	Exit	% Increase in profit	Code	Entry: Double-top Exit: Double-bottom Box x Rev.	Entry: Double-top Exit: Double-bottom or stop loss Box x Rev.	Exit	% Increase in profit
ABF	1.4% x 3	1.4% x 3	Double-bottom	0%	III	1.2% x 3	1.3% x 3	13.5% Stop	12%
AL-	1.3% x 3	0.9% x 3	13.5% Stop	32%	IMT	2.4% x 3	2.4% x 3	Double-bottom	0%
ALLD	1.6% x 3	2.1% x 3	15.0% Stop	15%	IPR	2.1% x 3	2.1% x 3	8.0% Stop	44%
ANTO	0.9% x 3	0.9% x 3	Double-bottom	0%	ITV	2.3% x 3	2.3% x 3	Double-bottom	0%
AUN	1.5% x 3	0.5% x 3 H/L	8.0% Stop	31%	JMAT	2.1% x 3 H/L	0.7% x 3 H/L	14.0% Stop	49%
AV-	2.2% x 3	2.2% x 3	Double-bottom	0%	KGF	2.2% x 3	2.0% x 3 H/L	11.5% Stop	38%
AVZ	2.4% x 3	2.5% x 3 H/L	15.0% Stop	32%	LAND	1.5% x 3	2.2% x 3	8.5% Stop	14%
AZN	1.5% x 3	2.4% x 3 H/L	12.5% Stop	38%	LGEN	1.9% x 3	1.9% x 3 H/L	14.0% Stop	17%
BA-	1.8% x 3	1.8% x 3	Double-bottom	0%	LLOY	1.0% x 3	2.2% x 3	8.5% Stop	37%
BAA	2.0% x 3	2.1% x 3 H/L	12.0% Stop	26%	MKS	2.5% x 3 H/L	2.5% x 3 H/L	14.0% Stop	5%
BARC	2.4% x 3 H/L	2.4% x 3 H/L	Double-bottom	0%	MRW	2.5% x 3	0.7% x 3	13.5% Stop	24%
BATS	2.5% x 3	2.5% x 3	Double-bottom	0%	NGT	2.4% x 3	2.3% x 3 H/L	10.5% Stop	37%
BAY	0.8% x 3	0.8% x 3	7.5% Stop	35%	NRK	1.5% x 3	1.5% x 3	11.0% Stop	16%
BG-	1.9% x 3	1.9% x 3	12.0% Stop	5%	NXT	1.1% x 3	1.1% x 3	Double-bottom	0%
BLND	1.4% x 3	1.4% x 3	Double-bottom	0%	PRU	2.2% x 3	2.4% x 3	15.0% Stop	55%
BLT	2.3% x 3	1.1% x 3	15.0% Stop	19%	PSON	2.1% x 3	2.1% x 3	Double-bottom	0%
BNZL	1.1% x 3	1.1% x 3	Double-bottom	0%	RB-	2.0% x 3 H/L	2.4% x 3 H/L	11.0% Stop	45%
BOC	2.4% x 3	2.4% x 3	Double-bottom	0%	RBS	2.5% x 3 H/L	0.5% x 3 H/L	15.0% Stop	14%
BOOT	1.3% x 3	1.9% x 3	10.0% Stop	18%	REL	2.5% x 3	2.3% x 3	11.5% Stop	39%
BP-	2.1% x 3	0.8% x 3	15.0% Stop	37%	REX	1.8% x 3	2.2% x 3	14.0% Stop	21%
BSY	2.1% x 3	2.1% x 3	Double-bottom	0%	RIO	1.9% x 3	1.6% x 3 H/L	13.0% Stop	26%
BT-A	2.5% x 3	2.5% x 3	Double-bottom	0%	RR-	1.7% x 3	1.7% x 3	Double-bottom	0%
CBRY	1.9% x 3	1.4% x 3	10.0% Stop	38%	RSA	1.8% x 3	1.8% x 3	Double-bottom	0%
CCL	0.7% x 3	0.6% x 3	10.5% Stop	31%	RTO	2.4% x 3	2.5% x 3	10.5% Stop	27%
CNA	1.6% x 3	1.6% x 3	Double-bottom	0%	RTR	2.5% x 3	2.5% x 3	Double-bottom	0%
CPI	0.7% x 3	0.7% x 3	Double-bottom	0%	SBRY	1.5% x 3	1.5% x 3 H/L	13.5% Stop	16%
CS-	2.5% x 3	2.5% x 3	Double-bottom	0%	SCTN	2.5% x 3	2.5% x 3	14.0% Stop	11%
CW-	2.5% x 3	2.5% x 3	15.0% Stop	0%	SDR	1.0% x 3	1.6% x 3	7.5% Stop	36%
DGE	2.2% x 3	2.4% x 3 H/L	14.5% Stop	16%	SGE	2.3% x 3	2.3% x 3	Double-bottom	0%
DMGT	2.2% x 3	1.0% x 3	7.5% Stop	64%	SHEL	2.3% x 3	2.3% x 3	11.0% Stop	9%
DXNS	1.6% x 3	1.0% x 3	15.0% Stop	12%	SHP	2.3% x 3	2.3% x 3	Double-bottom	0%
EMA	0.5% x 3	0.9% x 3 H/L	8.5% Stop	18%	SMIN	1.9% x 3	2.0% x 3 H/L	7.0% Stop	66%
EMG	1.7% x 3 H/L	1.2% x 3 H/L	15.0% Stop	63%	SN-	1.9% x 3	0.5% x 3 H/L	13.0% Stop	22%
ETI	0.9% x 3	0.5% x 3	15.0% Stop	50%	SPW	2.1% x 3	2.1% x 3 H/L	14.5% Stop	23%
EXL	2.3% x 3 H/L	2.0% x 3 H/L	13.5% Stop	20%	SSE	2.0% x 3	2.0% x 3	Double-bottom	0%
GLH	2.2% x 3	1.1% x 3 H/L	15.0% Stop	45%	STAN	1.1% x 3	1.1% x 3	Double-bottom	0%
GSK	1.4% x 3	1.9% x 3	9.5% Stop	18%	SVT	2.4% x 3	2.4% x 3	Double-bottom	0%
GUS	1.5% x 3 H/L	1.5% x 3 H/L	Double-bottom	0%	TATE	1.4% x 3	0.9% x 3	8.0% Stop	41%
HAS	2.5% x 3	2.5% x 3	Double-bottom	0%	TSCO	0.9% x 3	1.5% x 3	9.5% Stop	23%
HBOS	1.1% x 3	2.3% x 3	13.5% Stop	14%	ULVR	1.9% x 3 H/L	1.9% x 3 H/L	8.0% Stop	44%
HG-	1.0% x 3	0.5% x 3	4.0% Stop	3%	UU-	0.7% x 3	2.5% x 3	4.0% Stop	22%
HNS	1.8% x 3	1.8% x 3	Double-bottom	0%	VOD	2.0% x 3	2.0% x 3	8.0% Stop	24%
HSBA	2.4% x 3	1.1% x 3	12.0% Stop	35%	WOS	1.2% x 3	1.2% x 3	9.0% Stop	28%
ICI	2.2% x 3	2.2% x 3	Double-bottom	0%	WPP	2.4% x 3	1.2% x 3 H/L	15.0% Stop	86%
IHG	2.5% x 3 H/L	0.7% x 3 H/L	10.0% Stop	13%	WTB	0.8% x 3	0.8% x 3	Double-bottom	0%

Table 7-3: Optimisation of FTSE 100 constituents from January 1998

Table 7-3 shows the difference in box sizes when the exit is a double-bottom sell or a trailing stop loss. The columns are as follows:

1. The instrument code.[26]

2. The best box size for a 3-box reversal chart based on an entry signal of a double-top buy and an exit on a double-bottom sell.

3. The best box size for a 3-box reversal chart based on an entry signal of a double-top buy and an exit either on a double-bottom sell or % stop loss.

4. Which was the better exit: a double-bottom sell or a stop loss. If a stop loss, the percentage is shown.

5. The % increase in profit when a stop loss is used instead of a double-bottom sell to exit.

There are few things to notice:

- Although each instrument requires a different box size, the average box size is 1.8%. This is due to the long-term nature of the data under consideration. A similar optimisation (not shown) on 250 days of data yielded an average box size of 1.1%, showing that the box size decreases as your time horizon decreases.

- The average box size when a stop loss is used is only slightly different at 1.7%.

- In most cases, although not all, the results are improved by exiting on a stop loss, shown by the column showing the percentage increase in profit when a stop loss is used.

- Only 28% of the results required construction using high/low data. It is interesting to note, however, that this increased to 47% when the data under consideration is reduced to 250 days.

Once you have the ground rules for conducting Point and Figure optimisations, they can be performed on any group of instruments.

Optimisation of S&P 100 constituents for longs

Table 7-4 shows the results of a similar optimisation conducted on the S&P 100 constituents, using data from January 1998 to the present day. Once again, those with less data history have been excluded.

---

[26] A table of instrument names is shown in Appendix D.

Entry: Double-top Exit: Double-bottom or Stop loss			Entry: Double-top Exit: Double-bottom or Stop loss		
Code	Box x Rev.	Exit	Code	Box x Rev.	Exit
AA	0.6% x 3	14.0% Stop	INTC	2.3% x 3	10.0% Stop
AEP	1.9% x 3 H/L	6.0% Stop	IP	1.5% x 3 H/L	15.0% Stop
AES	0.5% x 3 H/L	8.5% Stop	JNJ	0.7% x 3	15.0% Stop
AIG	2.0% x 3	14.0% Stop	JPM	1.2% x 3	12.5% Stop
ALL	1.2% x 3 H/L	9.5% Stop	KO	2.3% x 3	13.0% Stop
AMGN	1.9% x 3	Double-bottom	LEH	0.7% x 3	Double-bottom
AVP	0.5% x 3 H/L	13.5% Stop	LTD	0.7% x 3	14.0% Stop
AXP	1.6% x 3	Double-bottom	LU	1.4% x 3	11.0% Stop
BA	1.0% x 3	9.5% Stop	MAY	1.6% x 3	14.5% Stop
BAC	0.7% x 3	9.0% Stop	MCD	2.5% x 3 H/L	11.0% Stop
BAX	2.1% x 3 H/L	10.0% Stop	MDT	2.5% x 3	12.0% Stop
BDK	0.9% x 3 H/L	10.0% Stop	MEDI	2.0% x 3	Double-bottom
BHI	1.4% x 3	Double-bottom	MER	1.4% x 3	10.0% Stop
BMY	2.4% x 3 H/L	15.0% Stop	MMM	0.9% x 3 H/L	15.0% Stop
BNI	2.2% x 3 H/L	15.0% Stop	MO	1.1% x 3	Double-bottom
BUD	0.5% x 3	13.0% Stop	MRK	2.2% x 3	15.0% Stop
C	2.4% x 3 H/L	14.5% Stop	MSFT	0.8% x 3	7.5% Stop
CCU	1.7% x 3 H/L	14.5% Stop	MWD	1.2% x 3	14.0% Stop
CI	2.1% x 3	Double-bottom	NSC	0.9% x 3 H/L	12.5% Stop
CL	0.7% x 3 H/L	15.0% Stop	NSM	1.7% x 3 H/L	14.0% Stop
CPB	1.6% x 3	Double-bottom	NXTL	2.5% x 3	Double-bottom
CSC	0.6% x 3	11.0% Stop	ORCL	1.6% x 3	Double-bottom
CSCO	2.5% x 3	Double-bottom	PEP	0.6% x 3	12.0% Stop
DAL	1.5% x 3 H/L	13.5% Stop	PFE	2.5% x 3	7.5% Stop
DD	0.8% x 3	14.5% Stop	PG	1.3% x 3 H/L	13.0% Stop
DELL	0.8% x 3 H/L	10.5% Stop	ROK	0.7% x 3 H/L	13.0% Stop
DIS	2.5% x 3	12.5% Stop	RSH	1.1% x 3	14.5% Stop
DOW	0.6% x 3 H/L	14.5% Stop	RTN	1.3% x 3	6.0% Stop
EK	0.5% x 3	11.5% Stop	S	1.2% x 3 H/L	11.5% Stop
EMC	2.5% x 3	Double-bottom	SBC	1.2% x 3	5.0% Stop
EP	0.7% x 3	Double-bottom	SLB	1.5% x 3 H/L	13.0% Stop
ETR	1.9% x 3 H/L	14.0% Stop	SLE	1.3% x 3 H/L	10.5% Stop
EXC	0.6% x 3	9.0% Stop	SO	0.5% x 3	12.5% Stop
F	2.2% x 3 H/L	13.5% Stop	T	2.3% x 3	5.5% Stop
FDX	2.0% x 3 H/L	Double-bottom	TOY	1.2% x 3	9.0% Stop
G	2.3% x 3	5.5% Stop	TWX	2.5% x 3	Double-bottom
GD	2.5% x 3	14.0% Stop	TXN	2.5% x 3	Double-bottom
GE	1.3% x 3 H/L	14.0% Stop	TYC	0.8% x 3	12.0% Stop
GM	1.5% x 3 H/L	14.0% Stop	UIS	1.2% x 3	Double-bottom
HAL	0.8% x 3	14.0% Stop	USB	0.7% x 3	8.0% Stop
HCA	1.8% x 3	12.5% Stop	UTX	0.5% x 3	14.0% Stop
HD	1.2% x 3	12.5% Stop	VZ	2.4% x 3 H/L	13.5% Stop
HET	1.6% x 3 H/L	14.5% Stop	WFC	1.0% x 3	Double-bottom
HIG	1.2% x 3 H/L	9.0% Stop	WMB	1.3% x 3	9.5% Stop
HNZ	2.1% x 3	4.5% Stop	WMT	1.1% x 3 H/L	13.5% Stop
HON	2.3% x 3 H/L	14.5% Stop	WY	0.8% x 3	14.5% Stop
HPQ	1.6% x 3	14.0% Stop	XOM	1.5% x 3 H/L	9.5% Stop
IBM	1.3% x 3 H/L	6.5% Stop	XRX	2.1% x 3	Double-bottom

Table 7-4: Optimisation of S&P 100 constituents from January 1998

Table 7-4 shows:

1.   The instrument code.[27]

2.   The best box size for a 3-box reversal chart based on an entry signal of a double-top buy and an exit either on a double-bottom sell or % stop loss.

3.   Which was the better exit: a double-bottom sell or a stop loss. If a stop loss, the percentage is shown.

The average box size is 1.4%, slightly smaller than the FTSE 100. In most cases, the results can be improved by exiting on a stop loss rather than a double-bottom sell. 36% of the results required construction using high/low data.

These tables show the best box size, and in some cases the best stop loss percentage, at the time the optimisation was conducted. Although it is likely that they will remain the best for a short time, they cannot be expected to remain so for any length of time and should, therefore, not be relied on.

Optimising for shorts

All the optimisations conducted so far have assumed that your position is opened by buying. Of course, it is just as easy to open a position by selling, called a 'short position'.

Optimisation of FTSE 100 constituents for shorts

Table 7-5 shows the results of an optimisation on the FTSE 100 constituents using a double-bottom sell as the entry signal and either a double-top buy or a stop loss as the exit signal.

Notice that the stop loss exit, in other words a buy based on a stop loss, is a far more common exit than one based on a double-top buy. Notice also that the box sizes are different from those achieved for longs and that the high/low construction method is less common.

This shows that if you intend shorting, you should be looking at a completely different Point and Figure chart. Optimisation will guide you to the best box size to achieve this because optimisation of shorts maximises the profit from shorts rather than longs.

---

[27] A table of instrument names is shown in Appendix D.

	Short Entry: Double-bottom Short Exit: Double-top or Stop loss				Short Entry: Double-bottom Short Exit: Double-top or Stop loss	
Code	Box x Rev.	Exit	Code	Box x Rev.	Exit
ABF	1.5% x 3	15.0% Stop	III	1.2% x 3	Double-top
AL-	2.3% x 3	7.5% Stop	IMT	2.4% x 3	5.0% Stop
ALLD	2.2% x 3	14.5% Stop	IPR	0.5% x 3	15.0% Stop
ANTO	1.6% x 3	3.5% Stop	ITV	2.5% x 3	12.5% Stop
AUN	2.0% x 3	1.0% Stop	JMAT	2.0% x 3	3.0% Stop
AV-	2.2% x 3	Double-top	KGF	2.5% x 3	8.0% Stop
AVZ	2.4% x 3	11.5% Stop	LAND	2.2% x 3 H/L	14.5% Stop
AZN	1.2% x 3 H/L	15.0% Stop	LGEN	2.4% x 3	13.5% Stop
BA-	2.1% x 3	Double-top	LLOY	0.8% x 3	15.0% Stop
BAA	2.4% x 3	8.0% Stop	MKS	1.9% x 3	14.0% Stop
BARC	2.3% x 3	1.5% Stop	MRW	2.5% x 3	8.5% Stop
BATS	2.5% x 3	Double-top	NGT	2.0% x 3	5.0% Stop
BAY	1.0% x 3	12.0% Stop	NRK	2.3% x 3	0.5% Stop
BG-	2.5% x 3	1.0% Stop	NXT	1.1% x 3	Double-top
BLND	1.4% x 3	13.5% Stop	PRU	2.2% x 3	13.0% Stop
BLT	2.5% x 3	10.0% Stop	PSON	2.1% x 3	Double-top
BNZL	1.7% x 3	2.5% Stop	RB-	2.2% x 3 H/L	13.5% Stop
BOC	2.4% x 3	Double-top	RBS	2.5% x 3	0.5% Stop
BOOT	1.3% x 3	Double-top	REL	2.5% x 3	Double-top
BP-	2.3% x 3 H/L	13.0% Stop	REX	2.5% x 3	7.0% Stop
BSY	1.2% x 3	11.5% Stop	RIO	1.7% x 3	12.5% Stop
BT-A	2.5% x 3	Double-top	RR-	1.7% x 3	13.0% Stop
CBRY	2.3% x 3	13.0% Stop	RSA	2.0% x 3	11.0% Stop
CCL	2.2% x 3	6.5% Stop	RTO	2.4% x 3	Double-top
CNA	1.6% x 3	13.0% Stop	RTR	2.4% x 3	12.0% Stop
CPI	2.3% x 3	7.5% Stop	SBRY	1.5% x 3	13.5% Stop
CS-	0.9% x 3	7.5% Stop	SCTN	0.7% x 3	14.5% Stop
CW-	2.5% x 3	Double-top	SDR	1.0% x 3	15.0% Stop
DGE	2.5% x 3	13.5% Stop	SGE	1.0% x 3	15.0% Stop
DMGT	2.2% x 3	14.0% Stop	SHEL	2.3% x 3	Double-top
DXNS	2.4% x 3	14.0% Stop	SHP	1.1% x 3	6.5% Stop
EMA	0.5% x 3	14.5% Stop	SMIN	1.4% x 3	6.0% Stop
EMG	2.3% x 3	1.0% Stop	SN-	2.5% x 3	4.0% Stop
ETI	0.8% x 3	4.5% Stop	SPW	2.3% x 3	4.5% Stop
EXL	1.4% x 3	2.0% Stop	SSE	1.8% x 3	11.5% Stop
GLH	2.4% x 3	2.0% Stop	STAN	1.2% x 3	7.5% Stop
GSK	1.2% x 3	11.5% Stop	SVT	2.2% x 3	6.0% Stop
GUS	2.1% x 3	Double-top	TATE	2.4% x 3	4.5% Stop
HAS	2.5% x 3	Double-top	TSCO	1.6% x 3 H/L	14.5% Stop
HBOS	2.5% x 3	5.0% Stop	ULVR	2.3% x 3 H/L	6.5% Stop
HG-	2.5% x 3	11.0% Stop	UU-	2.4% x 3	Double-top
HNS	1.8% x 3	4.0% Stop	VOD	1.7% x 3 H/L	8.5% Stop
HSBA	2.4% x 3	13.5% Stop	WOS	2.3% x 3	3.0% Stop
ICI	2.2% x 3	Double-top	WPP	2.1% x 3	12.5% Stop
IHG	2.5% x 3 H/L	5.5% Stop	WTB	1.1% x 3	9.0% Stop

Table 7-5: Optimisation of FTSE 100 constituents based on short trades

Optimisation of S&P 100 constituents for shorts

Table 7-6 shows the results of an optimisation conducted on the S&P 100 constituents using a double-bottom sell as the entry signal and either a double-top buy or a stop loss as the exit.

Once again, the trailing stop loss exit has proved best in most cases and the high/low construction method is only used in a few cases.

Short Entry: Double-bottom Short Exit: Double-top or Stop loss				Short Entry: Double-bottom Short Exit: Double-top or Stop loss		
Code	Box x Rev.	Exit		Code	Box x Rev.	Exit
AA	2.2% x 3	3.5% Stop		INTC	2.0% x 3	Double-top
AEP	1.3% x 3	8.0% Stop		IP	2.3% x 3	4.5% Stop
AES	1.5% x 3	8.5% Stop		JNJ	2.5% x 3	8.5% Stop
AIG	1.8% x 3	10.5% Stop		JPM	1.6% x 3	10.0% Stop
ALL	2.2% x 3	8.0% Stop		KO	1.3% x 3	7.0% Stop
AMGN	1.0% x 3	6.5% Stop		LEH	0.7% x 3	13.0% Stop
AVP	2.5% x 3	2.5% Stop		LTD	1.0% x 3	6.0% Stop
AXP	1.9% x 3	9.0% Stop		LU	0.5% x 3	Double-top
BA	1.6% x 3	6.0% Stop		MAY	1.7% x 3	15.0% Stop
BAC	2.3% x 3	1.0% Stop		MCD	2.4% x 3 H/L	Double-top
BAX	1.2% x 3	14.0% Stop		MDT	2.3% x 3	0.5% Stop
BDK	1.7% x 3	9.5% Stop		MEDI	2.3% x 3	7.0% Stop
BHI	2.5% x 3	2.5% Stop		MER	2.4% x 3	10.0% Stop
BMY	2.3% x 3 H/L	Double-top		MMM	2.1% x 3	4.0% Stop
BNI	2.5% x 3	10.0% Stop		MO	1.1% x 3	Double-top
BUD	2.2% x 3	5.5% Stop		MRK	2.2% x 3	Double-top
C	2.4% x 3	8.5% Stop		MSFT	0.5% x 3	11.0% Stop
CCU	1.8% x 3	6.5% Stop		MWD	2.0% x 3	14.0% Stop
CI	2.2% x 3	Double-top		NSC	1.6% x 3	8.0% Stop
CL	1.0% x 3	14.5% Stop		NSM	2.1% x 3	14.0% Stop
CPB	1.6% x 3	10.5% Stop		NXTL	1.3% x 3	2.5% Stop
CSC	1.6% x 3	9.5% Stop		ORCL	1.8% x 3	13.5% Stop
CSCO	2.4% x 3	15.0% Stop		PEP	2.3% x 3	8.0% Stop
DAL	1.0% x 3	13.0% Stop		PFE	1.1% x 3	14.5% Stop
DD	2.5% x 3	3.0% Stop		PG	2.2% x 3	11.5% Stop
DELL	1.2% x 3	9.0% Stop		ROK	2.3% x 3 H/L	5.0% Stop
DIS	1.7% x 3	Double-top		RSH	1.8% x 3	14.0% Stop
DOW	2.1% x 3	3.5% Stop		RTN	1.7% x 3	5.5% Stop
EK	2.3% x 3	3.5% Stop		S	0.8% x 3	Double-top
EMC	2.5% x 3	Double-top		SBC	1.4% x 3 H/L	9.0% Stop
EP	0.7% x 3	11.0% Stop		SLB	2.3% x 3	4.0% Stop
ETR	2.3% x 3	3.5% Stop		SLE	1.4% x 3	10.0% Stop
EXC	1.3% x 3	6.5% Stop		SO	2.1% x 3	2.0% Stop
F	2.5% x 3	13.5% Stop		T	0.7% x 3	15.0% Stop
FDX	1.9% x 3 H/L	7.5% Stop		TOY	0.8% x 3	6.5% Stop
G	2.3% x 3	Double-top		TWX	2.4% x 3 H/L	9.5% Stop
GD	2.4% x 3	14.5% Stop		TXN	2.4% x 3	0.5% Stop
GE	1.8% x 3 H/L	11.5% Stop		TYC	2.0% x 3	6.0% Stop
GM	1.3% x 3	4.5% Stop		UIS	1.2% x 3	Double-top
HAL	2.5% x 3	7.5% Stop		USB	1.4% x 3 H/L	6.5% Stop
HCA	2.1% x 3	3.5% Stop		UTX	2.3% x 3	4.5% Stop
HD	1.2% x 3	6.0% Stop		VZ	2.5% x 3	2.0% Stop
HET	2.2% x 3	14.5% Stop		WFC	2.4% x 3	0.5% Stop
HIG	1.8% x 3	6.0% Stop		WMB	0.7% x 3	11.0% Stop
HNZ	2.2% x 3	3.5% Stop		WMT	2.1% x 3	3.5% Stop
HON	2.5% x 3	4.0% Stop		WY	1.2% x 3	7.5% Stop
HPQ	1.9% x 3	Double-top		XOM	2.4% x 3	7.0% Stop
IBM	1.5% x 3	7.0% Stop		XRX	1.4% x 3 H/L	10.5% Stop

Table 7-6: Optimisation of S&P 100 constituents based on short trades

Optimising for specific patterns

As discussed earlier, the only pattern guaranteed to occur on every chart is the double-top buy and double-bottom sell. This does not mean that you have to limit your optimisations to these. You may prefer to enter your long trade on a less common pattern such as a triple-top or a catapult, provided you don't try to exit on one; they may never occur. Therefore, if you optimise for entry on either a catapult or a triple-top, the results will tell you the best box size and construction method to achieve the greatest profit from these patterns.

Catapult entry signals

Optimisation of FTSE 100 constituents for catapult entry for longs

Table 7-7 shows the results of an optimisation conducted on the FTSE 100 constituents again, but this time using a bullish catapult as the entry signal and either a double-bottom sell or a stop loss as the exit.

Code	Box x Rev.	Entry	Exit	Code	Box x Rev.	Entry	Exit
ABF	0.5% x 3 H/L	Catapult Buy	Double-bottom	III	2.1% x 3 H/L	Catapult Buy	13.5 % Stop
AL-	1.4% x 3 H/L	Catapult Buy	8.0 % Stop	IMT	2.1% x 3 H/L	Catapult Buy	12.0 % Stop
ALLD	1.9% x 3 H/L	Catapult Buy	Double-bottom	IPR	0.5% x 3 H/L	Catapult Buy	8.0 % Stop
ANTO	0.8% x 3	Catapult Buy	Double-bottom	ITV	1.5% x 3 H/L	Catapult Buy	8.0 % Stop
AUN	0.8% x 3 H/L	Catapult Buy	7.5 % Stop	JMAT	2.3% x 3	Catapult Buy	7.0 % Stop
AV-	0.5% x 3 H/L	Catapult Buy	7.5 % Stop	KGF	1.1% x 3	Catapult Buy	10.0 % Stop
AVZ	1.5% x 3 H/L	Catapult Buy	1.5 % Stop	LAND	1.3% x 3 H/L	Catapult Buy	8.0 % Stop
AZN	0.9% x 3	Catapult Buy	Double-bottom	LGEN	2.1% x 3	Catapult Buy	7.0 % Stop
BA-	1.8% x 3	Catapult Buy	Double-bottom	LLOY	2.0% x 3 H/L	Catapult Buy	9.0 % Stop
BAA	0.6% x 3	Catapult Buy	11.5 % Stop	MKS	1.1% x 3 H/L	Catapult Buy	14.0 % Stop
BARC	0.7% x 3 H/L	Catapult Buy	8.0 % Stop	MRW	0.5% x 3 H/L	Catapult Buy	11.0 % Stop
BATS	1.7% x 3 H/L	Catapult Buy	7.5 % Stop	NGT	1.8% x 3 H/L	Catapult Buy	6.0 % Stop
BAY	2.5% x 3 H/L	Catapult Buy	6.5 % Stop	NRK	2.2% x 3 H/L	Catapult Buy	8.0 % Stop
BG-	1.6% x 3 H/L	Catapult Buy	8.0 % Stop	NXT	0.6% x 3 H/L	Catapult Buy	8.5 % Stop
BLND	0.7% x 3 H/L	Catapult Buy	9.5 % Stop	PRU	0.5% x 3 H/L	Catapult Buy	5.5 % Stop
BLT	2.3% x 3 H/L	Catapult Buy	13.0 % Stop	PSON	1.1% x 3	Catapult Buy	Double-bottom
BNZL	1.0% x 3 H/L	Catapult Buy	9.0 % Stop	RB-	0.9% x 3 H/L	Catapult Buy	15.0 % Stop
BOC	1.7% x 3 H/L	Catapult Buy	10.5 % Stop	RBS	1.2% x 3 H/L	Catapult Buy	13.5 % Stop
BOOT	0.8% x 3 H/L	Catapult Buy	15.0 % Stop	REL	0.8% x 3 H/L	Catapult Buy	9.0 % Stop
BP-	1.9% x 3	Catapult Buy	7.5 % Stop	REX	0.8% x 3 H/L	Catapult Buy	9.0 % Stop
BSY	1.9% x 3	Catapult Buy	Double-bottom	RIO	0.7% x 3	Catapult Buy	Double-bottom
BT-A	1.8% x 3 H/L	Catapult Buy	6.0 % Stop	RR-	1.4% x 3 H/L	Catapult Buy	9.0 % Stop
CBRY	1.8% x 3 H/L	Catapult Buy	9.5 % Stop	RSA	2.4% x 3 H/L	Catapult Buy	5.0 % Stop
CCL	1.3% x 3 H/L	Catapult Buy	8.5 % Stop	RTO	1.9% x 3 H/L	Catapult Buy	10.5 % Stop
CNA	1.7% x 3	Catapult Buy	14.5 % Stop	RTR	1.9% x 3 H/L	Catapult Buy	15.0 % Stop
CPI	1.1% x 3	Catapult Buy	Double-bottom	SBRY	1.7% x 3 H/L	Catapult Buy	Double-bottom
CS-	2.2% x 3 H/L	Catapult Buy	2.5 % Stop	SCTN	0.7% x 3	Catapult Buy	7.5 % Stop
CW-	0.6% x 3 H/L	Catapult Buy	12.0 % Stop	SDR	1.1% x 3 H/L	Catapult Buy	7.5 % Stop
DGE	0.7% x 3 H/L	Catapult Buy	8.5 % Stop	SGE	0.5% x 3	Catapult Buy	7.0 % Stop
DMGT	0.7% x 3	Catapult Buy	12.0 % Stop	SHEL	0.8% x 3	Catapult Buy	1.0 % Stop
DXNS	0.6% x 3 H/L	Catapult Buy	12.5 % Stop	SHP	2.0% x 3	Catapult Buy	Double-bottom
EMA	1.3% x 3 H/L	Catapult Buy	Double-bottom	SMIN	2.1% x 3 H/L	Catapult Buy	9.0 % Stop
EMG	0.5% x 3 H/L	Catapult Buy	10.5 % Stop	SN-	1.5% x 3 H/L	Catapult Buy	14.0 % Stop
ETI	0.9% x 3 H/L	Catapult Buy	6.0 % Stop	SPW	0.7% x 3 H/L	Catapult Buy	11.0 % Stop
EXL	1.0% x 3 H/L	Catapult Buy	13.5 % Stop	SSE	0.5% x 3 H/L	Catapult Buy	6.0 % Stop
GLH	1.6% x 3 H/L	Catapult Buy	11.5 % Stop	STAN	1.1% x 3 H/L	Catapult Buy	13.0 % Stop
GSK	1.8% x 3 H/L	Catapult Buy	8.0 % Stop	SVT	1.8% x 3 H/L	Catapult Buy	6.5 % Stop
GUS	1.9% x 3 H/L	Catapult Buy	6.0 % Stop	TATE	1.9% x 3 H/L	Catapult Buy	3.5 % Stop
HAS	1.3% x 3	Catapult Buy	14.5 % Stop	TSCO	1.9% x 3 H/L	Catapult Buy	5.0 % Stop
HBOS	1.1% x 3	Catapult Buy	13.5 % Stop	ULVR	1.9% x 3 H/L	Catapult Buy	Double-bottom
HG-	0.6% x 3 H/L	Catapult Buy	11.0 % Stop	UU-	2.0% x 3 H/L	Catapult Buy	4.0 % Stop
HNS	0.5% x 3	Catapult Buy	6.0 % Stop	VOD	1.8% x 3 H/L	Catapult Buy	7.5 % Stop
HSBA	1.6% x 3 H/L	Catapult Buy	6.0 % Stop	WOS	2.1% x 3 H/L	Catapult Buy	9.0 % Stop
ICI	0.5% x 3 H/L	Catapult Buy	7.5 % Stop	WPP	2.2% x 3	Catapult Buy	13.0 % Stop
IHG	0.5% x 3 H/L	Catapult Buy	10.5 % Stop	WTB	1.4% x 3 H/L	Catapult Buy	14.5 % Stop

Table 7-7: Optimisation of FTSE 100 based on 3-box catapult buy signals & double-bottom or stop loss exits

Compare Table 7-7, which uses a catapult entry with Table 7-3, which uses a double-top entry. Notice that the high/low (h/l) construction method is found to be the best in most cases when the catapult is used, indicating that if you wish to trade on catapult entries, you are better off drawing high/low Point and Figure charts. This is one of the great benefits of optimisation; it can tell you how best to construct your charts.

Notice also that an exit based on a stop loss is preferred in most cases to an exit based on a double-bottom sell. The reason is that, having entered on a catapult buy, you will want to run the trade for as long as it is profitable. If you get closed out on a double-bottom sell signal, you have to wait for another catapult to occur before you can buy again. As you have seen, that may never happen again and you will have to forego a profit opportunity. Consequently, the less sensitive trailing stop loss ensures you remain with the trend for as long as possible.

Optimisation must, therefore, be tailored to suit your trading style. If you wish to know what box size and construction method is most likely to produce the most profitable catapult entry trades, then optimising based on these conditions is the only way to find out.

Although the Table 7-7 shows the results for long trades using catapult buys, a similar optimisation (not shown) may be conducted for shorts, where the entry signal is a catapult sell and the exit is a double-top buy or stop loss.

Optimisation of S&P 100 constituents for catapult entry for longs

Table 7-8 shows the results of a similar optimisation conducted on the S&P 100 constituents. The entry signal is a bullish catapult and the exit signal is either a double-bottom sell or a trailing stop loss.

Once again, the high/low (h/l) construction method is found to be the best in most cases. The trailing stop loss exit is also preferred to the double-bottom sell in most cases.

Code	Box x Rev.	Entry	Exit	Code	Box x Rev.	Entry	Exit
AA	1.3x 3 H/L	Catapult Buy	10.5% Stop	INTC	0.6x 3	Catapult Buy	14.0% Stop
AEP	1.1x 3 H/L	Catapult Buy	2.5% Stop	IP	0.9x 3 H/L	Catapult Buy	9.0% Stop
AES	2.0x 3 H/L	Catapult Buy	10.5% Stop	JNJ	1.7x 3	Catapult Buy	14.0% Stop
AIG	0.6x 3	Catapult Buy	12.5% Stop	JPM	1.4x 3 H/L	Catapult Buy	12.5% Stop
ALL	1.3x 3 H/L	Catapult Buy	11.0% Stop	KO	2.0x 3 H/L	Catapult Buy	7.0% Stop
AMGN	1.8x 3 H/L	Catapult Buy	9.5% Stop	LEH	1.5x 3 H/L	Catapult Buy	Double-bottom
AVP	0.7x 3	Catapult Buy	11.5% Stop	LTD	0.5x 3 H/L	Catapult Buy	14.0% Stop
AXP	0.7x 3 H/L	Catapult Buy	7.5% Stop	LU	1.1x 3 H/L	Catapult Buy	6.5% Stop
BA	2.1x 3	Catapult Buy	Double-bottom	MAY	2.0x 3 H/L	Catapult Buy	12.0% Stop
BAC	1.2x 3 H/L	Catapult Buy	5.5% Stop	MCD	0.5x 3 H/L	Catapult Buy	8.5% Stop
BAX	0.7x 3 H/L	Catapult Buy	14.0% Stop	MDT	0.8x 3 H/L	Catapult Buy	12.0% Stop
BDK	0.8x 3 H/L	Catapult Buy	10.0% Stop	MEDI	1.3x 3	Catapult Buy	11.5% Stop
BHI	1.9x 3 H/L	Catapult Buy	14.5% Stop	MER	1.0x 3 H/L	Catapult Buy	Double-bottom
BMY	1.4x 3 H/L	Catapult Buy	14.5% Stop	MMM	2.4x 3	Catapult Buy	6.0% Stop
BNI	0.6x 3 H/L	Catapult Buy	10.5% Stop	MO	1.8x 3 H/L	Catapult Buy	6.5% Stop
BUD	0.5x 3 H/L	Catapult Buy	15.0% Stop	MRK	1.3x 3 H/L	Catapult Buy	Double-bottom
C	2.2x 3 H/L	Catapult Buy	Double-bottom	MSFT	0.6x 3 H/L	Catapult Buy	Double-bottom
CCU	2.5x 3 H/L	Catapult Buy	13.5% Stop	MWD	1.0x 3 H/L	Catapult Buy	10.0% Stop
CI	2.1x 3 H/L	Catapult Buy	13.5% Stop	NSC	1.0x 3	Catapult Buy	9.0% Stop
CL	2.3x 3	Catapult Buy	6.5% Stop	NSM	1.6x 3 H/L	Catapult Buy	8.5% Stop
CPB	0.9x 3 H/L	Catapult Buy	Double-bottom	NXTL	1.6x 3	Catapult Buy	Double-bottom
CSC	2.2x 3 H/L	Catapult Buy	4.5% Stop	ORCL	2.5x 3 H/L	Catapult Buy	12.5% Stop
CSCO	1.1x 3 H/L	Catapult Buy	10.0% Stop	PEP	0.5x 3 H/L	Catapult Buy	9.0% Stop
DAL	1.1x 3 H/L	Catapult Buy	5.0% Stop	PFE	1.0x 3 H/L	Catapult Buy	6.0% Stop
DD	0.5x 3 H/L	Catapult Buy	9.0% Stop	PG	0.6x 3	Catapult Buy	6.0% Stop
DELL	0.7x 3 H/L	Catapult Buy	Double-bottom	ROK	1.0x 3 H/L	Catapult Buy	Double-bottom
DIS	1.4x 3 H/L	Catapult Buy	12.5% Stop	RSH	1.1x 3 H/L	Catapult Buy	1.0% Stop
DOW	0.7x 3 H/L	Catapult Buy	8.5% Stop	RTN	1.2x 3 H/L	Catapult Buy	9.0% Stop
EK	1.1x 3 H/L	Catapult Buy	3.5% Stop	S	0.7x 3	Catapult Buy	11.0% Stop
EMC	1.1x 3 H/L	Catapult Buy	12.5% Stop	SBC	1.0x 3 H/L	Catapult Buy	3.0% Stop
EP	0.9x 3 H/L	Catapult Buy	14.5% Stop	SLB	1.1x 3 H/L	Catapult Buy	13.0% Stop
ETR	1.0x 3 H/L	Catapult Buy	14.0% Stop	SLE	0.7x 3 H/L	Catapult Buy	7.5% Stop
EXC	1.0x 3 H/L	Catapult Buy	15.0% Stop	SO	0.7x 3 H/L	Catapult Buy	12.5% Stop
F	0.9x 3 H/L	Catapult Buy	13.0% Stop	T	0.6x 3 H/L	Catapult Buy	7.0% Stop
FDX	2.3x 3 H/L	Catapult Buy	Double-bottom	TOY	1.5x 3 H/L	Catapult Buy	7.5% Stop
G	0.9x 3 H/L	Catapult Buy	12.0% Stop	TWX	1.7x 3 H/L	Catapult Buy	14.5% Stop
GD	0.8x 3 H/L	Catapult Buy	14.0% Stop	TXN	1.3x 3	Catapult Buy	Double-bottom
GE	1.1x 3 H/L	Catapult Buy	14.0% Stop	TYC	1.5x 3 H/L	Catapult Buy	11.0% Stop
GM	1.2x 3	Catapult Buy	Double-bottom	UIS	1.4x 3 H/L	Catapult Buy	12.0% Stop
HAL	0.7x 3 H/L	Catapult Buy	5.0% Stop	USB	1.8x 3 H/L	Catapult Buy	Double-bottom
HCA	0.7x 3 H/L	Catapult Buy	11.0% Stop	UTX	1.1x 3 H/L	Catapult Buy	4.5% Stop
HD	1.8x 3 H/L	Catapult Buy	13.0% Stop	VZ	0.7x 3 H/L	Catapult Buy	12.0% Stop
HET	1.7x 3 H/L	Catapult Buy	11.5% Stop	WFC	0.7x 3 H/L	Catapult Buy	6.5% Stop
HIG	1.3x 3 H/L	Catapult Buy	8.0% Stop	WMB	1.2x 3 H/L	Catapult Buy	14.0% Stop
HNZ	1.5x 3	Catapult Buy	6.0% Stop	WMT	1.9x 3	Catapult Buy	9.0% Stop
HON	2.3x 3 H/L	Catapult Buy	7.0% Stop	WY	2.3x 3 H/L	Catapult Buy	14.0% Stop
HPQ	1.4x 3 H/L	Catapult Buy	14.0% Stop	XOM	0.6x 3	Catapult Buy	11.0% Stop
IBM	1.4x 3 H/L	Catapult Buy	10.5% Stop	XRX	2.1x 3 H/L	Catapult Buy	5.5% Stop

Table 7-8: Optimisation of S&P 100 based on 3-box catapult buy signals and double-bottom or stop loss exits

Triple-top entry signals

It is possible to run an optimisation based on any entry pattern, and the next logical one is a triple-top buy signal. As with catapults, they don't occur that often, but when they do, they tend to produce good gains.

Optimisation of FTSE 100 constituents for triple-top entry for longs

Table 7-9 shows the results of an optimisation conducted on the FTSE 100 constituents using a triple-top as the entry signal and either a double-bottom sell or a stop loss as the exit.

Code	Box x Rev.	Entry	Exit	Code	Box x Rev.	Entry	Exit
ABF	2.5% x 3	Triple-top	7.0 Stop	III	1.7% x 3	Triple-top	13.5 Stop
AL-	2.5% x 3	Triple-top	10.0 Stop	IMT	2.1% x 3	Triple-top	Double-bottom
ALLD	1.9% x 3 H/L	Triple-top	11.0 Stop	IPR	0.9% x 3 H/L	Triple-top	8.0 Stop
ANTO	2.1% x 3 H/L	Triple-top	14.0 Stop	ITV	0.9% x 3 H/L	Triple-top	13.0 Stop
AUN	1.7% x 3 H/L	Triple-top	7.5 Stop	JMAT	1.7% x 3	Triple-top	13.0 Stop
AV-	0.5% x 3	Triple-top	Double-bottom	KGF	1.5% x 3 H/L	Triple-top	11.5 Stop
AVZ	2.4% x 3	Triple-top	Double-bottom	LAND	0.6% x 3	Triple-top	8.0 Stop
AZN	2.0% x 3	Triple-top	10.5 Stop	LGEN	2.2% x 3	Triple-top	Double-bottom
BA-	2.1% x 3	Triple-top	Double-bottom	LLOY	1.1% x 3 H/L	Triple-top	3.5 Stop
BAA	0.6% x 3	Triple-top	12.0 Stop	MKS	1.1% x 3 H/L	Triple-top	14.0 Stop
BARC	2.5% x 3 H/L	Triple-top	Double-bottom	MRW	1.0% x 3 H/L	Triple-top	15.0 Stop
BATS	0.6% x 3	Triple-top	9.5 Stop	NGT	1.0% x 3 H/L	Triple-top	10.0 Stop
BAY	1.9% x 3	Triple-top	Double-bottom	NRK	2.4% x 3 H/L	Triple-top	11.0 Stop
BG-	0.5% x 3 H/L	Triple-top	9.0 Stop	NXT	1.9% x 3	Triple-top	Double-bottom
BLND	0.5% x 3	Triple-top	10.0 Stop	PRU	2.2% x 3	Triple-top	15.0 Stop
BLT	1.1% x 3 H/L	Triple-top	10.5 Stop	PSON	2.5% x 3	Triple-top	Double-bottom
BNZL	0.8% x 3	Triple-top	8.5 Stop	RB-	1.6% x 3 H/L	Triple-top	14.5 Stop
BOC	1.2% x 3	Triple-top	Double-bottom	RBS	0.6% x 3	Triple-top	12.5 Stop
BOOT	1.1% x 3	Triple-top	3.5 Stop	REL	0.6% x 3 H/L	Triple-top	10.0 Stop
BP-	0.7% x 3	Triple-top	Double-bottom	REX	0.8% x 3 H/L	Triple-top	14.0 Stop
BSY	2.0% x 3	Triple-top	Double-bottom	RIO	2.1% x 3 H/L	Triple-top	10.0 Stop
BT-A	2.5% x 3 H/L	Triple-top	11.5 Stop	RR-	1.7% x 3	Triple-top	Double-bottom
CBRY	1.2% x 3 H/L	Triple-top	10.0 Stop	RSA	2.0% x 3	Triple-top	Double-bottom
CCL	0.5% x 3 H/L	Triple-top	9.5 Stop	RTO	2.0% x 3 H/L	Triple-top	10.5 Stop
CNA	0.6% x 3	Triple-top	13.5 Stop	RTR	1.4% x 3 H/L	Triple-top	15.0 Stop
CPI	0.6% x 3	Triple-top	Double-bottom	SBRY	2.0% x 3 H/L	Triple-top	5.5 Stop
CS-	2.4% x 3 H/L	Triple-top	Double-bottom	SCTN	2.5% x 3 H/L	Triple-top	7.0 Stop
CW-	2.5% x 3 H/L	Triple-top	15.0 Stop	SDR	1.1% x 3 H/L	Triple-top	8.0 Stop
DGE	2.1% x 3	Triple-top	7.0 Stop	SGE	2.5% x 3	Triple-top	Double-bottom
DMGT	2.2% x 3 H/L	Triple-top	12.5 Stop	SHEL	1.9% x 3 H/L	Triple-top	11.0 Stop
DXNS	2.5% x 3 H/L	Triple-top	14.5 Stop	SHP	2.0% x 3	Triple-top	Double-bottom
EMA	0.8% x 3 H/L	Triple-top	7.5 Stop	SMIN	0.7% x 3	Triple-top	4.5 Stop
EMG	2.2% x 3 H/L	Triple-top	15.0 Stop	SN-	1.3% x 3 H/L	Triple-top	15.0 Stop
ETI	0.7% x 3	Triple-top	14.5 Stop	SPW	1.5% x 3	Triple-top	14.5 Stop
EXL	2.5% x 3 H/L	Triple-top	Double-bottom	SSE	1.0% x 3	Triple-top	6.0 Stop
GLH	2.3% x 3 H/L	Triple-top	15.0 Stop	STAN	1.8% x 3 H/L	Triple-top	12.0 Stop
GSK	2.5% x 3	Triple-top	8.0 Stop	SVT	1.4% x 3	Triple-top	Double-bottom
GUS	0.5% x 3	Triple-top	8.5 Stop	TATE	1.9% x 3 H/L	Triple-top	11.0 Stop
HAS	1.4% x 3 H/L	Triple-top	14.0 Stop	TSCO	1.5% x 3	Triple-top	9.5 Stop
HBOS	1.9% x 3	Triple-top	13.0 Stop	ULVR	0.5% x 3 H/L	Triple-top	8.5 Stop
HG-	0.7% x 3	Triple-top	3.5 Stop	UU-	2.0% x 3	Triple-top	4.0 Stop
HNS	0.6% x 3 H/L	Triple-top	15.0 Stop	VOD	1.8% x 3 H/L	Triple-top	Double-bottom
HSBA	1.7% x 3	Triple-top	14.0 Stop	WOS	1.7% x 3 H/L	Triple-top	9.5 Stop
ICI	1.8% x 3 H/L	Triple-top	10.5 Stop	WPP	2.2% x 3	Triple-top	13.5 Stop
IHG	1.9% x 3	Triple-top	Double-bottom	WTB	1.5% x 3 H/L	Triple-top	Double-bottom

Table 7-9: Optimisation of FTSE 100 based on triple-top buy signals and double-bottom or stop loss exits

Once again the stop loss is the favoured exit, although the choice of construction methods is evenly balanced between close only and high/low. This is because the high/low spikes are more likely to produce catapults, which are, in effect, triple-tops which have failed on the first break.

It is worth noting that when a triple-top occurs, a double-top is also occurring. This means that some of the triple-top buys may be at the same point as a double-top buy. Indeed, some of the triple-tops in Table 7-9 will also have been double-tops.

Optimisation of S&P 100 constituents for triple-top entry for longs

Table 7-10 shows the results of an optimisation conducted on the S&P 100 constituents using a triple-top as the entry signal and either a double-bottom sell or a stop loss as the exit.

Code	Box x Rev.	Entry	Exit	Code	Box x Rev.	Entry	Exit
AA	1.9x 3 H/L	Triple-top	11.5% Stop	INTC	0.7x 3 H/L	Triple-top	9.5% Stop
AEP	0.6x 3	Triple-top	6.0% Stop	IP	2.3x 3 H/L	Triple-top	Double-bottom
AES	1.3x 3	Triple-top	Double-bottom	JNJ	1.2x 3 H/L	Triple-top	14.0% Stop
AIG	1.9x 3	Triple-top	12.5% Stop	JPM	1.8x 3 H/L	Triple-top	12.5% Stop
ALL	1.2x 3 H/L	Triple-top	7.5% Stop	KO	1.1x 3 H/L	Triple-top	4.5% Stop
AMGN	1.0x 3	Triple-top	Double-bottom	LEH	0.7x 3 H/L	Triple-top	10.0% Stop
AVP	1.6x 3	Triple-top	Double-bottom	LTD	1.4x 3	Triple-top	14.0% Stop
AXP	1.3x 3	Triple-top	Double-bottom	LU	0.7x 3 H/L	Triple-top	11.0% Stop
BA	0.6x 3 H/L	Triple-top	9.5% Stop	MAY	2.0x 3 H/L	Triple-top	12.0% Stop
BAC	1.0x 3	Triple-top	4.5% Stop	MCD	0.7x 3 H/L	Triple-top	11.0% Stop
BAX	1.7x 3	Triple-top	9.5% Stop	MDT	1.6x 3 H/L	Triple-top	14.0% Stop
BDK	2.1x 3	Triple-top	10.0% Stop	MEDI	1.7x 3 H/L	Triple-top	14.0% Stop
BHI	1.6x 3 H/L	Triple-top	14.5% Stop	MER	1.3x 3 H/L	Triple-top	9.0% Stop
BMY	1.6x 3 H/L	Triple-top	15.0% Stop	MMM	0.7x 3 H/L	Triple-top	15.0% Stop
BNI	1.2x 3 H/L	Triple-top	11.0% Stop	MO	1.3x 3 H/L	Triple-top	10.0% Stop
BUD	0.5x 3	Triple-top	13.0% Stop	MRK	1.8x 3 H/L	Triple-top	8.0% Stop
C	2.0x 3 H/L	Triple-top	14.5% Stop	MSFT	1.0x 3 H/L	Triple-top	8.0% Stop
CCU	2.5x 3 H/L	Triple-top	13.5% Stop	MWD	2.4x 3 H/L	Triple-top	Double-bottom
CI	1.0x 3 H/L	Triple-top	13.5% Stop	NSC	1.0x 3 H/L	Triple-top	12.5% Stop
CL	2.3x 3	Triple-top	6.5% Stop	NSM	1.6x 3 H/L	Triple-top	13.5% Stop
CPB	1.0x 3	Triple-top	8.0% Stop	NXTL	1.0x 3 H/L	Triple-top	15.0% Stop
CSC	1.3x 3	Triple-top	15.0% Stop	ORCL	1.8x 3 H/L	Triple-top	13.5% Stop
CSCO	1.1x 3 H/L	Triple-top	11.0% Stop	PEP	0.6x 3 H/L	Triple-top	10.0% Stop
DAL	1.1x 3 H/L	Triple-top	3.5% Stop	PFE	1.0x 3 H/L	Triple-top	10.5% Stop
DD	0.6x 3	Triple-top	11.0% Stop	PG	1.1x 3 H/L	Triple-top	13.0% Stop
DELL	0.5x 3 H/L	Triple-top	10.0% Stop	ROK	0.8x 3 H/L	Triple-top	15.0% Stop
DIS	0.5x 3 H/L	Triple-top	13.0% Stop	RSH	0.7x 3 H/L	Triple-top	14.5% Stop
DOW	2.5x 3	Triple-top	10.5% Stop	RTN	0.7x 3 H/L	Triple-top	11.0% Stop
EK	1.2x 3 H/L	Triple-top	8.5% Stop	S	1.4x 3	Triple-top	10.0% Stop
EMC	0.9x 3 H/L	Triple-top	7.0% Stop	SBC	0.9x 3	Triple-top	Double-bottom
EP	1.1x 3	Triple-top	14.5% Stop	SLB	0.6x 3 H/L	Triple-top	14.0% Stop
ETR	1.3x 3 H/L	Triple-top	14.0% Stop	SLE	1.2x 3 H/L	Triple-top	3.5% Stop
EXC	0.6x 3	Triple-top	15.0% Stop	SO	0.7x 3 H/L	Triple-top	6.5% Stop
F	1.0x 3	Triple-top	Double-bottom	T	0.6x 3 H/L	Triple-top	7.5% Stop
FDX	1.6x 3	Triple-top	Double-bottom	TOY	1.5x 3 H/L	Triple-top	12.5% Stop
G	0.8x 3	Triple-top	4.5% Stop	TWX	0.8x 3 H/L	Triple-top	15.0% Stop
GD	0.8x 3	Triple-top	14.0% Stop	TXN	1.7x 3	Triple-top	13.5% Stop
GE	1.7x 3 H/L	Triple-top	14.5% Stop	TYC	1.2x 3 H/L	Triple-top	11.0% Stop
GM	0.7x 3	Triple-top	10.5% Stop	UIS	2.0x 3 H/L	Triple-top	12.0% Stop
HAL	1.5x 3	Triple-top	Double-bottom	USB	1.5x 3	Triple-top	Double-bottom
HCA	0.5x 3 H/L	Triple-top	11.5% Stop	UTX	1.1x 3 H/L	Triple-top	13.0% Stop
HD	0.5x 3 H/L	Triple-top	9.0% Stop	VZ	2.0x 3 H/L	Triple-top	12.0% Stop
HET	0.6x 3 H/L	Triple-top	14.5% Stop	WFC	1.7x 3 H/L	Triple-top	1.5% Stop
HIG	1.4x 3 H/L	Triple-top	8.0% Stop	WMB	1.4x 3 H/L	Triple-top	Double-bottom
HNZ	1.5x 3 H/L	Triple-top	6.0% Stop	WMT	2.2x 3 H/L	Triple-top	11.0% Stop
HON	2.5x 3 H/L	Triple-top	13.5% Stop	WY	1.4x 3 H/L	Triple-top	14.0% Stop
HPQ	1.4x 3 H/L	Triple-top	14.0% Stop	XOM	1.2x 3 H/L	Triple-top	9.5% Stop
IBM	1.9x 3	Triple-top	Double-bottom	XRX	1.1x 3 H/L	Triple-top	14.0% Stop

Table 7-10: Optimisation of S&P 100 based on triple-top buy signals and double-bottom or stop loss exits

The trailing stop loss continues to be the favoured exit, but it is significant to note that the high/low construction method has been used 70% of the time. This is a significant increase over that when the FTSE 100 was optimised. This says more about the state of the high/low data on FTSE 100 stocks than anything else.

Conclusion

If you think that optimisation will replace chart reading, you should think again; it will not. Optimisation will guide you to the best parameters to use, based on past performance, but it will not provide you with a formula for untold wealth. It can tell you whether an instrument's characteristics require the high/low construction rather than close only, but you must be aware that it can change. It will tell you what box size to start with, based on taking every buy and sell signal, but that does not mean that is the box size you must use, because you won't take every buy and sell generated from the chart.

Optimisation, therefore, gives you the parameters to get you started, from which point your subjective analysis and knowledge of Point and Figure charts should take over and adjustments be made. Remember when analysing Point and Figure charts there are many things to take into consideration, such as trend and pattern formation, but before doing that you have to make the decision about box and reversal. Optimisation can assist with that decision.

This chapter has only scratched the surface as far as optimisation is concerned. It is a vast subject and far more sophisticated optimisations need to be performed. Provided you understand that the 'holy grail' is not the prize, then further work on optimisation should be considered with an understanding of the following:

- Optimisation is only of value with 3-box reversal charts, because of their unambiguous signals.

- Unless you are looking very short-term, percentage box sizes should be used.

- Including uncommon Point and Figure patterns is fine for entry signals, but they should never be included as possible exit signals.

- Optimisation should always be conducted using the latest data because this allows the parameters to adjust as new data is received.

- The unrealised profit from any open position should be excluded from the optimisation, so box sizes are calculated on closed positions only.

- Dealing costs must be taken into account to prevent lots of small trades from being included.

- Optimisation can tell you what box size is working best, based on double-top and bottom signals. In doing so, it tells you about the characteristics of the instrument.

- In most cases, profits are increased considerably when trailing stop loss is used as the exit rather than a double-column signal.

- Optimisation can tell you whether the close only or high/low construction method is working best for the particular instrument.

- Optimisation results show that the shorter your time horizon, the smaller the box size is required.

- Optimisation does not tell you how to read the chart, but it gives you a starting point from where your subjective analysis must take over.

- Optimisation shows that the best box size for shorts is different from that for longs, requiring optimisations to be conducted for both longs and shorts, resulting in two different Point and Figure charts.

- Signal delay may need to be considered, although it is more difficult to administer with Point and Figure charts.

Finally, do not rely just on the tables of results. To really see how well they have worked in practice, you need to see them visually on the chart. Experience has shown that in a list of optimisation results, only a few will demonstrate consistently readable charts. Furthermore, you don't have to use the optimum box size, and often you wouldn't. Above all, optimisation tells you the range of box sizes you should be using. You may have to think again about using a 1% box size when a 2% has produced better results.

Chapter 8

Point and Figure's Contribution to Market Breadth

Introduction

Market breadth indicators are so called because they measure the action of a group of instruments – either the constituents of a sector or the whole market itself. Breadth, therefore, measures the market trend by looking at the action of all the instruments within a market index or sector each day.

The key to understanding the basis of breadth indicators is that they are calculated using the number of instruments that have fulfilled a predetermined condition. Therefore, every day, the number of shares fulfilling the condition is totalled, and this total used to plot the breadth indicator. The calculation is simple, but the management is complex. Ideally it should be performed every day or every week, and the total stored for use when required, but often this is not possible and so the calculation has to be performed in a sweep of many days to obtain the totals required to construct the breadth chart.

It is important to understand that breadth indicators do not and cannot analyse individual shares because they don't analyse the price. Furthermore, although breadth indicators tend to be used for the general analysis of equity markets, because indices are usually made up of shares, breadth can be assessed on any set of data, no matter what the make-up is. This is because breadth, in effect, creates an alternative index using the same constituents.

There are many indicators that measure breadth in slightly different ways, but the thinking behind all of them is the same. The advance decline line is one of the most popular. It calculates the number of shares that have advanced on the day and the number that have declined. The difference between the advances and declines is added to or subtracted from a running total, which is then plotted. Advance decline lines are drawn as line charts, but they can of course be drawn as Point and Figure charts. As they are not based on Point and Figure, however, they have no place in a book on Point and Figure charts. There is, in fact, only one breadth indicator that is purely Point and Figure and that is bullish percent, discussed below.

The point of breadth indicators is that they are an independent measure of the market or sector index. For example, if, on a day when all shares in the NASDAQ 100 fell or remained unchanged, one of the biggest shares in the index rose by 5%, the index itself would rise. Would that index rise be a true reflection of the market for that day? It would, in fact, be misleading. Market breadth, on the other hand, would count 99 shares down or unchanged and only 1 share up, giving a strong downward bias on the day. It brings another dimension to the analysis of indices and markets. If 99 shares have fallen and only 1 has risen, surely the direction of the market should be down rather than up. The essential difference between breadth and an index is that no account is taken of the amount by which a share has risen, only that it has risen. Breadth gives an equal weighting to every constituent.

A caveat

Before going any further, it is just as well to draw your attention to an important caveat. One of the major problems with any market breadth indicator, not just bullish percent, is that it is calculated by adding up, on a daily basis, the number of shares in an index, group or portfolio fulfilling a particular condition. That in itself is not a problem, provided that the constituents of the index remain constant. The fact is they don't. So assessing the bullishness or bearishness of a stock which is in the index today, and using it to construct a bullish percent chart is not a problem, unless at some stage in the past the share was not in the index or group. Traditionally, the calculation of market breadth indicators was started many years ago and a running total was kept for a few key charts, usually American indices. Doing it this way ensures that, each day, only those shares which are in the index on that day are assessed. The problem comes when you want to construct a market breadth indicator for an index or portfolio which has never been done before. You could, of course, find out the changes to the index constituents over the past ten years and then calculate your breadth indicators day by day, ensuring the correct constituents are used and name changes, mergers and de-mergers are accounted for. The alternative is to assume that the constituents have not changed over the years and construct the history based on today's constituents.

The former method is correct, and the latter is flawed, but the former is so difficult and so time-consuming that it is unlikely that anyone would take the time to do it. Does this mean that the breadth indicators should be avoided? The answer is no. What should be avoided is any index that changes its constituents regularly. The FTSE 100 Index, which is used as London's benchmark, is one such example. It only has 100 constituents, which are revised every 3 months, based on market capitalisation, making medium-term analysis of any market breadth indicator based on the Index meaningless. The best option with the FTSE 100 would be to start a new breadth chart every 3 months and only look back to the revision date. It cannot be stressed strongly enough, that indices like the FTSE 100 should not be assessed for any market breadth index, other than for the recent period for which the components have remained unchanged.

The bullish percent charts used in the next few pages of the broad FTSE All Share Index are not perfect, nor are its constituents constant, but what is important is that the vast majority do not change from one quarter to the next. It is, therefore, feasible to use it when constructing any market breadth chart of the London market, although it still suffers from constituent changes. In a similar vein, the S&P 500, Russell 1000 or NASDAQ Composite indices are feasible to use for US markets. Some would say that London's FT30 and New York's Dow Jones Industrial Average, although consisting of only 30 stocks, remain fairly consistent and can be used as well, although both have had a few changes in recent years. Essentially, indices that have a larger number of constituents will be better for market breadth calculations. Even though changes may still be regular, a smaller fraction are moving in and out of the index.

There are those that will find this unacceptable. If you are one, then you have two choices. Either use the market breadth indicator only for the period for which the index constituents are constant, meaning no medium- to long-term analysis, or accept that using a wide index with its current constituents is flawed, but is better than no breadth chart at all. If neither of these is acceptable, start recording the figures manually today so that in ten years' time, you can look back on an accurate breadth chart in the hope that some other index has not replaced the one you have been following.

Bullish percent

Point and Figure charts are either bullish or bearish – that is a major advantage of them – there is no half measure. A bullish Point and Figure chart is one where the last signal generated was at least a double-top buy signal. See page 115 for an explanation of the double-top buy signal. It does not matter how many columns back the signal occurred. Provided there has not been a double-bottom sell since, (in other words, provided a column of Os has not fallen below the previous column of Os) the double-top buy remains valid and the Point and Figure chart remains bullish.

Bullish percent was devised by A.W. Cohen of Chartcraft, and measures the percentage of shares comprising an index or a market, with charts showing bullish Point and Figure patterns. Because the double-top is the signal that decides the bullishness of the chart, bullish percent charts may only be constructed from 3-box reversal price charts, the reason being that double-top buy signals are a 3-box signal and not a 1-box signal.

To construct a bullish percent chart, therefore, you have to draw a Point and Figure chart of every share in the index you wish to study, on the day you wish to study it. You then have to count the number of shares that have, as the last signal, at least a double-top buy. The number is then expressed as a percentage of the total number of shares in the index. The resultant percentage is then used as the next data point to construct another chart, which is the bullish percent chart. The next day, the whole procedure is repeated, making the creation and maintenance of any breadth indicator a tedious task. Furthermore, in order to obtain back history, the procedure has to be carried out every day for which the history is required. It is here that a problem exists, which is explained in the caveat section above. Bearing in mind the caveat, computers can be used to calculate bullish percent on any index, even if it has never been done before.

It is traditional to draw a bullish percent chart as a Point and Figure chart, however, a line chart is also possible and practical. Each method adds something to the analysis.

Analysing bullish percent as a line chart

A line chart of bullish percent is not used often, but it should not be ignored by Point and Figure aficionados, because it can show things that the Point and Figure version does not. The main reason it is used is that it can be plotted below the index itself and thus compared on a day-to-day basis. Remember that although a line chart is plotted, the foundation of the indicator is still in Point and Figure because it uses the percentage of bullish Point and Figure charts each day throughout the entire history.

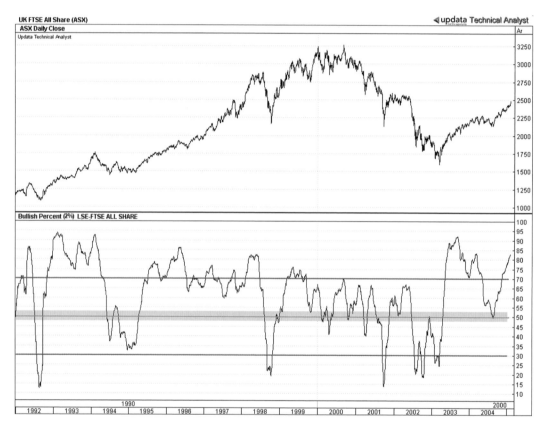

Chart 8-1: Price line chart of FTSE All Share Index with line chart of bullish percent based on 2% Point and Figure charts

The bullish percent Chart 8-1 is constructed as follows:

•   A log scale[28] 2% x 3 Point and Figure chart is drawn of each share in the FTSE All Share Index.

---

[28] See page 105 for details of log scaled Point and Figure charts.

- Each day, total the number of shares that display a bullish pattern (last signal a double-top buy).

- Express that number as a percentage of the total number of shares in the FTSEAll Share Index.

- Plot the bullish percentage each day.

Before trying to analyse the line, think what the chart is telling you. A rising line means that the number of shares with bullish charts is increasing, whereas as a falling line means the number of bullish charts is decreasing because more are turning bearish.

The bullish percent line chart can be regarded and analysed as if it is an overbought/oversold[29] oscillator, where anything above 70% is considered overbought and anything below 30% is considered oversold. These critical levels do vary from index to index. A break below 70% is not a sell signal. 'Overbought' itself is not a sell signal, just as 'oversold' is not a buy signal. Strong uptrends can stay overbought for months, even years. Provided the bullish percent remains above 70%, the uptrend in the underlying index is strong and intact. It means that 70% of its constituents have bullish Point and Figure charts. A break below 70% shows a slowing down and perhaps a weakness in the uptrend, but does not signal that the uptrend is at an end. Trends cannot accelerate forever; they need a period where the speed of the rise is constant or even slowing. A break below 70%, therefore, simply tells you that some of the overbought nature has been relieved by some shares turning bearish – most likely the overextended ones.

Because of their very nature, indices tend to remain overbought much longer than they remain oversold. Therefore, dips below the 30% level into oversold territory are usually short-lived, and a break back above the 30% level is a strong new bullish signal. It means that only 30% of stocks have bullish patterns but that number is increasing. The fact that it is increasing means that more charts are becoming bullish and less are turning bearish.

You will often see the line oscillate above and below the 70% level; this is normal bull market action where the market runs from being overbought to being neutral. This is clearly shown between the years 1995 and 1997.

It is the 50% line, however, that is the real indicator of trend change. A break above 50% indicates a change to a bull trend and a break below 50% indicates a change to a bear trend. It would, however, be wrong to assume that trends change at the 'flick of a switch' and so sticking rigidly to the 50% level as the indication of a trend change is unwise. It is better to draw a 2.5% band either side of the 50% level, as shown in Chart 8-1, and regard the crossing of the band edges as the signal. If the bullish percent falls to the band and bounces back towards the 70% level, it is a reinforcement of the uptrend in the index. It means that the previous overbought

---

[29] Overbought is a condition that occurs when a price has risen too far, too quickly, and is due for a pause or a correction. Oversold occurs when the price has fallen too far, too quickly.

nature has been removed by a correction, which reduces the number of bullish charts, but then the number of bullish charts has started to increase again. If, alternatively, it penetrates the band, but does not immediately bounce back again and instead falls towards the 30% level, this indicates that the uptrend has come to an end, as shown in 1998.

The area between 70% and 30% is the trend change area. If the bullish percent oscillates above and below the 50% band without ever reaching 70% or 30%, this indicates uncertainty about the prevailing trend, suggesting that it is ending and is in the process of being replaced by a trend in the opposite direction after a period of sideways movement. At this time, positions in the market are best avoided until the trend becomes clear again. This is shown between mid-1999 and early 2001, when the line eventually penetrated the 30% level. Notice that the period below the 30% level was short-lived, as is normally the case, and the line went back up through the 50% level but did not reach the 70% level. This indicates weakness. It means that, although the number of bullish charts increased, it was due to a short-term oversold situation rather than a resumption of the bull trend.

The strongest trend change signal that bullish percent can give is when it breaks below 70%, then goes on to break below the 50% and then the 30% level without much interruption. It is a clear signal that a bull trend has ended. The reason is that there is a steady decrease in bullish Point and Figure charts and consequently increase in bearish ones. To turn a bullish chart bearish requires a double-top buy signal to be reversed into a double-bottom sell signal. That is not as simple as it sounds. You may think that it requires a reversal of 3 boxes but that is not the case.

Once a double-top buy signal has been generated, the chart becomes bullish. In order to reverse the buy signal and turn the chart bearish, a double-bottom sell signal must be generated. In order to do that, the price must reverse by a minimum number of 5 Os as shown in Figure 8-1(a). The chart turns bullish when it breaks above the blue line and turns bearish when it breaks below the red line. In order to reverse from a bearish chart to a bullish chart, a double-bottom sell signal must be converted into a double-top buy signal. This also requires a minimum rise of 5 Xs as shown in Figure 8-1(b). Remember, this is the minimum condition; it could be many more boxes. If your individual stock charts are 2% x 3 Point and Figures, it means the price must reverse by 10% (5 x 2%) to change from bullish to bearish and vice versa. Therefore, once a sell signal has registered, the bias is down and only the strongest bull market can turn it around and make it bullish again.

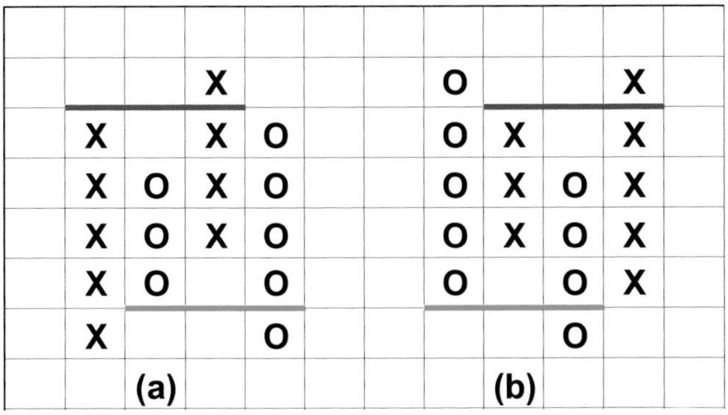

		X				O			X	
X		X	O			O	X		X	
X	O	X	O			O	X	O	X	
X	O	X	O			O	X	O	X	
X	O		O			O		O	X	
X			O						O	
	(a)						(b)			

Figure 8-1: (a) bullish into bearish (b) bearish into bullish

If bullish percent breaks above 30%, then through 50% and 70%, this is a clear signal that a bear trend has ended for the same reasons as given above. To keep increasing the number of bullish charts, more shares must be turning by 10% or more, which is bull market action. Examples of this are found in Chart 8-2 in 1994, 1998 and 2003. The move from oversold in 2003, straight through the 50% level and up to the 70% level without a pause, was the clearest indication of the end of the 2000 to 2003 bear market and the start of a new bull market. Notice that, in early 2004, the indicator broke below 70% and reached the 50% band where it turned and went straight back above 70%, confirming the resumption of the bull trend.

As with all oscillators – bullish percent is an oscillator – divergence with the price is another indication of strength or weakness. This divergence is impossible to see when bullish percent is plotted as a traditional Point and Figure chart because it cannot be lined up with the index.

Divergence occurs when the price is in a rising trend making higher highs, but the oscillator is falling, making lower highs. The price, in this case, is the underlying index, and the oscillator is the bullish percent that measures the percentage of shares with bullish Point and Figure charts on a day-to-day basis. The converse is true for downtrends; the price making lower lows but the oscillator making higher lows is a sign of strength.

Divergence tells you whether the rises or falls in the index are being supported by the number of bullish or bearish charts of the underlying shares in the index. Divergence itself is not a signal; rather it is a warning that the trend is experiencing weakness. Unlike normal oscillators, divergence above 70% and below 30% is not important, because these show strong trends. Divergence in the 70% to 30% trend change area is, however, important because in this area there is already uncertainty. If that uncertainty is coupled with an inability to regain the 70% level, this indicates weakness. This is shown in the years 1999 to 2000. Notice that the bullish percent chart broke below 70% and then 50%, signalling the end of the uptrend. It then immediately broke back above 50%, signalling a resumption of the uptrend, but did not break back above 70%, although at this stage the index itself was at a new high. This means that less than 70% of stocks in the FTSE All Share Index were bullish, despite the fact the index was making a new high. That is a worrying sign. The bullish percent broke below 50% again, and again it broke back up, but could not get near the 70% line.

Divergence is always easier to read after the fact, which makes it difficult to apply. As for all Technical Analysis, try to put yourself beyond the chart and try to understand what it is showing you. In this case, it was clear that there was divergence and clear that it was showing signs of weakness.

Adjusting the sensitivity of bullish percent

You will already know that you can adjust the sensitivity of any Point and Figure chart by adjusting its parameters, most especially the box size. Chart 8-1 was constructed by drawing 2% x 3 Point and Figure charts of all the constituents of the FTSE All Share Index. You can take a more sensitive, and hence shorter-term, view by reducing the box size to 1%. Chart 8-2 is a bullish percent constructed by drawing 1% x 3 Point and Figure charts of the constituents. Notice that the volatility of the bullish percent chart increases because to reverse from bullish to bearish, and vice versa, the price of any instrument must reverse by only 5% instead of 10%. This means that it is easier to turn from one condition to the other. Exactly the same observations apply with regard to the various levels.

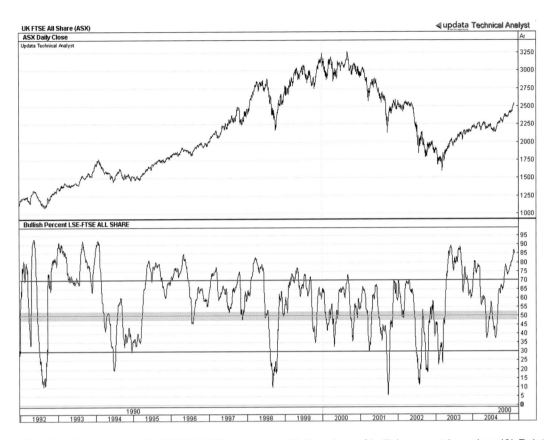

Chart 8-2: Price line chart of FTSE All Share Index with line chart of bullish percent based on 1% Point and Figure charts

The sensitivity may be further adjusted by drawing the bullish percent based on 0.5% x 3 Point and Figure charts of the constituents, as shown in Chart 8-3. The chart has been zoomed to show the last two years because it should be used for obtaining short-term information about the bullishness or bearishness of the index constituents. In this case, a share turns from bullish to bearish, and vice versa, by a reversal of only 2.5% (5 x 0.5).

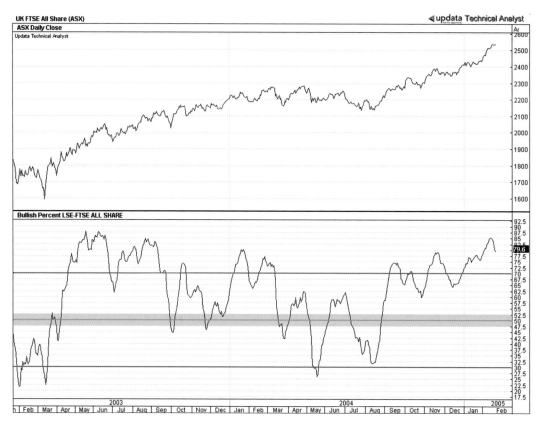

Chart 8-3: Price line chart of FTSE All Share Index with line chart of bullish percent based on 0.5% Point and Figure charts

As you have seen, the much neglected line charts of bullish percent do contain valuable information and should not be ignored. You can know more about what is going on in the broader market than the vast majority of the market participants at a stroke.

Analysing bullish percent as a Point and Figure chart

The original and traditional way to view bullish percent is to draw a Point and Figure chart of the percentages each day. The immediate disadvantage is that it is now impossible to compare the underlying index, because the Point and Figure columns will not line up with the price Point and Figure, but that does not mean you should ignore the Point and Figure version, as it has other important indications.

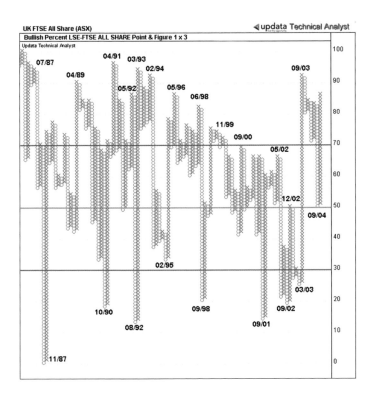

Chart 8-4: 1 x 3 bullish percent of the constituents of FTSE All Share Index based on 2% Point and Figure charts

Chart 8-4 is a Point and Figure version of the bullish percent line shown in Chart 8-1. It is based on 2% x 3 charts of the constituents and the bullish percent chart itself is a 1 point x 3 of the percentages. Since there is no time-scale in Point and Figure charts, keys dates have been placed on the chart. The same observations about the 30% and 70% level apply, but the fact that it is a Point and Figure chart can help you in your analysis of the chart.

Normal Point and Figure patterns and trend lines apply, so signals are easier to interpret. A double-top buy on the bullish percent chart is a signal to look for buying opportunities within the constituents of the index. A double-bottom sell is a signal to look for selling opportunities. The strength of these signals is defined by where they are on the 0 to 100 scale. A buy signal below 30 is a strong signal to buy shares, whereas one above 70 is a cautious buy with a quick exit strategy in place. Only stocks giving buy signals with positive relative strength should be considered at this level. In the same way, a sell signal above 70 is a strong signal but below 30 is a weak signal.

The 2% version of bullish percent shown in Chart 8-4 does not show many signals either below the 30 or above the 70 levels. In fact, there are always more above 70 than below 30. The dates of the important tops are shown and most coincide with a double-bottom sell above the 70 level. The only strong buy in the chart is the double-top buy in 03/03. It is for this reason that many switch to looking at the 1% version, in Chart 8-5, where the share charts are 1% x 3 instead of 2% x 3.

The power of the Point and Figure version of bullish percent is that the last column tells you the current status. If the last column is a column of Xs, this is bull status. A rising column of Xs indicates that more of the constituent Point and Figure charts are becoming bullish and reversing from bearish. Remember, a Point and Figure chart is either bullish or bearish; there is no middle position. To turn from bearish to bullish it must reverse by 5 boxes (see page 385 for a full description), which in this case is 10% – a strong turnaround. If the last column is a column of Os, this is a bear alert status. A falling column of Os indicates that more constituents are turning bearish.

If a column of Xs has given a buy signal by rising above a previous column of Xs, opportunities to take long positions are sought. If, however, a reversal into a column of Os takes place, this is an indication to stop any buying and wait for one of two things to occur: Either the column of Os falls below a previous column of Os, signalling that you should close long positions and look for shorts, or the column of Os reverses back into a column of Xs, indicating a resumption of the uptrend and buying can commence again. All the time, the position on the 0 to 100 scale tells you the risk of acting.

The 50 level is the dividing line between a bullish and bearish market breadth. If, after giving a buy signal below 50, a column of Xs rises up to and then through 50, this confirms a strong bullish status. This is shown after the 03/03 bottom and the subsequent rise. The converse applies when a column of Os falls through 50. This is shown after the 05/92 top, down to the 08/92 bottom.

If the rising column of Xs stops at the 50 level and reverses, this is a sign that the bullish nature has halted. You should be cautious, as you are on the borderline. All buying should cease. Short-term profits should be taken. Longer-term positions can remain open. It is a signal that the bulls do not have full control. Often it means that a second, lower bottom is about to be made. This is shown in 12/02. If, however, the reversal is short-lived and the column of Os is reversed into a column of Xs, at the same time giving a double-top buy signal, this is very bullish; having been pushed back, the bulls have re-asserted themselves and turned more shares bullish. This is shown in the rise from 09/98, which was rebuffed at the 50 level temporarily. The converse applies when sell signals are given above 50 and the column of Os falls and stops at the 50 level. If it turns back into a column of Xs, it means that the uptrend has resumed.

Although bullish percent based on 2% x 3 Point and Figure charts of the constituents is in common use, one based on 1% x 3 charts is actually more useful to the medium-term investor. Chart 8-5 shows the bullish percent calculated on 1% x 3 Point and Figure charts of the constituents. The key dates are again marked to allow comparison. In many cases, the 1% is better because it shows more double-top and bottom signals.

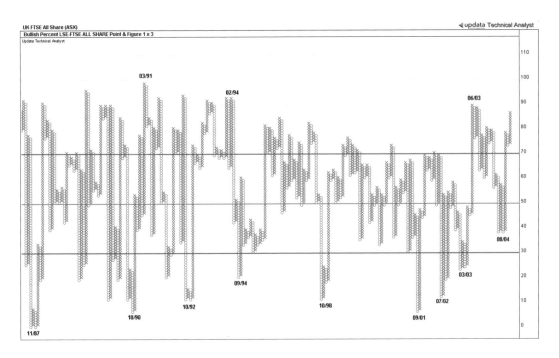

Chart 8-5: 1 x 3 bullish percent of the constituents of FTSE All Share Index based on 1% Point and Figure charts

Log or arithmetic scaling

All the bullish percent charts shown above are constructed by drawing log scale charts of each share, but you are aware that there are two ways to scale Point and Figure charts. Arithmetic scale uses the same number of points for each box, whereas log scale uses the same percentage. The question arises whether bullish percent charts can be constructed using arithmetic scaling of the individual shares. Arithmetic scaling presents a problem if a long history is being observed, because the box size is a fixed points size. As the price rises, therefore, so the chart becomes more sensitive because the box size is too small for the price level. This means that bullish percent should *never* be calculated using arithmetic scale (points box) when drawing Point and Figure charts of the constituents. Log scale should always be used.

Close only or high/low data

All the bullish percent charts drawn above are constructed using the daily close only for each of the individual shares. They could just as easily have been based on high/low data. A.W. Cohen, the inventor of bullish percent, used high/low charts because they were also his invention. There is no doubt that provided your high/low data is spike free, the high/low version of bullish percent contains more detail. Chart 8-6 is a bullish percent constructed using 2% x 3 Point and Figure charts of the constituents on high/low data. Compare and contrast this with Chart 8-4 using close only data.

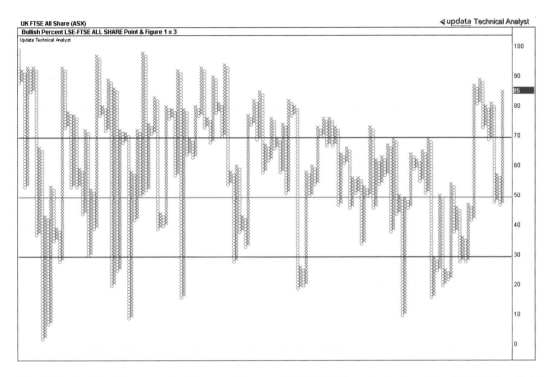

Chart 8-6: 1 x 3 bullish percent of the constituents of FTSE All Share Index based on 2% high/low Point and Figure charts

The point you should understand is that there is no single bullish percent chart for any index, as many believe. The variables are the box size of the individual share charts and whether they are constructed using close only or high/low data. You will find, as you do with all Point and Figure charts, that varying the parameters can often expose patterns in one chart that may not be obvious in another.

Chart 8-7 below is a bullish percent chart of the German Dax 30 Index constituents. Once again, key dates have been inserted on the chart, which may be compared with the line chart of the Dax 30 Index itself, in Chart 8-8.

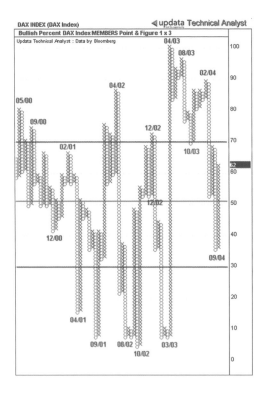

Chart 8-7: 1 x 3 bullish percent of Dax 30 Index constituents: constructed with data courtesy of Bloomberg

Notice the double-top buy signal in March 2003 below the 30 level. This is the strongest signal you can get from a bullish percent chart. Not only is the double-top buy important, but also the fact it is below 30 makes it more so. It is a signal to start accumulating positions in shares that make up the Index. Notice too that after the double-top buy, the column of Xs rises strongly, without pausing, through the 50 level and up above the 70 level. Compare and contrast this with the double-bottom buy in August 2002, which also occurred below the 30 level, but which stopped short of the 50 level, only to turn down and make a new low in October 2002. Double-top buys below the 30 level are indeed the strongest signals but it is vital that they carry up through 50 to confirm a new bull trend. In August 2002, this failed to happen and the column of Os puts a stop to any stock accumulation.

After the strong buy in March 2003, the bullish percent runs straight through to 100%. This is unusual but can easily occur when bullish percent is calculated on indices with only a few constituents, in this case 30. It means all 30 stocks have bullish Point and Figure charts. This is a strong indication of the start of a new bull trend; however, reaching 100% leaves newcomers to the market with nothing to buy, so it is an obvious place to take profits, or at least stop buying. Notice that the correction away from 100% is short-lived, and only to the 82% level, before it pushes higher, giving a repeat double-top buy signal. In August 2003, a double-bottom sell above 70% is an important signal to close long positions and look for short positions. Notice, however, that although a second double-bottom sell occurred, it failed to push below 70%. Instead, it bounced off 70% giving another double-top buy, albeit in an overbought area. Bounces off the top side of 70% are bullish and are a signal of a resumption of the bull trend.

Chart 8-8: Price line chart of the Dax 30 Index: data courtesy of Bloomberg

In February 2004, another double-bottom sell signal above 70, combined with the column of Os going through 70, signals the end of the bull run. Remember that the 50 level is the dividing line and the bounce off 50 is encouraging for the resumption of the bull trend. To signal the resumption, however, a column of Xs must give a double-top buy, which it was unable to do. Instead, a new column of Os forms, giving another double-bottom sell and falling below 50%. This means that more than half the Dax 30 Index stocks have bearish Point and Figure charts and consequently a bear trend is confirmed. This continues until early September, when the column of Os is halted above the 30% level. A new column of Xs forms and rises above 50%, confirming the resumption of the bull trend again. To confirm the new trend, however, a double-top buy is required and the column of Xs needs to rise through the 70% level.

Bullish percent on other indices

Bullish percent is not reserved for main market indices. It may be calculated on any group of shares, including shares in an industry sector, or a portfolio, bearing in mind the caveat above. All you need to know is the shares which comprise the index or portfolio on which you wish to calculate the bullish percent.

Summary

Bullish percent is another way of looking at the market. Its power is that it is constructed by looking at the status, either bullish or bearish, of the constituents of any index or market group. It performs two tasks: it tells you how overbought the market is, as well as flashing you signals to accumulate stock or dispose of it. Although its construction is based on Point and Figure charts, its representation may be either as a line chart or as a Point and Figure chart, which is the traditional way. Each has advantages and disadvantages. A line chart of bullish percent has the distinct advantage that it may be lined up below the price and read like any other oscillator. This is particularly useful for spotting divergences.

The more common Point and Figure version of bullish percent cannot be lined up with the price chart but it has two advantages: firstly, normal Point and Figure double-top and bottom signals apply; and secondly, the last column tells you the status of the market. A rising column of Xs means the market is bullish and is continuing to be so. A falling column of Os means the market is bearish because an increasing number of shares are turning bearish. This is far more important than simply a rising or falling line on a line chart, because, in order to change a column of Os into a column of Xs, the bullish percent chart itself must reverse by 3 boxes, or 3%, which means that 3% more share charts must be bullish than before.

A.W. Cohen, the originator of bullish percent, only used the Point and Figure version and never the line chart. His rules for reading it were simple:

- A rising column of Xs below 50% is a bull alert signal.

- When the column of Xs crosses above the 50% level, the bull trend is confirmed.

- However, if the column of Xs is below 50% and issues a double-top buy then the bull trend is confirmed earlier.

- A falling column of Os above 50% is a bear alert signal.

- When the column of Os crosses below the 50% level, the bear trend is confirmed.

- However, if the column of Os is above 50% and issues a double-bottom sell then the bear trend is confirmed earlier.

- He added that any turn up from below 10% is a signal for a new bull market.

Earl Blumenthal expanded on Cohen's work and produced six states of the bullish percent chart:

- Bull confirmed – occurs when there is a rising column of Xs after a double-top buy signal.

- Bear confirmed – occurs when there is a falling column of Os after a double-bottom sell signal.

- Bull correction – occurs when the last signal was a double-top buy, but the last column is a falling column of Os.

- Bear correction – occurs when the last signal was a double-bottom sell, but the last column is a rising column of Xs.

- Bull alert – occurs when there is a column of Xs rising up through 30% but the last signal is still the previous double-bottom sell.

- Bear alert – occurs when there is a column of Os falling down through 70% but the last signal is still the previous double-top buy.

Rules are there to be understood, not learnt. It is wise to go back, look again at the bullish percent charts with these rules in mind, and understand why Cohen and Blumenthal devised them.

Bullish percent is not a proxy for the market index you are studying. It adds an extra dimension to the analysis of the index, as do all other market breadth charts.

Chapter 9

Advanced Point and Figure Techniques

The standard way to establish and expose trends in Point and Figure charts is with trend lines. However, it is possible to apply other techniques instead, ones that are usually reserved for bar and line charts. This chapter will explore the application of moving averages[30], parabolic SAR[31] and Bollinger Bands[32] to Point and Figure charts with the aim of providing additional trend information, which will in turn enhance the validity of any standard Point and Figure buy or sell signals. The particular success of these techniques will stem from the unique way in which they are calculated when Point and Figure is the base chart on which they are applied.

Moving averages on Point and Figure

The concept of moving averages on Point and Figure charts is alien to most, as it is recognised that Point and Figure charts do not have a time-scale and, of course, everyone knows that moving averages are the price averaged over a time period. Kenneth Tower, however, introduced moving averages based on Point and Figure charts in his chapter on the subject in the book, *New Thinking in Technical Analysis*, edited by Rick Bensignor. The basis of the technique is that, whereas moving averages on bar, candle and line charts are based on a number of time periods, moving averages on Point and Figure charts are based on a number of columns. To clarify, you are averaging the price per reversal rather than price per unit of time. Price per reversal is price per column change, which is really price per change in intermediate trend. The more sensitive the Point and Figure chart, therefore, the more column changes there will be.

Tower calculates the price on which the moving average is based by taking the price at the centre of each column. In columns where there is an odd number of boxes it will be the centre box. For example, in a 10 x 3 Point and Figure chart where a column runs from 40 to 80 (see Figure 9-1), the centre box is 60, so 60 is used as the figure that represents the column.

---

[30] A moving average on a price chart is the average of a predetermined number of prices calculated on a moving basis, so that the average moves forward as the next price is included and the first price is excluded.

[31] The parabolic stop and reverse (SAR) that was developed by J. Welles Wilder in the mid-1970s. It is a trend definition system which has a parabolic shape which moves closer to the price as the price trend matures.

[32] Bollinger Bands were developed by John Bollinger. They are volatility bands around a central moving average, where the upper and lower bands are a predefined number of standard deviations away from the moving average.

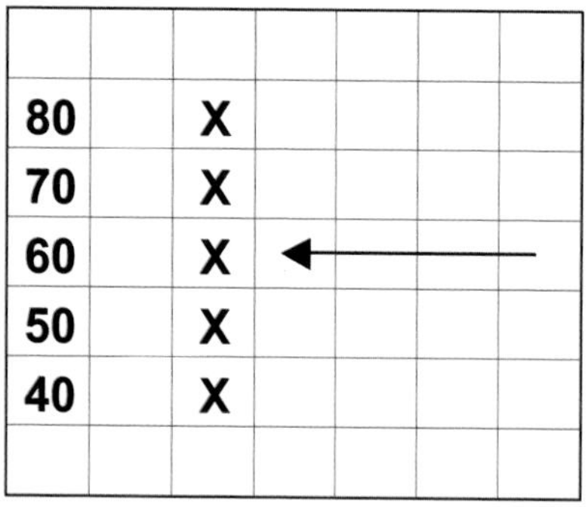

Figure 9-1: Showing the centre box in the column for moving average calculation

An even number of boxes in a column creates a problem, however, because there is no centre box. If the column runs from 40 to 70 with 4 boxes, then the centre of the column is taken, which is $(70+40)/2 = 55$. In essence this is the same logic as used on odd box columns above: $(80+40)/2 = 60$.

Once you have the representative, or proxy, value for each column, you may calculate moving averages using these values. Decide on the number of columns for the average and calculate it on a moving basis. There are many excellent texts on moving averages, so there is no point in discussing how these are calculated. As with moving averages on bar, line or candle charts, so moving averages on Point and Figure charts can, and should, use a number of calculation methods such as simple arithmetic, exponential, weighted, adaptive, regression, etc.

The first decision to make is how many columns to average. This is no different from having to decide how many days to average on a daily line or bar chart. With a Point and Figure chart, it is related to the width of the Point and Figure chart itself. Consequently, a moving average on a close only Point and Figure chart will trace a completely different path from one on a high/low chart. A moving average on a 3-box reversal chart will look completely different from one on a 1-box chart, even if the box size is the same.

Chart 9-1 is a 50 x 3 Point and Figure based on the end-of-day close of the FTSE 100 Index. Chart 9-2 is also a 50 x 3 Point and Figure chart but based on the end-of-day high/low. Chart 9-3 is a 50 x 1, based on the close. In each case a 21 column moving average has been drawn. Notice how well the 21 column moving average contains the price and traces out the trends in Chart 9-1, whereas in Chart 9-2 it is not quite as effective. Notice that the moving average in Chart 9-3, the 50 x 1 close chart, seems to trace out a similar path to that in Chart 9-2, the 50 x 3 high/low chart.

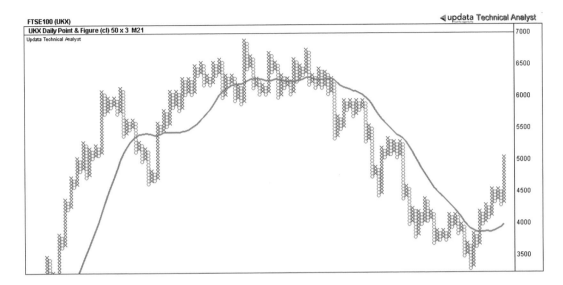

Chart 9-1: 50 x 3 of the FTSE 100 Index with a 21 column simple moving average

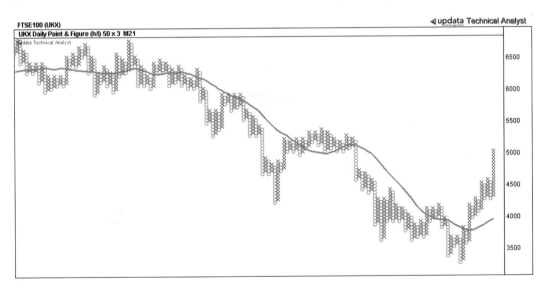

Chart 9-2: 50 x 3 (h/l) of the FTSE 100 Index with a 21 column simple moving average

Chart 9-3: 50 x 1 of the FTSE 100 Index with a 21 column simple moving average

What this means is that you cannot use the same length (measured in columns) moving average across different box sizes, different reversals and different construction methods. So, the choice of moving average length is much more complex for Point and Figure than it is when using line charts. The pay-off, however, is that existing Point and Figure signals are enhanced by the use of moving averages.

The main purpose of using moving averages on Point and Figure charts is to define the trend which may not be obvious at the time. An upward sloping moving average indicates the price is in an uptrend, and a downward sloping moving average indicates the price is in a downtrend. Moving averages expose trends that cannot be seen by looking at the raw price, in the same way that trend lines do. This is most useful in Point and Figure charts, because knowing the trend helps to decide whether an initial Point and Figure buy or sell signal should be taken. Remember, opening a trade with a buy signal in a downtrend is far riskier than opening a trade with a buy signal in an uptrend. If a moving average is used, therefore, the trend of the moving average needs to be ascertained.

The difficulty is knowing when the trend of the moving average has changed. The best and most common way to do this is to use two moving averages. When the lesser length moving average crosses above the greater length moving average, the trend changes to up; when it crosses below, the trend changes to down. What remains, therefore, is to decide what lengths of moving average to use. Remember, time has nothing to do with it. Moving average lengths are in columns. This means that the wider the congestion areas, the greater the number of columns that are required.

The benefit of Point and Figure charts over bar or line charts is that they already have an unambiguous signal generator with the standard double-top and bottom signals. Adding moving averages to the chart helps to confirm or reject a Point and Figure signal that is already there. This means that the length of the averages is not quite as critical, which is a good thing because the range of available lengths is far less. For example, while a 200 day moving average is quite useful in exposing the longer-term trend on a bar chart, a 200 column average on a Point and Figure chart is of no significance at all; it may actually be impossible to draw because there may not be 200 columns to average. In any case, to expose the longer-term trend in a Point and Figure chart, you may simply increase the box size. It is likely, therefore, that the range of moving average lengths will be somewhere between 5 columns and 50 columns in normal use. When using two moving averages with Point and Figure charts, the interplay tends to be best when one moving average is around double the length of the other. This means you could use 5 and 10, or 12 and 24, or 10 and 20, etc., but this allows too many combinations, making the choice and consistency more difficult. If you wish to narrow the choice, therefore, the use of Fibonacci numbers is a good option for moving average lengths. Combinations such as 3 and 5, 5 and 8, 8 and 13, 13 and 21, 21 and 34, 34 and 55 are recommended. You may also use a combination of these, such as 8 and 21, or 13 and 55.

Unfortunately, deciding which combination to use can only be assessed by trial and error and inspection. Remember, Technical Analysis is the study of the past in the belief that it can help with predicting the future. A chart with wide congestion areas may require longer moving averages, so 1-box reversal charts and charts constructed with high/low data will require longer length averages than 3-box charts using close only data. After drawing a few, you will quickly be able to predict which combination is best for the chart you are looking at and the trends you wish to expose. The shorter the moving average, the shorter-term the trend exposed.

Finally, there are many ways to calculate moving averages. Simple arithmetic moving averages assign equal weights to the prices in the series, whereas exponential moving averages assign a greater weight to the latest price. Exponential averages, therefore, react to the latest figure in the series quicker than simple averages and thus react quicker to any change in direction. This is especially important for moving averages of Point and Figure, because the representative price is the centre of the column, not the latest price, and the centre of the column will always lag the latest price, so simple moving averages will be slower to react to change.

How to use moving averages on Point and Figure charts

Before embarking on the use of moving averages, consider why they are being used in the first place. They are used to help you accept or reject any standard Point and Figure buy or sell signal by reason that the signal is with or against the trend. The trend, remember, is determined at the crossover point of the two moving averages you choose.

With bar and line charts, a buy signal is indicated immediately when the shorter moving average crosses above the longer and a sell when the shorter crosses below the longer. Point and Figure charts already have their own signalling mechanisms, which were discussed in chapter 3. Therefore, what the moving averages are doing is confirming or rejecting the Point and Figure signals as they occur.

As you are aware, the way signals are interpreted in 3-box reversal charts is different from 1-box charts. The double-top and double-bottom signals in 3-box charts are unambiguous and so are easier to interpret. This does not apply to 1-box charts where the signals are catapult and fulcrum patterns. Many would say 3-box chart signals are more clear-cut. That is true, but it is not a reason to ignore moving averages on 1-box reversal charts. Both are discussed below. Anything that applies to 3-box charts also applies to 2-box and 5-box charts, as their signalling mechanisms are the same.

Moving averages on 3-box reversal charts

With 3-box reversal charts, a buy signal is only registered by a double-top breakout which occurs after the shorter-length moving average has crossed above the longer-length. The converse is true for sell signals. The averages, therefore, should be used to filter out false signals using the following guidelines:

*   Take the first double-top buy signal after the shorter-length average has crossed above the longer.

*   Subsequent double-top buy signals remain valid while the shorter average remains above the longer.

*   Ignore any double-bottom sell signals when the shorter average is above the longer.

Conversely:

*   Take the first double-bottom sell signal after the shorter-length average has crossed below the longer.

*   Subsequent double-bottom sell signals remain valid while the shorter average remains below the longer.

*   Ignore any double-top buy signals when the shorter average is below the longer.

These are guidelines which may be adjusted according to your trading style. For example, a short-term trader may take double-bottom sell signals to close long positions while the moving averages are in bullish mode, but only open shorts on a double-bottom sell when the averages are in bearish mode. Conversely, double-top buys when the averages are in bearish mode may be used to close short positions.

Using a moving average filter greatly enhances the signals generated from your Point and Figure chart.

Chart 9-4 is a 50 x 3 close only Point and Figure chart of the FTSE 100 Index with exponential 5- and 8-column moving averages. Notice how well these relatively short-length moving averages define the main uptrend AB and downtrend CD. At no time during the long downtrend CD did the red shorter-length moving average cross above the longer blue moving average, keeping you from opening a long position during the downtrend. The section outlined in black is shown in greater detail in Chart 9-5.

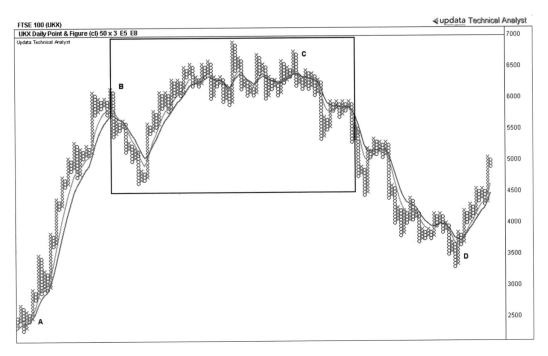

Chart 9-4: 50 x 3 of the FTSE 100 Index with 5- and 8-column exponential moving averages. Inset shown in Chart 9-5

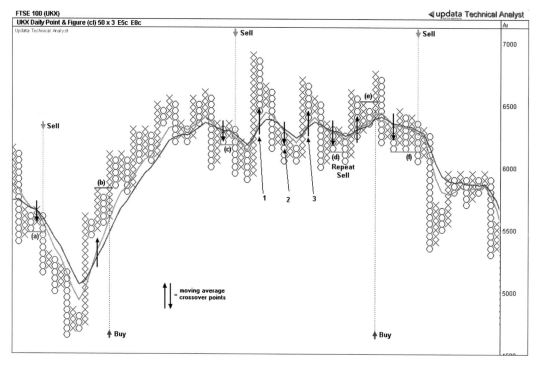

Chart 9-5: 50 x 3 of the FTSE 100 Index with 5- and 8-column exponential moving averages (zoomed)

The first double-bottom sell signal of trend AB from the 1987 low occurs at point (a) on Chart 9-5 when the 5-column average crosses below the 8-column and, thereafter, a double-bottom sell signal is indicated. Notice that this can only happen to the right of the crossover column, marked with the vertical line. The next buy signal occurs at point (b) when a double-top buy signal is generated after the 5-column average crosses above the 8-column average. Again, this can only occur after the crossover column is compete. The next sell is at point (c).

The 5-column average then crosses back above the 8-column again at point 1. This is a signal to look for buy signals. Any double-top buy signal to the right of the vertical line marked 1 must be taken, but none occurs and the averages cross back down again at point 2. There is no double-bottom sell signal after point 2 either, and the 5-column average crosses back above the 8-column at point 3. Once again the chart is on buy alert, but again there is no double-top buy signal, so the price remains in a sell mode governed by the last sell at point (c).

The averages cross down again, signalling a repeat double-bottom sell at point (d). Then the 5-column crosses above the 8-column again. Once again, any buy signal to the right of the crossover line must be taken, so the double-top buy at point (e) is valid. This is reversed by the double-bottom sell signal at point (f) when the 5-column crosses below the 8-column. Notice that this sell came before the big sell-off from the top.

Using moving averages, therefore, has allowed you to filter out the numerous buy and sell signals that occurred during the very difficult top that developed between 1999 and 2001. They are not perfect but it gives you an unambiguous way of deciding when to accept or reject the standard Point and Figure signals.

Shortening the moving average lengths to 3 and 5 columns in Chart 9-6 improves the signals without adding any additional false signals to the chart. Sell signal (a) is generated earlier, as is buy signal (b), as well as sell signals (c) and (f).

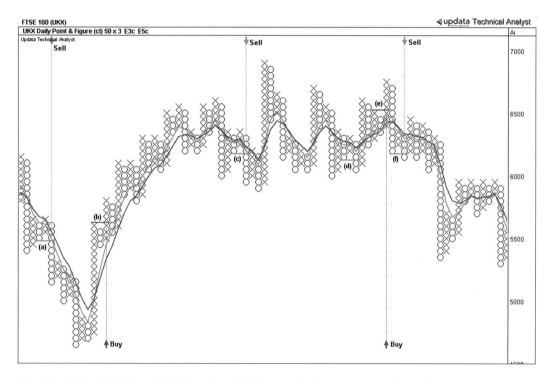

Chart 9-6: 50 x 3 of the FTSE 100 Index with 3- and 5-column exponential moving averages

Although the averages do cross-over during the CD downtrend, there are no false buy signals because no double-top buy is generated after the 3-column crossed above the 5-column, as shown in Chart 9-7. Despite crossover points at (g) and (h), no double-top buy signal occurred.

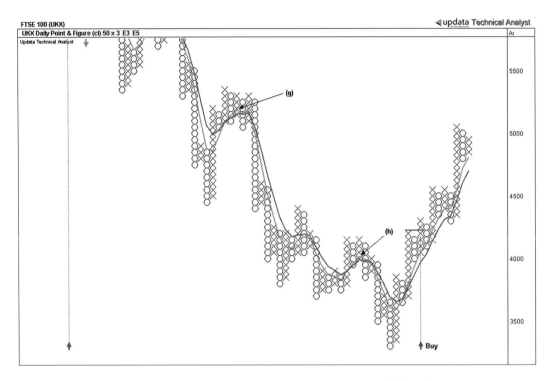

Chart 9-7: 50 x 3 of the FTSE 100 Index with 3- and 5-column exponential moving averages

There are two things you will have observed. The first is the added dimension of the position of the moving averages in determining if a Point and Figure buy or sell signal is valid. This greatly enhances the standard signals generated from a Point and Figure chart. The second is that the lengths of the moving averages are short. Trying 8 and 13 and 13 and 21, does nothing to improve the signals but does result in greater delays. The reason for this is that there are only a certain number of possible signal points within the trend.

Changing the box size changes the time horizon and produces wider congestion areas, but this does not require the averages to be lengthened. Chart 9-8 is a 25 x 3 chart using 5- and 8-column exponential averages. The valid buy and sell signals are marked by the blue (buy) and red (sell) horizontal lines.

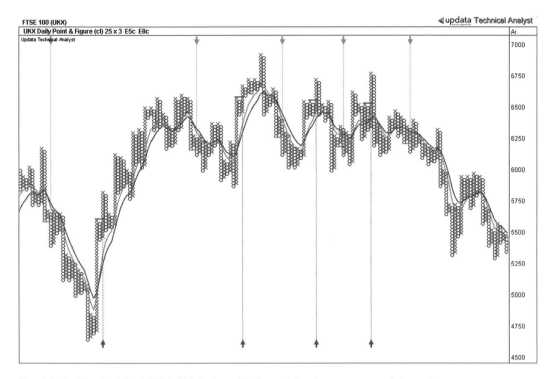

Chart 9-8: 25 x 3 of the FTSE 100 Index with 5- and 8-column exponential moving averages

Moving averages on 1-box reversal charts

In the same way that moving averages expose the trend in 3-box charts, they also expose them in 1-box charts. The use of moving averages on 1-box charts is slightly different because the characteristics of 1-box charts are different from those of 3-box charts. 1-box charts change columns every time the price changes direction by one box, and consequently the congestion areas are wider. Whereas a strong uptrend in a 3-box chart could be a single column of Xs, in a 1-box chart it could be a series of small ascending congestion areas.

When the shorter-length moving average crosses above the longer on a 1-box chart it does not mean you must take the very next double-top signal. It means you must turn your attention to looking for either bullish fulcrums or semi-catapults and must ignore any bearish ones. This brings a new dimension to 1-box analysis where, during the formation of a bullish fulcrum, there can be smaller bearish semi-catapults forming.

In general, because there are more columns per move from one price area to the next, the length of the moving averages normally needs to be increased, but this is not always the case.

Chart 9-9 is the same instrument again, the FTSE 100 Index, but this time the chart is a 1-box reversal 50 x 1 chart. The averages are the same lengths, 5 and 8. When the red average is above the blue you look for bullish semi-catapult and fulcrum signals, and ignore any bearish ones. Shaded area A shows a bearish inverted fulcrum which occurred after the break of trend line 1. Normally this would be a strong sell signal, but the moving averages show that the trend is still up and that the inverted fulcrum should be ignored.

Shaded area B shows a similar situation. The position of the moving averages allows you to ignore what would otherwise be a sell signal from a small fulcrum top.

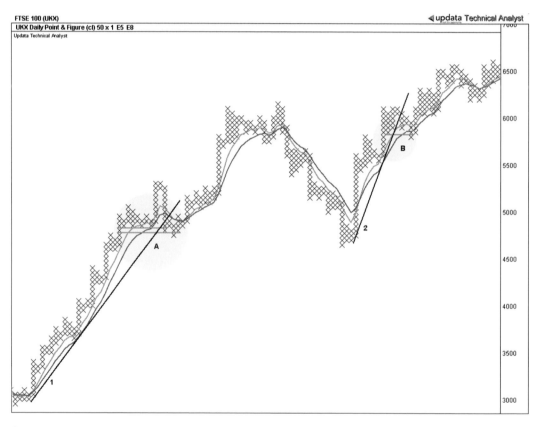

Chart 9-9: 50 x 1 of the FTSE 100 Index with 5- and 8-column exponential moving averages

Using such short-length moving averages on 1-box charts with their wider congestion areas does result in a number of false signals and whipsaws, which are buy and sell signals in quick succession. You will find that increasing the gap between the averages helps. Instead of using consecutive Fibonacci numbers, you will find that skipping one or two numbers produces very acceptable moving average combinations, such as 5 and 21, 8 and 21, or 5 and 13. As always, try drawing a few, look back on the chart, see how the averages have performed and that will tell you what to expect in the future. This is the very reason Technical Analysts draw charts; so they can look back and learn.

The false buy signal in shaded area A in Chart 9-10, using moving average periods of 5 and 8, is eliminated in Chart 9-11 when lengths of 8 and 21 are used. Don't be afraid to experiment. Lengthening averages does lead to a signal lag but it also improves the reliability of the signals.

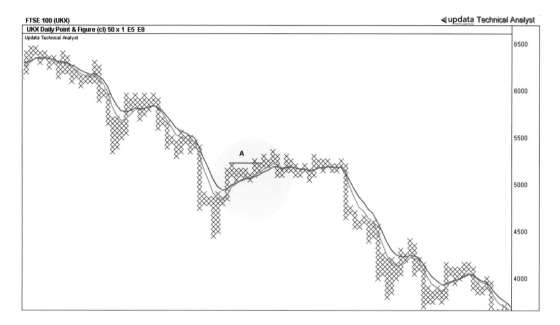

Chart 9-10: 50 x 1 of the FTSE 100 Index with 5- and 8-column exponential moving averages

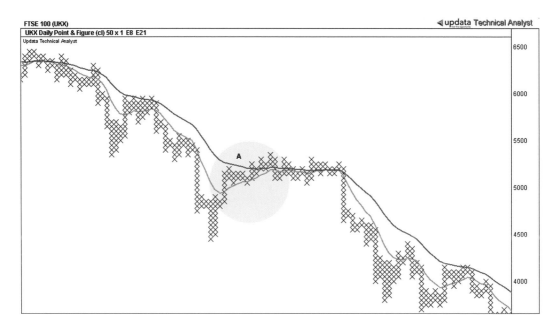

Chart 9-11: 50 x 1 of the FTSE 100 Index with 8- and 21-column exponential moving averages

It is not possible to show every single combination of box and reversal size as well as charts calculated on close or high/low. It is sufficient to say that it is likely that the moving average combinations will be different for each chart, which reinforces the view that the only way to determine which is best is to try various combinations until one suits. Although it has been suggested that exponential moving averages are best, there are a number of other ways to calculate moving averages, which you may wish to try.

As with trend lines, however, moving averages are an important enhancement to Point and Figure charts. Too often, a new student will query why one buy signal is ignored where another is taken. Using moving averages helps to answer that question.

Fine-tuning the guidelines

One of the problems in using moving averages is that once they have crossed one way, it can take a number of columns before they cross back the other way. For this reason, a sell signal cancelling a bad buy signal often occurs quite a few columns to the right of that signal. For this reason, the guidelines may be modified as follows:

- If, after a valid double-top buy signal, the shorter-length average turns down, take any double-bottom sell signal.

- If, after a valid double-bottom sell signal, the shorter-length average turns up, take any double-top buy signal.

Using these additional guidelines does improve many of the signals by shifting them a few columns to the left. Doing this, however, increases the risk of whipsaws.

Using a single moving average

The reason two moving averages were chosen above was that the crossover of the two moving averages signals a change in trend. Once signalled, you look for the next applicable Point and Figure signal. There are those, however, who prefer to use a single moving average instead and if this is used, then it needs to be read differently.

It has already been emphasised that it is very difficult to see changes in the direction of a single moving average, which is exactly why two were used. This being the case, the trend of the single moving average should not be the alert condition. Instead, the alert comes when an X or O column crosses through the moving average. This is only effective and unambiguous if used on 3-box reversal charts; 1-box chart patterns do not lend themselves to the column-crossover method employed when a single moving average is used.

You will find that you need to lengthen the moving average when using one on its own. Where you may have used 3- and 5-, or 5- and 8-column with double moving averages, you will need to use 13 or 21 as a single average.

So, when a column of Xs rises above the moving average, this places you on buy alert to take the very next Point and Figure buy signal. When a column of Os falls below the moving average, you are placed on sell alert to take the next Point and Figure sell signal. In 3-box terms, therefore, any double-top buy occurring above the moving average is valid, as is any double-bottom sell that occurs below the moving average. It is important to clarify what this means.

For a double-top buy to be valid, *both* Xs at the top of the pattern must be above the moving average. For a double-bottom sell to be valid, *both* Os at the bottom of the pattern must be below the moving average. This guideline will lead to some borderline cases for the simple reason that the moving average is calculated on the value of the box and plotted through the centre of the box. This means for an X to be above the moving average, the centre-line of the X must be above the moving average. In the same way for an O to be below, the moving average must be above the centre-line of the O.

Chart 9-12 shows a 50 x 3 Point and Figure of the FTSE 100 Index with a single 13-column exponential moving average. Sell signal A is valid as the double-bottom is below the moving average. Buy signal B is valid for the same reason, as are sell signals C and D, and buy signal E. The border-line cases are marked R, S, and T.

Chart 9-12: 50 x 3 of the FTSE 100 Index with 13-column exponential moving average

Buy signal R is not valid because the first X in the double-top is not above the moving average, as you can see in the enlarged Chart 9-13. Buy signal S is valid because the centre-line of both Xs in the double-top is above the moving average.

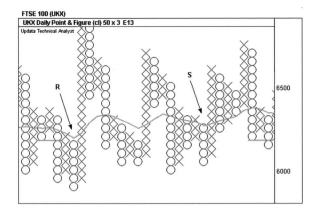

Chart 9-13: Enlarged 50 x 3 of the FTSE 100 Index with 13-column exponential moving average

Buy signal T in Chart 9-14 is also valid because both the Xs in the double-top are above the moving average.

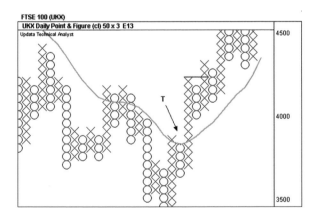

Chart 9-14: Enlarged 50 x 3 of the FTSE 100 Index with 13-column exponential moving average

If you find these signals too ambiguous, you will have to wait for the next double-top or bottom signal as the case may be. Furthermore it is easier to see the centre-line of an X than it is to see it of an O. If you are unsure, look left and see whether there is a larger pattern which will help you decide.

Final word on moving averages

Moving averages are powerful tools and one of the most popular Technical Analysis tools used. Using them in conjunction with Point and Figure signals enhances the signals produced by a Point and Figure chart. It has been suggested here that you use various moving average combinations. Do not presume that one of these combinations will work in all cases. The power of a computer allows you to try and test many different combinations and you are urged to do so.

Furthermore, moving averages have been used here in isolation without the aid of 45° and subjective trend lines. Trend lines are very effective with Point and Figure charts and you are urged to incorporate them, as well as moving averages, into your Point and Figure analysis.

Parabolic stop and reverse (SAR) on Point and Figure

When J. Welles Wilder devised the parabolic SAR, he wanted an indicator that kept you in the market, either long or short, hence the name 'Stop and Reverse'. The parabolic is either bullish or bearish which makes it well-suited to Point and Figure charts, which are also either bullish or bearish.

The calculation of the parabolic may be found in Wilder's book, *New Concepts in Technical Trading Techniques*. The only difference is that where Wilder used the period's high and low in the calculation, the Point and Figure version of the parabolic uses the column high and low. This is logical because when any type of calculation is attempted on a Point and Figure chart, it is the number of columns which are important. Also remember that, as the column is building, the latest box is always either the high or low of the column.

The parabolic is like a trailing stop but, unlike a simple trailing stop, it has an acceleration factor which allows it to start some distance away from the price after the initial signal, but get closer as the trend matures. This is the ideal situation. The parabolic tightens your stops for you as the trend matures.

The parabolic, therefore, shows trends in exactly the same way that moving averages do, except they are far easier to read. This is because the traditional way to draw the parabolic is with a series of dots. The dots then swap from one side of the price action to the other as the trend changes from up to down and vice versa. In an uptrend, the moment an O breaks below the trailing parabolic, the parabolic jumps above the price, signalling a trend change, and the calculation is re-initiated for the downtrend.

The acceleration factor determines how 'quickly' the parabolic catches up to the price. Wilder used a factor of 0.02, which continues to work well, but may need to be modified according to your requirements. The smaller the factor, the slower the parabolic is in catching up to the price. This is the equivalent of using a longer-length moving average.

Think of the parabolic as a switch. When the parabolic dots switch from red above the price to blue below the price, it switches you into 'buy signal' mode. You must then look at the Point and Figure chart and take the first buy signal you see, whether that is to close a short or open a long. When the parabolic switches from blue dots below the price to red dots above, it switches you into 'sell signal' mode so you must look for sell signals.

Chart 9-15 is the same 50 x 3 Point and Figure chart of the FTSE 100 Index used when moving averages were discussed. The parabolic is drawn using the standard 0.02 acceleration factor. The buy and sell signals are marked (a), (b), (c), (d), (e) and (f). As with moving averages, when the parabolic switches, you look for the next double-top buy or double-bottom sell signal as the case may be.

Notice that no false signals are given. Observe, too, the very early sell signal at point (e) which is 14 columns before the breakdown-column from the 1999 to 2000 top. In particular, notice the grey shaded area before (f), where the parabolic signalled an uptrend but no double-buy signal occurred to confirm it.

Chart 9-15: 50 x 3 of the FTSE 100 Index with a 0.02 parabolic SAR

Parabolic is a less subjective way of defining trend and, hence, makes it easier to decide on which Point and Figure signals to act.

Taking earlier signals

Although it can lead to many more false signals, it is possible to take earlier signals immediately when the parabolic triggers a trend change, without waiting for a traditional Point and Figure buy or sell signal. Chart 9-16 shows the same six signals lettered (a) to (f) again, but this time taken as soon as the parabolic switches from an up series of blue dots to a down series of red dots, and vice versa. In each case the point at which the switch occurs is marked with blue or red horizontal lines labelled (a) to (f). The black arrows show the parabolic dots switching sides. When they do, you buy or sell immediately, as the case may be, without waiting for a traditional Point and Figure buy or sell signal. You can see that taking the signals on the parabolic switch does result in earlier signals but, in the majority of cases, they occur at less favourable levels.

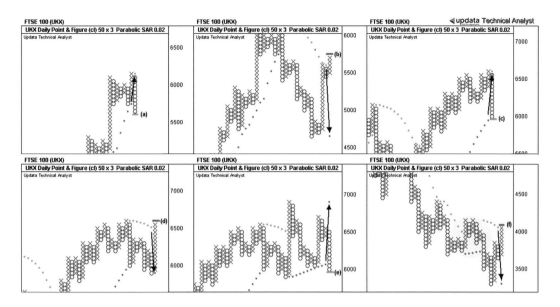

Chart 9-16: 50 x 3 of the FTSE 100 Index with a 0.02 parabolic SAR showing early signals

Notice that the area marked in grey in Chart 9-15, which did not produce a signal, did produce a whipsaw buy and sell. This is shown in detail in Chart 9-17 below.

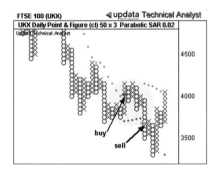

Chart 9-17: 50 x 3 of the FTSE 100 Index with a 0.02 parabolic SAR showing whipsaw details

There will, of course, be occasions when taking signals early will be beneficial. This is usually the case when the trend turnaround has been swift and sharp. The customary way to handle early signals is to commit a part of your allotted trade capital to the early signal and then commit the rest if the early signal is converted into a confirmed signal.

Parabolic on 1-box charts

The use of the parabolic is the same on 1-box charts. Remember the parabolic is a trend switch. When the trend is up, you look at the Point and Figure chart for any bullish pattern and act on it accordingly. When the trend is down, you look for bearish patterns.

As you know, patterns in 1-box charts are not quite as clearly defined as those in 3-box charts, so knowing whether you must look for either bullish patterns or bearish patterns makes the interpretation of the 1-box chart considerably easier.

Chart 9-18 is a 50 x 1 Point and Figure of the FTSE 100 Index. The shaded grey areas are those where you should be looking for bearish patterns and the white areas where you should be looking for bullish patterns. As you are already familiar with fulcrum and semi-catapult patterns, these have not been marked to avoid cluttering the chart. An important point is that once the mode changes from 'look for sell signals' to 'look for buy signals', you must look left to see if a larger pattern has developed, even if that means looking back into the imaginary grey (bearish) area as defined by the parabolic SAR. Most importantly, the trigger or catapult point must be in the white (bullish) area where the price is above the parabolic SAR. This is shown by bullish semi-catapult pattern A in Chart 9-18, where the catapult point is in the white (bullish) area but where the pattern started in the grey (bearish) area. The converse applies when looking for sell signals. Pattern B is triggered in the grey area, although it started to form in the white area. If the pattern had formed in the white area, but did not trigger in the grey area, it would have been ignored. There are, of course, other patterns on the chart which have not been marked.

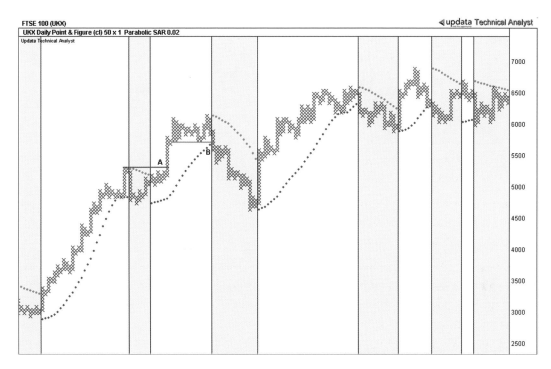

Chart 9-18: 50 x 1 of the FTSE 100 Index with a 0.02 parabolic SAR

1-box reversal charts and charts using high/low construction have wider congestion areas and, therefore, present a problem with the use of the parabolic. This is because the parabolic acceleration factor ensures that the parabolic stop 'catches up' to the price when the price runs sideways. Chart 9-19 overleaf is a high/low constructed chart (the Xs and Os have been reduced in size to show more history). Compare this to Chart 9-15, which is constructed using the close only. In general, there is not much change in the signals; however, notice that as the congestion areas become wider, they do induce false signals like the area marked AA, where a buy signal was given halfway through the congestion area, resulting in a sell well below it. This is an example where common sense should override any set of rules, such as the parabolic, and a stop below the black support line marked X should ensure all long positions are stopped out.

Chart 9-19: 50 x 3 (h/l) of the FTSE 100 Index with a 0.02 parabolic SAR

Parabolic acceleration factor

The standard parabolic acceleration factor is 0.02. Increasing the factor produces a shorter-term parabolic, whereas decreasing it produces a longer-term. Remember, however, that you may also alter the time horizon of Point and Figure charts by varying the box size. This gives you two ways of changing your trend time horizon and you should combine the two.

Chart 9-20 shows the FTSE 100 Index 50 x 3 again, but with a 0.01 parabolic acceleration factor, which traces out the longer-term trend changes very effectively without any of the lag that would be expected by increasing moving average lengths.

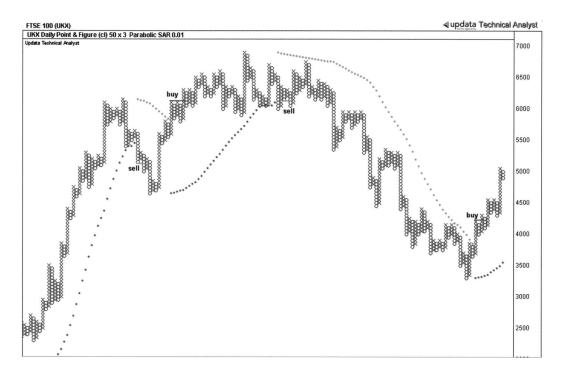

FTSE 100 (UKX) ◄updata Technical Analyst

UKX Daily Point & Figure (cl) 50 x 3 Parabolic SAR 0.01

Updata Technical Analyst

Chart 9-20: 50 x 3 of the FTSE 100 Index with a 0.01 parabolic acceleration factor

As you are aware, every instrument has its own characteristics. The strategy, therefore, is to decide on your box size and reversal first, then draw the standard 0.02 parabolic to see whether it has assisted you in seeing past trends. If it has not, then adjust the acceleration factor accordingly. You will find that where the chart has narrow congestion areas, the 0.02 parabolic is best and where it has wide congestion areas, the 0.01 factor is best. There is, however, no rule, other than the rule of inspection. Literally, any acceleration factor from 0.001 to 0.999 may be used, but, in reality, 0.005, 0.01, 0.02 and 0.05 are the most common.

0.02 is often the best factor to use, as the 0.25 x 3 Chart 9-21 of Intel Corporation. overleaf shows. The parabolic defines the trend with exceptional accuracy. Increasing the factor does not benefit the trend definition at all. The parabolic is better suited to sharp uptrends than 45° lines because the acceleration factor ensures that the parabolic curves towards the price as the trend progresses.

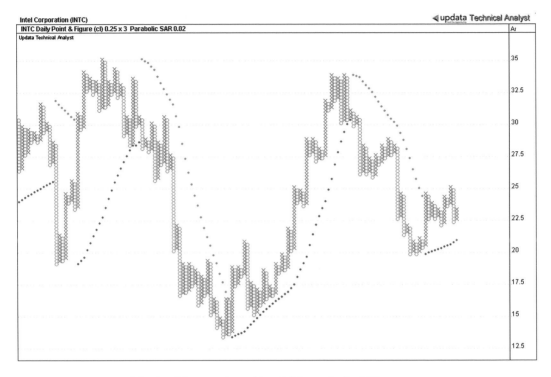

Chart 9-21: 0.25 x 3 of the Intel Corporation with a 0.02 parabolic SAR

Combining parabolics with trend lines

Although the parabolic is a stop and reverse system, you may feel that closing a long and opening a short is too severe an action. Normally longs are closed first, then shorts are only opened if there is a second opportunity to do so, or if a major trend has broken at the same time.

Determining the major trend may, therefore, be done with trend lines, where a parabolic sell above the main trend line is used to close a long and not to open a short. This emphasises the view that you should never rely on one technique when analysing Point and Figure charts; trend and pattern formation as well as techniques, such as parabolics or moving averages, should be used in conjunction with one another.

Bollinger Bands on Point and Figure

Now that there is an acceptable method for calculating and drawing moving averages on Point and Figure charts, other techniques, such as the popular Bollinger Bands, may be drawn as well. A full analysis of Bollinger Bands cannot be given here. Readers are, therefore, encouraged to read John Bollinger's excellent book, *Bollinger on Bollinger Bands*, for a full analysis of the technique.

Bollinger Bands are volatility bands, drawn a predefined number of standard deviations above and below a chosen moving average. With bar and line charts, either the closing price or the high and low are used to calculate the moving average and the bands; with Point and Figure, it is the centre of the column that is used instead. Bollinger used a 20-day simple moving average with 2 standard deviation bands. The reason that 2 standard deviations are used are that the Bands then contain approximately 95% of the data.[33] The upper and lower bands are calculated by adding or subtracting 2 standard deviations and these lines are then plotted above and below the moving average.

In column terms, you will find that around half the suggested moving average length is better for Point and Figure charts, although it is dependent on the make-up of the Point and Figure chart itself. 1-box reversal, and charts constructed with high/low data have wider congestion areas and, therefore, fewer long columns, requiring you to lengthen the moving average. Bollinger also suggests increasing or decreasing the number of standard deviations by a few decimal points when the moving average is increased or decreased. Point and Figure charts already compartmentalise the data into boxes, so altering the number of standard deviations by a few points makes no noticeable difference.

Bollinger Bands add to Point and Figure analysis in two ways. The first is that they show when the price is overbought or oversold, which a Point and Figure chart on its own cannot show. Secondly, although Point and Figure charts are very good at showing volatility by the length of the columns, Bollinger Bands enhance the chart as they show increasing or decreasing volatility by the widening or narrowing of the Bands.

Overbought or oversold

It is important to note, and Bollinger himself stresses this, that Bollinger Bands do not give buy and sell signals; they warn you when the price is overbought or oversold and whether it is behaving in a manner that confirms the trend. During strong uptrends, the price stays close to the upper Band, sometimes breaking above it. Conversely, during strong downtrends, the price remains close to the lower Band, often breaking below it. It is what the price does when it returns inside the Bands that gives you more information.

---

[33] Actually 1.96 standard deviations contain 95% of the data.

If the price breaks above the upper band, then returns inside the upper band but remains above the central moving average, this confirms the strength of the uptrend as shown by blue line AA in Chart 9-22 of the FTSE 100 Index. The chart is the standard 50 x 3 used so often before. The Bollinger Bands are based on a 13-column simple moving average with 2 standard deviation bands.

If the price breaks below the lower Band, then returns inside the lower Band but remains below the central moving average, this confirms the strength of the downtrend, shown by line BB.

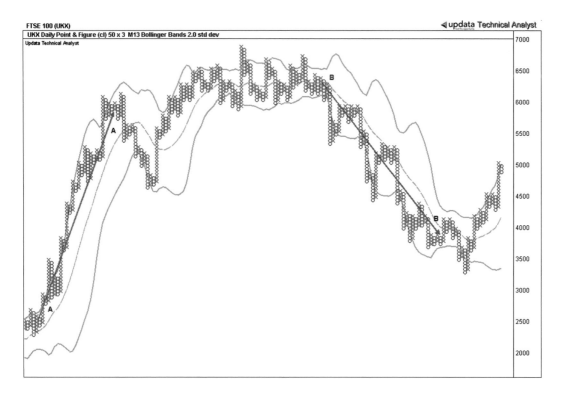

Chart 9-22: 50 x 3 of the FTSE 100 with 13-column, 2 standard deviation Bollinger Bands

You have seen already, when a single moving average was discussed, that if the price breaks below the moving average, it is an indication that the trend is changing from up to down and the next Point and Figure sell signal should be taken. Conversely, if the price breaks above the moving average, it is an indication that the trend is changing from down to up and the next Point and Figure buy signal should be taken. What this means, therefore, is that Bollinger Bands add an extra dimension to the use of the single moving average by informing you whether the trend is strong or weak and whether the price is overbought or oversold. In this respect alone, the Bands are very useful.

Weakness in an uptrend is indicated when the price fails to reach the upper Band but has not yet crossed below the central moving average. The same applies to downtrends. If the price fails to reach the lower Band, it indicates that the downtrend is weakening.

Uncertainty is demonstrated by the price 'bouncing' off the upper and lower Bands within one or two columns of each other, indicating that the price is alternating between overbought and oversold. This is typical trading range action, which brings us to the second part of Bollinger analysis.

Volatility and the squeeze

Representation of volatility is central to Bollinger Bands. The wider the Bands are, the higher the volatility; the narrower they are, the lower the volatility. Bands will, therefore, narrow during congestion areas and widen when the price is trending. Typically, when this happens, the price starts bouncing off the upper and lower bands, indicating a trading range. This action, together with the narrowing of the Bands helps you to identify that a congestion area is developing. As you know, in Point and Figure terms, congestion areas occur during times of accumulation and distribution when the price continually changes direction, creating short columns of Xs and Os. Remember, if the price doesn't move, the Point and Figure chart does not change. If the price moves up by a few boxes then down by a few boxes, it shows that no one is prepared to hold a position for long. Sometimes Point and Figure congestion areas are not that easy to see. Using Bollinger Bands to identify these areas helps with the analysis of the Point and Figure chart as a whole.

You will know already that congestion areas are wider when 1-box charts or 3-box charts constructed with daily high/low are drawn. Furthermore, reducing the box size also increases the sensitivity of the chart and, therefore, exposes congestion areas.

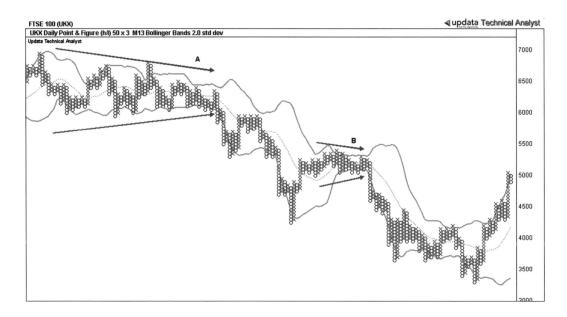

Chart 9-23: 50 x 3 of the FTSE 100 Index using high/low data with 13-column, 2 standard deviation Bollinger Bands

Chart 9-23 is a 50 x 3 of the FTSE 100 Index. It is the same box size and reversal as that in Chart 9-22, but this time it is constructed with daily high/low data instead of the close only. Notice how the Bollinger Bands converge during the congestion areas, showing volatility decreasing. The congestion area marked A is the 1999 to 2001 top. Without the Bollinger Bands it would have been harder to see the reduction in volatility. Notice the narrowing of the Bands in area B as well. At the time, without the assistance of the Bands, it would have been difficult to say that volatility was decreasing to such an extent.

Volatility cannot keep decreasing; it needs to revert to the mean at some stage. When the Bands come together, Bollinger calls it '*The Squeeze*' and suggests it may be identified when the Band width is the narrowest for 6 months. As time plays no part in Point and Figure construction or analysis, it is not possible to use that rule. Instead, you should look at the number of boxes between the bands. If the number of boxes is around the same or less than any previous squeeze, there is a high probability of a sharp move. In the case of area B on the chart, at no time in the history of the FTSE 100 had there ever been only 5 boxes between the Bands! 5 boxes means 250 points or around 5% of the price at the time. As you know, that percentage will not apply throughout the chart and so it is suggested that when volatility and the squeeze are assessed, log scale Point and Figure charts are used.

Chart 9-24 is a 1% x 3 of the FTSE 100 Index calculated with high/low data. Notice the significant squeezes, circled on the chart, that occurred prior to important moves. In each case, the squeeze came down to approximately 5 boxes.

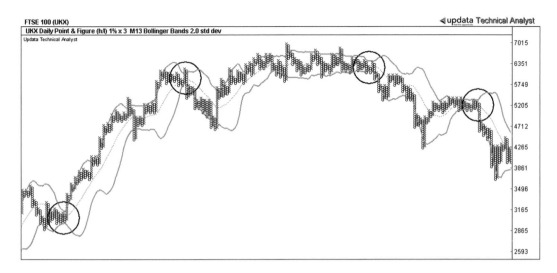

Chart 9-24: 1% x 3 of the FTSE 100 Index using high/low data with 13-column, 2 standard deviation Bollinger Bands

The other way to expose congestion areas is to switch to a 1-box reversal chart. Chart 9-25 below is a section of a 1% x 1 of the FTSE 100 Index. Once again, the circled squeezes can clearly be seen, with the exception of the one in 1998 marked with the arrow. In this case the 1-box chart did not show a squeeze. What this shows is that you need to look at more than one Point and Figure chart when doing your analysis. As has been said so many times before, you need to vary the drawing parameters to hide and expose patterns.

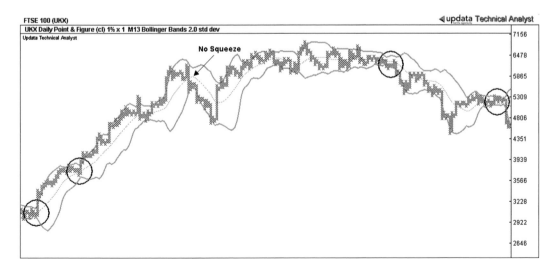

Chart 9-25: 1% x 1 of the FTSE 100 Index using close only data with 13-column, 2 standard deviation Bollinger Bands

As you have seen, adding Bollinger Bands to a Point and Figure chart can highlight congestion areas and warn you to be on the alert, but they do not tell you anything about the direction of the impending breakout. What they do tell you is that something is about to happen. If you do not have a clue as to the direction, then a derivative position, such as an options straddle,[34] may be considered.

Every chart you look at will require slightly different parameters. You will soon discover whether Bollinger Bands, based on a 13-column moving average, are better than those based on a 20-column moving average. It is worth spending the time experimenting with the instruments you are following to discover the right parameters to use.

More examples

Not all charts will exhibit squeezes and, even when they do, you may have to adjust your box size, reversal and construction method to expose them. Chart 9-26 is a 2% x 3 of Countrywide Financial Corporation, an S&P 500 company. The two squeezes marked show how volatility decreased during congestion following the uptrends.

Chart 9-26: 2 x 3 of Countrywide Financial Corporation using close only data with 13-column, 2 standard deviation Bollinger Bands

---

[34] An options straddle is a strategy used when a move is expected but the direction is uncertain. The strategy is to buy a call and a put at the same time.

During congestion, profits are taken and positions re-evaluated, but it is difficult to predict which way the price will break after the squeeze. The pattern created during the squeeze needs to be assessed, but, in most cases, a breakout is required to confirm the direction.

The use of Bollinger Bands should not be restricted to daily Point and Figure charts. Chart 9-27 of Apple Computer Inc. is a 0.1 x 3 using 5 minute data. Notice the squeeze as the price tries to exceed the previous top. Look at the pattern. It is a potential triple-top but there is weakness on the lower side of the pattern, giving you a clue as to the breakout direction. However, even if you wait for the break, it is not too late to trade. Chart 9-28 overleaf shows the position once the price breaks out of the pattern. There is lots of opportunity to enter a trade.

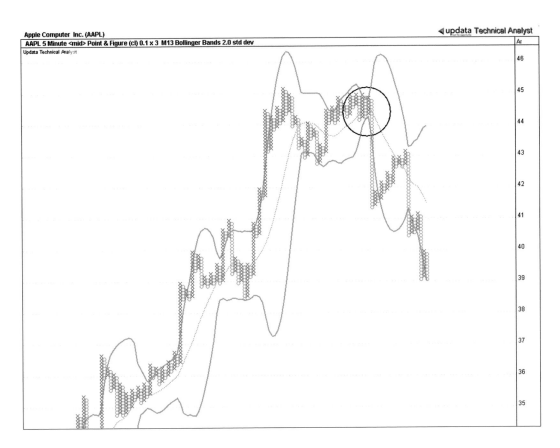

Chart 9-27: 0.1 x 3 of Apple Computer Inc. using 5 minute data with 13-column, 2 standard deviation Bollinger Bands

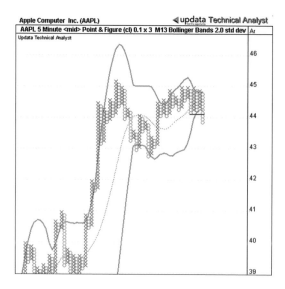

Chart 9-28: 0.1 x 3 of Apple Computer Inc. using 5 minute data with 13-column, 2 standard deviation
        Bollinger Bands

Bollinger stresses that there is no single way to use and read Bollinger Bands and that different people read them in different ways. The use of Bollinger Bands on Point and Figure charts is introduced here to encourage you to explore the technique further.

Summary

Point and Figure analysis may be enhanced by using tools usually reserved for the analysis of bar and line charts.

- Moving average periods (lengths) are measured by the number of Point and Figure columns.

- The centre price, not the last price, in each column is used in the calculation.

- The trend of the moving averages is best assessed by using two fairly short-length moving averages.

- Moving averages are not a substitute for Point and Figure signals.

- Moving averages simply tell you whether to look for a Point and Figure buy or Point and Figure sell signal.

- Parabolic SAR may be used in the same way, identifying trends and informing you which Point and Figure signal to look for.

- Bollinger Bands on Point and Figure demonstrate whether the price is overbought or oversold by its relative position to the bands.

- Prices tend to cluster at the upper Bollinger Band in uptrends and at the lower Bollinger Bands in downtrends.

- Bollinger Bands show the volatility of the Point and Figure chart, and, hence, the price.

- Squeeze points, where the column length between the bands is equal to or less than the previous squeeze, must be considered significant.

All the techniques discussed in this chapter are alternative ways of exposing the trend, for the purpose of enhancing the readability of your Point and Figure charts. They are not a substitute for pattern reading and standard Point and Figure signals. Before blindly accepting that a trend has changed because two moving averages have crossed over, or a parabolic has switched sides, always look at the underlying Point and Figure chart and the pattern that is forming. If that also indicates a trend change then you should act. If the pattern is not clear, then take account of the trend change signal, but wait for pattern clarification before acting.

Chapter 10

Chart Examples

Y ou can never have too many examples. This chapter is dedicated to drawing Point and Figure charts from a variety of markets and discussing a number of points. It is not a full analysis of each one. It is, however, a series of real life, rather than idealised, situations. Sometimes you will see something that has not been discussed. It may have been left out because it was not thought to be relevant, or I may have simply missed it, or it was so obvious it required no comment. All charts should be viewed with an open mind and without any preconceived idea. Labelling has been kept to a minimum so as not to clutter the chart.

To recap, the strategy with Point and Figure charts is:

- Look at the chart. Does it look right? If not, adjust the box and/or reversal size. In each chart chosen here, the box and reversal size have been adjusted to try to extract the information required for the analysis.

- Draw trend lines to define the bullish and bearish sections of the chart.

- Look for patterns, support and resistance levels.

- Establish counts and check past ones to see if they have been achieved or not.

- Look at the current trend. Draw internal and/or subjective trend lines.

- Weigh up the evidence obtained from the chart.

Spot Euro Dollar (daily) 0.01 x 1

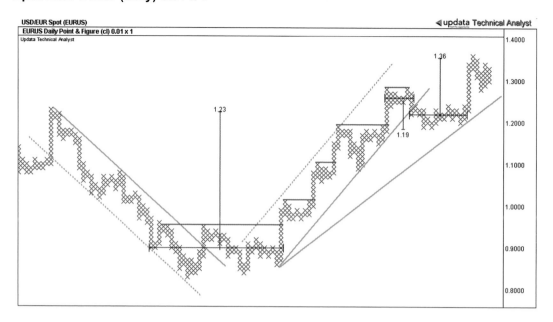

Chart 10-1: 0.01 x 1 spot Euro Dollar (daily)

The daily chart of Euro Dollar shows the formation and completion of a typical bullish fulcrum pattern. The price falls within the narrow channel, making new lows as it does. It then breaks out of the channel, running into resistance. The character of the chart has changed from a downtrend into a sideways congestion. It is during this sideways congestion that accumulation takes place. After the mid-pattern rally, notice that the price falls towards the lows of the pattern. Notice, also that the anchor or pivot of the pattern is evenly balanced around the middle, which means, at the time, you do not know whether it is a continuation or a reversal pattern. Only the break above the blue resistance line, where the catapult point is, confirms it to be a reversal pattern. As it rises out of the pattern, notice that once again it forms a channel with a number of semi-catapults. The horizontal count of 1.23 from the fulcrum is reached and the price moves sideways out of the channel, indicating profit taking and distribution. Notice the small inverted fulcrum within the channel with a downside target of 1.19. This leads into a small bullish fulcrum with a price target of 1.36, which has been achieved. You may also draw a new main uptrend line touching the bottom of the bullish fulcrum. Remember, because it is a 1-box reversal chart, trend lines are drawn to touch higher lows in the case of an uptrend, and lower highs in the case of a downtrend. The right-hand sides of patterns such as fulcrums and semi-catapults are normally where the trend lines would be placed.

For more detail of the last three columns in the chart, you can switch to the 60 minute chart opposite.

Spot Euro Dollar (60 minute) 0.01 x 1

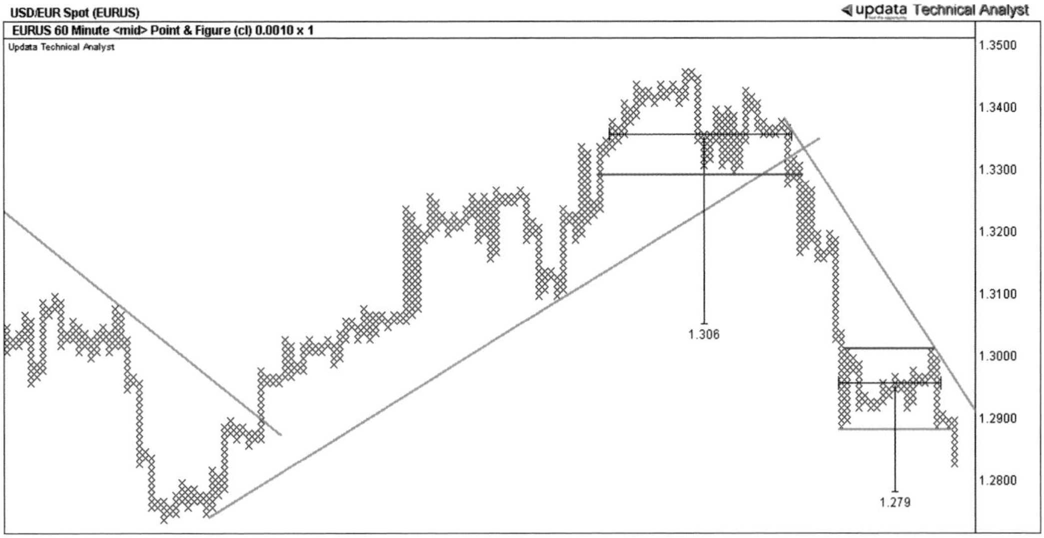

Chart 10-2: 0.01 x 1 spot Euro Dollar (60 minute)

The hourly chart of Euro Dollar shows the detail of the last three columns of the previous chart. There was a clear uptrend that was broken at the same time as the fulcrum top was completed. The horizontal count across the row with the most filled in boxes yields a target of 1.306, which was exceeded. Notice the inverted semi-catapult which formed between 1.29 and 1.30. This allows another downside count of 1.279 to be established across the most filled in row. Notice how equally balanced the pattern is, giving no clues to where the strength is. Once the semi-catapult breaks below the horizontal red support line, a new downtrend line may be drawn.

Gold PM Fix 5 x 1

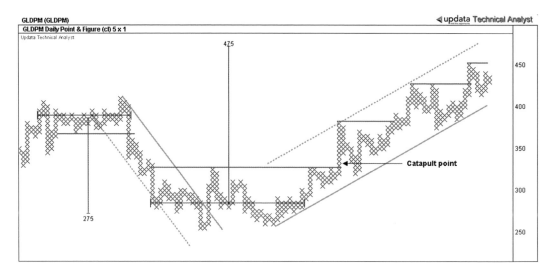

Chart 10-3: 5 x 1 gold pm fix (daily)

This is another example of how 1-box reversal charts show things that 3-box charts don't. Compare this chart of gold with Chart 10-4 on the next page. Notice the bearish fulcrum top, which yields a downside count of 275, achieved almost exactly. Notice the downtrend channel into the large fulcrum bottom which took five years to form. That is five years of accumulation. The mid-pattern rally established the level for the catapult point at the blue line. Notice how the price approaches, but does not reach, the lows of the fulcrum. Notice, too, that on the way out of the fulcrum the price made four attempts at breaking above the blue resistance line. Once broken, a new upside count of 475 across the row with the most filled in boxes may be established. Remember that, at the time of the breakout, the price was only 330. Notice also that the row with the most filled in boxes is in the lower half of the fulcrum pattern, showing strength towards the base. As the price exits the fulcrum it does so in a defined uptrend channel with main semi-catapults marked. There are some smaller ones you can try to spot for yourself.

The next chart is a 5 x 3 of the gold pm fix, to show how the 1-box and 3-box charts complement one another.

Gold PM Fix 5 x 3

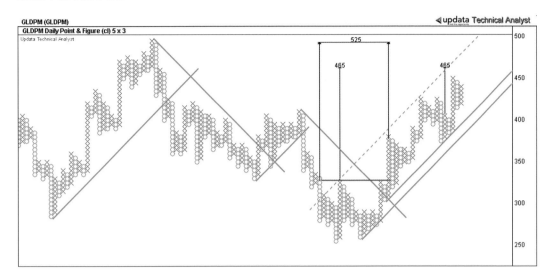

Chart 10-4: 5 x 3 gold pm fix (daily)

The 5 x 3 daily chart of gold looks completely different from the 5 x 1 chart on the previous page, even though the box size has been kept the same. It shows more history because 3-box charts compress the data. The low on the left is March 1985. It is a good idea to draw both 1- and 3-box charts, because often you will see something in one that is not apparent in the other.

The first thing to notice is how well the 45° lines define the bull and bear trends. The main 45° uptrend from the May 2001 low was tested immediately by the subsequent columns, but has not been tested since. Notice that the internal 45° uptrend line has also been tested, thereby giving it strength too. The price is following a well-defined channel as well. Notice that the vertical count of 465 from the bottom matches the 465 from the mini-bottom, making 465 an important target area.

Brent Crude Index (IPE) 2% x 1

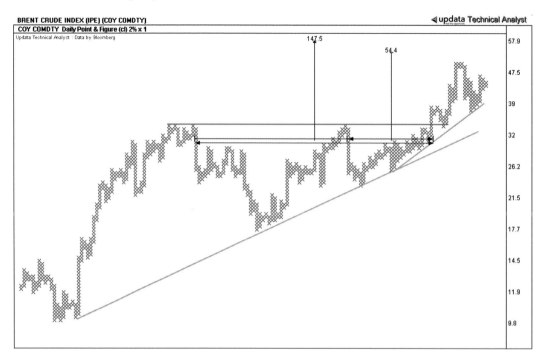

Chart 10-5: 2% x 1 of Brent Crude Index (daily): data courtesy of Bloomberg

The daily chart of Brent Crude Index (IPE) is a long-term 2% x 1 log scale chart, showing again that 1-box charts can be used for longer-term analysis where detail of the price movement is required. Notice the strong uptrend from the February 1999 low. Also notice the very strong resistance shown by the blue line from the 2000 highs around $34.5. That resistance is tested in March 2003, creating a huge continuation semi-catapult pattern with rising bottoms. The second half of the pattern yields a 54.4 upside target and the whole semi-catapult pattern yields a target of 147.5. Both targets were taken at the row at the base of the breakout column. At the time of writing, the 54.4 count seems possible but the 147.5 count seems improbable. Without more evidence, the 147.5 count is not a count to start getting excited about. Be aware that it exists, but understand that there are other counts, such as the 54.4 count, which must be achieved first. To see what other counts there are, you may change the box and reversal size. See Chart 10-6.

Brent Crude Index (IPE) 1% x 3

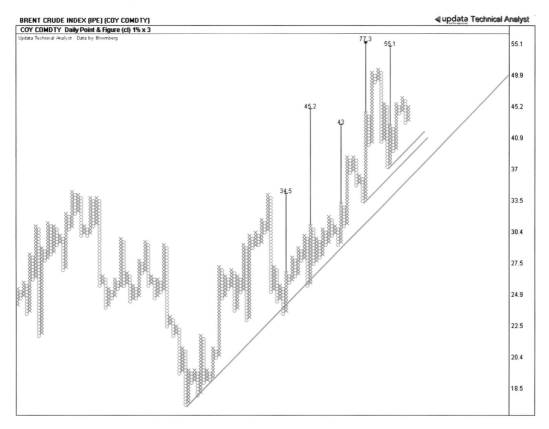

Chart 10-6: 1% x 3 of Brent Crude Index (daily): data courtesy of Bloomberg

To obtain nearer-term targets, you need to adjust the box size. In this case the box size has been halved from 2% to 1% and the reversal changed to 3-box so that some vertical targets may be obtained.

Notice how well the main 45° uptrend trend line from the November 2001 low has defined the bull trend in oil. A number of vertical targets have been placed on the chart, each at a mini-bottom. All, except two, have been exceeded, demonstrating bull market action. The 55.1 count is close to the 54.4 on the previous 1-box chart. The 77.3 count gives a target to aim for before the 147.5 target on the previous chart can be considered possible.

MIB 30 Index 1% x 3

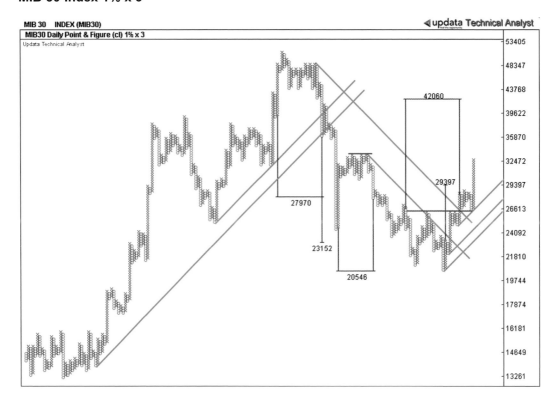

Chart 10-7: 1% x 3 MIB 30 Index (daily)

The first thing to do after drawing any Point and Figure chart is to add your trend lines. First, the main 45° trend from the August 1996 bottom, as well as the internal from the October 1998 low. The main uptrend was broken in July 2001 after providing good support prior to the break. That allowed a new 45° downtrend to be drawn from the November 2000 high. Significant resistance encountered in April 2002 allowed an internal 45° downtrend to be drawn as well. The price made a low but failed to break the internal line and was forced down to make a second low. The W pattern that formed is a typical 3-box fulcrum. Notice how the price ran into resistance from the mid-pattern peak. The triple-top that formed carried the price through the main 45° downtrend line, allowing a new 45° uptrend to be drawn. As the new uptrend matures, so additional internal 45° lines may be added, one of which has already provided support, thus elevating its status. The next thing to do is establish a few targets. Horizontal downside count 27970 was achieved, as was breakout vertical count 23152. Second horizontal count 20546 was achieved exactly. As far as upside counts are concerned, notice that the 29397 vertical count from the low has been exceeded, which is bull market action. There is a 42060 horizontal count from the W pattern, which is still to be achieved. Remember, just because a count is there, does not mean it will be achieved.

Nikkei 225 Index 100 x 3

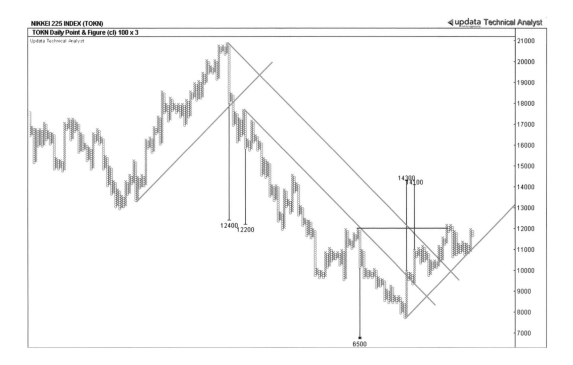

Chart 10-8: 100 x 3 Nikkei 225 Index (daily)

Once again, trend lines should be drawn first to divide up the chart into bullish and bearish trends. All trend lines are at 45° because it is a 3-box chart. Notice how the 45° internal downtrend provided resistance on the way down. When this happens, it makes the internal line more important. Counts are the next thing to establish. There is 12400 count from the top, which was exceeded, confirming the bear trend. In fact, after the 12200 count, which was also exceeded, there were no other significant down counts until the 6500 from the mini-top which touched the internal downtrend line. Then a thrust off the bottom breaks the internal 45° downtrend line, forming a small bearish pattern reversed and allowing a new upside count of 14300 to be established. A mini-bottom then allows another upside count of 14100 to be established. Note the counts clustering around the 14200 area. The character of the chart is changing. It is trending sideways towards the main downtrend line, showing accumulation after the severe downtrend. The main downtrend breaks, allowing a new uptrend to be drawn. The chart is now in an uptrend and the 6500 count looks less likely. When the price breaks above the blue horizontal resistance line, the 6500 count is cancelled and can be removed from the chart. The 14200 target becomes more likely. Its achievement or non-achievement will tell you a lot about the state of the new uptrend.

Hang Seng Index 100 x 3

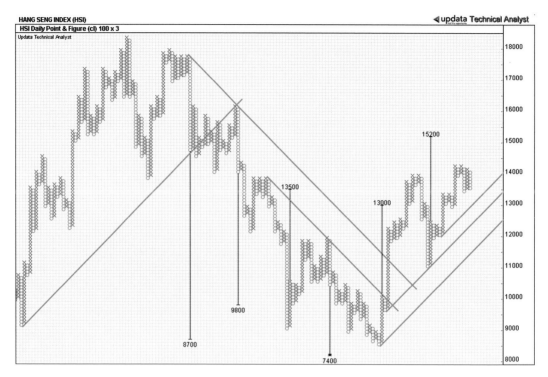

Chart 10-9: 100 x 3 Hang Seng Index (daily)

Observe how effective the 45° trend lines are in defining both the main trend as well as the internal support and resistance. A number of vertical counts have been placed on the chart so you can see where they should be taken. Remember, the achievement or non-achievement adds to your assessment of the bullishness or bearishness of the chart. For example, during the downtrend, the upside target of 13500 was not achieved, confirming the bear trend at the time.

Notice the last downside count of 7400 has been cancelled and the 13000 upside count has been exceeded, confirming bull market action. Mini-tops and bottoms that bounce off 45° trend lines are ideal places to establish counts during a trend. There are horizontal counts available as well. You should try establishing these yourself.

DJ Euro Stoxx 50 1% x 3

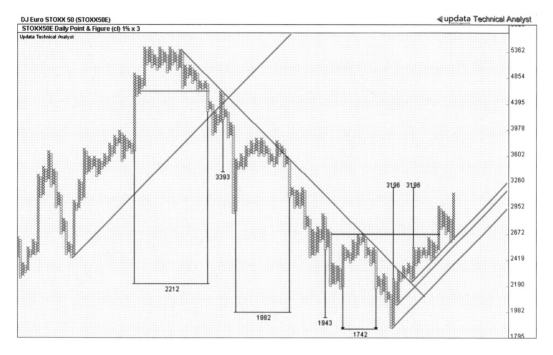

Chart 10-10: 1% x 3 DJ Euro Stoxx 50 (daily)

This is a 1% x 3 daily log scale chart. Notice how well the 45° lines have defined previous trends, lending weight to them being able to define future trends as well. The break of the red horizontal support line at the top allowed a horizontal downside count of 2212 to be established. It means that the size of the top is such that it can justify a target which is over 2000 points away! This simple fact on its own should make you take notice. Once the main 45° uptrend breaks as well, the target becomes a distinct possibility. Notice how other horizontal counts established during the downtrend were achieved. Once the main bearish resistance line is breached and the index moves to a bull trend, notice the two vertical upside counts taken from two completely different columns, yielding the same 3196 target. Notice the large fulcrum bottom with the catapult point at the blue horizontal line allowing a horizontal count (not shown) to be taken across that pattern. There are three valid support lines for the current uptrend. One has already been tested and held. Notice that a bearish pattern reversed has formed at the same time.

Infineon Technologies AG 2% x 3

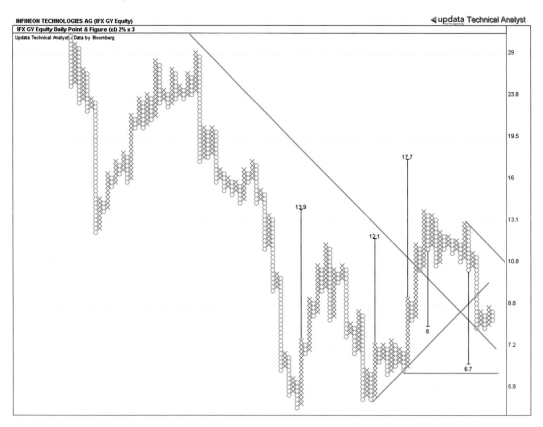

Chart 10-11: 2% x 3 Infineon Technologies AG (daily): data courtesy of Bloomberg

Notice the W bottom fulcrum pattern, which generates two upside counts of 12.1 and 13.9, both of which were achieved. Once the main 45° bearish resistance line is broken, a new bullish support line may be drawn. However, the trend did not last and was broken, placing the share in a new downtrend. New downside counts of 8 and 6.7 may be established from the new top. The fact that 8 was achieved confirms the current bearish status. The achievement of the 17.1 upside counts is looking less likely and will be cancelled if the price falls below the red horizontal line from the base of the count.

IBM 1% x 3

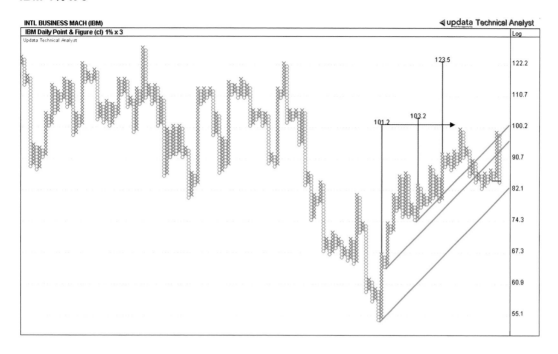

Chart 10-12: 1% x 3 IBM Corporation (daily)

This is a log scale 1% x 3 chart of IBM showing the strong rise from the October 2002 low. The first upthrust allows an upside vertical count of 101.2 to be established and the main 45° uptrend to be drawn. A number of internal 45° lines may also be drawn as the trend progresses. Another upside count of 103.2 can be established from the mini-bottom, reinforcing the 101.2 target. Notice the price reaches the target within a box, before turning down.

Observe the bullish catapult pattern just before the target is achieved. The thrust out of the catapult pattern is very bullish and the 123.5 count looks likely, but notice that the thrust is terminated by a retracement column of Os alongside the breakout column, forming a high pole. The price breaks two internal 45° lines and then forms another bullish catapult. There is a very long breakout column of Xs, which is again retraced by a column of Os. Another high pole is being formed. Some would close any long positions on a 50% retracement of the pole, others would wait until the double-bottom sell signal shown by the horizontal blue line. Ideally some congestion is required before the high pole, and the catapult provides that congestion. Buyers taking part in the move out of the catapult are distressed by the retracement in the next column.

Compuware Corporation 1% x 1

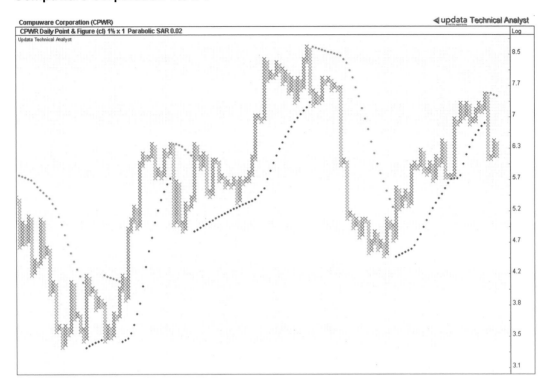

Chart 10-13: 1% x 1 Compuware Corporation (daily)

Although the drawing of trend lines is important in Point and Figure analysis, sometimes other trend definition techniques work better. The 1-box reversal chart of Compuware Corporation uses a 0.02 parabolic to define the trends. Notice how well it does this. Remember that when the parabolic swings below the price, and the dots turn blue, it puts you into 'buy' mode and you must look for next buy signal. When the parabolic swings above, and the dots turn red, you must look for sell signals. Without the aid of the parabolic, it would have been very difficult to define the trends of Compuware Corporation.

Intel Corporation 0.25 x 3

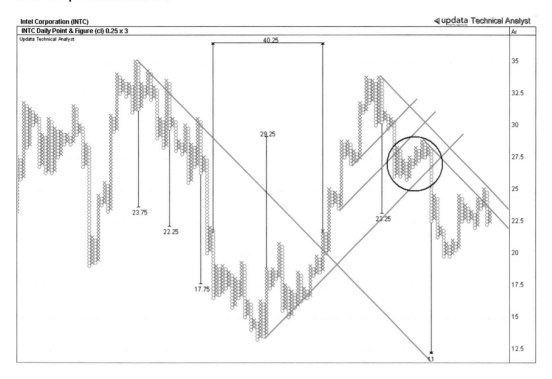

Chart 10-14: 0.25 x 3 Intel Corporation (daily)

Notice the 45° lines defining the main and internal trends. Counts during the downtrend taken from mini-tops were all exceeded, confirming the bear trend. You will have noticed that there are further downside counts from mini-tops which have not been shown because they were not achieved, thus confirming the end of the downtrend and the October 2002 bottom. The first move off the bottom yields a target of 29.25. Notice how the price falls back and finds support a number of times on the bullish support line from the October low. The large fulcrum bottom yields a horizontal upside count of 40.25. The upside target of 29.25 is achieved. Observe how the price consolidates at that level before pushing higher. Everything is in place for the achievement of the 40.25 target. The price forms a potential extended triple-top at 33.75 but does not breakout; instead, it falls and breaks the first two internal 45° uptrend lines. It forms a bullish trend reversed pattern (circled) and then breaks the main 45° bullish support line, exceeding the downside target of 23.25 from the top which is bear trend action. Notice how the price tried to recover to the 45° bearish resistance line from the top, but failed to break it. Refer also to the chart of Intel on page 426 to compare trends established with the parabolic SAR.

American Express Company 1.5% x 3

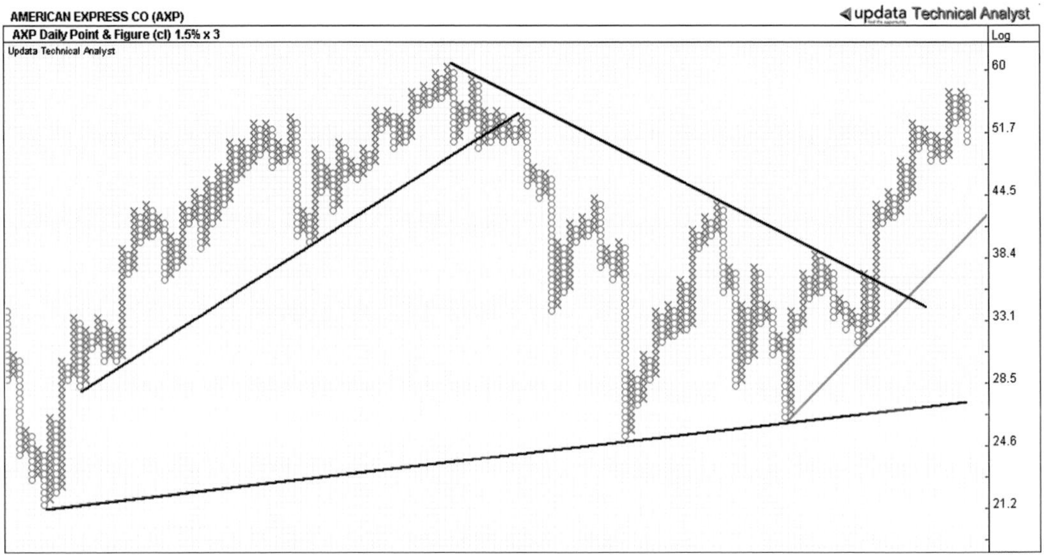

Chart 10-15: 1.5% x 3 of American Express Company (daily)

Although 45° trend lines are very good at defining trends on 3-box reversal charts, there may be times when subjective trend lines, joining higher lows or lower highs, are better. The log scale chart of American Express Company shows three subjective trend lines drawn in black, all showing the trend, and hence support and resistance, better than any 45° line would have done. They are, therefore, preferred on this chart. Notice that after the lines were drawn initially, using two touch points, they were tested afterwards increasing their validity. Notice, too, the double-top buy signal that coincides with the break of the downtrend.

There is no reason why you can't mix 45° trend lines with subjective ones. Look at how the red 45° line from the low has already been tested, increasing its strength and validity.

Three Month Sterling Interest Rate Future (June 2005) (60 minute) 0.025 x 1

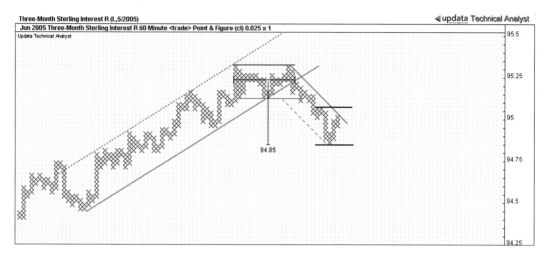

Chart 10-16: 0.025 x 1 Three month Sterling Interest Rate Future (June 2005) (60 minute)

This is an hourly chart from June 2004. Notice the clear uptrend channel so typical of 1-box reversal charts. Distribution takes place each time the price hits the upper channel and moves sideways across the channel. What occurs after will either be a continuation semi-catapult or an inverted fulcrum. The inverted fulcrum usually occurs as the price drifts sideways out of the channel. Notice how resistance was encountered twice at 95.3 at the blue horizontal resistance line. At this stage it could either be a continuation pattern or a top. Only when the price breaks below the red support line is the inverted fulcrum top confirmed and a downside count of 94.85 can be established. The target has been achieved and the price has rallied up to the downtrend line. As this is a short-term chart, profits should be taken close to targets.

The price is in a downtrend channel. There are no clues on the chart at this stage to tell you whether it will continue lower or whether it will form a bottom. Price action subsequent to this chart will tell you. You need to wait to see whether it forms a fulcrum bottom or a continuation semi-catapult. The black horizontal lines are the key support and resistance levels.

Summary

There is no better way to practise Point and Figure analysis than drawing charts yourself. This chapter should have given you some idea how to view a Point and Figure chart, how to proceed and what to look for.

Chapter 11

Conclusion

Can Point and Figure replace all other charts? Are they indeed 'desert island' charts? The reality is that it would be naïve to expect a single chart type to satisfy all the needs of a trader or investor, but there is no other single chart that is more useful. Before being introduced to Point and Figure charts, you would have used other chart types. Stop for a moment and consider whether you would be prepared to take any one of those to a desert island and trade the markets using it. It is unlikely that any single one would suffice, but Point and Figure would.

Point and Figure charts answer more questions than any other chart. They come from the market, and that is important because it is the market that you are trading. They only 'move' when the price moves and not just because time has passed. When the market is quiet, the Point and Figure chart falls silent.

They show the forces of supply and demand better than other charts and it is this supply and demand that pushes prices down and up respectively. In their own way they simulate volume, because only volume behind the demand or supply can make the price move and plot another box. They can be used for short-term as well as long-term analysis, even using the same series of data, by changing the construction parameters.

The great thing about Point and Figure charts over any other method is that they are unambiguous, especially when the 3-box reversal method is used. The buy and sell signals are unambiguous; you cannot argue that you didn't see the signal. It is clear-cut. This does not imply accuracy; that is another matter. They may not always be right, but if they are not, you will know soon enough. The same applies to trend lines, the bread and butter of Technical Analysis. Provided you can see a top or a bottom on a Point and Figure chart, you can draw unambiguous, objective 45° trend lines and, as a result, trends are defined much earlier. Targets are also unambiguous, whether they are taken from tops and bottoms or breakouts. No other chart provides such an objective way of establishing targets. An unambiguous method of establishing the potential reward from any trade allows risk-reward ratios to be calculated. Stops are also easier to establish when looking at Point and Figure patterns.

You may find it hard to agree with what you are seeing when you look at a Point and Figure chart, but you cannot argue with the chart once the trend lines and counts have been placed on it. Point and Figure is not a method for picking tops and bottoms. That is a 'mug's game' and best left to those foolhardy enough to attempt it. It is just as well to remember that a top or a bottom can only be fact after the event, which makes picking them a risky and foolish business. Point and Figure is a trend following system. It is best to ride with the trend, observe when the trend is about to change, act when it has changed and ride it in the other direction.

You will have seen that the analysis of Point and Figure charts is an evidence-gathering procedure. The evidence from trend lines, patterns and targets help you to decide when trend changes are about to occur. Of course, there will be mistakes along the way, but that is the way of the market. No method is foolproof. Mistakes are, however, essential to good analysis because you only ever learn from mistakes. No one truly learns from their successes. What you will learn is what to look for and watch out for next time you see a similar picture emerging. The purpose of this book has not been to define a prescribed method, but rather to encourage thought whilst analysing your charts.

You have seen that there are many ways to construct a Point and Figure chart, all of which are valid, and each way extracts something different from the data. The traditional 1-box reversal method, which has fallen out of favour, shows things that the more common 3-box method does not. It helps you to see the interplay between the bulls and the bears. Although Point and Figure charts were designed to be constructed from tick data, you have seen that any time-frame, from 1 minute to daily, may be used and in each case you may either use the close at the end of each period or the high/low.

Point and Figure charts may be drawn on an arithmetic scale where each X and O has the same value, or on a log scale where each X and O is a percentage. This makes longer-term Point and Figure charts much more valid because the box size adjusts as the price rises and falls.

You have seen that the Point and Figure method of drawing charts can be extended to drawing charts of calculated lines, such as relative strength, on-balance volume and others. The Point and Figure representation of these indicators does make them easier to interpret.

You have also seen that Point and Figure contributes to market breadth with the bullish percent oscillator, which measures the percentage of stocks in an index which are showing bullish Point and Figure charts.

Tools such as moving averages, parabolics and Bollinger Bands may all be adapted to Point and Figure charts, and you have seen that they provide additional help in evaluating and interpreting the Point and Figure chart itself by showing when to look for traditional Point and Figure buy and sell signals.

You will see, in Appendix E, that the fact that a Point and Figure chart is either bullish or bearish makes it the ideal condition on which to search for stocks. Scans based on the last Point and Figure signal allow a group of stocks to be quickly sorted into bullish and bearish.

Finally, any Technical Analyst worth his or her salt will ensure that they are familiar and conversant with Point and Figure charts. Whether you have decided you like them or not, you cannot choose to ignore understanding them, so if you want to call yourself a Technical Analyst, you must start using Point and Figure charts now. You will find that the more you do, the more you will appreciate them.

Applying Point and Figure analysis to the real market and real money will take you along the next path to success. Although it is extreme to believe that Point and Figure charts are the only charts you will ever need, it is not an exaggeration that Point and Figure charts do tell you a lot more about the market than any other single chart. In previous chapters, the use of technical indicators in Point and Figure format has been discussed and you are encouraged to use these as well.

It is hoped that you have enjoyed reading this book and that it has given you a taste of Point and Figure charts. The hard work starts from today.

You must remember that Technical Analysis and the use of Point and Figure is like learning to ride a horse. It's no good sitting down and reading a book on how to do it. You have to get on the horse, ride around, and perhaps fall off a few times, until you can claim to know anything.

Chapter 12

References and Further Reading

The following books have been read and referenced in writing this work. The author wishes to thank those that have gone before and laid out the path so clearly.

Aby, Carroll D., Jr., *Point & Figure Charting*, Traders Press Inc, Greenville. 1996

Bensignor, Rick (Editor), *New Thinking in Technical Analysis*, Bloomberg Press, Princeton, 2000

Blumenthal, Earl, *Chart for Profit Point and Figure Trading*, Investors Intelligence, New York, 1975

Bollinger, John, *Bollinger on Bollinger Bands*, McGraw-Hill, New York, 2001

Burke, Michael L., *Three Point Reversal Method or Point & Figure Construction and Formations*, Chartcraft Inc., New York, 1990

Cohen, A.W., *How to use the Three-Point Reversal Method of Point and Figure Stock Market Trading*, Chartcraft, 1978

Cole, George, *Graphs and their Application to Speculation*, Bernbee Press, Peoria, 1936

De Villiers, Victor, *The Point and Figure Method of Anticipating Stock Price Movements* [Windsor Books, 1933] Wiley, New York, 2000

De Villiers, Victor and Taylor, Owen, *De Villiers and Taylor on Point and Figure Charting*, FT Prentice Hall, 2000

Dines, James, *How the Average Investor can use Technical Analysis for Stock Profits*, Dines Chart Corporation, 1972

Dorsey, Thomas J., *Point and Figure Charting* (2nd Ed), Wiley Trading, New York, 2001

Hoyle, *The Game in Wall Street, and How to Play it Successfully*, Oglivie Publishing Co. 1898 and Fraser Publishing Co., Burlington, 1968

Jiler, William, *How Charts Can Help You in the Stock Market*, [Trend line, New York, 1970] McGraw-Hill, New York, 2003

Markstein, David L., *How to Chart Your Way to Stock Market Profits*, Arco Publishing, New York, 1972

Mackay, Charles, (*Memoirs of*) *Extraordinary Popular Delusions & the Madness of Crowds*, London 1841 and Harriman House, 2003

Murphy, John J., *Technical Analysis of the Financial Markets*, New York Institute of Finance, New York, 1999

Pring, Martin, *Technical Analysis Explained*, McGraw-Hill, New York, 2002

Rollo Tape (Richard Wyckoff), *Studies in Tape Reading*, Traders Press 1910 & Fraser Publishing, 1997

Schabacker, Richard W., *Technical Analysis and Stock Market Profits* – A Course in Forecasting, Schabacker 1932 and Harriman House, 2005

Wheelan, Alexander, *Study Helps in Point and Figure Technique*, Morgan Rogers and Roberts, New York, 1954 and Traders Press, Greenville, 1990

Wilder Jr, J. Welles, *New Concepts in Technical Trading Systems*, Trend Research, Greensboro, NC, 1978

Wyckoff, Richard D, *Stock Market Technique: Number One*, 1933 and Fraser Publishing Co. Burlington, 1984

Wyckoff, Richard D, *Stock Market Technique: Number Two*, 1934 and Fraser Publishing Co. Burlington, 1989

Zieg, Kermit C., *Point & Figure Commodity & Stock Trading Techniques*, Traders Press, Greenville, 1997 c

Appendix A

Construction of 2-Box Reversal Charts

Example of a 10 x 2 Point and Figure chart

It may seem tedious, but the construction of 2-box charts must be shown. The reason is that 2-box charts have not been written about before, so it is important that the reader has a reference point. The best way to do this is to use the same set of data used in constructing the 3-box examples.

No.	Price		No.	Price
1	1100		26	1122
2	1105		27	1133
3	1110		28	1125
4	1112		29	1139
5	1118		30	1105
6	1120		31	1132
7	1136		32	1122
8	1121		33	1131
9	1129		34	1127
10	1120		35	1138
11	1139		36	1111
12	1121		37	1122
13	1129		38	1111
14	1138		39	1128
15	1113		40	1115
16	1139		41	1117
17	1123		42	1120
18	1128		43	1119
19	1136		44	1132
20	1111		45	1133
21	1095		46	1147
22	1102		47	1131
23	1108		48	1159
24	1092		49	1136
25	1129		50	1127

Table A-1: Table of close prices for construction of a 2-box reversal chart

As before, because the prices are in the thousands, you are going to use a box size of 10. The chart you are going to construct will be called a 10 x 2 Point and Figure chart. This means that each X and O is worth 10 points and the reversal required to change columns is 2 boxes or 20 points.

As before, the first thing you have to do is to decide whether the first box will be an X or an O. It will be an X if the initial price trend is up and an O if the initial price trend is down. This is the same procedure outlined when the 1- and 3-box charts were plotted, and is shown in Figure A-1.

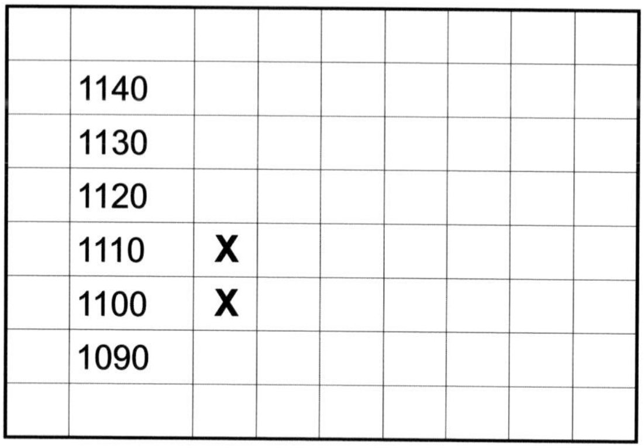

1140							
1130							
1120							
1110	X						
1100	X						
1090							

Figure A-1: 2-box reversal construction exercise

- The 4th price is 1112, so ignore it because it is not 10 points higher than the last plotted box of 1110.

- The 5th price is 1118, which is also not 10 points higher than the last plotted box of 1110.

- The 6th price is 1120. This is 10 points higher than the last plotted price of 1110 and so an X can be placed into the 1120 box. See Figure A-2.

	1140							
	1130							
	1120	X						
	1110	X						
	1100	X						
	1090							

Figure A-2: 2-box reversal construction exercise

- The 7th price is 1136, so another X can be placed in the 1130 box. See Figure A-3.

	1140							
	1130	X						
	1120	X						
	1110	X						
	1100	X						
	1090							

Figure A-3 2-box reversal construction exercise

- The 8th price is 1121. Remember, the last plotted box was 1130. This means that to plot another X, the price must be 1140 or higher, or to plot an O it must be 1110 or lower; that is 2 boxes or 20 points lower. It is neither, so the 8th price is ignored.

- The 9th price is 1129. Again this is ignored.

- The 10th price is 1120. This is 10 points away and against the price direction of the last plotted box of 1130, but because you are plotting a 10 x 2 chart, the price must reverse by 2 boxes or 20 points to change columns. It has not done this, so it is ignored.

- The 11th price is 1139 which is neither 10 points above nor 20 points below our last plotted box of 1130, so it is ignored. Remember, what you are doing now is looking for 1140 or higher to plot another X or 1110 or lower to plot 2 Os.

- The 12th, 13th, 14th, 15th, 16th, 17th, 18th, 19th and 20th prices are neither 1140 or higher, nor 1110 or lower, and so are ignored as well.

- The 21st price is 1095, which is 35 points lower than the last plotted box of 1130. This means there has been a reversal in the price of at least 20 points (more in this case), which is enough to plot a column of Os. You plot this by moving to the next column and plotting three Os down to the 1100 box. See Figure A-4.

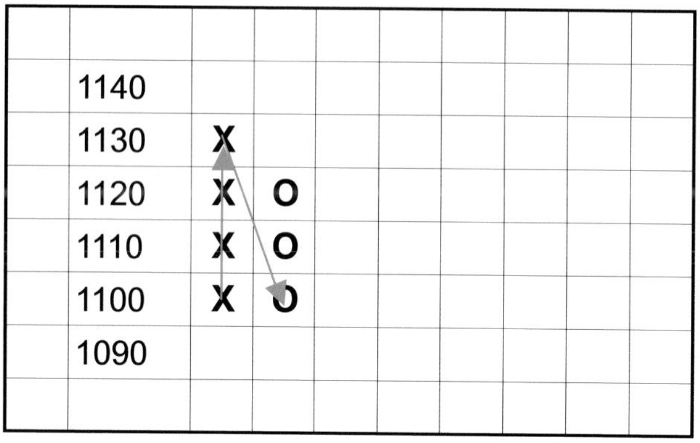

1140							
1130	X						
1120	X	O					
1110	X	O					
1100	X	O					
1090							

Figure A-4: 2-box reversal construction exercise

- The 22nd price is 1102. This is neither 10 points below the last plotted box of 1100, nor 20 points above it, so it is ignored.

- The 23rd price is 1108 and is ignored as well, as is the 24th price of 1092. Remember, with the last plotted box having been 1100, you either have to receive a new price of 1090 or lower, or a reversal price 2 boxes away at 1120 or higher.

- The 25th price is 1129. This is 20 points higher than the last plotted box of 1100. This means that there has been a reversal in the price of 20 points, which is enough to plot a column of Xs. You plot this by moving to the next column and plotting two Xs up to the 1120 box. You can't plot to the 1130 box because the price only got to 1129. Remember the glass of water is not quite full enough to stack it. See Figure A-5.

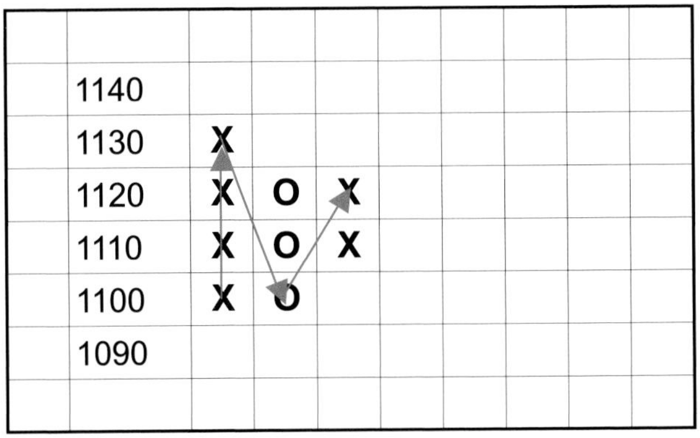

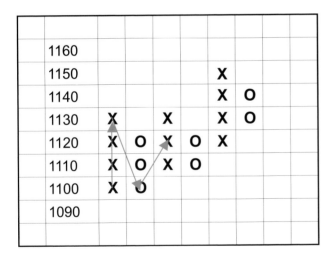

Figure A-5: 2-box reversal construction exercise

Figure A-5 shows the chart after the first 25 prices. Notice that there are now 9 Xs and Os in total, which is two more than the 3-box reversal chart.

As before, there are 25 prices left in the series. It is suggested that you use the template in Figure A-5 to complete the chart and see if yours looks like the completed chart in Figure A-6.

1160								
1150					X			
1140					X	O		
1130	X		X		X	O		
1120	X	O	X	O	X			
1110	X	O	X	O				
1100	X	O						
1090								

Figure A-6: 2-box reversal construction exercise

Table A-2 shows the completed plots.

No.	Price	Plot Box	X/O		No.	Price	Plot Box	X/O
1	1100	1100	X		26	1122		
2	1105				27	1133	1130	X
3	1110	1110	X		28	1125		
4	1112				29	1139		
5	1118				30	1105	1110	O
6	1120	1120	X		31	1132	1130	X
7	1136	1130	X		32	1122		
8	1121				33	1131		
9	1129				34	1127		
10	1120				35	1138		
11	1139				36	1111		
12	1121				37	1122		
13	1129				38	1111		
14	1138				39	1128		
15	1113				40	1115		
16	1139				41	1117		
17	1123				42	1120		
18	1128				43	1119		
19	1136				44	1132		
20	1111				45	1133		
21	1095	1100	O		46	1147	1140	X
22	1102				47	1131		
23	1108				48	1159	1150	X
24	1092				49	1136		
25	1129	1120	X		50	1127	1130	O

Table A-2: Table showing the result of the 2-box reversal construction exercise

Once again, compare your new 10 x 2 chart in Figure A-6 with the 10 x 1 chart in Figure 2-21 on page 74 and the 10 x 3 chart in Figure 2-32 on page 84. Notice how the 2-box reversal chart condenses the price movement of the 10 x 1 but not as much as the 10 x 3.

Appendix B

Construction of 1-Box Reversal
High/Low Charts

Example of a 10 x 1 Point and Figure chart using high/low prices

Table B-1 shows 50 high/low prices from which a high/low Point and Figure chart may be constructed. Because the prices are in the thousands you are going to use a box size of 10. This means that any movement less than 10 is ignored. The chart will be called a 10 x 1 Point and Figure chart (h/l), which means that each X and O is worth 10 points and the reversal required to change columns is 1 box. The (h/l) tells the person looking at the chart that it is constructed with high/low prices instead of close only.

Day no.	Day's high	Day's low		Day no.	Day's high	Day's low
1	1100	1099		26	1125	1120
2	1105	1102		27	1136	1129
3	1115	1109		28	1127	1124
4	1115	1110		29	1141	1133
5	1124	1115		30	1107	1100
6	1131	1110		31	1133	1128
7	1136	1130		32	1125	1118
8	1129	1115		33	1132	1126
9	1129	1121		34	1128	1123
10	1125	1113		35	1140	1135
11	1141	1134		36	1119	1100
12	1122	1118		37	1125	1120
13	1132	1123		38	1114	1108
14	1143	1135		39	1130	1124
15	1113	1108		40	1115	1110
16	1140	1136		41	1119	1111
17	1128	1121		42	1124	1116
18	1141	1126		43	1120	1117
19	1139	1133		44	1134	1129
20	1112	1096		45	1137	1130
21	1096	1087		46	1149	1143
22	1105	1100		47	1135	1130
23	1110	1105		48	1162	1153
24	1095	1089		49	1139	1132
25	1132	1127		50	1130	1125

Table B-1: Table of high/low prices for 1-box construction exercise

The procedure to construct a 10 x 1 Point and Figure chart using the high/low data in the Table B-1 is as follows:

As before, the first thing you have to do is to decide whether the first box will be an X or an O. It will be an X if the initial price trend is up and an O if the initial price trend is down.

- Take note of the 1st high/low, 1100/1109, and look at the 2nd high/low, 1105/1102. If the 2nd high is 1110 or higher, then the first plot is an X. If it is not 1110 or higher, then compare lows. If the 2nd low is 1090 or lower, then the first plot is an O. Neither applies in this case, so the 2nd high/low is ignored.

- Look at the 3rd high/low, 1115/1109, and apply the rule. The 3rd high is 1115, which is more than 10 points higher than the first high, so the Point and Figure chart can be started by plotting two Xs in the 1100 and 1110 boxes, ignoring the 2nd price. You could also have started at 1090, but this is not important.

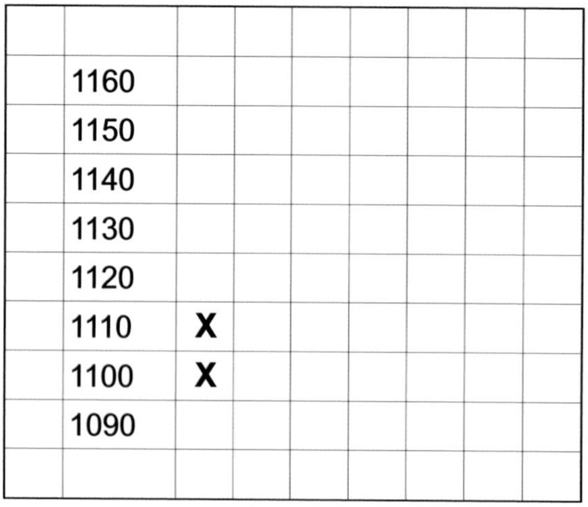

1160							
1150							
1140							
1130							
1120							
1110	X						
1100	X						
1090							

Figure B-1: 1-box reversal high/low construction exercise

- The 4th high/low is 1115/1110. The rule is that if you are plotting a column of Xs, you must look at the high to see if it generates a new X. To do this, the high would have to be 1120 or higher, which it is not, so you must look at the low to see if it generates a reversal. The low is 1110, so no new O can be plotted and the 4th high/low is ignored.

- The 5th high/low is 1124/1115. Once again, you are looking for a high of 1120 or higher. An X may, therefore, be placed in the 1120 box and the low ignored. See Figure B-2.

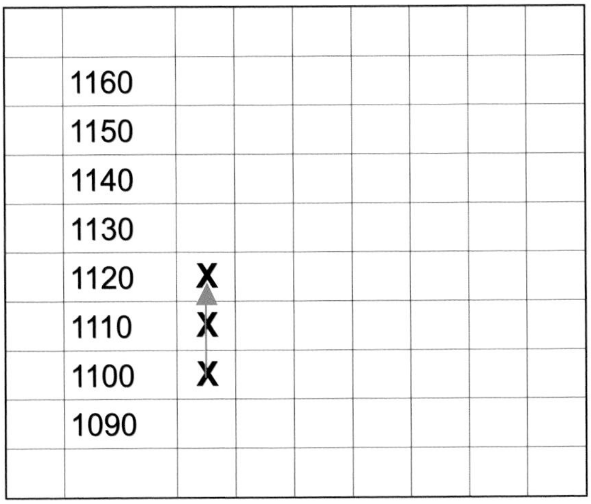

1160							
1150							
1140							
1130							
1120	X						
1110	X						
1100	X						
1090							

Figure B-2: 1-box reversal high/low construction exercise

- The 6th high/low is 1131/1100. You are in a column of Xs, so you must look at the high to see if it generates a new X, which it does at 1130. The low of 1110 is then ignored; see Figure B-3. It is just as well to note that this shows one of the plotting difficulties of high/low Point and Figure charts. The high generates a new X but the low is also low enough to generate a reversal and a new O at 1110. However, once the high is plotted, the low must be ignored. This does not mean that the high always takes precedence; it only does so when the last plotted box is an X. If the last plotted box is an O, then the low takes precedence.

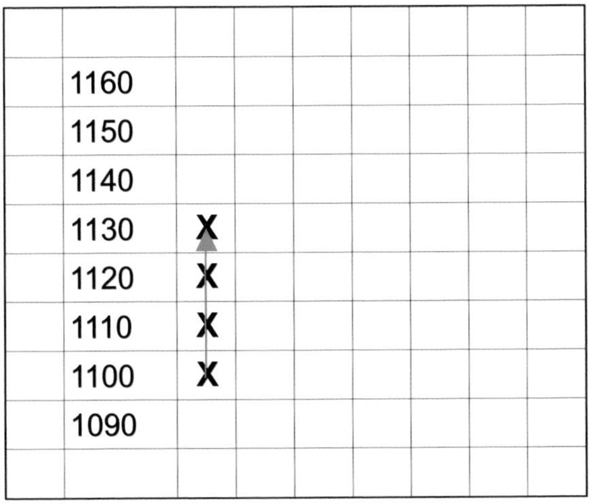

1160							
1150							
1140							
1130	X						
1120	X						
1110	X						
1100	X						
1090							

Figure B-3: 1-box reversal high/low construction exercise

- The 7th high/low is 1136/1130, so you must look at the high to see if it produces a new X, which it does not. The low does not produce a reversal and so the 7th price is ignored.

- The 8th high/low is 1129/1115. You are still in a column of Xs, so you must look to see if the high is 1140 or higher. It is not; therefore, you must look at the low, to see if there is a reversal. To do this, the low must be 1120 or lower, which it is. You must, therefore, plot an O in the 1120 box. See Figure B-4.

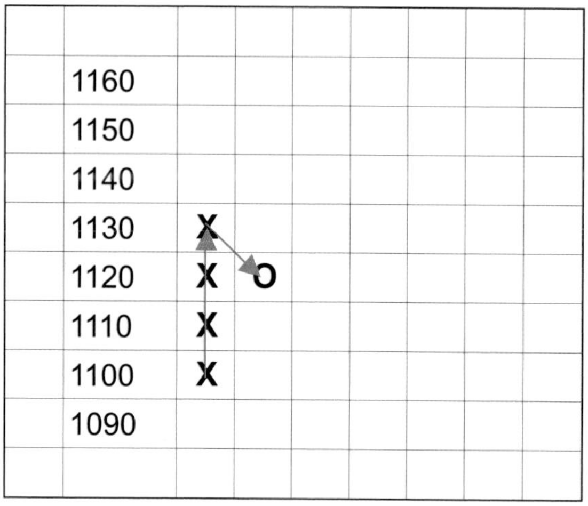

1160							
1150							
1140							
1130	X						
1120	X	O					
1110	X						
1100	X						
1090							

Figure B-4: 1-box reversal high/low construction exercise

- The 9th high/low is 1129/1121. Because you are now in a column of Os, you must first look at the low to see if it produces a new O at 1110 or lower. It does not, so you must look at the high to see if it produces a new X at 1130 or higher. It does not, so the 9th high/low is ignored.

- The 10th high/low is 1125/1113. You are still looking at the low. 1113 does not produce a new O, so you must look at the high, which does not produce a new X either, so the 10th high/low is ignored.

- The 11th high/low is 1141/1134. The low, which you must look at first, does not produce a new O, but the high of 1141 does produce a reversal. You need to plot 2 Xs at 1130 and 1140. See Figure B-5. Note that you do not have to change columns because the 1130 box above the O is vacant. The Xs are, therefore, plotted above the O in column 2. This is the one-step-back rule discussed on page 62.

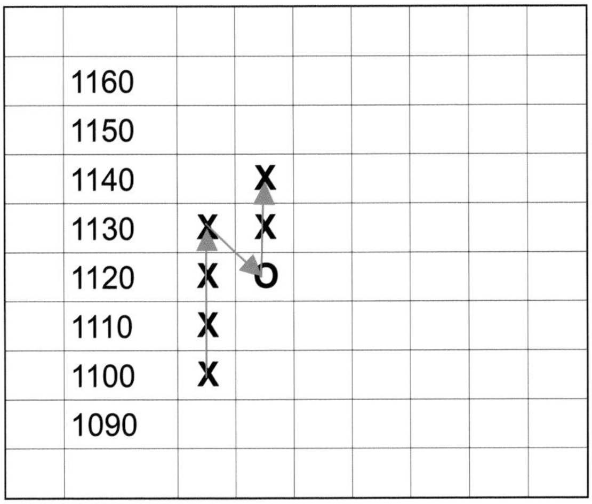

1160								
1150								
1140			X					
1130	X	X						
1120	X	O						
1110	X							
1100	X							
1090								

Figure B-5: 1-box reversal high/low construction exercise

- The 12th high/low is 1122/1118. Your last plot was an X, so look at the high. This does not produce a new X, so look at the low to see if there is a reversal. The low is 1118, so a reversal can take place and 2 Os can be plotted in the 1130 and 1120 boxes. See Figure B-6.

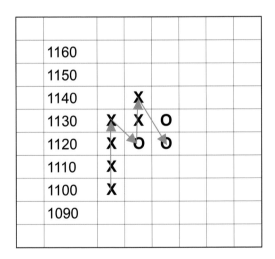

1160								
1150								
1140			X					
1130	X	X	O					
1120	X	O	O					
1110	X							
1100	X							
1090								

Figure B-6: 1-box reversal high/low construction exercise

- The 13th high/low is 1132/1123. Since your last plot was an O, you must look at the low first. The low does not produce a new O, so you must look at the high to see if there is a reversal. The last plotted box was at 1120. The high is 1132, so there is a reversal, and an X can be plotted in the 1130 box and to do this you must change columns. See Figure B-7.

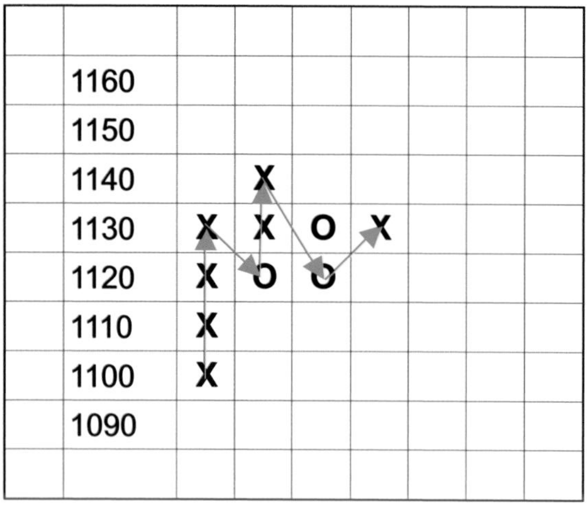

1160							
1150							
1140		X					
1130	X	X	O	X			
1120	X	O	O				
1110	X						
1100	X						
1090							

Figure B-7: 1-box reversal high/low construction exercise

- The 14th high/low of 1143/1135 produces another X at 1140. See Figure B-8.

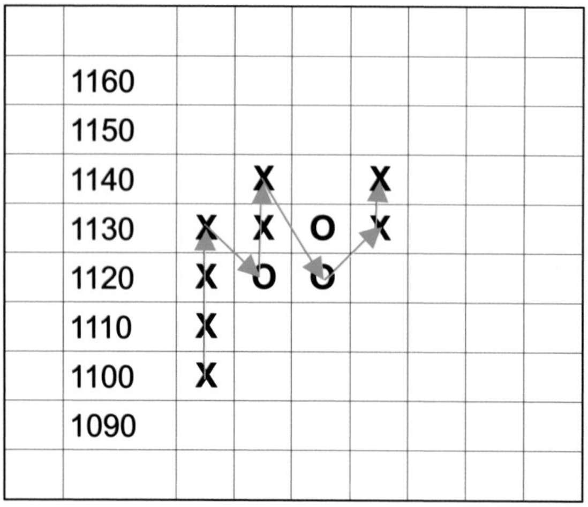

1160							
1150							
1140		X		X			
1130	X	X	O	X			
1120	X	O	O				
1110	X						
1100	X						
1090							

Figure B-8: 1-box reversal high/low construction exercise

- The 15th high/low of 1113/1108 does not produce a new X, so the low is checked and this produces a new column of Os down to 1110. See Figure B-9.

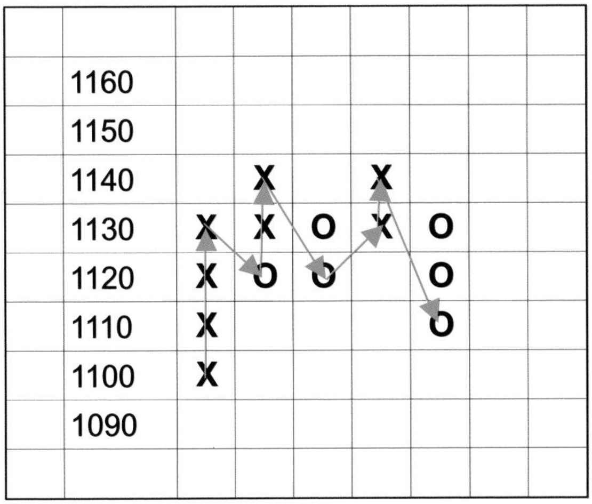

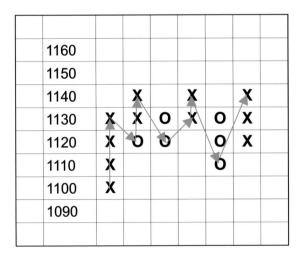

1160							
1150							
1140		X		X			
1130	X	X	O	X	O		
1120	X	O	O		O		
1110	X				O		
1100	X						
1090							

Figure B-9: 1-box reversal high/low construction exercise

- The 16th high/low of 1140/1136 does not produce a new O, but the high does produce a new column of Xs up to 1140. See Figure B-10.

1160							
1150							
1140		X		X		X	
1130	X	X	O	X	O	X	
1120	X	O	O		O	X	
1110	X				O		
1100	X						
1090							

Figure B-10: 1-box reversal high/low construction exercise

- The 17th high/low of 1128/1121 does not produce a new X, but the low does produce a new O at 1130. See Figure B-11.

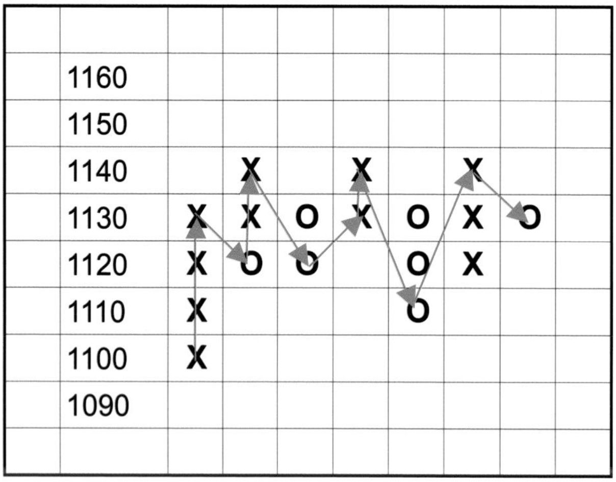

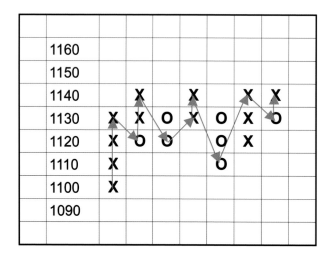

Figure B-11: 1-box reversal high/low construction exercise

- The 18th high/low is 1141/1126. The low does not produce a new O so the high is checked to see if there is a reversal. There is a reversal and an X can be placed in the 1140 box. Note that the X may be placed in the same column as the last O, which is a one-step-back. See Figure B-12.

1160									
1150									
1140		X		X		X	X		
1130	X	X	O	X	O	X	O		
1120	X	O	O		O	X			
1110	X				O				
1100	X								
1090									

Figure B-12: 1-box reversal high/low construction exercise

- The 19th high/low does not produce a new X or a new column of Os and is therefore ignored.

- The 20th high/low is 1112/1096. The high must be looked at first, but this does not produce a new X, so the low is considered for a reversal. The low is 1096, which means that a column of Os can be plotted down to 1100. See Figure B-13.

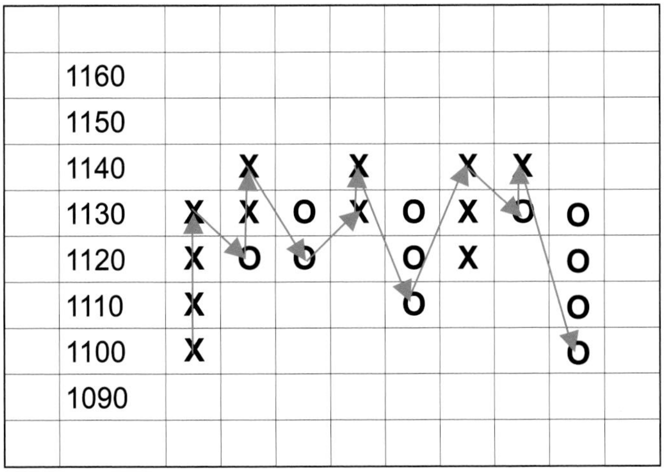

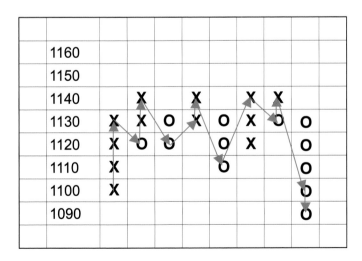

Figure B-13: 1-box reversal high/low construction exercise

- The 21st high/low produces another O at 1090. See Figure B-14.

Figure B-14: 1-box reversal high/low construction exercise

- The 22nd high/low is 1105/1100. No new O is produced from the low, but a new X column at 1100 is produced from the high. See Figure B-15.

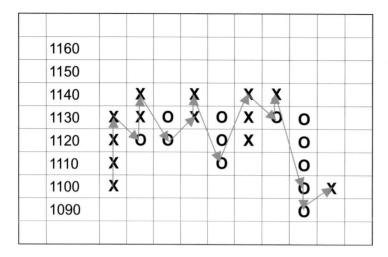

Figure B-15: 1-box reversal high/low construction exercise

- The 23rd high/low produces another X at 1110. See Figure B-16.

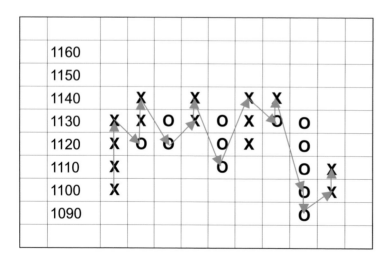

Figure B-16: 1-box reversal high/low construction exercise

- The 24th high/low is 1095/1089. No new X can be plotted from the high, but a new column of Os can be plotted down to 1090. See Figure B-17.

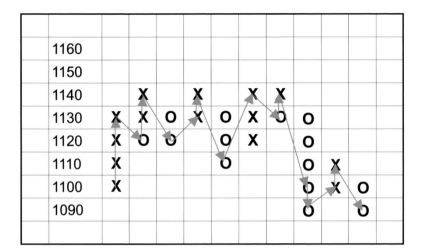

Figure B-17: 1-box reversal high/low construction exercise

- The 25th high/low is 1132/1127. The low does not produce a new O, but the high does produce a column of Xs up to 1130.

Figure B-18 shows the chart after the first 25 days of prices. Notice that the chart is far wider than any plotted so far. This is because there are many more reversals when high/low data is used.

Once again, there are 25 prices left in the series in Table B-1. It is a good exercise to complete the chart using the template below in Figure B-18. When finished it should look like the chart in Figure B-19.

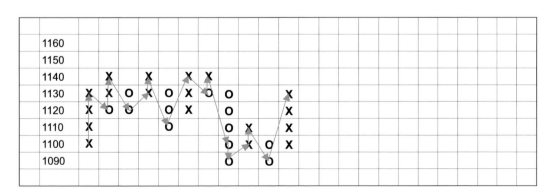

Figure B-18: 1-box reversal high/low construction exercise

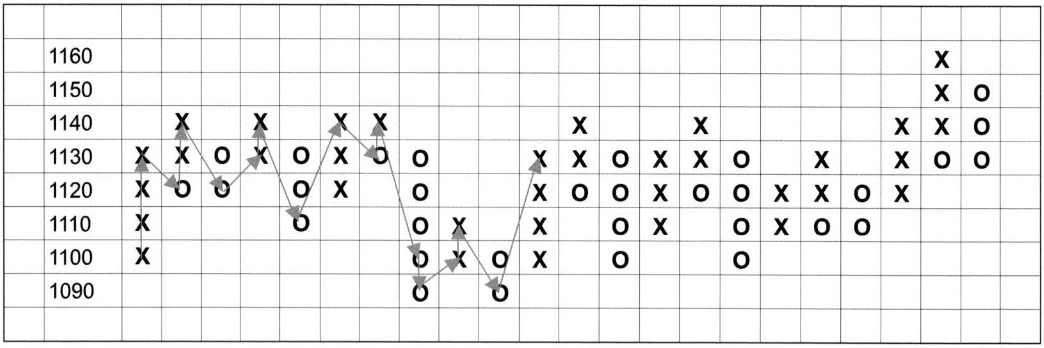

1160																		X		
1150																		X	O	
1140		X		X		X	X			X		X				X	X	O	
1130	X	X	O	X	O	X	O	O		X	X	O	X	X	O		X	X	O	O
1120	X	O	O		O	X		O		X	O	O	X	O	O	X	X	O	X	
1110	X			O				O	X		X		O	X		O	X	O	O	
1100	X							O	X	O	X			O			O			
1090								O		O										

Figure B-19: 1-box reversal high/low construction exercise

Appendix C

Construction of Log Scaled Charts

There are a number of ways to take the log of a number. The two most common are log base 10 and log base e, or natural log, (ln). The natural log is preferred for log scaled charts.

To construct a log scaled chart you must proceed as follows:

- Decide on a box size. This is done by either deciding on a logged value, or, better still, a percentage change in price, because this is easy to understand and apply.

- The box increment is, therefore, (1 + % change). For example, if you have chosen a box size of 1%, the box increment is 1.01. In other words, the next box value is 1.01 times the previous box.

- Take the ln of the box increment. The ln of 1.01 is 0.00995.

- Take the ln of the starting price in your data series. This is now the start of your logged series.

- Add the ln (1.01) to the ln of the starting price to find the value of the next box.

- Continue to do this for the full range of prices you encounter. This gives you the framework, or scaling, on which to construct the chart. This is exactly the same procedure you would go through when constructing an arithmetic chart.

- Take the ln of every price in your data series, so that you have a data series of logged prices.

- Finally, plot a normal Point and Figure chart using the series of logged prices, using a box size of ln(1 + % increment) which is 0.00995 in this example. You are, in effect, plotting a 0.00995 x 3 Point and Figure chart of the logged prices.

Table C-1 shows the construction of a 1% x 3 Point and Figure chart, where the first price in the series is 500:

- Log of start price ln(500) = 6.214608098

- Log of the increment ln(1.01) = 0.009950331

- Column 1 shows the logged value being incremented by the ln of the box increment (0.009950331). This gives the logged value of each box on which the Point and Figure chart is constructed. It is the scaling framework for the chart.

- Column 2 shows the exponential, or anti-log, of the logged value. This gives the actual price of each box and is used for scaling purposes only; it has no part in the construction.

- Column 3 shows the % increase in the price from one box to the next. As expected, it is 1% in all cases.

- Column 4 shows the percentage change for 3 rising boxes; in other words, the percentage increase in price required to achieve a 3-box reversal of Xs, which is 3%.

- Column 5 shows the % decrease in price from one box to the next. It is 0.99% in all cases.

- Column 6 shows the percentage change for 3 falling boxes; in other words, the percentage decrease in price required to achieve a 3-box reversal of Os, which is 2.97%.

Log value incremented by .009950331	Price is anti-log of the log value	% change in price per box when price is rising	% change for a 3-box reversal of X's	% change in price per box when price is falling	% change for a 3-box reversal of O's
6.274310084	530.760	1.00%	3.00%	0.99%	
6.264359753	525.505	1.00%	3.00%	0.99%	
6.254409422	520.302	1.00%	3.00%	0.99%	2.97%
6.244459091	515.151	1.00%	3.00%	0.99%	2.97%
6.23450876	510.050	1.00%		0.99%	2.97%
6.224558429	505.000	1.00%		0.99%	2.97%
6.214608098	500.000				

Table C-1: Showing how log scaled charts are calculated

Appendix D

Codes and Instrument Names

For FTSE 100 stocks

Code	Name
ABF	A.B.FOOD ORD 5 15/22P
AL-	ALLIANCE & LEIC ORD 50P
ALLD	ALD.DOMECQ ORD 25P
ANTO	ANTOFAGASTA ORD 5P
AUN	ALLIANCE UNICHM ORD 10P
AV-	AVIVA ORD 25P
AVZ	AMVESCAP ORD 25P
AZN	ASTRAZENECA ORD SHS $0.25
BA-	BAE SYS. ORD 2.5P
BAA	BAA ORD 1
BARC	BARCLAYS ORD 25P
BATS	BR.AMER.TOB. ORD 25P
BAY	BR.AIRWAYS ORD 25P
BG-	BG GRP. ORD 10P
BLND	BR.LAND ORD 25P
BLT	BHP BILLITON ORD $0.50
BNZL	BUNZL ORD 25P
BOC	BOC GRP. ORD 25P
BOOT	BOOTS GROUP ORD 25P
BP-	BP $0.25
BSY	BSKYB ORD 50P
BT-A	BT GROUP ORD 5P
CBRY	CADBURY-SCH. ORD 12.5P
CCL	CARNIVAL ORD USD 1.66
CNA	CENTRICA ORD 6 14/81P
CPI	CAPITA GROUP ORD 2P
CS-	CORUS GROUP ORD 10P
CW-	CABLE & WIRE ORD 25P
DGE	DIAGEO ORD 28 101/108P
DMGT	DAILY MAIL'A' 'A'ORD(NON.V)12.5
DXNS	DIXONS GRP ORD 2.5P
EMA	EMAP ORD 25P
EMG	MAN GROUP USD0.18
ETI	ENT.INNS ORD 5P
EXL	EXEL ORD 27 7/9P
GLH	GALLAHER GRP. ORD 10P
GSK	GLAXOSMITHKLINE ORD 25P
GUS	GUS ORD 25P
HAS	HAYS ORD 1P
HBOS	HBOS ORD 25P
HG-	HILTON GROUP ORD 10P
HNS	HANSON ORD 10P
HSBA	HSBC HLDGS.UK ORD $0.50 (UK REG
ICI	IMP.CHEM. ORD 1
IHG	INTERCON. HOTEL ORD 112P

Code	Name
III	3I GRP. ORD 50P
IMT	IMP.TOBACCO GRP ORD 10P
IPR	INTL POWER ORD 50P
ITV	ITV ORD 10P
JMAT	JOHNSON MATTH. ORD 1
KGF	KINGFISHER ORD 15 5/7P
LAND	LAND SECS. ORD 10P
LGEN	LEGAL&GEN. ORD 2 1/2P
LLOY	LLOYDS TSB GRP. ORD 25P
MKS	MARKS & SP. ORD 25P
MRW	MORRISON (WM) ORD 10P
NGT	NATIONAL GRID ORD 10P
NRK	NTHN.ROCK ORD 25P
NXT	NEXT ORD 10P
PRU	PRUDENTIAL ORD 5P
PSON	PEARSON ORD 25P
RB-	RECKITT BENCKSR ORD 10 10/19P
RBS	ROYAL BANK SCOT ORD 25P
REL	REED ELSEVIER ORD 12.5P
REX	REXAM ORD 64 2/7P
RIO	RIO TINTO ORD 10P
RR-	ROLLS-ROYCE ORD 20P
RSA	ROYAL&SUN ALL. ORD 27.5P
RTO	RENTOKIL INITL. ORD 1P
RTR	REUTERS GRP. ORD 25P
SBRY	SAINSBURY(J) ORD 28 4/7P
SCTN	SCOT.&NEWCASTLE ORD 20P
SDR	SCHRODERS VTG SHS 1
SGE	SAGE GRP. ORD 1P
SHEL	SHELL ORD 25P(REGD)
SHP	SHIRE PHARMCTCL ORD 5P
SMIN	SMITHS GROUP ORD 25P
SN-	SMITH&NEPHEW ORD 12 2/9P
SPW	SCOT.POWER ORD 50P
SSE	SCOT.&STH.ENRGY ORD 50P
STAN	STAND.CHART. ORD USD0.50
SVT	SEVERN TRENT ORD 65 5/19P
TATE	TATE & LYLE ORD 25P
TSCO	TESCO ORD 5P
ULVR	UNILEVER ORD 1.4P
UU-	UTD UTILITIES ORD 1
VOD	VODAFONE GRP. ORD SHS $0.10
WOS	WOLSELEY ORD 25P
WPP	WPP GRP. ORD 10P
WTB	WHITBREAD ORD 50P

Table D-1: Codes and instrument names for FTSE 100 stocks

For S&P 100 stocks

Code	Name
AA	ALCOA INC
AEP	AMER ELECTRIC POW CO
AES	AES CP INC
AIG	AMERICAN INTERNATIONAL GROUP IN
ALL	ALLSTATE CORP
AMGN	AMGEN INC.
AVP	AVON PRODUCTS INC
AXP	AMERICAN EXPRESS CO
BA	BOEING CO
BAC	BK OF AMERICA CP
BAX	BAXTER INTL INC
BDK	BLACK DECKER CP
BHI	BAKER HUGHES INTL
BMY	BRISTOL MYERS SQIBB
BNI	BURLINGTON SANTE FE
BUD	ANHEUSER BUSCH COS INC
C	CITIGROUP INC
CCU	CLEAR CHANNEL COM
CI	CIGNA CP
CL	COLGATE PALMOLIVE
CPB	CAMPBELL SOUP CO
CSC	COMPUTER SCIENCES CP
CSCO	CISCO SYSTEMS INC.
DAL	DELTA AIR LINES INC
DD	DU PONT E I DE NEM
DELL	DELL COMPUTER CORP.
DIS	WALT DISNEY-DISNEY C
DOW	DOW CHEMICAL
EK	EASTMAN KODAK CO
EMC	E M C CP
EP	EL PASO CORPORATION
ETR	ENTERGY CP
EXC	EXELON CORPORATION
F	FORD MOTOR CO
FDX	FEDEX CORP
G	GILLETTE CO
GD	GEN DYNAMICS CP
GE	GENERAL ELECTRIC CO.
GM	GEN MOTORS
HAL	HALLIBURTON HLDG CO
HCA	HCA INC.
HD	HOME DEPOT INC
HET	HARRAH'S ENTERTAIN
HIG	HARTFORD FIN SVC
HNZ	HEINZ H J CO
HON	HONEYWELL INTERNATIONAL
HPQ	HEWLETT PACKARD CO
IBM	INTL BUSINESS MACH

Code	Name
INTC	INTEL CORPORATION
IP	INTL PAPER
JNJ	JOHNSON AND JOHNS DC
JPM	J.P. MORGAN CHASE CO
KO	COCA COLA CO THE
LEH	LEHMAN BR HOLDINGS
LTD	LIMITED BRANDS INC
LU	LUCENT TECH INC
MAY	MAY DEPT STORES
MCD	MCDONALDS CP
MDT	MEDTRONIC INC
MEDI	MEDLMMUNE INC,
MER	MERRILL LYNCH & CO INC
MMM	3M COMPANY
MO	ALTRIA GROUP INC
MRK	MERCK CO INC
MSFT	MICROSOFT CORP
MWD	MORGAN STANLEY
NSC	NORFOLK SO CP
NSM	NATL SEMICONDUCTOR
NXTL	NEXTEL COMM INC
ORCL	ORACLE CORPORATION
PEP	PEPSICO INC
PFE	PFIZER INC
PG	PROCTER GAMBLE CO
ROK	ROCKWELL AUTOMAT INC
RSH	RADIOSHACK CORP
RTN	RAYTHEON CO NEW
S	SEARS ROEBUCK CO
SBC	SBC COMMUNICATIONS
SLB	SCHLUMBERGER LTD
SLE	SARA LEE CP
SO	SOUTHERN CO
T	AT&T CP NEW
TOY	TOYS R US HLDG
TWX	TIME WARNER INC
TXN	TEXAS INSTRUMENTS
TYC	TYCO INTERNATIONAL
UIS	UNISYS CP
USB	US BANCORP
UTX	UNITED TECHNOLOGIES CORP
VZ	VERIZON COMMUN
WFC	WELLS FARGO & CO NEW
WMB	WILLIAMS COS
WMT	WAL-MART STORES INC
WY	WEYERHAEUSER CO
XOM	EXXON MOBIL CP
XRX	XEROX CP

Table D-2: Codes and instrument names for S&P 100 stocks

Appendix E

Dividing your Stocks into Bullish and Bearish

You have seen that 3-box reversal Point and Figure charts are either bullish, where the last signal was a double-top buy, or bearish, where the last signal was a double-bottom sell. There is no neutral position. This is powerful because it allows the hedge fund manager to divide his horizon of stocks very quickly into those that are bullish and those that are bearish. Of course the power of the computer allows this to be done without actually looking at a chart, if you think carefully about what you want from it.

It has already been stressed that more than one time horizon is necessary for good Point and Figure analysis. It requires your chosen time horizon, plus perhaps two others to help with timing. For example, if your chosen time horizon chart gives a buy signal, you may wish to consult your shorter-term horizon charts to see whether it is best to wait before entering the trade. For this purpose, time horizons are defined by the box size. It is best, when dealing with a number of stocks with different histories and characteristics, to use log scale Point and Figure charts, where the box size is a percentage rather than a fixed points size. This allows you to define your time horizon by the percentage.

Normally 2% x 3 is considered to be a medium- to long-term horizon, 1% x 3 to be a medium-term horizon and 0.5% x 3 a short-term horizon. You may decide, therefore, to search for a list of stocks where the medium-term horizon, signified by 1% x 3 Point and Figure charts, is either bullish or bearish as follows:

- Fix the reversal at 3-box, because the signals are unambiguous.

- Set the box size to 1% for all charts.

- Search for stocks where the last signal from the Point and Figure chart was a double-top buy signal, meaning that a column of Xs has broken above the previous column of Xs and this has not been cancelled by a double-bottom sell signal. This places the chart in the bullish camp.

- At the same time, search for stocks where the last signal from the chart was a double-bottom sell signal, meaning that a column of Os has broken below the previous column of Os and this has not been cancelled by a double-top buy signal. This places the chart in the bearish camp.

Each chart has to be one or the other. It is either bullish or bearish: it cannot be both. It is a very quick way of separating the bullish stocks from the bearish ones.

Refining the search

The search above only considers one time horizon. You may refine it by considering two time horizons at once, by searching for bullish and bearish on both 1% and 0.5% box sizes as follows:

- Fix the reversal at 3-box.

- Set the box size to 1% and search for stocks where the last column of Xs has broken above the previous column of Xs, but where there is no O column to the right of the last X column. This means there has been no reversal since the X column breakout. Again, this places the chart in the bullish camp.

- At the same time, search for stocks where the last column of Os has broken below the previous column of Os, but where there is no X column to the right of the last O column. This means there has been no reversal since the O column breakdown. This places the chart in the bearish camp.

These two conditions define the medium-term bullishness or bearishness of the chart. At the same time, you need to establish the shorter-term position by setting the box size to 0.5%. Once again, you need to search for the bullish, as well as the bearish, condition. But this time there is no need to filter out any columns to the right of the signal column.

- Set the box size at 0.5% and search for stocks where the last column of Xs has broken above the previous column of Xs, but it does not matter if there is an O reversal column to the right of last X column. If there is, it is a 'wait' signal.

- Set the box size at 0.5% and search for stocks where the last column of Os has broken below the previous column of Os. It does not matter if there is an X reversal column to the right of last O column. If there is, it is a 'wait' signal.

The result is that your horizon of stocks will be divided into 4 sections:

1. Buy signal on the 1% chart and a buy signal on the 0.5% chart. These are stocks to put on today's buy list. See Chart E-1.

2. Buy signal on the 1% chart but a column of Os reversing against the signal on the 0.5% chart. These are stocks to place on a watchlist to buy, but only when the 0.5% chart generates a buy signal, provided the 1% buy signal is still in place. See Chart E-2.

3. Sell signal on the 1% chart and a sell signal on the 0.5% chart. These are stocks to put on today's sell list. See Chart E-3.

4. Sell signal on the 1% chart but a column of Xs reversing against the signal on the 0.5% chart. These are stocks to place on a watchlist to sell, but only when the 0.5% chart generates a sell signal, provided the 1% sell signal is still in place. See Chart E-4.

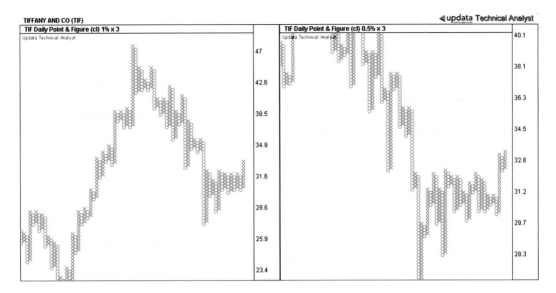

Chart E-1: Buy on 1% and buy on 0.5%

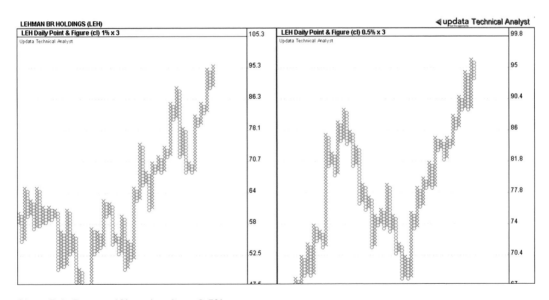

Chart E-2: Buy on 1% and wait on 0.5%

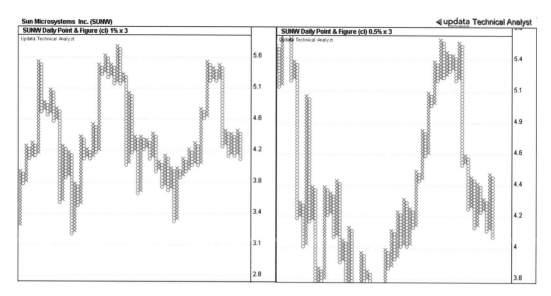

Chart E-3: Sell on 1% and sell on 0.5%

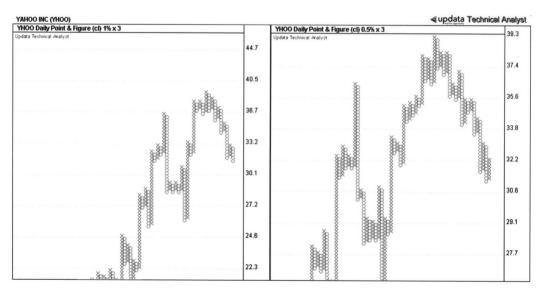

Chart E-4: Sell on 1% and wait on 0.5%

No other technique is able to divide up your portfolio of stocks so objectively. Even if you use the technique simply to separate the bullish charts from the bearish, it is clearly an objective way of doing it.

Adding relative strength to the search

The division of your horizon of stocks into those which are bullish and those which are bearish, based on the position of their Point and Figure charts, may be enhanced by including bullishness or bearishness of the Point and Figure of relative strength at the same time. This is done in exactly the same way. If the last signal on the relative strength Point and Figure chart was a double-top buy, the relative strength chart is considered bullish. If the last signal was a double-bottom sell, it is considered bearish.

A bullish stock combined with a bullish relative strength places the stock in a much stronger position than a bullish stock combined with a bearish relative strength. Conversely, a bearish stock combined with a bearish relative strength places the stock in a much weaker position than a bearish stock combined with a bullish relative strength.

Once again, you may assess more than one time horizon by drawing 0.5% and 1% Point and Figure charts of the relative strength and matching them with the 0.5% and 1% Point and Figure charts of the stock. This way, you will find stocks where not only the price chart is bullish, but the relative strength chart is as well. This helps to narrow down the selection and focus on the small section of stocks which are bullish on price and relative strength, and bearish on price and relative strength. The first group provides a shortlist of stocks to go long of, the second those to go short of.

Index

A

B

E

F

G

H

I

IBM Corporation, 350, 451

Impossible counts, 241

Improbable counts, 241

Indexia, 6, 7, 9

Indicators, 337

Infineon Technologies AG, 450

Instrument names, 495, 496

Intel Corporation, 46, 425, 426, 453

Internal 45° trend lines, 188, 189, 190, 195, 198, 202, 288, 289, 290, 291, 297, 300, 303, 304, 305, 306, 308, 310, 311, 312, 319, 321, 323, 326, 341, 342, 439, 443, 446, 447, 448, 451, 453

Intra-day Point and Figure charts, 104

Introduction to Technical Analysis, 11

Inverted catapult, 293

Inverted charts, 294-295, 300, 320

J

Jiler, William, 5, 465

K

Keynes, John Maynard, 12

L

Land Securities plc, 140

Last plotted box, 67, 68, 80

ln, 106, 249, 491

Log Scale charts, 105-111
    Choosing, 108
    Construction, 491-492
    Counts on, 246
    Naming, 107
    Stops on, 110

Looking left, 126, 133, 167, 262, 289-290, 301

Low pole, 155-164, 309-310

M

M pattern, 116

MACD, 337, 350

Mackay, Charles, 14, 465

Manhattan swing charts, 37

Marconi plc, 108-110

Market breadth, 379-398
    Caveat, 380

Market Technicians Association, iii

Markstein, David L., 42, 465

MIB 30 Index, 446

Mini-bottom, 147, 188, 190, 221-222, 225, 229, 233, 244, 288, 289, 302, 304, 308, 445, 450

Mini-top, 190, 221, 226, 228, 236, 289, 292, 293, 297, 303, 304, 447, 453

Minor move chart, 37

Mobilisation Stage, 14

Momentum, 337, 350

Month numbers, 48, 55-56

Moving averages, 401-418
    Calculation, 401-402
    Exponential, 402-405
    Fibonacci, 412
    Fine tuning, 414-415
    How to use them, 405
    Lengths, 404
    on 1-box charts, 411-414
    on 3-box charts, 406-410
    Simple, 403-405
    Using a single average, 414

N

Name Point and Figure, 43-44

Naming your Point and Figure charts, 56, 107

NASDAQ 100, 379

NASDAQ Composite Index, 214, 215, 216, 217, 218, 273, 313, 314, 316, 318, 319, 320, 322, 323, 324, 325, 326, 327, 328, 329

Natural log, 106, 249, 491

Negating counts, 238

Nikkei 225 Index, 447

Noise, 86, 337